Principles and Practice of Sex Therapy

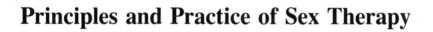

Principles and Practice of Sex Therapy

EDITED BY
Sandra R. Leiblum
Rutgers Medical School

and

Lawrence A. Pervin
Rutgers University

FOREWORD BY **Harold I. Lief, M.D.**

THE GUILFORD PRESS
New York

© 1980 The Guilford Press, New York
A Division of Guilford Publications, Inc.
200 Park Avenue South, New York, N.Y. 10003

Printed in the United States of America

Library of Congress Cataloging in Publication Data

Main entry under title:

Principles and practice of sex therapy.

      Includes bibliographies and index.
      1. Sex therapy.   I. Leiblum, Sandra Risa.
      II. Pervin, Lawrence A.
RC556.P743   616.8'583'06   79-20062
ISBN 0-89862-600-5

To Our Spouses, Julian and Bobbie

Contributors

BERNARD APFELBAUM, Ph.D., Director, Berkeley Sex Therapy Group, 2614 Telegraph Avenue, Berkeley, California

LONNIE BARBACH, Ph.D., Department of Psychiatry, University of California, San Francisco, California

DAVID H. BARLOW, Ph.D., Department of Psychology, State University of New York at Albany, Albany, New York

ENID H. CAMPBELL, Ph.D., Department of Psychology, Trenton State College, Trenton, New Jersey

ALBERT ELLIS, Ph.D., Executive Director, Institute for Rational-Emotive Therapy, New York, New York

CAROL RINKLEIB ELLISON, Ph.D., Psychologist in private practice, 2938 McClure Street, Oakland, California

ARNOLD A. LAZARUS, Ph.D., Graduate School of Applied and Professional Psychology, Rutgers University, New Brunswick, New Jersey, and Director, Multimodal Therapy Institute, Kingston, New Jersey

SANDRA R. LEIBLUM, Ph.D., Department of Psychiatry and Director of Sexual Counseling Service, College of Medicine and Dentistry of New Jersey–Rutgers Medical School, Piscataway, New Jersey

LESLIE LoPICCOLO, M.S., Long Island Research Institute, State University of New York at Stony Brook, Stony Brook, New York. Currently, psychologist in private practice, San Francisco, California

ANDREW M. MATTISON, Ph.D., Psychologist in private practice, Clinical Institute for Human Relationships, 3821 4th Avenue, San Diego,

California, and Department of Community Medicine, School of Medicine, University of California at San Diego, La Jolla, California

DAVID P. McWHIRTER, M.D., Medical Director, Clinical Institute for Human Relationships, 3821 4th Avenue, San Diego, California, and Department of Psychiatry, School of Medicine, University of California at San Diego, La Jolla, California

MICHAEL A. PERELMAN, Ph.D., Director of Research, Human Sexuality Program, Payne Whitney Clinic, Cornell–New York Hospital Medical Center, New York, New York, and Chief of Training, Institute for Behavior Therapy, New York, New York

LAWRENCE A. PERVIN, Ph.D., Department of Psychology, Livingston College, Rutgers University, New Brunswick, New Jersey

RICHARD A. STEIN, M.D., Department of Medicine, Downstate Medical Center, State University of New York, and Director, Cardiac Exercise Laboratory and Medical Service, State University Hospital, Brooklyn, New York

JOHN P. WINCZE, Ph.D., Department of Psychiatry, Brown University, Providence, Rhode Island

BERNIE ZILBERGELD, Ph.D., Psychologist in private practice, 6209 Buena Vista Avenue, Oakland, California

Foreword

Sex counseling can be practiced by a wide variety of health professionals. Clergymen, educators, nurses, social workers, clinical psychologists, and physicians, including specialists of all sorts as well as family practitioners, having acquired some basic sexual information and interviewing skills, have the opportunity to make a beginning appraisal of the patient's sexual concerns. They can provide an understanding and compassionate atmosphere, correct misinformation, help the patient identify and label or relabel his or her feelings and attitudes, and, if the problems presented by the patient (or patient couple) seem to be complicated, the health professional can make a referral to someone with greater skills.

The person with greater skills is the sex therapist. A sex therapist is a psychotherapist. And a competent sex psychotherapist must be able to use a variety of therapeutic approaches and from among these to choose methods of intervention that fit the special and often unique circumstances found in a given clinical situation. This ability requires understanding of the individual patient and the dynamics of that person's intimate relationships. It is possible to state these simply, but it is another matter to understand often complex relations and their reciprocal transactions with sexual functioning while, at the same time, guarding against the possibility that one's theoretical orientation, and perhaps even one's own personal life, may lead to blind spots and erroneous conclusions.

In reading this book edited by Drs. Leiblum and Pervin, two words kept suggesting themselves. These were *flexibility* and *humility*. The many methods of treatment described—for example, behavioral therapy of different sorts such as sensate focus and systematic desensitization, cognitive therapy, the use of imagery, paradoxical intention, various group methods, conjoint marital therapy, social skills training, and, to a lesser degree, some conventional psychodynamic psychotherapy—make the reader aware of the many different ways that sex therapy can be practiced. Only additional sophisticated research will inform us as to which methods are superior for each sexual dysfunction. In the meantime, each of us can expand his or her potential range of therapeutic techniques by careful perusal of these pages. Not that we all can or should try to master every possible approach, but we should examine our clinical failures and wonder if a different therapeutic method might have been more beneficial than the one we used.

Of one thing I can be sure: This book is not intended for the "cookbook" enthusiast. No single recipe will suffice to help every one of our suffering patients. The enormous number of practitioners who have staked out their own turf and claim that they have "the" answer for the millions of people who need assistance with the sexual side of their lives, even if not unexpected, is disappointing to those of us who recognize the complexities of this field. The serious student who wants to increase his or her understanding of sex therapy and who, at the same time, has the healing intent and the desire to alleviate anxiety, misery, and despair and to restore a natural function, will find much of interest in these pages.

The large number of professionals insufficiently trained in sex therapy and the outright quacks who have invaded the field create a need for standards. At the same time, there is a fear that standardization will prematurely foreclose on the possibilities of new, potentially valuable treatment methods. This problem occurs whenever a new clinical specialty is in the developing stage, but in sex therapy the possibility of fraud and incompetence is much greater. The specialty of "sexology" must find a way to monitor itself while standards are being developed and until accreditation procedures are adopted. In the meantime, we have the obligation to study and to try new treatment approaches with an open mind—and this volume helps us do that.

In the editors' concluding chapter, many of the issues confronting sex therapists are set forth. These include problems in diagnosis, assessment of results, use of different scientific methods, incidence, etiology, the effect of subjective perception on the labeling of problems, and the role of anxiety. Of special research interest to me are the connections between anxiety, psychophysiologic processes, and specificity of dysfunction. We have a long way to go to understand these phenomena.

The complexity of individual sexual behaviors, affects, sensations, imagery, and cognition (Lazarus' useful achronym BASIC ID) is multiplied by the complexity of the dyadic interaction. From research in our laboratories (Harold Persky *et al.*), we are beginning to recognize that interpersonal psychological phenomena are reflected in hormonal events, and vice versa; we are fascinated by what we have labeled the "psychobiology of the dyad." In brief, the sexual processes in a couple's interactions involve the transfer of information from one partner's neurohormonal system to the other's in ways that are almost completely mysterious to us at present. Systems theory and systems analysis is probably the best scientific model to deal with these phenomena; any theory, psychoanalytic or behavioral, that focuses only on the individual will be inadequate to conceptualize much of sexual functioning.

For so many years, psychotherapy has contained a gallimaufry of approaches; it is an easy task to find at least one form of psychotherapy for each letter of the alphabet: analysis, behavior therapy, cognitive therapy, etc., down to zootherapy. Each approach has its zealous supporters insisting on its superiority over all others. I hope that sex therapy, promoting the idea of flexibility—of finding the right method for the right patient at the right time, of the possibility of multiple approaches over time—and the integration of individual with marital therapy (it is impossible to be a capable sex therapist without being a capable marital therapist) would serve as a model for the rest of psychotherapy. If psychodynamic psychotherapy, cognitive therapy, and behavioral therapy can be integrated in sex therapy, why not in all of psychotherapy?

Moreover, the great importance of biogenic factors in sexual function and dysfunction requires the integration of psychotherapy with medicine in more ways than in any other area of psychotherapy. I see sex therapy, therefore, serving also as an integrative force in the delivery of health care, helping to bridge the illusory gap between the mental and the physical.

Harold I. Lief, M.D.
Professor of Psychiatry
University of Pennsylvania
Director, Marriage Council of Philadelphia

Preface

It is a decade since the publication of Masters and Johnson's *Human Sexual Inadequacy,* a book that radically altered therapeutic approaches to the treatment of sexual dysfunction. The impressive success rates achieved in the short-term, directive treatment of sexual difficulties so impressed clinicians and the lay public alike that sex therapy as a distinctive therapeutic specialty was launched. Workshops proliferated, and therapists flocked for training in the "new sex therapy." Patients with long-standing sexual problems felt optimistic that, at last, their difficulties could be overcome both rapidly and effectively.

The enthusiasm accompanying the Masters and Johnson report still continues, although in a somewhat modified form. Today, there seems nothing radical about time-limited, problem-focused approaches for resolving sexual problems. What is different, though, is our expectations for their success. We realize that short-term approaches work well for some patients, with some problems, and only some of the time. As failures become apparent, new approaches and methods were adopted, and these, too, have become part of the therapeutic armamentarium for dealing with sexual difficulties.

Principles and Practice of Sex Therapy was conceived as an opportunity to take stock of the current alternative approaches in the practice of sex therapy. Within this context, three goals were set. The first involved presenting the various conceptual and treatment approaches characteristic of current practitioners in the field of sex therapy. The diversity of theoretical orientations existing today accounts for the uniqueness in the actual practice of sex therapy despite the utilization of certain standardized procedures for treating specific dysfunctions.

A second goal involved the presentation of sex therapy, as it is practiced, through a focus on actual clinical cases. Often, there is a significant disparity between theory and practice. While many people erroneously believe that sex therapy is the routine execution of established prescriptive procedures, in actuality it involves the skillful assessment and selection of considered interventions designed to facilitate behavioral and affective change. Treatment plans are continually modified to fit the circumstances presented by particular clients. The most effective method for understanding what is really done in the new sex therapies is the in-depth presentation of case studies.

Finally, this volume attempts to identify some of the factors leading to varying degrees of success with different problems and patients. Questions concerning such factors remain the basis for ongoing research in the broader field of psychotherapy and behavior change. What is the thinking of sex therapists in this regard? While few would challenge the effectiveness of problem-focused procedures for resolving sexual difficulties, it is quite difficult to determine the critical agents of change. Why does the same intervention work with one client and fail miserably with another? The contributors to this volume were asked to speculate about the factors influencing success and failure in their practice and to consider what they might have done differently to avert failure in particular cases.

In short, the goals for this volume included the presentation of case studies of varying degrees of therapeutic success by leading representatives of alternative approaches to sex therapy. Each contributor was asked to identify the principles involved in treating a specific dysfunction or clinical problem and to illustrate the general principles with selected case histories. Failures were regarded as important as successes.

In reading through this volume, certain characteristics of the new sex therapy will become evident. The sophistication of and concern about assessment are noteworthy, as is the ingenuity in overcoming obstacles to treatment. Equally noteworthy is the observation that sex therapy is not always brief and usually not linear. Resistances emerge, and the route to problem resolution is often marked by detours and plateaus. Often, specific behavioral changes occur but other problems remain. Such is the current state of the art! Sex therapy is enormously complex, and the field is as yet in its infancy.

The contributors to this volume have been remarkably open in sharing their thoughts and methods, their disappointments as well as their successes. We wish to thank them for their honesty and willingness to examine their work critically. Additionally, we wish to thank our editor, Seymour Weingarten, for his advice and support throughout this volume, and our secretaries, Agnes Bertelsen, Libby Brusca, Harriet Cohen, Janice Fusco, and Mary Anne Grandinetti, for their unfailing efforts in typing and retyping drafts. Those offering cheer, support, and encouragement throughout the many months of labor are particularly deserving of our appreciation and gratitude, in particular, our colleagues, Drs. Raymond Rosen and Julian Kassen.

Sandra R. Leiblum
Lawrence A. Pervin

Contents

Chapter 9
The Diagnosis and Treatment of Retarded Ejaculation

BERNARD APFELBAUM   263

Part IV: Sex Therapy with Special Populations 299

Chapter 10
Sexual Counseling and Coronary Heart Disease

RICHARD A. STEIN   301

Principles and Practice of Sex Therapy

Introduction: The Development of Sex Therapy from a Sociocultural Perspective

SANDRA R. LEIBLUM AND LAWRENCE A. PERVIN

Although sex therapy has assumed the status of an independent psychotherapeutic specialty, practitioners of many disciplines and theoretical persuasions have been treating sexual problems for centuries. Despite active efforts to limit research and clinical practice in the area, interest in human sexual functioning and concern with sexual dysfunctions refuse to go away. Both the efforts to maintain certain myths concerning sex and the efforts to change these myths attest to the importance of sex in our lives. A historical review of these efforts also gives testimony to the extent to which research and treatment invariably reflect the cultural and moral dictates of their times. Scientific and clinical pursuits never occur in a social vacuum. Whatever the general importance of this fact, however, it becomes particularly significant when considering efforts to understand and treat human sexual functioning. Three decades ago, it would have been inconceivable to bring groups of women together in order to instruct them in the techniques of successful masturbation! Masturbation, which once was viewed as an insidious perversion leading to acne, blindness, impotence, insanity, and other pernicious behaviors, has now come to be considered a legitimate, even therapeutic, source of physical relaxation and sexual satisfaction. A short while ago, showing films of methods of sexual intercourse would have been considered immoral and perhaps unethical, whereas today it is a common practice in most sex therapy centers.

Not only our methods of treatment but also the underlying statement concerning "what is wrong" are affected by shifts in societal values and norms. Behaviors that once were considered perverse or deviant are now viewed as variations of normal sexuality and even as positive additions to one's sexual repertoire. Homosexuality is no longer considered a psychiatric disorder, and we more frequently hear patients complain of not enough sexual interest than of excessive interest. To a certain extent, the work and writings of practitioners themselves affect what the general public considers normal. The woman who does not have multiple orgasms and the man who cannot endlessly delay ejaculations may both wonder what is wrong with them. Thus it is that our work as clinicians and practitioners is inextricably intertwined with what is going on in the surrounding society—it is both influenced by and in turn influences what people believe and what they practice in the area of sexual functioning.

To appreciate the enormous shifts in societal attitudes and beliefs about human sexuality, as well as the changing philosophies of the treatment of sexual dysfunction, it is useful to undertake a brief historical review.

The Victorian Heritage

Nineteenth century sexual ideology provided us with much of the underpinnings of our sexual heritage—our notion of what is normal and proper. On the surface, Victorian sexual ideology was grounded in clear moral imperatives. Adult men and women married and practiced heterosexual, monogamous coupling for the sole purpose of procreation. Men, with their lustful, impulsive sexual appetites, might enjoy sex, and women usually did not. The lack of sexual fulfillment for women was not especially critical since women were not viewed as having sexual needs. In fact, women were seen as inferior and subordinate to men in all respects. The Victorian woman went from the rule of her father to that of her husband, and the maintenance of her virginity was critical to making that transition. Once married, the woman was not expected to be erotic, but was enjoined to offer herself dutifully to her husband without actively participating in sex itself. For the most part, sexuality was associated with dirtiness. Sexual behaviors other than intercourse, such as cunnilingus, masturbation, or fellatio, were unnatural at best and wicked at worst. Homosexuality was considered a perversion, and masturbation assuredly led to every imaginable disorder.

Interestingly, the Victorian era, which cherished the ideal of sexual propriety, was often more prurient than pure in its behavior (Ruitenbeck, 1974). The double standard was alive and well, and hypocrisy flourished. An extramarital pregnancy was believed entirely due to the woman's weakness or depravity. The male's contribution was regarded with tolerance, and there was little social disgrace attached to him. Male indulgence with prostitutes and other sexually licentious women was acknowledged, if not encouraged. In fact, both prostitution and pornography were readily available, and other forms of sexual entertainment were widespread. *The Pearl,* a popular English underground magazine, proclaimed itself the journal of unblushing erotica for every taste, though, on the surface, any expressed interest in erotica was viewed as vulgar and indecent. Public morality reflected church tenets and tended to be repressive, judgmental, and intolerant.

Richard von Krafft-Ebing (1840–1902), a leading representative of the Victorian "ethos," stands as a good illustration of bourgeois attitudes toward sex. Krafft-Ebing was a psychiatrist who worked as a consultant to the courts. In his widely read book *Psychopathia Sexualis* (Krafft-Ebing, 1886/1902), he depicted sex in almost every respect as a collection of loathsome acts indulged in by degenerate people (Brecher, 1969). Krafft-Ebing was a pioneer in attempting to systematically study sex, but his emphasis was on categorizing— enumerating and describing the various sexual perversions he encountered in his work. He coined the term "sadism" and appeared to relish illustrating each example of fetishism, homosexuality, sadism, and masochism with sensational case histories. He emphasized the hereditary taint and moral degeneracy of the people he described. Perhaps he did his greatest harm in swaying public opinion by insisting that masturbation was the critical factor in the development of *all* sexual deviations, from simple fetishism and homosexuality to vicious and violent lust murder!

Early sex educators reinforced the view of sex as a dangerous force that needed watching. English writers such as Edward Lyttelton and the Baden-Powells cautioned their contemporaries to view adolescent sexuality with alarm. Lyttelton, headmaster of Eton, wrote a letter to the *London Times* in which he said:

> Those who are working and hoping, however feebly, to encompass the lives of our boys and girls with a wholesome atmosphere must know that in regard to sexuality, two facts stand out. First, that in proportion as the adolescent mind grows absorbed in sex questions wreckage of life ensues. Secondly, that sanity and upright manliness are destroyed, not only by the reading of obscene stuff, but by a premature interest in sex matters, however it be excited. (Lyttelton, 1913)

Lyttelton's views were supported by Sir Robert Baden-Powell, for many years leader of the Boy Scouts. He regarded sex as he regarded smoking and spectator sports—unhealthy practices that good Scouts should avoid if they wished to become good English citizens! In *The Handbook for Girl Guides* (Baden-Powell & Baden-Powell, 1912), written with his sister, Agnes Baden-Powell, adolescents are warned against "secret bad habits" that lead to hysteria, lunatic asylums, and serious illness (Ruitenbeck, 1974).

Open discussion of sexual practices and behaviors was practically unknown. The conspiracy of silence that surrounded explicit discussion of sex led to much needless suffering. Those few adventuresome sexologists who dared to report on cross-cultural sexual practices were either banned from polite society or had their writings censored. Mantegazza (1831–1910), a versatile Italian physician, surgeon, and anthropologist, wrote that when he first published his book *Hygiene of Love* in 1877,

> it was looked upon as a veritable offense to modesty, one to be punished in accordance with the laws governing the press, and particularly, those having to do with the public welfare. One of the most renowned men of letters in Italy even went so far as to exclaim that, were he to catch sight of the book in question in a lady's drawing room, he would never call upon her again. (Mantegazza, 1935, p. iv)

Even within the medical profession, sexuality was regarded as a "dirty secret." If physicians discussed sexual pathology with each other, it was with the protection of Latin terms. The general consensus was that the less men and women knew about sexuality, the better, since the dissemination of scientific information about sex would inflame and corrupt young minds.

Sex "therapy," such as it was at the turn of the century, centered on controlling sexual expressiveness in all areas, whether that involved suppressing masturbation in children, imprisoning sexual perverts (and homosexuals were included in this category), or finding ways to discourage too frequent indulgence in intercourse.

The Beginnings of Sexual Modernism

The turn of the century gave rise to several key figures who radically transformed our thinking about sex. Comtemporary sexologists agree that sexual modernism in theory and research was introduced by Sigmund Freud in Austria, Henry Havelock Ellis in England, Magnus Hirschfeld in Germany, and Alfred Kinsey in the United States. With the exception of Freud, all of these men were sexual enthusiasts who sought to broaden the range of legitimate sexual behavior, to acknowledge the existence of female sexuality on a parity with male sexuality, and to question the traditional institutional contexts of human sexuality—marriage and family.

Henry Havelock Ellis (1859–1939)

Henry Havelock Ellis started his career as a physician, but gave up his medical practice to devote his time to sex research. The product of that research, his six-volume encyclopedic work *Studies in the Psychology of Sex,* which he published and revised between 1896 and 1928, reflected his attempt to introduce into society a new attitude toward sex—an attitude encompassing biological, sociological, historical, and anthropological views. Ellis emphasized sex as a natural human instinct rather than a pathological force that needed censorship, and felt that all individuals were entitled to sexual information. He introduced two important, but unpopular ideas into Victorian England: Sexual deviants were not vicious criminals; judgments about sexual behavior needed to be relativistic and based on natural and humane considerations rather than on social and legal ones (Ruitenbeck, 1974).

Ellis was more accepting of masturbation than most of his contemporaries. He challenged the popular view that masturbation caused illness, insanity, and depravity, a doctrine introduced into European medicine in the 18th century by a Swiss physician, Samuel Auguste André David Tissot.[1] Further, he defended homosexuality and strenuously rejected Krafft-Ebing's view that it was a "functional sign of degeneracy." He argued that homosexuality was congenital and hence could not be considered a vice since it was not willfully chosen. His method of persuasion was the case history, and he compiled case reports of 33 British and American men who were admirable, productive, and sane. He was convinced that "inversion" was permanent and that most homosexuals had no desire to be relieved of their sexual orientation.

Ellis was also sympathetic to female sexuality. He felt it was more elusive and complex than male sexuality, which he viewed as "predominantly open and aggressive." Ellis maintained that female sexuality was essentially passive; while men were propulsive, women were receptive. However, Ellis recognized the necessity of what he termed "courtship" to get the female fires going. He emphasized the need for extensive foreplay, perhaps even cunnilingus, an activity that Krafft-Ebing had condemned as a masochistic perversion!

Although Ellis shared some common Victorian assumptions about sex, he went far beyond his contemporaries in suggesting that sex could and should be enjoyable. Unfortunately, his views were not widely embraced. In fact, when *Sexual Inversion* first appeared in 1896, it was suppressed as obscene and, even until 1935, his volumes were available only to the medical profession. Nevertheless, his interest in the sexual lives of "fairly normal people" and his recognition that a full understanding of sexuality depended on moving attention away from sexual criminals, lunatics, and people in therapy helped inspire, in the early decades of the 20th century, small-scale sex surveys and inquiries about sexual health.

Magnus Hirschfeld (1868–1935)

Magnus Hirschfeld completed his medical school studies in 1894 in Germany and became interested in the problems of sexuality and the relation between sexual problems and prevalent trauma and taboos. He subsequently founded the Institute of Sexual Science in Berlin, which was very active in sex research in the early decades of the 20th century. Hirschfeld displayed a humane attitude toward sexual deviants. His studies included books on homosexuality and cross-cultural studies of sex as well as the sexual life of adults. Much of the research and writings of Hirschfeld and his colleagues at the Institute of Sexual Science was lost in the 1930s when Hitler came to power. However, Hirschfeld did inspire the German sexual reform movement and was more interested than many of his sexology colleagues in investigating the possiblity of medical, rather than criminal, management of people with sexual problems. He eventually became a member in good standing of the Berlin Psychoanalytical Society (Ruitenbeck, 1974).

Sigmund Freud (1856–1939)

Freud's momentous contribution to 20th century sexuality was his emphasis on the centrality of sex in every aspect of human development. The publication of *Three Contributions to the Theory of Sex* in 1905 has been acknowledged as one of his most original contributions to human knowledge, though it resulted in his being labeled as an evil and wicked man with an obscene mind. Medical institutions were boycotted for tolerating Freud's views, and an early follower, Ernest Jones, was forced to resign his neurological appointment for inquiring into the sexual life of his patients.

In his three essays, Freud elaborated his theory that infantile sexual experiences and behaviors contribute to both the neurotic and the normal person's adult life and behavior in a far-reaching and comprehensive manner. His study of the impact of prepubertal sexuality on adult life fundamentally challenged the then prevailing notion of the child as a peculiarly pure creature.

> If any being on earth were innocent, it was the infant in his cradle or the toddler at his mother's knee. To suggest that the infant drew in libidinous delight with his mother's milk, and to assert that the toddler expressed enjoyment, anger, and many other pleasura-

ble emotions in his refusal to be housebroken was, as Ernest Jones comments, a "calumny on the innocence of the nursery." (Ruitenbeck, 1974, p. 43)

Freud's theory of infantile sexuality was received as a revolutionary idea and even now shocks and offends members of our society, yet few today can doubt that children have sexual desires, experiences, and fantasies.

Many of Freud's theoretical constructs have become an established part of our intellectual heritage, from the importance of the early developmental years in psychological development to the role of the unconscious in determining behavior. However, Freud, like Ellis, was both ahead of and part of his historical milieu, and many of his ideas reflect the impact of Victorian ideology. While he did not stigmatize it as evidence of sin or corruption, Freud believed that homosexuality was evidence of a failure to repress the polymorphously perverse feelings of childhood and characterized it as immature.

Homosexuality is assuredly no advantage, but it is nothing to be ashamed of, no vice, no degradation, it cannot be classified as an illness; we consider it to be a variation of the sexual functions produced by a certain arrest of sexual development. (Freud, 1935/1960, letter 277, p. 423)

It is Freud's views about women and female sexual functioning that best illustrate the influence of his culture on psychosexual theory. Freud reported difficulty in understanding women and emphasized biological and psychodynamic explanations of female sexuality where social and cultural explanations were possible. He considered penis envy and female masochism as cardinal constructs in understanding the psychology of women. More damaging for female sexuality was Freud's belief in the superiority of the vaginal orgasm. Basing his views on a paucity of physiological data, Freud argued that in the course of female psychosexual development, there was a shift in erogenous zones, particularly from the clitoris to the vagina. From this premise, he postulated that women have two distinct kinds of orgasms: the clitoral orgasm, the hallmark of infantile sexuality, and the more mature vaginal orgasm, which represented the renunciation of the clitoris as a major source of sexual excitement. Women who did not make the shift, who continued to experience orgasm only through clitoral stimulation and not through coitus, were considered to be neurotic. This theory, definitively rejected by Masters and Johnson's physiological studies of the orgasm, did much to undermine female sexuality for generations.

Freud's theorizing about female sexuality was attacked and subsequently revised by neo-Freudians, particularly Karen Horney, Clara Thompson, and Mary Jane Sherfy, who emphasized Freud's masculine bias and his failure to acknowledge the influence of patriarchal Western culture on his theorizing. If turn-of-the-century sexual treatment consisted of limiting sexual behavior to conform to the moralistic dogmas of Judeo-Christian culture, the rise in popularity of psychoanalysis led to a treatment focus that attempted to make sexual behavior conform to Freud's notions of sexual normality (LoPiccolo & Heiman, 1978). To a large extent, this involved treating the underlying neurotic and characterological causes of sexual dysfunction, resolving unconscious conflicts, and undertaking time-consuming and exhaustive investigations into the patient's past. In some ways, Freud set standards of sexual normality which encouraged both men and women to conform to gender and sex roles that now seem anachronistic and stultifying, especially for women.

Sexual "Freedom" Movements

The early decades of the 20th century saw the publication of the works of Ellis and Freud, anthropological and cross-cultural surveys of sex, and ideological movements to free sex from the rigid and punitive sexual morality of both the present and the past. After World War I, movements for sexual reform were active in Europe, where such men as Forel and Hirschfeld were leading figures. The World League for Sex Reform, which organized annual conferences between the years 1928 and 1932, tried to achieve complete equality of rights for both sexes and the liberation of sexual love from the sole objective of procreation. However, the movement had its political adversaries who retarded the push for sexual reform and liberation (Wood, 1961).

In America, there were similar efforts to free sex, and especially women, from Victorian shackles. Margaret Sanger, an early reformer, advocated the creation of birth-control clinics, saying, "A woman's body belongs to herself alone." World War I contributed to the emancipation of women as they became active in all aspects of the war effort and demonstrated their mettle in fields heretofore closed to them. Nevertheless, sexual frustration was still the common complaint of women, perhaps best documented by the work of Dickinson and Beam. Dickinson, a gynecologist, accumulated meticulously recorded case histories of his female patients and published his findings in *One Thousand Marriages* (Dickinson & Beam, 1932) and *The Single Woman* (Dickinson, 1934). He noted:

The characteristic coitus of these couples is brief and physiologically male, the female remaining passive and isolated. Once or twice a week there takes place, without preliminaries, an intromission lasting up to five minutes, at the end of which the husband has an orgasm and the wife does not. Both man and woman know that the woman has no animating desire. She submits without welcome to the embrace, it may occur without excitement and she expects it to terminate without orgasm. (cited in Brecher, 1969, p. 154)

Female sexuality continued to be, as it had been in the past, maligned, misunderstood, and subordinated to male expectations.

From Speculation to Fact: Alfred Kinsey (1894–1956)

We have said that what gets defined as normal and pathological in human sexual behavior is a function of both the societal climate and the writing of sexologists. It also is influenced by, and in turn influences, what people *do* sexually. Prior to Kinsey, little was known about the actual sexual practices of Americans. Although there had been several surveys of sexual and marital functioning before Kinsey (Dickinson & Beam, 1932; Hamilton, 1929), most of them failed to have a significant impact on the lay public. Kinsey's two classic works, *Sexual Behavior in the Human Male* (Kinsey, Pomeroy, & Martin, 1948) and *Sexual Behavior in the Human Female* (Kinsey, Pomeroy, Martin, & Gebhard, 1953), profoundly influenced society's notion of acceptable sexual behavior, and his generalizations about the sexual practices of Americans have not been significantly replaced or rejected by more recent studies (Robinson, 1977). In 1937, under the prodding of Robert Latou Dickinson, Kinsey began his systematic survey of sexual behavior.

Kinsey's investigation of the sexual practices of Americans was achieved through the use of probing personal interviews, involving hundreds of questions and lasting several hours. Between 1938 and 1956, Kinsey and his three collaborators, Wardell Pomeroy, Paul Gebhard, and Clyde Martin, secured 18,000 such individual histories, which provided a compelling cross-sectional sample of what people of various ages and socioeconomic, religious, and educational backgrounds *did* sexually.

The original Kinsey books are expressive of the thoroughness of his research. They reveal the extraordinary extent of variation in sexual behavior that exists within members of a society, including at least occasional experiences of homosexual arousal and sexual dysfunction among significant numbers. His studies of sexual behavior in the human female (Kinsey *et al.*, 1953) undermined the belief that females typically were "frigid" and disinterested in sexual gratification. Among his many findings, he found that women were capable of rapid sexual arousal (less than 4 minutes in 75% of cases with masturbation) and capable of arousal leading to orgasm from a very early age. Kinsey found that 62% of women masturbated at some time in their life and that 84% of them relied primarily on labial and clitoral stimulation. He emphasized the considerable individual variation among women in terms of when they started to have sex, the kinds of sexual experiences they enjoyed, and the quality and quantity of their orgasmic experiences. In his book on male sexual behavior (Kinsey *et al.*, 1948), Kinsey shocked and provoked considerable negative reactions by his report that 37% of all males have at least one homosexual experience to the point of orgasm at some point in their life, and that only 50% of the male population reach old age with neither a homosexual orgasm nor homosexual arousal.

Kinsey's studies were the most extensive effort ever made to establish normative standards of sexual behavior. His attempts to solicit a representative sample of people across age, sex, social class, educational, religious, and geographical lines resulted in an impressive taxonomy of sexual practices, their frequencies, and their relationship to demographic variables. Many of his findings evoked considerable shock and resulted in a wealth of outraged criticism and journalistic attack. The high rate of orgasmic response women reported through oral, manual, and self-stimulation challenged the popular belief that intercourse was the biologically "natural" means of sexual satisfaction, a belief cherished by many of Kinsey's contemporaries. The extent of extramarital sex—in 50% of the men interviewed and 25% of the women—questioned the sanctity of monogamous marriage in satisfying sexual desires. Kinsey's data on the extent of masturbation and homosexuality in "normal" adult men and women helped legitimize these and other sexual practices.

Although Kinsey prided himself on being objective, he did evidence certain biases. One was an *insistence* on *toleration* and a rejection of a normal–abnormal dichotomy in human behavior. Rather, he believed that all sexual behavior was part of the same continuum. He did not seriously consider the factors that led to the differences in the nature and extent of male and female sexual behavior helping, indirectly, to foster his beliefs in the *naturalism* of sexual behaviors. His belief in the naturalism of sex suggested that sex differences between males and females were not due to cultural/social learning and expectations, but rather were basic biological differences between them.

Nevertheless, despite these shortcomings in his work, Kinsey's studies helped legitimize and normalize the sexual practices of Americans and challenged the prohibitions exerted by religion and the law. However, prior to the pioneering work of Masters and Johnson, myths and misconceptions continued to characterize the public's understanding of, and attitudes toward, sex. Women were considered "neurotic" or immature if they did not experience the "vaginal" orgasm, masturbation was still regarded as taboo and unnecessary for adult men and women, and sexuality was widely regarded as the legitimate province of only the young and the married. An active sex life for those over 50 was regarded as somewhat indecent and quite likely impossible. Directive sex therapy was unavailable. Sexual problems were regarded as symptomatic of some more basic underlying pathology and were typically treated, for those individuals bold enough to seek relief, in long-term individual psychodynamic psychotherapy. Little emphasis was placed on the role of the partner in either causing or maintaining sexual dysfunction.

Sex Therapy Comes of Age: William Masters (1915–   ) and Virginia Johnson (1925–   )

If Kinsey must be credited with describing and empirically substantiating the sexual practices of Americans, Masters and Johnson must be singled out both for their development of a method for the brief treatment of sexual dysfunctions and for their physiological studies of sexual response. They were not the first to study and observe the response of humans to sexual stimulation. Prior to their work, a number of American and European investigators had studied sexual physiology, from Felix Roubaud in France in 1855 to Robert Latou Dickinson in the United States. Dickinson studied female sexual responses during masturbation and even introduced the electrical vibrator (massager) into gynecological practice. His findings are summarized in the classic *Atlas of Human Sex Anatomy* (1933), the first modern book by a gynecologist to contain illustrations of sex positions. Kinsey and his Indiana University associates also observed male and female bodily responses during masturbation and coitus, but decided not to publish the explanation of where, how, or by whom the observations were made, although their data are presented in Chapter 15 of the 1953 report. Prior to Masters and Johnson, however, reports often were fragmentary, they were based on few cases or on isolated aspects of the response cycle, and physiological recording instruments coupled with visual observations were not undertaken. Further, there were few complete reports on male responses to sexual stimulation (Brecher, 1969).

From the start of his medical career, William Masters had displayed an interest in problems of human sexuality. As a medical student, he studied under an outstanding authority on the biology of sex, George Washington Corner. In his subsequent work as a gynecologist, Masters was intrigued by the use of hormone replacement therapy for aged and aging women and published many papers in this area. He became increasingly aware of the inadequate knowledge of the physiology of normal human response to erotic stimuli. Just before Kinsey's death in 1956, Masters launched his studies on sexual physiology, in part because of the generally favorable public response to Kinsey's work, and in part because of his conviction that basic research in human sexual functioning was essential.

The history of Masters' efforts to pursue his work in human sex research illustrates the place of these efforts in relation to the broader society. Despite his excellent professional credentials, Masters met with vehement opposition from his medical colleagues: "As people first and doctors second, many physicians have the same restrictive attitudes about sex as the rest of the public" (Belliveau & Richter, 1970, p. 18). Just as most past sex researchers had met with resistance, Masters found that his colleagues felt either that sexual disorders were not important to study or that sexual functioning could not be studied directly. Whereas previously he was offered chairmanships at several medical schools, those offers stopped once his sex research began. While initially he received a small grant from the National Institutes of Health, subsequently he was repeatedly turned down in his grant requests. University support was limited, and research articles were rejected for journal publication. Despite the tremendous interest in Kinsey's results, professionals were not completely receptive to open inquiries into human sexuality.

Human Sexual Response by Masters and Johnson was published in 1966 and was a comprehensive laboratory report of how the human body reacts to sexual stimulation. In all, 694 individuals, including 276 married couples, participated in the research program. In this book, Masters and Johnson describe the events that comprise the physiological response to erotic stimulation in terms of a pattern of four phases: excitement, plateau, orgasm, and resolution. Masters and Johnson attempted to illustrate the parallelism between the male and female sexual response by describing in considerable detail the analogous changes in males and females during each phase of the cycle. For instance, erection in the male and vaginal lubrication in the female are evidence of excitement-phase responses to sexual stimulation, whether fantasy or tactual. There are difficulties in Masters and Johnson's conceptual use of the four-phase model of human sexual response (e.g., the distinction between phases is often arbitrary and the important element of sexual desire is omitted altogether), and other models have since been suggested (Kaplan, 1974). However, the model did serve as a descriptive reference and provided some basis for their conceptualization of treatment.

Perhaps the major contribution of this first book was in challenging and rejecting the earlier theory of the physiological distinction between the vaginal and clitoral orgasm. Masters and Johnson compared female orgasms following clitoral stimulation and following vaginal stimulation and demonstrated that the so-called clitoral and vaginal orgasms were physiologically indistinguishable! Psychologically, of course, orgasms experienced with a partner during coitus and those experienced during masturbation might be perceived and interpreted differently by the woman, but *physiologically,* an orgasm is an orgasm, however induced. This finding proved tremendously liberating for scores of women who felt inadequate, incomplete, or immature if they had been unable to experience the so-called vaginal orgasm during intercourse.

In their second book, *Human Sexual Inadequacy* (1970), Masters and Johnson reported on the therapeutic techniques developed in their work with 790 persons who came to St. Louis for the treatment of sexual disorders. They conceptualized sexual problems as stemming primarily from anxiety, specifically fears of performance, and suggested that they might be eliminated through specific reeducation procedures designed to remove the debilitating performance anxiety. Unlike many of their predecessors, Masters and Johnson believe that sexual dysfunctions may be separated from other neurotic and characterological disorders and treated directly with favorable outcome. They treated sex as a natural rather than a learned phenomenon, one which the person who was free of anxiety could capably perform. Thus, successful sexual performance is a *natural* ability that gets interfered with through various sociocultural influences and ignorance, and if these are removed appropriate responsiveness will occur:

> It should be restated that fear of inadequacy is the greatest known deterrent of effective sexual functioning, simply because it so completely distracts the fearful individual from his or her *natural* responsivity by blocking reception of sexual stimuli either created by or reflected from the sexual partner. (Masters & Johnson, 1970, p. 13)

The therapy format developed by Masters and Johnson contains a number of elements which have since been incorporated into a variety of other treatment programs. First, and perhaps most significant, is their emphasis on sexuality as a source of pleasure and the shared contribution of both partners to the individual and joint sexual experience: "There is no such thing as an uninvolved partner in a marriage where sexual dysfunction exists" (1970, p. 31). The development of the sensate focus program represented a considerable achievement in providing an exercise that would help to alleviate anxiety, increase pleasure and communication, and point up problems interfering with the couple's sexual relationship. The use of a dual therapy team and focus on the couple's interaction helped to destigmatize the individual with the most obvious sexual difficulty, helped to limit blame as a central focus, and helped to establish the equal place of the needs and responsibilities of both partners in the treatment program. Along with the specific treatment exercises, the overall approach to treatment represented a radical departure from previous therapeutic strategies. It emphasized that the primary cause of sexual dysfunction in most cases is psychological, rather than physical, and that sexual problems could, in fact, be overcome in a rapid manner through reeducation rather than through intensive individual psychotherapy designed to elucidate and eliminate specific intrapsychic conflicts. It not only assumed that women were equal to men in their ability to enjoy sexual experiences but assigned to women a significant role in many of the treatment programs.

Beyond Masters and Johnson: Directive Sex Therapies

Masters and Johnson's development of a short-term directive treatment program for the remediation of problems of sexual dysfunction both excited the general public and inspired therapists of varying theoretical backgrounds to take a fresh look at problems of human sexuality. Sex therapy as a distinctive psychotherapeutic specialty was launched. Several factors contributed to its growth: Advances in birth-control technology in the 1950s had helped free sexuality from a primarily procreative emphasis to a recreative one; the increasing autonomy and changing life-styles of women encouraged them to consider "liberating" their sexuality along with the rest of their lives; the free-wheeling "flower and drug" cultures of the 1960s emphasized spontaneity and sensuality and the rejection of authoritarian and restrictive inhibitions in general; and the proliferation of popular magazine articles devoted to sex helped destigmatize discussion of, and fostered interest in, sexual satisfaction for all individuals, not just the young and beautiful. Medical schools began including human sexuality in their curricula, and graduate students in psychology and related disciplines were exposed to the work of Masters and Johnson.

Therapists began being approached by "normal" individuals and couples for assistance in overcoming dysfunction and enhancing satisfaction. Since the two-week intensive and expensive treatment format developed by Masters and Johnson was prohibitive for most people, new treatment formats and therapeutic strategies had to be developed.

Behavioral Approaches to Sex Therapy

Since its inception, behavior therapy had recognized the importance of learning and conditioning in creating and maintaining both adaptive and maladaptive sexual behavior. Nevertheless, behavior therapy in the late 1950s and early 1960s focused primarily on the treatment of deviant sexual behavior. Aversion therapy (Feldman, 1966; Feldman & MacCullough, 1971; Marks & Gelder, 1967) and systematic desensitization (Wolpe, 1958) were the principal techniques employed, and the goal was the elimination of the undesired behavior rather than the development of more appropriate options (Bancroft, 1977).

By and large, early behavior therapists paid little attention to problems of sexual dysfunction, though there were exceptions. Lazarus (1963) reported on the use of systematic desensitization in the treatment of "chronic frigidity," Friedman (1968) achieved success in a small number of males with erectile impotence using desensitization combined with methohexotal relaxation, Hastings (1963) advocated using masturbation techniques for some anorgasmic women, and Schultz (1951) had been alleviating anxiety in sexually dysfunctional couples by forbidding intercourse in the early stages of treatment.

Even before the publication of *Human Sexual Inadequcy,* Albert Ellis had written extensively on the critical role that an individual's cognitions played in perpetuating sexual difficulties. More than any of the early behaviorists, Ellis recognized that sexual problems were not simply a question of technique, but also of the unique attitudinal and belief systems an individual brought to bed (Ellis, 1952, 1958, 1961).

Nevertheless, the publication of *Human Sexual Inadequacy* in 1970 inspired many more behavior therapists to turn their attention to the application of behavior therapy techniques to individuals and couples with sexual difficulties. Although not self-described behavior therapists, Masters and Johnson had provided a clinical approach that was uniquely appealing to behavioral clinicians, an approach that incorporated many explicitly behavioral strategies and principles: the identification of anxiety as the primary cause of dysfunctional behavior; viewing overt, symptomatic behavior as the target of change, rather than hypothetical underlying intrapsychic conflicts; changing undesired behaviors through step-by-step successive approximation to the desired end goal; and using active, directed behavioral assignments for promoting behavioral change, rather than insight and interpretation.

Since 1970, there has been a plethora of publications by behavior therapists describing techniques for modifying sexual dysfunction. Almost all approaches incorporate strategies for sexual reeducation designed to eliminate sexual myth and misinformation, attitude-change techniques, marital and communication enhancement methods, and specific prescriptions for behavior change. Basic techniques include the following:

1. *Anxiety-reduction techniques,* specifically, progressive relaxation (Jacobson, 1938), systematic desensitization (Wolpe, 1958), occasionally with the adjunctive use of brevital, a fast-acting muscle relaxant (Brady, 1966, 1971), and assertive training procedures (Albert & Emmons, 1970; Phelps & Austin, 1975).

2. *Directed masturbation* (Kohlenberg, 1974; LoPiccolo & Lobitz, 1972) for treatment of both anorgasmia and impotence.

3. *Orgasmic reconditioning* (Davison, 1968; Marquis, 1970), the use of directed fantasy in conjunction with masturbation to modify the kinds of sexual stimuli associated with arousal.

4. *Imagery techniques* (Lazarus, 1977) for assessment and rehearsal of desired sexual responses.

5. *Explicit homework assignments* such as massage, self-stimulation, or couple communication exercises.

Current behavioral methods are more sophisticated conceptually than those popular even a decade ago. Assessment is often multimodal (Lazarus, 1976), and psychophysiological (Heiman, 1978; Hoon, Wincze, & Hoon, 1976; Rosen & Kopel, 1977, 1978), and attention is paid to the many contributing factors involved in creating sexual compatability. Treatment programs are tailor-made to meet the particular needs and goals of the client. Many behavior therapists are even sensitive to, and questioning of, what were formerly considered acceptable treatment aims. For instance, some behavior therapists are reluctant to enter into a therapeutic contract to change a homosexual orientation to a heterosexual one (Davison, 1976). Even if this were possible, they feel that it reinforces the view that homosexuality is an illness. Sexually deviant behavior is treated with a wide variety of psychophysiological and imaginal procedures, ranging from covert sensitization (Cautela & Wisocki, 1971) to the use of testosterone-suppressing drugs

(Walker, 1978). While the basic Masters and Johnson sensate-focus exercises are often prescribed as one part of treatment, many other methods are employed, including bibliotherapy and sexually explicit audiovisual aids.[2]

Kaplan's New Sex Therapy

Helen Singer Kaplan (1974) is the leading synthesizer of psychoanalytic and behavioral approaches in sex therapy. Kaplan has a multicausal conceptualization of the etiology of sexual dysfunction, which includes both remote and immediate causes. Factors such as ignorance, anxiety, and sexual communication failures, as well as less apparent internal conflicts between sexual wishes and fears, are all seen as potential contributors. She rejects the psychoanalytic position that holds "that early incestuous experiences are the only causes of sexual conflict, and that sexual dysfunctions are always caused by unconscious conflict, which is the only etiologic factor, and that cure must be predicated on resolution of these specific underlying conflicts" (Kaplan, 1974, p. 144) while recognizing that unconscious conflict may be instrumental in leading to sexual dysfunctions if "it evokes disorganizing anxiety at the moment of love-making or mobilizes perceptual and obsessive defenses against arousal" (Kaplan, 1974, p. 145).

In treatment, Kaplan typically focuses on the "here and now" rather than the past. She states that symptom relief can be obtained by modifying the immediate products of conflict, typically anxiety, without eliminating the underlying conflict. The techniques she suggests are an eclectic blend of Masters and Johnson's sensate-focus exercises, marital therapy techniques, dynamic counseling, and prescribed behavioral exercises, such as masturbation. Unlike Masters and Johnson, Kaplan advocates the use of individual therapists of either gender and is amenable to experimenting with various treatment formats, from conjoint couple therapy to same-gender groups (Kaplan, Kuhl, Pomeroy, Offit, & Hogan, 1974). Patients are seen weekly, rather than in an intensive two-week program, and techniques are prescribed on an individualistic basis to meet the needs of the particular presenting case.

What is noteworthy about Kaplan's approach is her effort to combine behavioral and psychodynamic concepts and approaches. While many therapists feel that such a combination is incompatible and unsound, others find it challenging and useful. They feel that sex therapy, as a specialized form of psychotherapy, is doomed to failure unless cognizance is paid to the less apparent intraindividual issues that might be operating to inhibit change.

New Formats in Sex Therapy: Group and Weekend Approaches

As the demand for sex therapy services escalated, the need for more economical and efficient approaches became apparent. Group methods for treating sexual problems have become popular and appear to be effective. To date, success has been achieved in group treatment for premature ejaculators with and without their partners, anorgasmic women, and couples with a variety of different sexual dysfunctions. Such approaches have had a significant impact in reducing the cost and increasing the accessibility of treatment, though research on long-term efficacy and comparison with other formats need to be done.

The weekend sexual-enhancement workshop for the purpose of instruction in self-help methods and sex education has also been used successfully to foster attitude change and enhance couple communication in the area of sexuality (Leiblum & Rosen, 1979).

The Self-Help Movement

Long before the popularity of sex therapy as a therapeutic specialty, individuals have consulted books and manuals for suggestions on enhancing sexual satisfaction. The earliest sources of sexual advice came through marriage manuals. One of the most popular was *Ideal Marriage* (1930), written by Van de Velde, a Dutch gynecologist. It became the bible which newly married couples consulted as they entered the kingdom of sexual delight.

Today we have a literal explosion of sex manuals providing graphic illustrations and encouragement to experiment and enjoy. *The Joy of Sex,* Alex Comfort's (1972) answer to *Ideal Marriage,* has been on the best-seller list for years and attests to the dramatic change in sexual attitudes and values in the last decade. Comfort's "gourmet guide to sex" is an endorsement of sex as recreation and pleasure—any activity that is humanly possible and mutually agreed upon is condoned, from mild forms of bondage and discipline to swinging and group sex.

In addition to marriage and sex manuals designed to encourage variety and enhance satisfaction for "functional" couples, there exists an everincreasing array of self-help books for overcoming sexual dysfunction. The feminist movement helped legitimize women's desire for sexual fulfillment, and a host of books have been published instructing her on ways of achieving it.[3] Paralleling the trend in self-help books for women has been an increasing number of books for men[4] and specialized populations.[5]

The impact of these books on reducing the incidence of sexual dysfunction is unknown, since there is an absence of research documenting either the efficacy of the techniques prescribed or the extent to which their advice is followed. Nevertheless, self-help manuals are visible contenders to professional health services for individuals and couples in sexual distress.

Conclusion

Several themes emerge from this brief review of the history of sexual thought and therapy. While Victorian sexual ideology was characterized by almost universal agreement on the purpose of sex and on acceptable sexual behavior, today there exists an open arena for thought and action where almost anything goes. Men and women of the 1970s enjoy an almost infinite choice in the selection of life-styles and sex roles. In the absence of an imperative moral order to guide and determine behavior, individuals are free to experiment with a host of behaviors formerly considered deviant, immoral, or criminal. In part, the absence of agreed-upon social sanctions leaves a vacuum for some individuals in determining personal sexual conduct and creates doubt and confusion. For some, not engaging in a wide repertory of sexual behaviors creates as much anxiety as engaging in these same behaviors would have created 50 years ago.

The changing definition of sexual normality and pathology plagues both individuals and health professionals. As Gagnon (1977) points out, our labels describing sexual conduct vary with the times. During the Victorian age, good/evil and virtue/vice were common designations of sexual acts, while during national crisis, approved sex becomes "patriotic" and disapproved sex, "unpatriotic." Homosexual behavior was initially regarded as sinful, then deviant; today, it is regarded as a sexual variation. Less than 40 years ago, it was regarded as unnatural and unhealthy to masturbate. Today, it is far less common to find young adults who confess to a "hands-off" approach to their bodies. Yesterday's cherished virgin could easily become today's patient.

As we have indicated, societal attitudes about sexual behavior interface directly with clinical practice. In a time where women are not expected to enjoy sex or achieve orgasm, there is little point in treating early ejaculation or anorgasmia. Conversely, where sexual expectations and demands are high, individuals and couples tend to evaluate negatively their sexual abilities and to seek sexual counseling and advice. Current expectations enjoin women to be well versed in their sexual preferences, lubricate promptly, enjoy a variety of sexual acts, experience a minimum of one orgasm at some point during a sexual encounter (and preferably more), and take active delight in pleasuring their partner. Men are expected to know the full theme and variation of female sexual responsiveness in addition to being able to delay ejaculation until their partner is both physiologically and psychologically ready. If possible, they should supply a second erection if she has not climaxed during intercourse and, at the very least, pleasure their companion extensively following ejaculation. These expectations, popularly disseminated, have raised insecurity for many and created new performance pressures and, of course, new patients. With 50% of married couples expressing sexual dissatisfaction and/or dysfunction (Frank, Anderson, & Rubinstein, 1978), we may well ask to what extent the growing liberalization of sexual attitudes and behaviors has led to iatrogenic sexual problems. We may also ask whether, with all of the liberalization of our sexual attitudes, people today are basically more free to enjoy sex without conflict, tension, and guilt.

The enthusiasm accompanying Masters and Johnson's work and the ready acceptance of sex therapy as a clinical speciality in the last 10 years have also created problems. Sex therapy was regarded as a panacea for all kinds of sexual difficulties in all kinds of people. Both clinicians and the lay public regarded short-term active sexual treatment as incredibly successful and the "answer" to difficulties that traditional therapists had unsuccessfully struggled with for years. To some extent, active sex therapy deserved its accolades. However, many of us are more skeptical today. We recognize that brief treatment can work effectively with some individuals and couples some of the time. We have become increasingly aware of its limitations, and the task of the future is to determine which techniques and approaches work with which kind of person and when.

While recognizing our continuing limitations, it is clear that some legitimate and significant changes in attitude and treatment have occurred. The recognition that the sick and old, the institutionalized, the mentally and intellectually deprived have a right to sexual enjoyment and advice, as well as the young and advantaged, must be applauded. The acknowledgment that sexual "minorities" have a right to treatment has been a long time coming and is to be valued.

To a certain extent, the chapters in this book are indicative of recent developments in theory and practice. They reflect the changing nomenclatures, views of dysfunction, and approaches to treatment that have mirrored societal changes in norms and values. The problems dealt with in these chapters are different from those worrisome 50 years ago, and the treatment procedures described reflect the diversity of approaches and techniques currently available.

In reading through this book, however, it may be well to keep in mind that the problems and approaches will undoubtedly be different 50 years from now and will reflect yet another order of sexual ideology, societal climate, and therapeutic philosophy.

NOTES

1. Tissot, in turn, borrowed and incorporated many of the ideas presented earlier in England by an anonymous author, thought to be a clergyman who abandoned the cloth for medicine. This author published his treatise with the descriptive title *Onanism,* or "the Heinous Sin of Self-Pollution and all its frightful consequences, in both sexes, considered with spiritual and physical advise to those who already have injur'd themselves by this abominable practice, to which is subjoin'd a letter from a lady to the author, concerning the use and abuse of the marriage bed, with the author's answer." By 1764, this book had reputedly gone through 80 editions (Caird & Wincze, 1977).
2. Readers interested in a more extended discussion and elaboration of behavior therapy approaches to sex therapy should see Annon (1976); Caird and Wincze (1977); Fisher and Gochros (1977); and LoPiccolo and LoPiccolo (1978).
3. Some illustrative titles are *For Yourself: The Fulfillment of Female Sexuality* (Barbach, 1975); *Liberating Masturbation* (Dodson, 1974); *Woman's Orgasm—A Guide to Sexual Satisfaction* (Kline-Graber & Graber, 1975); and *Becoming Orgasmic: A Sexual Growth Program for Women* (Heiman, LoPiccolo, & LoPiccolo, 1976).
4. Current titles include *Male Sexuality* (Zilbergeld, 1978); *Sex and the Liberated Man* (Ellis, 1976); *What You (Still) Don't Know about Male Sexuality* (McCarthy, 1977).
5. Books on homosexual sex include *The Joy of Gay Sex* (Silverstein, 1977) and *The Joy of Lesbian Sex* (Harris & Sisley, 1977). Books on sex and aging include *Sex after Sixty: A Guide for Men and Women for Their Later Years* (Butler & Lewis, 1976) and *Good Age* (Comfort, 1976).

References

Albert, R., & Emmons, M. *Your perfect right! A guide to assertive behavior.* San Luis Obispo, Calif.: Impact Books, 1970.

Annon, J. *The behavioral treatment of sexual disorders.* Baltimore: Harper & Row, 1976.

Baden-Powell, A., & Baden-Powell, R. *The handbook for girl guides.* London: Thomas Nelson, 1912.

Bancroft, J. The behavioural approach to treatment. In J. Money & H. Murphy (Eds.), *Handbook of sexology.* Amsterdam: Elsevier/North Holland, 1977.

Barbach, L. *For yourself: The fulfillment of female sexuality.* New York: Signet, 1975.

Belliveau, F., & Richter, L. *Understanding human sexual inadequacy.* Boston: Little, Brown & Co., 1970.

Brady, J. P. Brevital-relaxation treatment of frigidity. *Behaviour Research and Therapy,* 1966, *4,* 71.

Brady, J. P. Brevital-aided systematic desensitization. In R. D. Rubin, H. Fensterheim, A. Lazarus, & C. M. Franks (Eds.), *Advances in behavior therapy*. New York: Academic Press, 1971.

Brecher, E. M. *The sex researchers*. Boston: Little, Brown & Co., 1969.

Butler, R. N. & Lewis, M. *Sex after sixty: A guide for men and women for later years*. New York: Harper & Row, 1976.

Caird, W., & Wincze, J. *Sex therapy: A behavioral approach*. New York: Harper & Row, 1977.

Cautela, J. R., & Wisocki, P. Covert sensitization for the treatment of sexual deviations. *The Psychological Record*, 1971, *21*, 37–48.

Comfort, A. *The joy of sex*. New York: Crown, 1972.

Comfort, A. *Good age*. New York: Crown, 1976.

Davison, G. C. Elimination of a sadistic fantasy by a client-controlled counter-conditioning technique. *Journal of Abnormal Psychology*, 1968, *73*, 84–90.

Davison, G. C. Homosexuality: The ethical challenge. *Journal of Consulting and Clinical Psychology*, 1976, *44*, 157–162.

Dickinson, R. L. *Atlas of human sex anatomy*. Baltimore: Williams & Wilkins, 1933.

Dickinson, R. L. *The single woman*. Baltimore: Williams & Wilkins, 1934.

Dickinson, R. L., & Beam, L. *One thousand marriages*. London: Williams & Worthgate, 1932.

Dodson, B. *Liberating masturbation*. New York: Bodysex Designs, 1974.

Ellis, A. Applications of clinical psychology to sexual disorders. In L. E. Abt & D. Brower (Eds.), *Progress in clinical psychology*. New York: Grune & Stratton, 1952.

Ellis, A. *Sex without guilt*. New York: Lyle Stuart, 1958.

Ellis, A. Frigidity. In A. Ellis & A. Abarbanel (Eds.), *The encyclopedia of sexual behavior*. New York: Hawthorn Books, 1961.

Ellis, A. *Sex and the liberated man*. New York: Lyle Stuart, 1976.

Feldman, M. P. Aversion therapy for sexual deviations: A critial review. *Psychological Bulletin*, 1966, *65*, 65–79.

Feldman, M. P., & MacCullough, M. J. *Homosexual behaviour: Theory and assessment*. Oxford: Pergamon Press, 1971.

Fisher, J., & Gochros, H. (Eds.). *Handbook of behavior therapy with sexual problems* (Vols. 1 & 2). New York: Pergamon Press, 1977.

Frank, E., Anderson, C., & Rubinstein, D. Frequency of sexual dysfunction in "normal couples." *New England Journal of Medicine*, 1978, *299*(3), 111–115.

Freud, S. *Letters of Sigmund Freud* (E. L. Freud, Ed.). New York: Basic Books, 1960. (Originally published, 1935.)

Friedman, D. The treatment of impotence by brietal relaxation therapy. *Behaviour Research and Therapy*, 1968, *6*, 257–261.

Gagnon, J. *Human sexualities*. Glenview, Ill.: Scott, Foresman, 1977.

Hamilton, G. *A study in marriage*. New York: Alfred & Charles Boni, 1929.

Harris, B., & Sisley, E. *The joy of lesbian sex*. New York: Simon & Schuster, 1977.

Hastings, D. W. *Impotence and frigidity*. London: Churchill, 1963.

Heiman, J., LoPiccolo, L., & LoPiccolo, J. *Becoming orgasmic: A sexual growth program for women*. Englewood Cliffs, N.J.: Prentice-Hall, 1976.

Heiman, J. R. Uses of psychophysiology in the assessment and treatment of sexual dysfunction. In J. LoPiccolo and L. LoPiccolo (Eds.), *Handbook of sex therapy*. New York: Plenum Press, 1978.

Hoon, P., Wincze, J., & Hoon, E. Physiological assessment of sexual arousal in women. *Psychophysiology,* 1976, *13,* 196–204.

Jacobson, E. *Progressive relaxation.* Chicago: Chicago University Press, 1938.

Kaplan, H., Kuhl, R., Pomeroy, W., Offit, A., & Hogan, B. Group treatment of premature ejaculation. *Archives of Sexual Behavior,* 1974, *3,* 443–452.

Kaplan, H. S. *The new sex therapy.* New York: Brunner/Mazel, 1974.

Kinsey, A. C., Pomeroy, W. B., & Martin, C. E. *Sexual behavior in the human male.* Philadelphia & London: W. B. Saunders, 1948.

Kinsey, A. C., Pomeroy, W. B., Martin, C. E., & Gebhard, P. H. *Sexual behavior in the human female.* Philadelphia & London: W. B. Saunders, 1953.

Kline-Graber, G., & Graber, B. *Woman's orgasm—a guide to sexual satisfaction.* New York: Bobbs-Merrill, 1975.

Kohlenberg, R. Directed masturbation and the treatment of orgasmic dysfunction. *Archives of Sexual Behavior,* 1974, *3,* 349–356.

Krafft-Ebing, R. von. *Psychopathia Sexualis.* Brooklyn: Physicians & Surgeons Books, 1902. (Originally published, 1886.)

Lazarus, A. The treatment of chronic frigidity by systematic desensitization. *Journal of Nervous and Mental Disorders,* 1963, *136,* 272–278.

Lazarus, A. *Multimodal behavior therapy.* New York: Springer, 1976.

Lazarus, A. *In the mind's eye: The power of imagery for personal enrichment.* New York: Rawson Associates, 1977.

Leiblum, S., & Rosen, R. The weekend workshop for dysfunctional couples: Assets and limitations. *Journal of Sex and Marital Therapy,* 1979, *5,* 57–69.

LoPiccolo, J., & Heiman, J. The role of cultural values in the prevention and treatment of sexual problems. In C. B. Qualls, J. P. Wincze, & D. H. Barlow (Eds.), *The prevention of sexual disorders: Issues and approaches.* New York: Plenum Press, 1978.

LoPiccolo, J., & Lobitz, W. C. The role of masturbation in the treatment of primary orgasmic dysfunction. *Archives of Sexual Behavior,* 1972, *2,* 153–164.

LoPiccolo, J., & LoPiccolo, L. (Eds.). *Handbook of sex therapy.* New York: Plenum Press, 1978.

Lyttelton, E. Letter. *London Times,* November 22, 1913, p. 11.

Mantegazza, P. *The sexual relations of mankind.* New York: Eugenics Publishing Co., 1935.

Marks, I. M., & Gelder, M. G. Transvestism and fetishism: Clinical and psychological changes during faradic aversion. *British Journal of Psychiatry,* 1967, *113,* 711–729.

Marquis, J. N. Orgasmic reconditioning: Changing sexual object choice through controlling masturbation fantasies. *Journal of Behavior Therapy and Experimental Psychiatry,* 1970, *1,* 263–271.

Masters, W. H., & Johnson, V. E. *Human sexual response.* Boston: Little, Brown & Co., 1966.

Masters, W. H., & Johnson, V. E. *Human sexual inadequacy.* Boston: Little, Brown & Co., 1970.

McCarthy, B. *What you (still) don't know about male sexuality.* New York: Crowell, 1977.

Phelps, S., & Austin, N. *The assertive woman.* San Luis Obispo, Calif.: Impact Books, 1975.

Robinson, P. *The modernization of sex.* New York: Harper & Row, 1977.

Rosen, R. C., & Kopel, S. A. Penile plethysmography and biofeedback in the treatment of a transvestite–exhibitionist. *Journal of Consulting and Clinical Psychology,* 1977, *45,* 900–916.

Rosen, R. C., & Kopel, S. A. Role of penile tumescence measurement in the behavioral treatment of sexual deviation: Issues of validity. *Journal of Consulting and Clinical Psychology,* 1978, *46,* 1519–1521.

Ruitenbeck, H. *The new sexuality.* New York: New Viewpoints, 1974.

Schultz, J. H. *Autogenic training.* New York: Grune & Stratton, 1951.

Silverstein, C. *The joy of gay sex.* New York: Simon & Schuster, 1977.

Van de Velde, T. *Ideal marriage, its physiology and technique.* Random House, 1930.

Walker, P. A. The role of antiandrogens in the treatment of sex offenders. In C. B. Qualls, J. P. Wincze, & D. H. Barlow (Eds.), *The prevention of sexual disorders: Issues and approaches.* New York: Plenum Press, 1978.

Wolpe, J. *Psychotherapy by reciprocal inhibition.* Stanford: Stanford University Press, 1958.

Wood, R. Sex reform movement. In A. Ellis and A. Abarbanel (Eds.), *Encyclopedia of sexual behavior* (Vol. 2). New York: Hawthorn Books, 1961.

Zilbergeld, B. *Male sexuality.* Boston & Toronto: Little, Brown & Co., 1978.

Treatment of Sexual Desire Disorders

I

Introduction: Treatment of Sexual Desire Disorders

While much of the early work in the field of sex therapy focused on the resolution of problems of sexual dysfunction, increasingly interest is being paid to problems of desire. The current emphasis on desire disorders is the outgrowth of several related trends. Whereas considerable success had been achieved in treating specific male and female sexual dysfunctions, clinicians across the country were bewailing the difficulties encountered in resolving problems of low sexual interest. Many centers witnessed an increase in referrals of individuals and couples complaining of too little sexual interest. Whether the increase in such referrals was a result of the media's insistence on enjoying an active sexual life, a real increase in the incidence of low sexual desire resulting from an increasing emphasis on sexual performance, or an artifact of generally more sophisticated diagnostic and assessment procedures on the part of sex therapists is not clear. Whatever the cause, the demand for a solution was considerable.

A serious look at the problem resulted in a host of new dilemmas. What constitutes a diagnosis of desire deficit or excess? In the absence of agreed upon norms for sexual behavior, it was difficult to determine just how much or how little sexual behavior constituted a problem that demanded treatment. Various therapists handled the issue differently. Some felt that diagnosis rested with the individual or couple requesting treatment, while others felt the need to establish more absolute criteria. Still others felt that the problem should not be labeled a dysfunction at all. Nevertheless, there was general agreement that we had ignored and now must recognize the importance of the desire phase in our conceptualization of the sexual response cycle. Deficiencies and excesses in sexual interest were every bit as problematic as erectile or orgasmic disorders.

Other problems became apparent. Investigation revealed that some individuals had active sexual lives but reported little satisfaction, while others reported low sexual frequencies but satisfaction, and still others reported prompt physical arousal and moderate sexual activity but little subjective pleasure. More and more therapists were forced to acknowledge the role of subjective satisfaction in determining sexual activity and arousal.

When clinicians attempted to treat problems of sexual desire, they often encountered failure. Whether because of inadequate assessment of the parameters of the presenting problem or deficiencies in their therapeutic armamentarium, the outcome often left much to be desired.

In light of the complex conceptual, assessment, and treatment issues, we have included two chapters on problems of sexual desire in this volume. There are areas of agreement as well as evidence of disagreement in the viewpoints expressed. Both LoPiccolo and Zilbergeld and Ellison acknowledge the diagnostic confusion present in this area and note that the absence of established norms on sexual frequencies for individuals of varying ages, socioeconomic groups, and relationship status complicates the issue. The authors emphasize the importance of cognitive and subjective factors, among other variables, in contributing to both the cause and the treatment of the problem. LoPiccolo stresses the importance of cognitive variables in affecting what is perceived as sexually arousing and in determining expectations about one's ability to become sexually aroused. In a similar vein, Zilbergeld and Ellison assist clients in relabeling states of physiological activation as indicative of, or leading to, sexual arousal. Zilbergeld and Ellison suggest that a diagnosis of sexual desire difficulty must be based on the discrepancy between the partners in a dyad—it cannot exist independently. Therapeutic work is consequently directed at both the individual with little and the individual with considerable desire. LoPiccolo also treats the couple, but greater attention appears to be paid to the individual with low sexual interest. Neither chapter addresses the treatment approach adopted with the single individual or the individual without a current partner.

Both chapters offer a salient discussion of the problem and indicate the multiple treatment options available for dealing with desire discrepancies. They indicate the necessity of going beyond circumscribed assessment and intervention methods if the outcome is to be favorable. While many questions remain concerning the cause and resolution of sexual desire difficulties, the chapters by LoPiccolo and by Zilbergeld and Ellison make useful suggestions for the treatment of this problem.

2

Low Sexual Desire

LESLIE LOPICCOLO

In her chapter on low sexual desire, LoPiccolo summarizes the various theorists and theories that have attempted to account for the perplexing problem of diminished or low sexual interest. She is drawn to the conclusion that the host of psychological, physiological, sociological, learning/conditioning, hormonal/neuroendocrine, and cognitive factors that may be implicated in cases of low sexual interest contribute to the complexity of diagnostic and treatment issues involved in such cases.

LoPiccolo emphasizes that low sexual interest is not a unitary syndrome. Rather, each case may reflect a particular aspect of the problem, and require a unique treatment program. Given the variety of factors involved in the genesis and maintenance of the problem, assessment is particularly critical. If assessment is inadequate, incomplete, or incorrect, failure may result despite the best intentions of client and therapist. Conversely, even where assessment adequately identifies the multicausal determinants of the difficulty, if therapist–client power struggles exist or if change results in disrupting an implicit balance between partners, problem resolution may be less than satisfactory.

The variety of treatment interventions necessary in cases of low sexual interest parallels the variety of contributing etiological factors. LoPiccolo describes the range of interventions that may be employed in treatment, including self-stimulation exercises, fantasy training, couple sensual exercises, relationship-enhancement techniques, anxiety-reduction techniques, and exploration of intrapsychic and interpersonal conflict. The cases she presents to illustrate her therapeutic approach are good examples of the complexity of assessment and treatment and the clinical acumen needed by the therapist.

Leslie LoPiccolo is currently a psychologist in private practice in San Francisco, California, and the coauthor of several books on sex therapy, including the Handbook of Sex Therapy *and* Becoming Orgasmic: A Sexual Growth Program for Women.

Since the pioneering work of Alfred Kinsey and his associates in the 1940s, human sexual behavior has become the subject of increasingly sophisticated scientific investigation. What is emerging from this research is a view of human sexuality as an exquisitely complex phenomenon determined and influenced by a myriad of physiological, sociological, and psychological factors.

Until now, most of our information about sexual functioning has come from work done primarily with two groups of people: sociological studies of people whose sexual functioning is unimpaired or "normal" and clinical studies of those who experience problems or are "dysfunctional" and, therefore by implication, "not normal." However, researchers and clinicians working in the area of sexuality have become increasingly aware of the limitations of such a dichotomy. They are being challenged to develop effective intervention strategies for individuals who do not fit neatly into either category, for example, individuals who have little desire for sexual expression with their partner or spouse but who are usually not "dysfunctional" at those times when they do engage in sex with their partner. In other cases, a specific dysfunction such as erectile problems may exist, but it is clearly secondary to a lack of desire for, or an aversion to, sex.

The distinction between "normal" and "not normal" and "functional" and "dysfunctional" makes it difficult to define precisely, and indeed conceptualize, what we are talking about when we refer to problems of low sexual desire. Part of the difficulty stems from the lack of clarity with which we talk about sexual desire or drive in humans. What are the possible etiologic factors that may contribute to disinterest in sex? Is there a biological sexual drive or instinct which is innate but capable of being repressed in some individuals? Or is sexual desire a product of an individual's learning and experiences, with only the physiology of sexual arousal being innate? How can the phenomenon of low desire be assessed, and what treatment strategies seem to be effective? The purpose of this chapter is to address some of these questions and present illustrative case material.

Theoretical Perspectives on the Etiology of Low Desire

In *Three Essays on the Theory of Sexuality*, Freud (1905/1962) wrote of the existence in humans of a "sexual instinct" or libido. According to Freud, libido is determined by a number of factors, such as chemical processes within the individual and individual variations in constitution and heredity. This innate sexual instinct is not static but is subject to modification and even suppression.

According to Freud's formulations, low sexual desire can be conceptualized as a dissociation of the sexual instinct. This dissociation is the result of excessive defensive inhibition during sexual maturation or certain constitutional factors within the individual. Low sexual desire would be more likely to occur in women, since Freud believed that there was a greater tendency toward inhibition and repression in girls than in boys. He also believed that males possessed a greater intensity of innate libido.

Along with these factors, Freud also postulated a relationship between unresolved oedipal conflicts coupled with unacknowledged homosexual desires and suppression of libido or aversion to heterosexual sex (Freud, 1920).

Freud, of course, based his formulations on a small number of clinical cases drawn from a basically homogeneous socioeconomic group. Alfred Kinsey's research, in contrast to Freud's, was based on case histories of over 12,000 males and females from a wide range of socioeconomic, religious, and geographical groups (Kinsey, Pomeroy, Martin, & Gebhard, 1965).

Unlike Freud, Kinsey did not postulate the existence of sexual instinct or drive. Rather, he believed individuals were born merely with an innate capacity to respond to physical or psychologic stimuli and that most aspects of human sexual behavior were the product of learning and conditioning. The attitudes which an individual developed as a result of learning and conditioning would "have considerable significance in determining subsequent acceptance or avoidance of particular types of overt sexual activity" (Kinsey *et al.*, 1965, p. 649).

While discounting the notion of an innate sexual drive, Kinsey, like Freud, believed that gender differences between males and females accounted for a greater desire in males for regular and frequent sexual activity. Kinsey felt that even given individual variations, males are generally more responsive to psychologic sexual stimuli which exist in the environment and experience greater desire for sexual expression. Although he believed that biologic, psychologic, and sociologic factors all influenced rates of sexual activity, he also believed that certain individuals "never were equipped to respond erotically" (Kinsey, Pomeroy, & Martin, 1948, p. 209). These individuals would, in a sense, be unresponsive to sexual stimulation or would fail to be conditioned even by positive sexual experiences. Such individuals would tend to experience little sexual desire.

In *Human Sexual Inadequacy* (Masters & Johnson, 1970), there are two brief sections on low sexual tension as a clinical entity. Both discuss the problem as it relates to a subgroup of women who would be

classified as situationally orgasmic. These women have "random orgasmic inadequacy" problems in that they "are rarely orgasmic and
usually are aware of little or no physical need for sexual expression"
(Masters & Johnson, 1970, p. 240). The tendency up till now to see
problems of low desire primarily in relation to women is reflected in
the fact that no mention is made of this phenomenon in males in *Human
Sexual Inadequacy* (Masters & Johnson, 1970).

Sexual functioning is viewed by Masters and Johnson as a natural
physiological process that can be inhibited or denied expression. One
hypothesis they put forth as to possible etiology in cases of random
orgasmic inadequacy is that prior negative conditioning experiences
(psychosocial influences) interfere with the woman's ability to respond
to positive sexual stimuli. These women do not give themselves "permission" to function sexually. This "blocking of receptivity to sexual
stimuli is an unfortunate result of factors which deprive her of the
capacity to value the sexual component of her personality or prevent
her from placing its value within the context of her life" (Masters &
Johnson, 1970, p. 315).

Not all individuals with low sexual desire have a history of negative or traumatic experiences, however. Also, the fact that in the
nonclinical population there are individuals with traumatic histories
who do not experience sexual problems suggests the influence of other
factors.

The lack of an adequate conceptualization of etiology in such
cases is reflected in the relatively high failure rates for treated cases of
random orgasmic inadequacy reported by Masters and Johnson. It is
possible that one problem in treating such cases may stem from the
assumption that desire is always part of the natural physiological
process of sexual functioning for all individuals.

The general success of the Masters and Johnson approach to the
treatment of sexual dysfunctions led to the questioning of earlier
psychoanalytic formulations about sexual problems. In *The New Sex
Therapy,* Kaplan (1974) attempts to integrate psychoanalytic and behavioral concepts of sexual dysfunction and treatment. Although she
does not talk about libido as such, she does refer to a "sexual urge" or
"craving for sexual expression":

[This sexual urge] can be suppressed and diverted and a person
can survive indefinitely without any sexual release at all. This
dichotomy between the urgent craving to seek erotic pleasure and
the ability to delay, divert, or modify sexual expression indefinitely sets the groundwork for prolonged and extensive sexual

frustration, inhibitions, variations, and compromises in sexual expression. (p. 45)

According to this view, the root of sexual problems is unconscious sexual conflict which arises in childhood out of the desire to act on sexual and aggressive wishes and the fear of doing so. For some individuals, subsequent sexual behavior evokes anxiety and unconscious guilt which is dealt with through the mechanism of repression. However, the sexual conflicts remain in the unconscious, and sexual wishes are often "denied, and then delayed, diverted, and expressed in distorted and neurotic ways" (Kaplan, 1974, p. 140). One result of this process may be alienation of individuals from their own sexuality. These individuals would tend to avoid erotic stimulation and intimacy as a way of coping with feelings of anxiety and guilt which these situations arouse. Certain cases of low sexual desire, where feelings of anxiety and guilt are expressed, might be conceptualized in this way.

More recently, Kaplan (1977) specifically addressed the phenomenon of low-libido disorders or what she calls, "hypoactive sexual desire." These disorders are seen as an impairment of the desire phase of the sexual response cycle. Kaplan describes desire for sex as an "appetite" which originates in the brain and which is dependent on testosterone in both males and females. Anything which acts as a central nervous system depressant or interferes with testosterone and the balance between estrogen and testosterone, such as illness or stress, can decrease sexual desire.

A useful typology is suggested by Kaplan for classifying cases of low sexual desire. Cases can be primary, secondary, and either global or situational. In cases of primary hypoactive sexual desire, there has been a total lack of sexual desire throughout the individual's life. Secondary hypoactive desire refers to those cases in whom desire was present at some point in the individual's life but then disappeared, such as after the birth of a child. Situational hypoactive desire refers to individuals who experience a lack of desire in particular situations while not in others—for example, those who experience desire only in extramarital relationships—while global hypoactivity would indicate a current lack of desire regardless of situational variables.

These distinctions would seem to have important implications for the development of an effective treatment program in cases of low sexual desire. It seems reasonable to assume that the etiology of the various forms of hypoactive sexual desire Kaplan identifies may differ, as well as the psychological components which may be involved in maintenance of this disorder.

Psychological Components of Low Sexual Desire

The experience of anxiety is frequently implicated in the etiology and maintenance of sexual dysfunction and would seem to have relevance for understanding certain cases of low sexual desire as well. Sufficient anxiety can interfere with the processes of arousal and orgasm and may also inhibit the experience of sexual desire.

Sexual anxiety can stem from many sources, such as feelings of guilt, performance fears, and fears of intimacy or commitment. For those individuals in whom anxiety is associated with the arousal process, suppression of sexual thoughts and feelings and avoidance of sexual situations and stimuli will serve to reduce anxiety and maintain a pattern of low sexual desire. The presence of anxiety in all cases of low desire, however, has not been demonstrated, and its role needs to be clarified by further research.

Like anxiety, depression is often associated with a decrease in sexual behavior and desire for sex. Important variables may be severity and duration of depression as well as etiology. In some cases, depression and low desire may be a result of a dysfunction in one or both partners or a reaction to some particular life event or stress. The prognosis for such cases, in response to sex therapy, is often more optimistic than for those cases in whom depression preceded the sexual dysfunction, or in whom it is identified as chronic and a major cause of low sexual desire (Kaplan, 1974; Lobitz & Lobitz, 1978).

The fact that depression may actually interfere with the physiological processes of menstruation, arousal, and orgasm points out the intricate relationship between gonadal steroids, the central nervous system, and the regulation of affects and behaviors (Bardwick, 1971; Kaplan, 1974). Because of the feedback nature of the neurohormonal system, affects, cognitions, and other inputs can influence central nervous system functioning as well as be influenced by it.

Recently, numerous studies have attempted to investigate the neurohormonal basis of sexual behavior (Davidson, 1977; Everitt, 1977; Herbert, 1974). The majority of this research, however, has been done with animals, and extrapolation from these data to the study of human sexuality is problematic.

Research with humans tends to implicate testicular androgens (testosterone in particular) as the biological substrate for sexual drive and behavior in men. The effect of androgens on facilitating sexual responsiveness in women has also been shown (Carney, Bancroft, & Mathews, 1977). However, data in this area are extremely complex and often contradictory. Consequently, there is relatively little that can be said with certainty about the relationship between the levels of the various hormones and the level of sexual desire. Research seems to indicate that certain threshold levels of androgen may be necessary but not sufficient to elicit sexual desire and activity, at least in males. However, no reliable association between circulating levels of androgens and sexual behavior has been found.

A variety of factors make interpretation of research data in this area extremely difficult. For example, there are problems with looking only at circulating levels of testosterone without considering other factors, including the role of neurotransmitters which might mediate the effects of hormones on sexual behavior. Davidson (1977) also mentions the action of binding proteins which render some of the circulating androgens ineffective. Measures of androgen levels must, therefore, distinguish between bound and unbound androgen. The metabolism of androgen within the cell through the process of aromatization, as well as the role of tissue sensitivity and the function of receptor sites in the brain, need to be clarified by further investigation. In addition, research needs to focus on the relationship of the gonadal hormones to the pituitary and thyroid hormones which have also been implicated as biochemical correlates of sexual behavior.

Research in the area of sexual dysfunction has been focused largely on the processes involved in sexual function and dysfunction, with particular emphasis on the ability to attain orgasm and erection and to delay ejaculation. The process of arousal and the subjective dimension of sexual desire have been largely ignored. Cognitions, however, can have a profound effect on what is perceived as sexually arousing by an individual and in ultimately determining the subjective experience of pleasure. For this reason, an exploration of the role of cognitions in sexual arousal is particularly relevant to the study of low sexual desire.

Heiman and Morokoff (1977) studied female sexual arousal and experience as correlates of what they term "sexual malaise." On the basis of their data, they speculate that although subjective sexual arousal and physical sexual arousal are independent components of the erotic experience, one dimension can influence the other. That is, an individual's expectations and cognitions can alter his or her perception of the physical experience, and perceptions of the physical experience can alter future expectations and cognitions. In some women, disagreement between subjective and physiological sexual arousal levels may be due to a "diminished subjective erotic experience of these physical feelings" (Heiman & Morokoff, 1977, p. 12).

Rook and Hammen (1977) suggest a variety of cognitive processes that can affect sexual arousal. These include, among others, perception and misperception of internal and external cues associated with arousal, labeling of sensations and stimuli as arousing or erotic, and the effect of expectations on arousal. Applying cognitive formulations to cases of low sexual desire would predict that certain individuals with low desire:

1. Have not learned to perceive or perceive *accurately* their own levels of physiological sexual arousal. Perception of arousal (such as genital sensations) is diminished or mislabeled.

2. Have not learned how to facilitate arousal in themselves.

3. Use a limited set of cues to define a situation as sexual.

4. Use a limited set of cues to define their own sexual arousal.

5. Have limited expectations for their own ability to be aroused.

6. On the basis of the above, tend not to perceive themselves as very sexual.

Some cases of low sexual desire indeed seem to fit this pattern. These individuals, in effect, tune out or mislabel internal and external sources of sexual stimulation. They may see themselves as not very sexual and generally experience disinterest in sex. Once in a situation defined by them as sexual, however, they may be able to experience arousal and pleasure. The presence or absence of anxiety, once in a sexual situation, may be an important mediating factor in such an individual's ability to experience arousal and pleasure.

A review of the literature, then, implicates psychological, physiological, sociological, learning/conditioning, hormonal/neuroendocrine, and cognitive factors as determinants of sexual arousal and behavior. The differential influence of these factors in determining the sexual experience of a given individual complicates the issues of diagnosis and treatment in cases of low sexual desire.

Issues in the Diagnosis of Low Sexual Desire

Exactly what constitutes a low frequency of sexual desire, and what is the incidence of such problems in the population? Kinsey's data provide some information as to the actual frequency of sexual activities among various groups of people. Total outlet (sexual activity that results in orgasm) for females was reported separately for single, married, and previously married women. For our purposes, the data on married women are most useful. Not surprisingly, after marriage, frequency of total outlet for the women studied increased. However, this increase steadily declined after age 20. Kinsey notes that these "aging effects" largely reflect changes in the sexual functioning of the males in these couples (Kinsey *et al.,* 1965, p. 528). Decade of birth, education, and religious background all correlated with frequency of total outlet among married women. For the first two factors (decade of birth and education level), there was a positive correlation with higher frequency of total outlet. For the last factor (religious background), there was a negative correlation.

The range of variation in sexual responsiveness and frequency of total outlet in the females was greater than the range in the males studied. However, while Kinsey's data showed three-quarters (77.7%) of the males falling within a range of 1.0 to 6.5 sexual outlets per week, there was still nearly a quarter (22.3%) of the males who fell into the extreme ranges. The extremes ranged from a man who had ejaculated only once in 30 years to others who averaged 20 or more ejaculations per week. Of the females studied, about 2% had never experienced sexual arousal under any condition.

In the volume on male sexual behavior (Kinsey *et al.,* 1948), Kinsey devotes a section to data on 179 males with low frequency of total outlet. These males were under 36 years of age, and their rates of total outlet averaged once in 2 weeks, or lower, for periods of at least 5 years. There is no such section in the volume on female sexual behavior (Kinsey *et al.,* 1965), perhaps reflecting Kinsey's belief that low sexual outlet is a more unusual condition for males. Kinsey found average frequencies of total outlet of once in 2 weeks, or lower, in 11.2% of the males under age 31 and average frequencies of between 0.0 and once in 10 weeks in 2.9% of the population under 31. He also found that the number of low-frequency males increased after age 35. Although males with low outlet were found in a cross section of the population studied, certain associations did emerge. Low sexual outlet was more often associated with less education, religious activity (especially Catholics and Orthodox Jews), and males who reached adolescence after age 11 (as measured by age at first ejaculation unless clearly preceded a year or more by physical development).

According to Kinsey, certain of these 179 males can be characterized as sexually "apathetic." These men have a consistent history of low sexual activity:

> After these apathetic persons have had orgasm, they may go for some days or weeks without further arousal. There are few, if any, psychologic stimuli which will excite them, and even when these males deliberately put themselves in erotic situations which involve active petting and genital manipulation, they may be unable

to respond more than once in several weeks. (Kinsey *et al.*, 1948, p. 209)

Other males with low rates of sexual outlet did not appear to be apathetic, but inhibited. Inhibited males actively avoid certain sexual situations and experience anxiety and fear in many sexual contexts.

The tremendous range of sexual variation among males and females convinced Kinsey of the meaninglessness of such terms as "normal" and "abnormal" in describing human sexual behavior. Rather, he viewed sexual frequency as falling along a curve, no portion of which could be designated as "normal."

No individual has a sexual frequency which differs in anything but a slight degree from the frequencies of those placed next on the curve. Such a continuous and widely spread series raises a question as to whether the terms "normal" and "abnormal" belong in a scientific vocabulary. At best, abnormal may designate certain individuals whose rates of activity are less frequent... but in that case, it is preferable to refer to such persons as rare, rather than abnormal. (Kinsey *et al.*, 1948, pp. 199, 201)

More recent data (Fisher, 1973; Hunt, 1974) indicate an increase in the frequency of activities such as marital and extramarital coitus and masturbation for both men and women since Kinsey collected his data.

There are several factors that argue for caution when interpreting these data as measures of sexual desire. First, figures on frequency of coitus, for example, are not necessarily an accurate measure of sexual desire, since numerous other factors such as marital status and desire to please one's partner may influence coital frequency. Second, it is necessary to distinguish between *actual* frequency of a particular sexual behavior and *desired* frequency, something which Kinsey, for one, does not do. An individual may be engaging in a sexual activity more or less than he or she actually desires to. Also, just looking at activities *engaged in* does not provide data on desire in relation to other activities which the individual might like to try. A third factor, that of the subjective experience of the individual in terms of arousal, pleasure, or discomfort, is not assessed by measures of frequency.

An additional problem with using normative data as a criterion for diagnosis is that in order for a comparison to be meaningful, individuals should be assessed with reference to the norms most relevant for them. Kinsey's data demonstrated that norms can vary with age, race, socioeconomic status, and other factors. Detailed norms, however, are usually not available. For example, what are the norms for masturbation, intercourse, and other sexual activities among male, middle-aged, religiously active Catholics in Suffolk County on Long Island?

Another way to approach diagnosis would be to use the individual's or couple's own definition of low sexual desire, but this is also problematic. Often, a complaint of low sexual desire may be due to unrealistic expectations about sexual functioning ("A male should always feel aroused by the sight of his wife's nude body") or disagreements about desired frequency of sexual activity. When disagreements over frequency arise, a pattern of daily (or more often) initiation by one partner and frequent refusal by the other often becomes established. In such cases, the partner who refuses is defined by the couple as having a lack of desire for sex, even though he or she may desire and engage in sexual behavior fairly often.

Recently, some data (Frank, Anderson, & Rubinstein, 1978) on the incidence of problems of desire and aversion to sex in a normal population were gathered. Analysis of the data from a sample of 100 predominantly white, nonclinical couples showed a surprisingly high incidence of sexual dysfunctions and sexual "difficulties."

Comparison of the sexual difficulties showed that 35% of the women and 16% of the men complained of "disinterest" in sex, and 28% of the women and 10% of the men experienced being "turned off" by sex. The strong influence of such difficulties on sexual satisfaction is shown by the fact that the number of difficulties reported by a couple was "more strongly and consistently related to overall sexual dissatisfaction than the number of 'dysfunctions' " (Frank *et al.,* 1978, p. 111). In terms of frequency of intercourse, 33% of the couples were having intercourse two to three times a month or less. In general, the more sexual dysfunctions and difficulties a couple had, the lower the frequency of intercourse.

Certain limitations of this and similar studies, however, should be kept in mind when attempting to apply results to the problem of low sexual desire. Frequency of intercourse, for example, was the only sexual behavior measured. No data were gathered on the incidence of masturbation, nocturnal emission, sexual fantasies or erotic dreams, extramarital relations, or other forms of sexual activity such as petting to orgasm which presumably reflect the presence of some level of sexual desire. Also, measures of desired frequency for intercourse as well as other sexual behaviors are lacking. However, it is clear that these data indicate that the incidence of disinterest and distaste for sex in a nonclinical population may be higher than has previously been assumed.

Informal data on the incidence of problems of desire are also available from those working in the field of sex therapy. A review of the 39 most recently completed cases involving a specific dysfunction at the

Sex Therapy Center, Department of Psychiatry, State University of New York at Stony Brook, showed that in 27 of the cases there was a complaint of low sexual desire. Seventeen of the men (63%) and 10 of the women (37%) indicated that low sexual desire was a problem for them:

| | Low desire | |
Presenting problem	*Male*	*Female*
Male dysfunction	7	2
Female dysfunction	2	4
Both male and female dysfunction	8	4

Analysis of 16 cases of low sexual desire without the presence of a dysfunction, seen over the same time period, showed that in four cases the male experienced low desire and in 12 cases the female experienced low desire.

What factors may account for what appears to be an increase in the number of clinical cases which involve disorders of the desire phase of the sexual response cycle? One factor may be that the seeming increase is actually an artifact of more sophisticated typology and assessment in the area of sexual problems. In certain cases, resistance in therapy is a clue to the presence of problems of desire. Indeed, Kaplan (1977) states:

> I first became interested in hypoactivity of sexual desire while studying failures in sex therapy. As I reviewed the records of those patients who had failed to improve in the course of psychosexual therapy, it became apparent that lack of sexual desire contributed heavily to our failure population. In addition, aversive reactions to sex therapy sometimes took the form of loss of desire; that is, some patients and/or their partners reported that they lost interest in sex after the target symptom had improved. (pp. 3–4)

A second factor in the increase in the number of people with problems of desire seeking sex therapy may be changes in cultural values regarding sexuality. Currently, sexual functioning is valued in our culture, and individuals with low sexual desire may be under increasing pressure to enter therapy. "As much as recent sex researchers have repudiated many of the destructive myths of the past, revised values have placed new demands on individuals' sexual expectations" (J. LoPiccolo & Heiman, 1978, p. 61).

It is interesting to speculate on whether or not any commonalities can be found among cases of low sexual desire. The only published data on this are Kinsey's (Kinsey *et al.*, 1948) data that low sexual outlet was associated with less education, religious activity, and age at adolescence. Kaplan (1977) suggests:

> Patients exhibiting hypoactivity of sexual desire tend to be, as a group, more injured, more vulnerable, and, therefore, more rigidly defensive than those whose orgasm and/or erection are impaired while desire remains active. (p. 8)

A review of cases involving low sexual desire that applied for therapy to the Sex Therapy Center at the State University of New York at Stony Brook revealed some interesting patterns. These findings are not based on a systematic analysis of all cases of low sexual desire presenting to the center, but on a subsample selected at random by the author. Therefore, the presence of such patterns in cases of low sexual desire should be regarded as speculative at present. In the cases reviewed, low sexual desire was often associated with:

1. A history of depression or current complaints of depression.

2. Catholicism (active or inactive).

3. The presence of a sexual dysfunction.

4. Aversion to oral–genital contact.

5. Aversion to female genitals (in both men and women with low sexual desire).

6. A history of never masturbating or masturbation at one time which was discontinued.

7. The presence of marital problems as assessed by the clinician but denied by the couple.

Certainly, further research is needed to substantiate the presence or absence of these or similar factors in cases of low sexual desire. Careful assessment is the first step in accurate diagnosis. Assessment also forms the basis for conceptualizations about etiology and maintenance which are vital for the formulation of effective treatment strategies.

Assessment in Cases of Low Sexual Desire

The theoretical framework with which one approaches the problem of low desire will influence which dimensions one chooses to assess and focus on, and to what degree. Assessment for the purpose of *client evaluation* and *treatment formulation* will focus on those dimensions which are likely to have the greatest therapeutic relevance. Assessment and *research* for the purpose of increasing our knowledge and understanding of this problem will necessarily be broad in focus. The fact that so little is known in this area and that success with such cases has been minimal argues for implementation of the multimodal approach whenever possible. Ideally, complete assessment would include:

1. A measure of the couple's and individual's *actual* sexual behavior, including such things as frequency of intercourse, manual stimulation, oral–genital contact, and so on. A good instrument for this is the Sexual Interaction Inventory (SII) (LoPiccolo & Steger, 1974). Certain items particularly relevant to low-desire cases are not included, however, and need to be assessed, for example, the frequency of occurrence, content, and subjective reaction to sexual thoughts, fantasies, or erotic dreams; spontaneous erections or nocturnal emissions; masturbation; reaction to erotic films, books, or magazines; initiation and refusal of sexual activity; and occurrence of extramarital sexual behaviors. How situational variables affect behaviors also needs to be assessed.

2. A measure of *desired* frequency for each of the various activities engaged in *and* a measure of interest in or desired frequency for sexual activities currently not engaged in. It cannot be assumed that because a couple or individual does not engage in a particular sexual behavior, they have no desire to do so. The SII can be used to measure desired frequency for the range of 17 behaviors it covers.

3. Subjective measures of emotional response to the sexual behaviors engaged in, and measures where the individual predicts his or her responses to behaviors not engaged in. For females, the Sexual Arousability Inventory (Hoon, Hoon, & Wincze, 1976) would be useful. The SII also provides a measure of some of these dimensions. However, although it measures pleasure in relation to the various sexual activities included, it does not assess arousal. Arousal may be a totally distinct dimension from pleasure, especially in cases of low desire. Therefore, additional questions assessing arousal responses to the sexual activities should be included, as well as an assessment of what situational variables influence responsiveness and in what direction. The SII also provides information on the satisfaction/ dissatisfaction dimension. Three of the scales, frequency of dissatisfaction, self-acceptance, and mate-acceptance, are difference scores based on the discrepancies between the way an individual says things are sexually and how he or she would like them to be.

4. Psychophysiological assessment of vasocongestion as a measure of sexual arousal (Heiman, 1977, 1978b). The relationship between the subjective experience of arousal or lack of arousal and psychophysiological measures of arousal yields important information about cognitions and misperceptions which may be contributing to the problem of low sexual desire.

5. Assessment of sexual functioning through medical examination and psychophysiological measurement. The possible effects of drugs, illness, fatigue, and aging need to be evaluated. Genital plethysmography appears to be useful in evaluating cases where impotency is a problem (Karacan, 1978). Gynecological and urological exams should also be performed.

6. Evaluation of the neuroendocrine/hormonal component of sexual functioning. Relevant workups would include plasma testosterone levels taken on at least two separate occasions, levels of estrogen and prolactin, estrogen/testosterone ratio, and the percentage of circulating unbound testosterone. Tests to detect diabetes and evaluate thyroid functioning should be done, as well as a buccal smear evaluation for detecting Klinefelter's syndrome.

7. Measures of anxiety or aversion in relation to various body parts and functions, such as male and female genitals, vaginal lubrication, and semen; measures of inhibiting attitudes such as guilt; and measures such as Annon's Sexual Fear Inventory (Annon, 1975) and Mosher's Sex Guilt Scale (Mosher, 1968).

8. Measures of anxiety and depression, such as the SCL-90 (Derogatis, Lipman, & Covi, 1973), the Profile of Mood States (McNair, Lorr, & Droppleman, 1971), and the Zung Scale (Zung, 1973).

9. Measures of psychosexual development through the use of a life-history questionnaire or interview (Heiman, 1978a; L. LoPiccolo & Heiman, 1978).

10. Measures of marital satisfaction and other aspects of the couple's relationship which are relevant, such as trust, physical attraction, intimacy, communication, anger and resentment, and power conflicts and disagreements. The Locke–Wallace Marital Inventory (Kimmel & Van Der Veen, 1974) is useful as a measure of general marital satisfaction. The "P" Questionnaire (Nowinski, 1978) is particularly useful to assess factors more relevant to the area of sexual satisfaction.

11. Assessment of knowledge, cognitions, and expectations in the areas of sex and marriage, moral and religious value systems, and sex-role expectations which may influence sexual desire and behavior. The "P" Questionnaire (Nowinski, 1978) and the Attitudes toward

Women Scale (Spence, Helmreich, & Stapp, 1973), as well as a life-history questionnaire, are such measures.

12. Assessment of defensiveness and/or rigidity. The Marriage and Sexual Defensiveness Scales (Jemail, 1977), designed to measure defensiveness specific to marriage and sex, would be such a measure.

13. Measures of psychopathology, such as the MMPI (Dahlstrom, Welsh, & Dahlstrom, 1972).

14. A general personality measure, such as the 16 Personality Factor Questionnaire (Cattell, Eber, & Tatswoka, 1970) or the Jackson Personality Research Form (Jackson, 1965).

Such detailed assessment is not always possible or necessary in every case. The clinician may choose to focus on those areas which will directly influence the therapy process. More informal clinical evaluation is also an alternative to paper-and-pencil measures of the areas cited above.

Treatment of Low Sexual Desire

There are three bases from which to begin formulating treatment for cases of low sexual desire:

1. Knowledge of human sexual function and dysfunction.

2. Knowledge of the various theoretical formulations and conceptual frameworks with which to approach the problem of low sexual desire.

3. Knowledge of the individual and the particular client couple based on a thorough assessment.

On the basis of this knowledge, therapy would focus on those dimensions which are most relevant for each particular case. Treatment could incorporate any of the following elements and interventions:

1. Hormonal therapy in cases where hormonal deficits have been established.

2. Treatment of a specific dysfunction if present.

3. Anxiety reduction—desensitization of aversive or phobic responses, relaxation training, sensate-focus exercises, flooding, education and information, rational-emotive therapy (RET), guilt reduction, removal of performance demands, dealing with issues concerned with conception and contraception.

4. Treatment of depression—medication, RET, behavioral techniques such as increasing activity levels and reinforcement, social and interpersonal skill training, assertiveness training, dealing with environmental/life factors.

5. *Increasing sensory awareness*—biofeedback techniques, sensate-focus exercises, tracking sexual thoughts and feelings, Gestalt techniques, increasing accuracy of perception and accurate labeling of sensations and responses, education about sexual responses, increasing awareness of situational variables and environmental influences.

6. *Improving the relationship*—conflict resolution, communication training, increasing level of trust and sharing, assertiveness training, increasing positive reinforcers and decreasing negatives, reduction of negative affect such as anger and resentment and facilitation of positive affect.

7. *Enhancing sexual/sensual experiences*—education and information, sexual communication, encouraging the use of facilitating fantasies, increasing comfort and skill of initiation and refusal of sexual activity, expanding the sexual repertoire, removing performance demands, increasing effectiveness of sexual technique, creating a sensual environment.

8. *Facilitation of erotic responses*—improving body image, fantasy training, encouraging masturbation, exercises on "letting go," increasing expressiveness during sex (physical movement as well as verbal and nonverbal communication), exposure to erotic stimuli, learning particular techniques to enhance arousal.

9. *Dealing with intrapsychic conflicts* such as fears of intimacy, dependence/independence conflicts, fears of the opposite sex, and fears of loss of control.

These interventions are not unique to cases of low sexual desire, but are used at various times in treatment of sexual dysfunction or general sexual dissatisfaction. The distinction may be one of degree in terms of a need to focus in greater depth on particular dimensions of the problem. Indeed, it seems helpful for therapy to conceptualize cases of low desire (where there is no apparent hormonal or physiological basis) as a sexual dysfunction. As in the case of other dysfunctions, the psychological determinants of low desire can be thought of as "multicausal," including intrapsychic conflict, dyadic or relationship causes, learned causes, and immediate causes such as failure to communicate (Kaplan, 1974).

If it is true that problems of low desire are etiologically similar to other sexual dysfunctions, what accounts for the low rates of successful treatment when compared to the relatively high rates for other dysfunctions? One reason may be inadequate attention to the possible biological determinants of such syndromes; another, the tendency to focus on treatment of specific dysfunctions without attending to (or recognizing) problems of desire; third, inadequate assessment which contributes to failure to discriminate among cases of low desire; and fourth, the presence of certain therapy issues which make therapy particularly difficult. These issues will be discussed later in relation to the two cases presented.

Two Cases of Low Desire

The two cases to be described were seen for 15 sessions of therapy at the Sex Therapy Center, Department of Psychiatry and Behavioral Science, State Univeristy of New York at Stony Brook.[1] Although both involve male clients, they are sufficiently different to illustrate some of the many dimensions involved in cases of low desire.

Case A

Mr. and Mrs. A. were referred to the center by a therapist with whom they had been working on marital problems. The presenting complaint was low frequency of intercourse due to lack of desire on Mr. A.'s part. The couple had been married 5 years and felt the sexual problem had existed from the beginning of their marriage. Both were in their 30s at the time they were seen.

Assessment

The frequency of intercourse at intake was once every 2 weeks to once a month. Mrs. A. usually initiated sex, and when she did, Mr. A. would accept reluctantly. Mr. A. had masturbated only very rarely in the past and currently did not masturbate. Within the last several months, he had begun to experience erectile difficulties both before and during intercourse. Mr. A. would occasionally have morning erections but was not aware of any nocturnal emissions and rarely had explicit sexual fantasies. Occasionally, he would wonder about how it would be to have sex with other women. Both Mr. and Mrs. A. expressed negative feelings about masturbation and what they called the "kinkier" aspects of sex. They also expressed fears about what they would be asked to do as part of therapy.

When seen alone, Mr. A. confided that he found his wife very unappealing physically and that he was often turned off at the idea of having sex with her. His score on the Locke–Wallace Marital Inventory was 66, indicating a great deal of dissatisfaction with the marriage.

On the Sexual Interaction Inventory (SII), Mr. A.'s scores indicated low self-acceptance and a lack of pleasure from those sexual activities in which they engaged. Both expressed some dissatisfaction with the frequency with which they engaged in various sexual activities. Mrs. A.'s scores indicated some lack of pleasure in their sexual activities and poor perceptual accuracy in terms of awareness of her husband's sexual preferences.

Before treatment, both Mr. and Mrs. A. were referred for medical evaluation. Findings on both were negative, and a diagnosis of psychogenic loss of libido in the case of Mr. A. was made by the consulting physician.

History

Mrs. A. had a relatively uneventful childhood. She was the youngest of three children. Her father was rather reserved and withdrawn and was somewhat uncomfortable around the children. However, she felt the relationship between her parents was warm and affectionate.

Sex was rarely mentioned at home, and when Mrs. A. began to menstruate, she was given a book to read which was never discussed. She was self-conscious about menstruation and resented what seemed to be only a discomfort and inconvenience. She experienced cramps with menstruation for many years, and although these have disappeared, she seemed to have retained negative feelings about her genitals and mestruation, which she viewed as nature's "mistake."

Mrs. A. never went to her parents with questions about sex and she never masturbated. She first heard a description of intercourse in the ninth grade from friends. She recalled thinking it sounded horrible, "something someone did to you." The idea of being passive and the possibility of pain frightened her. She would kiss and pet (including breast touching) on dates, but would never allow genital touching.

Mr. A. was an only child who spent a great deal of time with his parents. He led an extremely secure, settled life and always felt "unusually close" to his parents, particularly his mother, whom he viewed as like him in many ways. His mother was the more affectionate parent, while his father was the disciplinarian. Mr. A.'s parents never spoke with him about sex, and he did not recall any negative experiences. He recalled being aroused by reading erotic magazines and experiencing wet dreams around age 13 or so. He would occasionally masturbate, but never did so on a regular basis.

On dates, Mr. A. would kiss and pet, including genital fondling, and would experience orgasm at times in this way. He never attempted intercourse, out of feelings that it was special and should be reserved for marriage.

Once married, the couple attempted intercourse for the first time. Mr. A. described this experience as "floundering in the muck and the mire." Both were tense, and entry was difficult. Mrs. A. expected her husband to know what to do and resented his inexperience. Over the years, the frequency of intercourse steadily declined. Other marital problems also emerged. Mr. A. felt confined by his wife's need to "plan and regiment" their lives. He was working longer hours and the couple was spending little time together. Conflicts over Mr. A.'s attentions to his mother also arose.

During arguments, Mrs. A. was the more verbal, emotional one. Her husband's lack of response would cause her to escalate her remarks in an attempt to get a response. These bitter quarrels had left Mr. A. feeling humiliated and with "emotional scars."

Once therapy began, the personalities of both clients came into focus. Mr. A. presented an interesting mixture of qualities: attractive yet overweight, modest and somewhat self-effacing yet humorous and teasing, inhibited yet flirtatious. He proved to be very responsive to therapeutic interpretations and suggestions. Although these made him uncomfortable at times, he seemed to thrive on the challenge of therapy. In his interactions with his wife, he tended to be unassertive, cautious, and protective of her feelings.

Mrs. A. took a more defensive stance in therapy. She appeared less secure, in general, than Mr. A. and seemed to want confirmation from the therapist of the validity of her ideas and expectations for her husband. She frequently compared herself and her husband to what she believed to be an external standard of normalcy. She had difficulty accepting therapeutic interpretations and suggestions and was less insightful and reflective than Mr. A. She evidenced strong needs to remain in control of herself and situations and tended to dominate interactions with Mr. A. by being more verbal and offering rational arguments to counter his feelings.

Course of Therapy

The therapist began by formulating for herself a hypothesis of the possible etiology of low sexual desire in Mr. A.'s case. It seemed reasonable to assume that at the time of their marriage, both had some negative feelings about sex which were unacknowledged (for example, Mrs. A.'s feelings about menstruation and her fear of intercourse, and the association in Mr. A.'s mind between too much sexual interest and homosexuality). Anxiety was also probably a component for both of them in the awkward attempts at intercourse during their honeymoon. An initial discomfort with intercourse may have been intensified in Mr. A. by feelings of incompetence and inadequacy as a lover which were reinforced by his wife.

The therapist also hypothesized that the structure of the relationship between the couple also made it difficult for them to relate as lovers. Mrs. A. was cast as the practical, reliable, mature one in the relationship, and this was offset by Mr. A.'s more spontaneous, irresponsible style. Their relationship had an almost mother–son quality to it which may have played a part in the maintenance of low sexual desire in Mr. A.

On the basis of this formulation, several treatment interventions were employed.

Increasing Sensory Awareness.   Both Mr. and Mrs. A. began a series of exercises aimed at self- and mutual exploration and pleasuring following the basic program for treatment of inorgasmic women (Heiman, LoPiccolo, & LoPiccolo, 1976). It was hypothesized that Mr. A. was out of touch with or denying his own sexuality. It was reasoned that encouraging him to accept and get pleasure from masturbation would be a useful first step in enabling him to experience sexual desire. Since masturbation did not involve relating to his wife, the therapist felt it would be easier for Mr. A. to get in touch with sexual feelings in this context.

While Mr. A. was able to accept the rationale for the self-exploration and pleasuring sessions, Mrs. A. was extremely upset by the thought of her husband masturbating. Exploration of her feelings led to the next treatment intervention.

Bringing into Awareness the Couple's Ambivalent Feelings about Sex and Encouraging Attitude Change.   Mrs. A.'s extreme reaction to the idea of her husband masturbating was explored, and revealed an association in her mind between masturbation and homosexuality (an interesting parallel to her husband's association of "inordinate interest" in sex with homosexuality). Also, it became apparent that her insecurity extended beyond the relationship and included concerns about herself. This became clearer later in therapy when Mrs. A. admitted that she did not really enjoy intercourse. It was extremely important, therefore, that her husband desire intercourse as a way of reassuring her about her normalcy. One of her fears was that she would enjoy other forms of stimulation more than intercourse and, therefore, they would never have intercourse. Infrequent coitus was connected in her mind with being "abnormal." It became clear, then, that she projected her negative feelings about sex onto her husband and pressured him to desire sex in order to reassure herself that they were "normal."

In the early stages of therapy, awareness of ambivalent feelings about sex was achieved through exploring the reactions of the couple to the sexual assignments that were suggested by the therapist. Both Mr. and Mrs. A. evidenced an aversion to female genitals. Mrs. A., particularly, responded negatively to the suggestion that Mr. A. look at and explore her genitals as a way of becoming more comfortable and familiar with this part of her body. She also had a negative reaction to films on male and female sexual response. She felt that knowing the "nitty-gritty" of sex would detract from her experience of pleasure.

Mr. A. denied feeling uncomfortable with his wife's genitals but, during the first weeks of therapy, he avoided looking at them and touching them, except briefly. He also experienced a negative reaction to a film on male sexual response which included some scenes of self-stimulation.

Throughout the early stage of therapy, the therapist continued to point out examples of ambivalent feelings about sex in both Mr. and Mrs. A. This challenged Mrs. A.'s role as the sexual one in the relationship. It was hoped that encouraging both to express discomfort would also facilitate sharing and deepen the level of trust between them.

Both Mr. and Mrs. A. were encouraged to continue self-pleasuring, and Mr. A. was able to find a method of rubbing his penis against a pillow which felt pleasurable and resulted in orgasm. Mrs. A., however, got little pleasure from her individual pleasuring sessions and became more and more negative about them as time went on. Around session 5, she expressed feeling pressured and angry about this part of the therapy program. Because of Mrs. A.'s strong resistance and rather rigid defenses, the therapist decided not to assign further individual pleasuring sessions at that time, but to try and help her achieve orgasm in the couple sessions. This served to defuse what had become a power struggle between Mrs. A. and the therapist. In a sense, the therapist was siding with Mrs. A.'s resistance and her need to appear competent and in control by agreeing that perhaps individual pleasuring sessions were not helpful to her. It was hoped that this would also facilitate Mrs. A.'s progress in the couple sessions, as this provided Mrs. A. with a chance to prove that she had been right and the therapist wrong about the necessity of the individual sessions.

During the next 10 sessions, Mrs. A. used Kegal exercises, orgasm triggers, and role-played orgasm (Heiman *et al.*, 1976) in order to enhance arousal. Although she was able to reach increasingly higher levels of arousal in the couple sessions, she still had not achieved orgasm by the end of therapy. Progress was made, however, in accepting the idea of her husband's individual sessions and in changing her negative feelings about her own genitals. She also became more accepting of other forms of mutual pleasuring aside from intercourse and expressed an interest in experimenting with oral–genital stimulation. Although Mr. A. became increasingly comfortable with looking and touching his wife's genitals, he remained uncomfortable with the idea of oral–genital stimulation.

Facilitation of Erotic Responses and Enhancing Sexual/Sensual Experiences. Along with the individual and couple sensate-focus exercises, the therapist explored the use of erotic literature and fantasy in enhancing erotic responses.

Between sessions 4 and 5, both Mr. and Mrs. A. were asked to look through erotic magazines and note their reactions. Mr. A.'s reactions were intellectualized and distancing and he denied any arousal. This distancing was also evident at other times. When looking at his genitals, he focused on their "construction" and in writing about a masturbation session, he spoke of the use of "the hands" and "the penis" rather than "my hands" and "my penis." This disassociation of himself from anything sexual was focused on throughout therapy.

Encouraging Mr. A. to continue looking at erotic pictures and reading erotic literature enabled him to become more comfortable with it and experience arousal. He was encouraged to include the use of erotic literature in his individual sessions and to begin fantasizing.

Around session 7, the therapist asked Mr. A. to write down what was a particularly arousing fantasy for him. The substance of this fantasy was that two women would be fighting over who would go to bed with him. Each would have time alone to arouse him, and he would choose the "winner" to make love to. The women would arouse him by baring their breasts and rubbing them against him, massaging his thighs, and by being dressed in seductive and provocative ways.

The therapist encouraged Mr. A. to continue using fantasy during his individual masturbation sessions and at a point of high arousal to begin fantasizing about his wife. This was extremely difficult for him to do, however, and attempting to fantasize about his wife would rapidly diminish his arousal.

Discussion of Mr. A.'s difficulty in visualizing his wife as sexual was very fruitful for therapy. He was able to become aware of certain fears about becoming more sexual: first, that his wife would become more demanding sexually; second, that sex would become boring; and third, that they would start to experiment with oral or anal sex. This last fear was interesting, given Mr. A.'s strong negative feelings about "kinky" sex which were expressed at the beginning of therapy. The therapist began to feel that on some level Mr. A. actually had some desires in this direction which were unacceptable to him and contributed to his denial of sexual feelings and desires. Indeed, toward the end of therapy, Mr. A. admitted a desire to try anal intercourse.

Discussion of Mr. A.'s fantasies was also helpful in enabling him to articulate things that excited him. These included a female in a sexy dress, a large-breasted woman in a bikini, short skirts, and "a female who successfully uses her attributes to become a tease." With this list, the therapist was able to encourage Mr. A. to think about what things his wife could do that would excite him. He was able to come up with some ideas, such as her wearing more sensuous underwear and nightgowns.

Around this point in therapy, the interactional component of the sexual problem became apparent. Mrs. A. became increasingly uncomfortable as Mr. A. became more sexual and started to take more initiative. She began to find fault with their sessions and expressed a great deal of pessimism about changes being maintained after therapy. Attempts to confront Mrs. A.'s own ambivalence and fears about sexual changes were generally unsuccessful.

Dealing with Intrapsychic Conflicts.   As therapy proceeded, it became clear that both Mr. and Mrs. A. feared the changes involved in becoming more sexual. Being sexual was associated in both of their minds with becoming "perverted" and losing control over oneself.

Associated with these fears were conflicts within each of them about intimacy and trust. Intimacy seemed equated in both of their minds with a loss of self and a dependence on the other person. Rather than dealing with these conflicts by exploring possible intrapsychic bases in childhood, the therapist chose to focus on how they were acted out in the couple's current relationship.

Improving the Relationship.   Around the sixth session, the therapist saw both Mr. and Mrs. A. alone. Mr. A.'s feelings about the marriage were explored, and the therapist confronted him with the idea that he might work against changes in therapy as a way of avoiding commitment to the marriage. The idea that an improved sexual relationship did not mean further commitment seemed important for therapy to proceed. Given the connection in Mr. A.'s mind between intimacy and dependence, which became clearer as therapy proceeded, this intervention was probably crucial to the success of therapy.

Throughout therapy, the total relationship of the couple was focused on. Mrs. A. tended to relate to her husband in a parental way, anticipating his needs and analyzing his behavior (for example,

"You're tired and hungry"). He responded by feeling anger and with-drawing, which aroused her anxiety. The therapist was able to point out the interactional nature of this pattern, which went like this: Mr. A. shared very little with his wife. Due to her own insecurity, this would make her anxious and prompted the behaviors in her (angry confronta-tion) which caused him to withdraw. Mr. A. withdrew and avoided his wife out of anger and a sense of failure ("When I'm at home, I feel insignificant"). He also felt guilty that he was not meeting his wife's expectations and that he never would. Rather than express anger or annoyance directly, he defied her in rather juvenile ways (for example, by being irresponsible) which maintained the parent–child interactions.

Some of the things which the therapist did in order to enable the couple to deal with this pattern were encouraging more communica-tion, encouraging Mr. A. to be more assertive, helping the couple to be more reinforcing of each other, and helping Mr. A. to feel more effec-tive and competent in his interactions with his wife.

In session 8, the therapist directly confronted the couple with her interpretation of the mother–son pattern and the fact that this pattern was contributing to the problem of lack of desire. Deliberately phrasing the words bluntly, the interpretation was made that sex would not improve unless their interactions changed, because "one doesn't go to bed with one's mother." Mr. A. had an extremely strong reaction to the therapist's words which he had heard, at first, as an accusation that he unconsciously desired to have sex with his mother. However, he was able to accept the point the therapist was trying to make and in the next few sessions began to assert himself more in the relationship. Interestingly, as Mr. A.'s pleasure ratings of their couple sessions began to indicate an increase in pleasure, Mrs. A.'s began to indicate a decrease.

Anxiety Reduction. Although Mr. A. did not admit initially to feeling anxious in sexual situations or in response to sexual thoughts or feelings, the therapist assumed this to be a possibility. Relaxation train-ing was begun for both Mr. and Mrs. A., and Mr. A. was asked to construct a hierarchy of "tense" situations. Rather than ask him to restrict the items to sex, the therapist did not attempt to structure the content in any way. This yielded some very important information about Mr. A.'s concerns. He produced a list of 11 items which included such things as "knowing it will be hard to produce something which has been promised by me," "public displays of affection, expecially in large groups," "being corrected or 'talked at' by wife in social situa-tions," and "when I'm in a sexual situation with [Mrs. A.] and for some reason I'm concerned whether I can hold an erection and reach climax." Desensitization was conducted, with the items arranged from "least" to "most tense" regardless of content.

In addition to relaxation training, desensitization, and the *in vivo* desensitization of the sexual sessions, a great deal of information and education about sexuality was imparted in therapy through discussion and the use of books and films.

By the end of therapy, Mr. A. had recommitted himself to the relationship, and the couple had agreed to try and conceive a child. Mr. A. expressed amazement that at the beginning of therapy, the focus had been on sexual problems, since it now seemed to him that sex was not the major issue in their relationship.

Three-Month Follow-Up

At the end of therapy, Mr. A. felt that his attitudes toward sex were still changing. He was aware of actively enjoying time with his wife instead of dreading it because of the implicit demand that they have sex. He was aware of feeling more relaxed in general, and sex seemed more like a natural part of his life. The couple was engaging in intercourse once a week, which Mr. A. felt was his desired frequency for intercourse. They would also occasionally engage in sexual activity which did not include intercourse. Both were initiating sexual activity, and Mr. A. was now responding to his wife's initiations with pleasure. Mr. A. was masturbating about once every 2 weeks and was rarely experiencing erectile difficulties. Although Mrs. A. reported experiencing more pleasure during sex, she was still preorgasmic. Oral–genital and anal stimulation had still not been explored by the couple, although they had shared some feelings about this.

Now that sex was going reasonably well for the couple, other problems were being focused on. There seemed to be some conflicts around a new desire on Mrs. A.'s part for independence and a career and a desire on Mr. A.'s part for reassurance from her as to her commitment to the relationship and relationship goals. In a sense, there had been a form of role reversal: Mr. A. was now more concerned with commitment and family responsibilities, and Mrs. A. with exploring opportunities for personal growth. Mrs. A. was still preorgasmic and again expressed an interest in trying oral stimulation, which she believed would be arousing for her. Mr. A. still had some reluctance in this area and, so far, this had not been explored.

Case B

Mr. and Mrs. B. applied for therapy because of Mr. B.'s inability to retain an erection or ejaculate and his lack of desire for sex. Both were in their 30s, religiously active, and had been married for 3 years.

At the time of intake, the couple had had no sexual contact for a period of about a year. Before then, when they did have sex, it consisted of some kissing, breast and genital manipulation, and attempts at intercourse. Mr. B. usually was unable to obtain an erection or would lose it during what they described as "clumsy and awkward" attempts at insertion, Mr. B. had ejaculated on only one occasion, early in their marriage. Neither partner had ever masturbated, and Mrs. B. had never experienced orgasm.

Mrs. B. usually initiated sexual activity, and when she did, her husband would often refuse. Mr. B. reported having erectile problems before or during intercourse 90% of the time. Both felt their marriage to be free of problems in all areas except sex. Mr. B.'s medical records indicated no organic problems which could account for his erectile problems or lack of desire for sex.

History

Mr. B. was the middle child in a family of three. He had an extremely close relationship with his mother and one of his grandmothers, in contrast to his relationship with his father, whom he felt was still very critical and hostile toward him. Mr. B. felt that there were large differences in outlook between himself and his father and described, with pride, a certain rebelliousness in his own nature which resulted in many conflicts between the two.

Although Mr. B. saw his parents kiss and hug affectionately, sex was not mentioned in his family throughout his whole childhood and adolescence. Nudity was also forbidden, and he could never recall seeing his parents or anyone else in the family nude.

Mr. B. had always been very involved with his religion. He received a great deal of religious training while growing up and recalled being instilled with negative attitudes toward certain sexual activities such as masturbation and premarital intercourse. He insisted, however, that as an adult, he was able to reject the teachings of his church with regard to sexuality. He therefore felt that there was no connection between his lack of desire for sex and previously instilled negative attitudes.

Mr. B. began having nocturnal emissions around the 10th grade and remembered finding these pleasurable, frightening, and confusing. He never masturbated, however, and reported being unaware that other boys did. Although he interacted with girls, this was mostly in group situations, and he was not aware of any sexual interest in girls during adolescence.

At one point, Mr. B. entertained the idea of becoming a minister. He made some initial steps in that direction and then changed his mind because he felt he could not cope with what he saw as the authoritarian church hierarchy. However, he often experienced regret that he had not followed through on his plans to devote his life to the church.

Mr. B. was still sexually inexperienced in his late 20s when he made the decision to get married. He was attracted to Mrs. B. because she was intelligent and shared his interest in maintaining an active role in the church. In the period before Mr. and Mrs. B. married, their sex life consisted of short kisses and an occasional hug. Mrs. B. would have liked to have intercourse, but Mr. B. felt that premarital intercourse was morally wrong.

On their honeymoon, the couple engaged in intercourse, and Mr. B. ejaculated for the first time. However, Mrs. B. expressed anxiety on subsequent occasions and seemed to turn off to sex altogether. Although very upset by the sexual problems initially, Mrs. B. resigned herself to the idea of a marriage without sex.

The therapists were initially concerned about the possibility of promoting change in this case for three reasons: Mr. B.'s denial of, and lack of insight into, likely causes of his sexual problems; his extremely negative feelings about sexual activities, particularly his strong aversion to female genitals and to oral–genital sex; and his insistence that he was asexual and desired therapy to reassure himself that this was true. The fact that he had a history of rebellion against authority figures also raised the possibility that resistance to therapy might become a real issue.

Course of Therapy

The couple was seen by a dual-sex cotherapy team for 15 sessions. The treatment plan included:

1. Use of a self-pleasuring program, including reading *Becoming Orgasmic* (Heiman *et al.,* 1976) and seeing films which would facilitate Mrs. B. reaching orgasm.
2. Graded nondemand pleasuring sessions plus individual self-pleasuring sessions for Mr. B. to restore erectile functioning and reduce anxiety.
3. Dealing with religious conflicts which may have been inhibiting Mr. B.'s sexual responsiveness.

Throughout therapy, Mr. B. was resistant to following behavioral assignments, even when (or perhaps because) they were producing arousal in him. One of Mr. B.'s fears about therapy had been that he would be pressured into engaging in "objectionable" sexual behaviors, and this fear of loss of control over himself probably played a part in his resistance to therapy. Indeed, the experience of arousal during sessions in a given week would invariably lead to his avoidance of sessions during the next week. Around the seventh session, Mr. B. began accepting some responsibility for his sexuality and he gradually came to view himself as having desires but blocking them.

During therapy, Mrs. B. attained orgasm through masturbation. Reaching orgasm was, in a sense, frustrating for her because it seemed pointless to her if she had no sexual relationship with her husband. Following Mrs. B.'s attainment of climax, her individual self-pleasuring sessions were made optional, and she did not masturbate at all during the remainder of therapy. Her participation in therapy sessions also declined, as they became more focused on Mr. B.'s issues which were not being resolved.

Toward the end of therapy, Mr. B. seemed to withdraw from the therapy process, and the couple considered terminating therapy. They did agree to remain in therapy until the end of the 15 sessions, however, but only when it was agreed that the therapists would not place any demands on them for continued sexual activity.

In reviewing the case, it was clear that Mr. B. experienced severe conflicts about sexual feelings in relation to his identity as a religious person. This area of conflict was extremely upsetting to him, however, and he became highly defensive whenever therapeutic attempts were made to explore the possible association between his religious beliefs and his lack of sexual desire. The therapists were thus unable to deal with what was probably a major factor shaping his lack of sexual response.

At termination, Mr. B. felt that the major contribution of therapy had been to make him aware that he did, in fact, have sexual feelings. He had learned that he was capable of obtaining an erection when he would allow himself to be stimulated and to experience arousal. However, he still typically refused Mrs. B.'s initiation of sexual activity and rarely initiated on his own.

Mrs. B. had essentially resigned herself to not having a sexual relationship. She seemed to have again repressed her frustrations to a point where she could be supportive of her husband's fears and ambivalences. As a result of therapy, she gained the ability to reach climax through manual self-stimulation, but was not making use of this ability. The couple further felt that therapy had allowed them to communicate much more fully, particularly in the area of sexuality and, as a result, they felt closer and were more affectionate with each other.

Discussion

Although differing in certain dimensions, both of these cases had a number of elements in common: The wives in both cases were pre-orgasmic; both men had limited sexual experience, in that neither had engaged in intercourse premaritally; initial attempts at intercourse were stressful and, to some degree, unpleasant; both men evidenced some anxiety about intercourse and aversive reactions to female genitals and the idea of oral–genital stimulation; both were experiencing sexual dysfunction; both men had a history of an extremely close emotional attachment to their mothers, with whom they seemed to identify more closely than with their fathers; both had fears of losing control and seemed to equate being sexual with engaging in "deviant" sexual behaviors.

A connection between any of the factors cited above and problems of low sexual desire has, of course, not been demonstrated. The differential rates of improvement in therapy between the two cases also points to the need to attend to factors in the two cases that differentiated between them.

The first factor that may account for differences in treatment outcome is differences between the two men in the dimensions of *defensiveness* and *denial*. Mr. A. evidenced little defensiveness and was willing to accept interpretations and confrontations within therapy. Mr. B.'s rigidly defensive style, on the other hand, made it difficult for the therapists to have much impact on him. Because of the likely association between Mr. B.'s religious upbringing and his feelings about sex (which he denied), the therapists might be seen as challenging the church whenever they confronted him in the sexual area. Given that the church was a tremendously important part of Mr. B.'s life, a great deal of resistance was elicited by attempts to deal with his negative feelings in the area of sex.

A second factor is differences between the two in the dimension of *anxiety*. It seems clear that sexual feelings and activity engendered more extreme anxiety in Mr. B. than in Mr. A. Support for this comes from the fact that Mr. B. had *never* masturbated and was not engaging in any sexual activity with his wife at the time of intake. Additionally, on the one occasion in therapy when Mr. B. attained an erection from his wife's stimulation, he experienced this as unpleasant and her manipulation as somewhat painful. This experience elicited anxiety and avoidance of sexual activity thereafter. Mr. A., however, had masturbated at one time, did engage in sex with his wife at least once a month, and experienced arousal as pleasurable. It is possible that more extensive intervention in the dimension of anxiety in the case of Mr. B. would have been beneficial.

The third factor accounting for the differential rate of improvement is the extreme *resistance* to therapy in Mr. B.'s case. In part, this was due to the anxiety that he experienced while engaging in sexual activities that were encouraged as part of therapy. Another facet of this resistance probably had to do with his tendency to rebel against authority figures, in this case, the therapists.

A fourth difference between the two cases was the probable impact of *relationship factors* on the maintenance of low desire. In the case of Mr. A., relationship issues were clearly a factor in his avoidance of sex with his wife. Improving some of the nonsexual areas of Mr. and Mrs. A.'s relationship was facilitative of improvement in the sexual area. Relationship conflicts were not admitted to in Mr. B.'s case, and both Mr. and Mrs. B. expressed strong feelings of satisfaction with their marriage. Although the therapists were aware of areas of resentment in the marriage, the couple was resistant to dealing with those issues. This meant that therapy focused almost exclusively on the sexual aspect of their marriage, which was the area of most resistance for Mr. B.

The reactions of the two wives to the problem of low desire also probably played a part in treatment outcome. Mrs. A. was extremely upset about the problem and, therefore, provided strong motivation for her husband to change, once he resolved his ambivalence about commitment to the relationship. Mrs. B., on the other hand, had been able to resolve herself to a marriage without sex without experiencing extreme distress. Her primary motivation for treatment was to prevent the recurrence of anxiety in her husband, which the couple believed was due to his unhappiness with the sexual situation.

Lastly, the factor of *motivation* was experienced differently by the two men. Mr. A. was aware of arousal in response to other women and had, at first, attributed some of his problem to lack of attraction to his wife. He did not see himself, therefore, as totally without sexual desire. Mr. B., on the other hand, was not aware of arousal by any sexual stimulus and believed that he had no sexual desires in the same way that other people have no athletic or mathematical ability. This total denial of any sexual desires seemed comfortable to him, and he seemed to be seeking therapy, in effect, to prove to his wife that he was indeed not sexual. The cognitions and expectations, then, in the two men differed markedly.

The presence of these factors to varying degrees in the two cases suggests the usefulness of differentiating cases of low desire along certain dimensions. Dimensions which seem relevant in cases of low desire are:

 1. Anxiety/guilt

 2. Depression

 3. Aversion/avoidance

 4. Defensiveness/denial/resistance

 5. Pleasure

 6. Arousal

 7. Cognitions/expectations

 8. Global/situational

 9. Primary/secondary

 10. Hormonal/physiological

 11. Satisfaction/dissatisfaction/motivation

 12. Dysfunction in self or partner

 13. Relationship factors

Therapy Issues

Therapy issues which seem particularly relevant to cases of low sexual desire are the relationship of the clients with the therapist, the relationship between the couple, ambivalence about therapy and resistance to change, and the problem of maintenance. Again, as with treatment interventions, these issues are not unique to cases of low desire.

The relationship between clients and therapist is particularly important if, as was speculated earlier, individuals with low sexual desire tend to be highly defensive. These individuals may deny or intellectualize when confronted in therapy or show an almost hysterical lack of awareness of themselves and events. The relationship with the therapist may then become a struggle for power and control. These factors seem to have been particularly true in the case of Mr. B. Such struggles tend to interfere with the establishment of trust between clients and therapist.

The sex of the therapist (if there is not a cotherapy team) may also present issues, depending on whether the client with low desire is of the same or opposite sex. Such issues may be seductiveness (given the safety of the therapeutic environment), withdrawal because of fear or hostility, or competiveness or defiance. Focusing on the client's interactions with the therapist of the same or opposite sex seems crucial in cases of low desire.

The relationship between the couple must also be explored for its role in maintaining the problem of desire. Avoidance of sex, for example, may be reinforcing because it means avoidance of the partner. In this sense, lack of desire serves a functional role in the marriage. Difficulty may arise when interventions in the area of the marriage, for the purpose of improving the sexual problems, meet with strong resistance. This is often the case when one partner wants to see himself or herself as "uninvolved" or "the victim" in the relationship. As in other cases of sexual dysfunction, an increase in the level of desire (or functioning) may lead to resistance or distress in the supposedly "non-dysfunctional" partner.

Ambivalence about therapy and resistance to change should also be a major focus in therapy. Depending on the amount of satisfaction/dissatisfaction the individual experiences in relation to the level of desire, the motivation for change may be strong or weak. Relationship factors, of course, play a role in motivation, especially if the relationship is in jeopardy because of the problem of desire. If there are ambivalent feelings in either partner with regard to commitment to the relationship, therapy will be more difficult. Resolution of the sexual problem may be equated with being trapped in the relationship, and resistance to therapy will increase as things improve.

Fears of intimacy or trust and conflict around dependence/independence and loss of control may make it particularly difficult for a client with low desire to participate unambivalently in therapy. A tendency to deny or repress conflictual material and resistance to change in either partner can result in resistance to therapy and attempts to undermine or disqualify the impact of the therapist. In some clients, resistance is more obvious and can be dealt with directly. In other cases, there may be a form of passive resistance, with the client cooperating fully with therapeutic suggestions, but with no real engagement in therapy or therapeutic change occurring. These are the cases that are most likely to relapse after therapy and point out the need for dealing with the issue of maintenance as part of therapy.

Maintenance of therapy gains seems to be particularly difficult in cases of low desire. In cases where low desire plays a functional role in the relationship, we would expect reversal of treatment gains if this aspect of the problem is not dealt with as part of therapy. In other cases, treatment gains are undermined by partners who are forced by improvement in the problem of low desire to confront their own ambivalent feelings about sex.

Still other cases will respond well to therapy where assignments are structured and where sex is made more salient through the use of fantasy, masturbation, and so on. Once out of therapy, these cases are likely to falter without continued therapeutic support.

Lastly, a tendency toward denial and difficulty accepting responsibility for sexuality in some clients with low desire may make it difficult for these clients to internalize changes. These clients may respond well in therapy, where they are able to place responsibility for change on the therapist or the particular therapy techniques, but experience a recurrence of low desire upon termination.

Conclusion

The cases presented highlight the need for innovative approaches in the treatment of low sexual desire. Analysis of cases along the various dimensions suggested and a multimodal therapy orientation also seem crucial to successful outcome. Although both cases involved low sexual desire in men, it has been the experience of the author that the same issues are involved in the treatment of women with low desire. Possible differences between the syndromes of low desire in men and women should, however, be investigated in future research.

Research in the area of problems of desire is just beginning. It seems likely that just as knowledge about sexual function and dysfunction contributes to our understanding of problems of low desire, the reverse will also be true. What we learn about the processes of arousal and desire will enhance our understanding of human sexual expression.

ACKNOWLEDGMENT
Preparation of this chapter was supported in part by a grant from the National Institute of Mental Health, U.S. Public Health Service.

NOTE
1. The therapists for these cases were Leslie LoPiccolo, Joseph LoPiccolo, and Patricia Morokoff.

References

Annon, J. S. *The sexual fear inventory—female and male forms.* Honolulu: Enabling Systems, 1975.
Bardwick, J. M. *Psychology of women. A study of bio-cultural conflicts.* New York: Harper & Row, 1971.

Carney, A., Bancroft, J., & Mathews, A. *The combination of hormonal and psychological treatment for female sexual unresponsiveness: A comparative study*. Unpublished manuscript, 1977.

Cattell, R. B., Eber, H. W., & Tatswoka, M. M. *Handbook for the 16 personality factor questionnaire*. Champaign, Illinois: Institute for Personality and Ability Testing, 1970.

Dahlstrom, W. G., Welsh, G. J., & Dahlstrom, L. E. *An MMPI handbook* (Vol. 1), *Clinical interpretation*. Minneapolis: University of Minnesota Press, 1972.

Davidson, J. M. Neurohormonal bases of male sexual behavior. In R. O. Greep (Ed.), *International review of physiology* (Vol. 13), *Reproductive physiology II,* Baltimore: University Park Press, 1977.

Derogatis, L. R., Lipman, R. S., & Covi, L. SCL–90: An outpatient psychiatric rating scale. *Psychopharmacology Bulletin*, 1973, *9* (1), 13–28.

Dodson, B. *Liberating masturbation: A meditation of self love*. New York: Bodysex Designs, 1974.

Everitt, B. J. Cerebral monoamines and sexual behavior. In J. Money & H. Musaph (Eds.), *Handbook of sexology*. Amsterdam: Elsevier/North-Holland, 1977.

Fisher, S. *The female orgasm*. New York: Basic Books, 1973.

Frank, E., Anderson, C., & Rubinstein, D. Frequency of sexual dysfunction in "normal" couples. *New England Journal of Medicine,* 1978, *299* (3), 111–115.

Freud, S. *Psycho-genesis of a case of homosexuality in a woman*. Standard Edition, 1920, *17*, 147–171.

Freud, S. *Three essays on the theory of sexuality* (J. Strachey, Ed.). New York: Avon Books, 1962. (Originally published, 1905.)

Heiman, J. R. A psychophysiological exploration of sexual arousal patterns in females and males. *Psychophysiology*, 1977, *14* (3), 266–274.

Heiman, J. R. *The personal history questionnaire (PHQ-A)*. Department of Psychiatry and Behavioral Science, State University of New York at Stony Brook, 1978.(a)

Heiman, J. R. Uses of psychophysiology in the assessment and treatment of sexual dysfunction. In J. LoPiccolo & L. LoPiccolo (Eds.), *Handbook of sex therapy*. New York: Plenum Press, 1978.(b)

Heiman, J. R. LoPiccolo, L. J., & LoPiccolo, J. *Becoming orgasmic: A sexual growth program for women*. Englewood Cliffs, N. J.: Prentice-Hall, 1976.

Heiman, J. R., & Morokoff, P. *Sexual arousal and experience as correlates of sexual malaise*. Paper presented at American Psychological Association Meeting, San Francisco, California, 1977.

Herbert, J. Some functions of hormones and the hypothalamus in the sexual activity of primates. In D. F. Swaab & J. P. Schadi (Eds.), *Progress in brain research* (Vol. 41), *Integrative hypothalamic activity*. Amsterdam: Elsevier, 1974.

Hoon, E. F., Hoon, P. W., & Wincze, J. The SAI: An inventory for the measurement of female sexual arousal. *Archives of Sexual Behavior*, 1976, *5*, 208–215.

Hoon, P., Wincze, J., & Hoon, E. Physiological assessment of sexual arousal in women. *Psychophysiology*, 1976, *13*, 196–204.

Hunt, M. *Sexual behavior in the 1970's*. New York: Playboy Press, 1974.

Jackson, D. N. *Personality research form*. New York: Research Psychologists Press, 1965.

Jemail, J. A. *Response bias in the assessment of marital and sexual adjustment: I. Development of the marriage and sexual defensiveness scales*.

II. Suppressing response bias in the Locke–Wallace and Sexual Inter-action Inventory. III. Faking in the Locke–Wallace and Sexual Interaction Inventory. Doctoral dissertation, State University of New York, 1977.

Kaplan, H. S. *The new sex therapy.* New York: Brunner/Mazel, 1974.

Kaplan, H. S. Hypoactive sexual desire. *Journal of Sex and Marital Therapy,* 1977, *3* (1), 3–9.

Karacan, I. Advances in the psychophysiological evaluation of male erectile impotence. In J. LoPiccolo & L. LoPiccolo (Eds.), *Handbook of sex therapy.* New York: Plenum Press, 1978.

Kimmel, D., & Van Der Veen, F. Factors of marital adjustment in Locke's Marital Adjustment Test. *Journal of Marriage and the Family, 1974, 2,* 57–63.

Kinsey, A. C., Pomeroy, W. B., & Martin, C. E. *Sexual behavior in the human male.* Philadelphia: W. B. Saunders, 1948.

Kinsey, A. C., Pomeroy, W. B., Martin, C. E., & Gebhard, P. H. *Sexual behavior in the human female.* New York: Pocket Books, 1965.

Lobitz, W. C., & Lobitz, G. K. Clinical assessment in the treatment of sexual dysfunctions. In J. LoPiccolo & L. LoPiccolo (Eds.), *Handbook of sex therapy.* New York: Plenum Press, 1978.

LoPiccolo, J., & Heiman, J. The role of cultural values in the prevention and treatment of sexual problems. In C. Qualls, J. P. Wincze, & D. H. Barlow (Eds.), *The prevention of sexual disorders.* New York: Plenum Press, 1978.

LoPiccolo, J., & Steger, J. C. The sexual interaction inventory: A new instrument for assessment of sexual dysfunction. *Archives of Sexual Behavior,* 1974, *3*(6), 585–595.

LoPiccolo, L., & Heiman, J. Sexual assessment and history interview. In J. LoPiccolo & L. LoPiccolo (Eds.), *Handbook of sex therapy.* New Plenum Press, 1978.

Masters, W. H., & Johnson, V. E. *Human sexual inadequacy.* Boston: Little, Brown & Co., 1970.

McNair, D. M., Lorr, M., & Droppleman, L. F. *Profile of mood states (POMS).* San Diego: Educational and Industrial Testing Service, 1971.

Mosher, D. Measurement of sex guilt in females by self-report inventories. *Journal of Consulting and Clinical Psychology,* 1968, *32,* 690–695.

Nowinski, J. *"P" questionnaire.* Department of Psychiatry and Behavioral Science, State University of New York at Stony Brook, 1978.

Rook, K. S., & Hammen, C. L. A cognitive perspective on the experience of sexual arousal. *Journal of Social Issues, 1977, 33*(2), 7–29.

Spence, J. T., Helmreich, R., & Stapp, R. A short version of the Attitudes toward Women Scale (AWS), *Bulletin of the Psychonomic Society,* 1973, *2*(4), 219–220.

Zung, W. W. From art to science. The diagnosis and treatment of depression. *Archives of General Psychiatry,* 1973, *29,* 328–337.

3

Desire Discrepancies and Arousal Problems in Sex Therapy

BERNIE ZILBERGELD AND CAROL RINKLEIB ELLISON

In their chapter, Zilbergeld and Ellison tackle two problems that have plagued the discussion of desire issues in sex therapy. First, there is the failure of writers to distinguish between desire and arousal, and the resulting tendency to use a variety of terms interchangeably when discussing desire problems. Second, there is the failure to pay sufficient attention to the subjective element in sexuality. To remedy the first problem, Zilbergeld and Ellison differentiate between problems of sexual desire or interest, *which involves the frequency with which an individual wants to have sex (and which implies nothing about ability to do so or arousal experienced during it), and* arousal, *which refers to the subjective experience of excitement. They point out that physiological arousal may or may not mirror subjective arousal and suggest that neglect of the subjective element in sexuality has resulted in some therapists holding the naive assumption that increasing physical stimulation will result in increased arousal, and possibly, sexual interest.*

Based on their distinction between arousal and interest, the authors suggest that difficulties can result from a variety of combinations of arousal and interest, the most obvious being instances of discrepancy between the two.

Zilbergeld and Ellison propose that in the course of development various situations or cues are associated with sexuality, and erotic significance is attached to them. Individuals with low sexual interest are presumed to have an overly limited or narrow range of cues which trigger sexual interest, while individuals with high sexual interest may associate a multitude of situations with erotic meaning. The authors point out that the more functions sex serves for an individual, the more cues will be endowed with sexual meaning. Treatment then becomes a process of increasing or decreasing the number of stimuli to which sexual meaning is attached.

Zilbergeld and Ellison's treatment approach encompasses traditional sex therapy techniques along with concepts and interventions adopted from the brief therapy orientation of Milton Erickson and the Mental Research Institute. Their approach is an innovative, eclectic one in which reframing, relabeling, and indirect suggestions are actively utilized in treatment.

Bernie Zilbergeld is a psychologist in private practice in Oakland, California, as well as the author of Male Sexuality. *Carol Rinkleib*

Ellison is a clinical psychologist in private practice in Oakland, California, a member of the clinical faculty of the Human Sexuality Program, University of California, San Francisco, and coauthor of Understanding Human Sexuality.

Introduction

The publication of Masters and Johnson's *Human Sexual Response* (1966) and *Human Sexual Inadequacy* (1970) was received with great optimism by health professionals. At last there was a sensible and non-Freudian conceptual scheme (the sexual response cycle) for understanding sexuality and, more important, brief and effective methods for dealing with common sexual problems. To many, it seemed that all the questions were answered and all the problems solved. All that remained to be done was to train enough clinicians to use the new understandings and new approaches with the many clients who were already knocking at the doors asking for help.

While unblemished optimism is still the prevalent mood in the sex field, problems have surfaced. Some writers questioned the conceptual adequacy and clinical usefulness of the sexual response cycle (Apfelbaum, 1976; Kaplan, 1974; Robinson, 1976; Singer, 1973; Zilbergeld, 1978). Clinicians across the country started to see clients with problems regarding sexual frequency—these problems were not dysfunctions and could not be understood in terms of the sexual response cycle; they also could not be effectively treated by the now familiar methods. Even the dysfunctions were becoming more difficult to resolve with these methods. More and more clients were emotionally unaroused during sex and this, more than anything else, seemed to be what maintained their problems. Surprisingly, continued doses of sensate focus, genital massage, and non-performance-oriented intercourse did not help.

Obviously, something important was missing in the conceptual apparatus and in the treatment approaches—a concern for the subjective elements of sex. This chapter is devoted to the consideration of two subjective variables: sexual desire and arousal. Since these areas have not been the subjects of much research or even attention, and since we have been seriously concerned with them in our own work for only the last 2 or 3 years, we regard our understandings and formulations as tentative. Although the work is in its formative stages, we share it in the hope that it will help others to think more clearly about these issues and to develop more effective ways of dealing with the problems now being brought to sex therapy.

The most vexing difficulty in discussing the topics at hand is the lack of a common vocabulary. Many words are used to refer to desire and arousal, but they are used and understood in different ways. Among the most common terms employed are "drive," "libido," "excitement," "interest," "lust," "passion," "horniness," and "turn-on." To add to the confusion, many of these have more than one meaning. Thus, Masters and Johnson (1966) use "excitement" to refer to the first phase of their sexual response cycle, but excitement as they use it has little relationship to the way most people understand the word. They define the term solely by physiological reaction and not at all by subjective experience. Men with erections and women with vaginal swelling/lubrication are considered to be in the excitement phase, whether or not they *feel* excited.

In order to avoid adding to the confusion and to lay the basis for a more or less orderly discussion of the relevant issues, we have had to make some distinctions. We believe clarity is served if the area of desire–arousal is broken down into two relatively distinct categories.

Sexual Desire or Interest
This category refers exclusively to frequency, how often a person wants to have sex. Sexual interest can vary in intensity from a largely cognitive, at-a-distance position ("I guess I wouldn't mind having sex more often" or "No, I don't think I'd like more sex") to a more emotionally laden stance ("I'm so horny I have to have sex every day" or, on the other hand, what is sometimes called sexual aversion). Incidentally, there may be a temptation to assume that the horny person quoted above is aroused as well as interested. He may well be, but it is important to consider the possibility that he may not be. As we discuss later, it seems best to assume at least potential autonomy between the various components of sexuality.

Sexual desire has received some attention in the last few years because of the increasing numbers of couples coming to therapy complaining of desire discrepancies. One hears more and more about desire deficits or hypoactive sexual desire (e.g., Goldberg, 1973; Kaplan, 1977). This issue requires some clarification.

To say that there is more or less of something, a surplus or a deficit, necessitates a standard of comparison: more than what or less than what? But there are no standards of sexual desire; we do not know what is right, normal, or healthy, and it seems clear that such standards will not be forthcoming. Given this, how can we possibly say of a person that his interest is too much or too little?

Take a man who desires sex once a month and is content with this.

Is this too little? We could refer to a study of sexual frequency and compare our man with those in the study. Suppose most of the men his age want and have sex three times a week. Can we now say that our man has a desire deficit? If so, would we also be willing to say that a man who does not consume as many calories per day as his peers suffers from a calorie-desire deficit? Assume that our man has a partner who wants sex once every 4 or 5 months. Now we can see that from the partner's viewpoint, the man does have a problem—he wants sex too often. To add a bit more complication, say our man finds a new partner who wants sex at least twice a week. The man now has too little interest, and his partner may wonder what is wrong with him. But also note the other side of the issue. Her desire is too high, at least according to him.

This example offers some pointers for the framing of desire problems. They are almost invariably relationship problems. It is not that one person has too much desire and another too little on some absolute scale; it is rather a discrepancy in two people's styles or interests. Such discrepancies have much in common with other relationship differences—how to raise the children, how often to dine out or have company in, where to spend the vacation, etc.—that therapists have been dealing with for years.

This way of viewing desire discrepancies suggests a focus on both partners rather than the more common practice of working only on the partner with less interest. It is striking how one-sided the recent concern with desire has been, almost always on ways of increasing the appetite of the less interested partner (Kaplan, 1977; Masters & Johnson, 1978). Rarely has attention been directed at the partner who wants more sex. We suggest that this is because sex professionals have fallen for a common cultural myth—that wanting more sex, given a few limits, of course, is normal and healthy, while a lesser appetite indicates pathology. We believe that such thinking is inappropriate and misleading. Neither more nor less is better. What is needed is a satisfactory or at least tolerable compromise. Given this point of view, we attend to both partners, trying to increase the desire of the one while at the same time trying to decrease that of the other.

Sexual Arousal or Turn-On

Whereas desire refers to how often one wants sex, arousal denotes how high (excited, turned on) one gets during sex. As we use the term, arousal is subjective and can be ascertained only by self-report. It should not be confused with what the person thinks or with physical changes. While physiological changes—for example, in GSR or heartbeat—do indicate physical activation or excitation, they do not tell us how the person interprets his or her experience. What looks like sexual arousal on our machines is often interpreted as anxiety, anger, or something else by the individual, and sometimes it is not noticed at all (Heiman, 1977; Zuckerman, 1971). And, as we should know by now but somehow keep forgetting, erections and vaginal lubrication/ swelling can and do occur in the absence of any sexual feeling (Apfel-baum, 1976; Zilbergeld, 1978).

Unfortunately, the term "arousal" is not without problems. As indicated above, it is often used to refer to a state of nonspecific activation of the nervous system, for which excitation is probably a less confusing word. In our discussion, unless otherwise specified, arousal refers only to excitation to which the person attaches erotic significance. Another difficulty with arousal is that some of its common synonyms, such as drive and libido (which usually fuse desire and arousal), convey the impression that they are fixed entities which are properties of people. This is evident in many discussions of sex drive and libido, entities that presumably men possess in greater quantity than women. We do not view arousal in this static way. Rather, we see it as a meaning or label that persons attach to some internal and external stimuli and, as such, it is reasonably flexible, capable of being manipulated by changing the number and kinds of stimuli to which it is applied.

Arousal problems are usually presented in therapy in two ways. Sometimes clients complain that they do not feel much in sex. Such clients may function without difficulty; the problem is simply that the feelings are not intense.

More commonly, arousal problems are embodied in functional complaints: Clients report trouble with erections, orgasms, or ejaculations, but have not given any thought to how turned on they are. With increasing frequency, however, therapists are noticing that many clients like this are not aroused or are operating at very low levels of arousal ("I guess I wasn't really excited. But she was willing, so I figured what the hell, might as well give it a try"). While it is true that many men and women function quite well in the absence of arousal, after they develop a dysfunction, increasing arousal can be very beneficial in restoring satisfactory functioning.

Desire and Arousal in Perspective

Before discussing the relationship between desire and arousal, it may help to put these topics in a larger perspective. We are suggesting that human sexuality is far more complex than was anticipated a decade ago when Masters and Johnson's work was made public. Far from being a culmination, their work is best viewed as a promising and fruitful beginning. Their orientation was too heavily on the physiological. Most professionals and textbook writers seem unaware that there are few subjective data anywhere in *Human Sexual Response* (Masters & Johnson, 1966). As Kaplan (1977) noted, in neither of Masters and Johnson's books nor in her own *The New Sex Therapy* (1974) is sexual desire even mentioned. Kaplan did discuss lack of arousal in her book, but it was completely ignored in Masters and Johnson's two volumes.

Of course, in clinical work Masters and Johnson and most other therapists have dealt with the subjective—with how clients felt and how they interpreted their experiences. But because of the powerful influence of the Masters and Johnson paradigm, the sexual response cycle—which, to repeat, consists almost entirely of physiological data—we have been slow to recognize the tremendous importance of subjective factors like interest and excitement, despite the fact that both desire and arousal problems are quite common (Kaplan, 1977; Zilbergeld, 1978).

Because conceptual schemes exert great influence on clincial practice by telling us what legitimate problems are and where to look for solutions, we offer a few ideas toward a more adequate paradigm. The sexual response cycle not only leaves out too much but the very notion of sexual response as a cycle of phases, with each phase flowing from and building on the previous one, is misleading and does not fit the data. It does not, for example, explain how a man can ejaculate without an erection or how a woman can reach orgasm without vaginal swelling/lubrication, that is, without going through the excitement phase.

Following Kaplan (1974) and Apfelbaum (1976), we believe sexual behavior is best conceived of as a number of related but more or less autonomous components. Apfelbaum gives three such components or systems: arousal (used in the same way that we use it), readiness (which encompasses Masters and Johnson's excitement and plateau phases), and orgasm. While we do not doubt that Apfelbaum's scheme is a great improvement over previous ones, it still seems incomplete. It is not clear, for one thing, where desire discrepancies should go.

We think a classification scheme should at the least have a place for all the major problems clients present and should put things together in a way that does not confuse clinicians about what they are doing. Such a scheme should also include both of the major aspects of human sexuality—the physiological and the psychological. The outline

we use has five components, each of which is considered to be at least potentially autonomous of the others. The components are interest, arousal, physiological readiness (vaginal lubrication/swelling and erection), orgasm, and satisfaction (how one feels about or evaluates what has gone before). Even finer distinctions are needed—for example, orgasm includes both physiological and subjective reactions, either one of which can be problematic—but since our concern here is only with the first two areas, we do not stop to make them.

The Relationship between Desire and Arousal

To illustrate the complexity of sexuality and what is meant by the relative autonomy of the components of sex, we turn to the relationship between desire and arousal. Both can be high in an individual at a given time, both low, or one can be high and the other low. Since the first two combinations—high desire and arousal or low desire and arousal—are easily understood, we focus only on situations in which one is high and the other is low.

Consider a woman who wants sex frequently but who has trouble getting aroused, a pattern that is by no means uncommon. The lack of arousal may be the result of many factors—for example, a fear of letting go or a lack of trust in her partner—but in the short run it may not hinder her interest. In fact, she may desire sex quite frequently, desperately hoping that the next time she has sex things will be better. In the long run, of course, it is likely that lack of arousal will result in decreased interest. A woman who is constantly struggling to get excited and who is frequently frustrated by the absence of arousal and perhaps also by the absence of orgasm may adapt by losing interest in the whole subject.

The combination of high desire and low arousal is similar in many ways to the better-known pattern of high arousal and lack of physiological response (erection or lubrication/swelling). The factors that block physiological response are often similar to those that block arousal.

The other discrepant pattern, low desire and high arousal, sounds strange at first. The woman in this case is easily and highly turned on but she does not want to be, at least not often. She may believe that having sex more often will bring about more closeness than she wants; to maintain the distance she desires, she cannot allow herself to have sex frequently. She might also view sex as a distraction, taking her away from other things—work, being with the kids, etc.—that have a higher priority. Or she may use her lack of interest as a way of getting back at her partner for real or imagined wrongdoing. Her lack of interest puts him in a one-down position vis-à-vis her, which gives her satisfaction.

We are no in position to say why the same factor that causes one woman to lose interest in sex may allow another to keep her interest but be unable to get aroused. The simplest, but by no means satisfying, explanation is that different people have different points of vulnerability. The situation is similar to that regarding the causes of dysfunction. Why is it that the same degree of anxiety that prevents one man from getting erections allows another to have erections but be unable to maintain them, while a third man has no trouble with erections but finds himself ejaculating quickly? The state of the art is not sufficiently advanced to permit answers to such questions at this time.

General Principles of Therapy

Before presenting some cases, a few words are in order about our general style of therapy. While we have benefited and borrowed liberally from the work of many of the leaders in the sex field—Apfelbaum, Barbach, Kaplan, and Masters and Johnson—we have also learned much from the practitioners of what is often simply called brief therapy, especially from Milton Erickson (Haley, 1967, 1973) and the Mental Research Institute (Watzlawick, 1978; Watzlawick, Weakland, & Fisch, 1974). The following principles that inform and guide our therapy seem most relevant to our work with desire and arousal problems.

1. There are few, if any, universal rules of sexual behavior. The same stimulus that decreases one person's sexual appetite or excitement will have the opposite effect on another person; it may even have a different effect on the same person at a different time. Anxiety and anger are both correctly said to inhibit desire, arousal, and physiological reaction, but not for everyone and not all the time. Some people do quite well when they are nervous or angry. In fact, some couples have their best sexual experiences when they are fighting. Therefore, cookbook approaches are often ineffective. Each case must be understood on its own terms and treatment must be tailored to its specific needs and patterns.

2. Client resistance should be circumvented or minimized whenever possible. This statement may sound so obvious as to not warrant comment, but the fact is that much resistance in therapy is generated by the therapist trying to force clients to do what they cannot or will not do, in other words, trying to force clients to fit the therapist's approach. We prefer to let clients guide us. We assume that they want to resolve their problems provided we can help them find *acceptable* ways of doing so. If clients are not able or willing to do the things that have helped others, we need to discover what they can do. This may involve the reframing of assignments (e.g., calling masturbation "self-exploration" or some other term that is understandable and acceptable) or the creation of new approaches that better fit the clients' situations.

3. The goal of therapy is to change the behavior the client wants changed and not to promote insight unless, of course, the latter will facilitate the former. Generally, it is the therapist, not the client, who needs insight. Accordingly, we tell clients only those things we think will help them achieve their goals. Everything else is used to increase the therapist's understanding but is not shared.

4. Indirect suggestions are often more effective, especially in new or difficult areas, than direct ones. Oblique or circuitous statements are not as easily defended against as are more straightforward ones. They are therefore useful in determining the client's receptivity to new ideas without the risk of provoking strong resistance; when the client does seem receptive, the suggestions can later be built upon with more direct discussion and assignments.

A Case of Desire Discrepancy

(Neither this nor the cases that follow it are complete reports. Only issues relevant to the subject of the chapter are reported in detail; other matters are mentioned in passing or omitted.)

Mary and Bob came to therapy complaining of constant arguments about sex and of their whole relationship going downhill. Both in their late 20s, they had been married 2 years.

From the beginning of their relationship, Mary had wanted more sex than did Bob. For a few months after the wedding, Bob's sexual desire increased but then returned to its former level. This disappointed Mary, who found herself initiating sex more and more often. Her husband usually went along with her advances, but he gradually stopped initiating sex and stopped touching her outside of sex. The more he withdrew, the more Mary initiated. Then Bob started getting angry when she made sexual overtures. One day he announced that he had lost all interest in sex. He refused to discuss the subject, and soon arguments about sex and his refusal to talk about it became daily occurrences. The marriage was deteriorating—there was no sex, almost no touching, less and less communication, and fewer shared activities of any kind.

Mary had felt comfortable with her sexuality since adolescence. She first masturbated to orgasm when she was 16 and has continued the practice to the present. Her first sexual partners were experienced and had good ejaculatory control; with them she learned to be easily aroused, orgasmic with many types of stimulation, and to heartily enjoy sex. And, without her being aware of it, she had also learned to interpret a wide variety of stimuli as being sexual.

Of her physical relationship with Bob, she said, "Sex was one of the few times I had his undivided attention. Our sex life used to be good; there wasn't as much of it as I wanted, but otherwise it was fine. I know he enjoyed it, too. I can't understand why he didn't want to do it more often. Now he never wants sex. He doesn't even want to hold hands or touch anymore. We used to do lots of touching. Now we hardly do anything together. He spends every evening watching TV, doing work, or sleeping. I don't know what I'll do if things don't change."

Before meeting Mary, Bob's sex life had been relatively free of problems. He had noticed even as a teenager that his interest in sex seemed less that that of his peers, but this had not been of much concern. The women he dated seemed satisfied with the amount of sexual activity he desired.

Sex was usually good for Bob. He had no trouble getting an erection and having an enjoyable time. What happened after sex—in what we have called the satisfaction area—was something else. Bob often felt a bit sorry that he had engaged in sex because this meant he had less time to devote to his work. Bob's view of sex was ambivalent: On the one hand, it felt good almost every time but, on the other hand, it diverted time and energy from his work.

Bob's thinking about sex and the functions it served was somewhat narrow. Sex was a way of enjoying oneself and expressing love, but it was a grand event that had to be done well and according to plan, that is, with lots of foreplay before intercourse, which itself should be long-lasting, and with orgasms for him and Mary. As such, it was an event which consumed a lot of time and energy. Bob did not think of sex as a way of playing, as a way of reducing tension or recharging one's batteries, or as something that could be enjoyed even if the goals—intercourse and orgasm—were not reached. In short, although sex was enjoyable, in many ways it diminished Bob, taking from him valuable time and strength; it did not replenish his resources in any significant way.

When Mary started initiating, Bob often was not in a sexual mood but did not know how to get himself in the mood or how else to handle the situation. At first, he went along with her requests, but he felt very pressured and later reacted by withdrawing from her, sexually and otherwise.

Treatment of Mary and Bob focused on three areas that are discussed separately.

Resumption of Touching and Other Intimate Activities

These issues were dealt with first because Bob was not ready to do anything about sex. He felt estranged from his wife, a result of his withdrawal from her, but was willing to consider doing things short of sex that might help the two of them get closer. The therapist accepted Bob's refusal to work on sex, saying it was only natural given how he felt, and in fact encouraged Bob not to have sex until he was absolutely certain he was ready to do so. The therapist also sympathized with Mary, saying she could understand her desire to have sex, but that she would have to accept continued frustration in this area for a while. Since she was not getting sex, perhaps she could get something else she wanted. After a brief discussion, Mary said that she wanted Bob's undivided attention several times a week and also some nonsexual touching. Bob agreed to the compromise.

Since Bob was always concerned about having enough time to do his work, it was suggested that he pick three or four times during the week when he could devote no more than 15 to 20 minutes to being with his wife. They could do anything they wanted—talk, walk, touch, and so on—as long as it was not sexual. They were also to have one "date" on the weekend, a date being a shared activity that lasted no more than 4 hours. At first, Mary planned the dates, but later she alternated with Bob.

The therapist mentioned that they might want to do some touching during their times together—holding hands, rubbing feet under a table at the restaurant, light massages, and so on. In Mary's presence, Bob was told that many men had certain desires to touch their women but refrained from doing so because of various prohibitions. These desires included grabbing or patting the woman's buttocks while walking down the street, rubbing her thigh while sitting in the car or elsewhere, coming up behind her and kissing her neck or cupping her breasts. (The therapist had previously been told by Mary that she loved this kind of attention and could resist the temptation to make it into foreplay.) Bob was told that this would be a good time to carry out such desires, but he had to be certain to fight Mary off if she got carried away and wanted sex.

This part of treatment progressed rapidly and without incident.

Mary and Bob really did like each other, and therapy gave them opportunities to get back together in nonthreatening ways and to resume activities they had enjoyed in the past and would have liked to continue were it not for the distance that had developed between them. It also gave Bob a chance to experiment with something new. He had always been somewhat straitlaced, playing and enjoyment not being high priorities. But he was intrigued by the "daring" suggestions given by the therapist and found himself thoroughly enjoying patting Mary's behind as they walked and rubbing her leg while they drove in the car.

Mary enjoyed the dates, the touching, and Bob's new daring. She missed sex, but she felt hopeful and looked forward to the time when they could again have sex. Bob said that he felt closer to Mary than he had in many months and that he enjoyed the touching and the time they spent together. (The therapist noted but never commented on the fact that Mary and Bob had broken the rules and were spending much more time together than had been agreed upon.) Bob also said that he was getting tired of the ban on sex and wanted to know why the therapist felt it necessary to proscribe something the couple clearly wanted.

During the 3 or 4 weeks when touching was the main focus of therapy, a number of direct and indirect suggestions were given. Those directed at Bob implied that being together in the suggested ways might not only feel good but could also reduce tension, thus giving him more energy to devote to his work. It was also suggested, though quite indirectly at first, that sex could serve the same purposes. Mary, on the other hand, was given suggestions that sex was not the only way to get attention, to be close, or to feel good.

Increasing Bob's Sexual Interest

Bob's renewed sexual desire was thought by the therapist to be largely a product of the ban on sex. People often get interested in something as soon as they are told they cannot have it. Since both Mary and Bob were almost begging to have sex, the therapist reluctantly agreed. But, she warned, if they went about sex in the old ways, things would soon return to the condition they were in before therapy. New ways of understanding and having sex would have to be found. At this point, the couple seemed willing to try anything.

The first issue dealt with was Bob's reaction to a sexual advance from Mary. There was no problem when he initiated. Mary was almost always ready and willing. But when she initiated and Bob was doing something else, he felt pressured to go along even when he felt differently, or to quickly get into a sexual mood even when he needed more time. This pressure, it will be recalled, was what caused him to withdraw sexually and otherwise from his wife.

In the touching exercises given earlier, Bob was the initiator. Now that he felt closer to Mary, he was ready to deal with something more threatening—her advances. The therapist explained that an invitation opened the door to a number of possibilities and that, in the long run, the relationship would be enhanced if Bob would use Mary's overtures as opportunities to discover what he wanted. When she initiated, he was not to respond immediately; rather, he was to take a few seconds to think about his feelings and desires. The first question to ask himself was whether he was interested in being with her in any way or if he preferred continuing what he was doing without interruption. If he wanted the latter, was he willing to set a time when he would be available to her? How could he let her know? If he welcomed her company, what specifically was he interested in—touching, talking, sex, or something else? If she was making a clear sexual invitation and he wanted to be with her but not have sex, how could he tell her? (The answer came from Mary, who demonstrated ways of refusing advances that she could best tolerate.) If Bob was interested in sex but needed some time to get in the mood, what were the best ways of accomplishing this? All of these options were discussed and role-played in the office, then practiced at home.

This work was often difficult and sometimes caused Bob to withdraw or Mary to feel angry and frustrated. It wasn't easy for Bob to refuse his wife's overtures, but he gradually learned to do so with a reasonable degree of comfort. Mary helped to facilitate Bob's progress by repeatedly saying that although it hurt when he turned her down, she felt honesty was far more important. She had reason to be cooperative, for Bob refused her outright only a few times, most of the times accepting her company although not always for sex. The options presented above were eye-openers for both of them. Bob had not previously thought it possible to counter a sexual proposal with an alternative (e.g., "I'm not in the mood for sex but I'd be happy to lie here and talk with you" or "I'm not ready for sex now but if we mess around a while I might get in the mood"). And Mary had not fully realized that a rejection of sex need not be disastrous, that others ways of being together were still possible.

Mary and Bob were told to get into sexual activity very slowly and in small doses so that signs of discomfort or trouble could be quickly spotted and dealt with. Specifically, sex should not last more than 15 minutes and should not include intercourse at this time. Bob could pleasure Mary for up to 15 minutes in ways of her choosing, and vice versa. Each had to initiate to get what she or he wanted. (When Mary initiated, Bob was to think about what he wanted and let her know, as discussed above.) After each experience, they should separately take a minute or so to determine how they felt. To give Bob further opportunity to practice refusing Mary, he was instructed to turn her down at least once a week, without totally withdrawing from her.

The main reason for the 15-minute limit was to give Bob the chance to understand that sex need not be a long, drawn-out activity which consumed lots of energy. Asking him to assess his feelings after sex was an attempt to get him to take a more realistic look at what sex did and did not do for him. Bob generally found he felt quite good after sex ("warm, close, and relaxed"), but this was often marred by a strange sense of restlessness which he at first could not identify but which he later associated with repeated injunctions from his parents that work should always come before pleasure. He was told to resist the temptation to jump up and get to work; he should stay where he was and tell Mary about his feelings and his associations to them. This led to some long conversations in bed, with Bob telling Mary for the first time about the work ethic that enveloped his childhood and how it had affected many areas of his life. These conversations led to greater understanding on Mary's part and brought both of them closer.

But all was not roses. The sixth week of therapy went quite badly. Mary came to the session angry at both Bob and the therapist. Shortly after the previous session, Bob had been stimulating her and she was close to orgasm when he quit because 15 minutes were up and refused to continue despite her entreaties. They had a bitter fight about this. Mary felt "raw" after the fight and thought that Bob rubbed salt in her wounds when later in the week he rejected one of her sexual overtures. In discussing his refusal, she realized that it reminded her of all the times he had turned her down in the past. (This is a good example of how the past affects present behavior; Mary was responding to Bob's refusal as it was experienced in the context of past rejections and what had happened earlier in the week.) She said she knew that both the time limit and the refusal were assigned by the therapist and therefore should not bother her, but she felt bad nonetheless. Surprisingly, Bob came to the rescue. He took her hand during the session and said he felt terrible for what had happened. He blamed his own "obsessiveness" for stopping the stimulation just before her orgasm and promised not to do it again no matter what the assignment was. Mary was taken by his reaction and felt better. She thought she could better deal with refusals as long as he kept his promise.

The therapist also sought to expand the range of cues Bob regarded as sexual. He was asked to notice times during the day when he felt slightly excited, restless, or in need of something to help him unwind, whether or not these feelings seemed sexual. As Bob noted such cues and reported them, it was suggested, at first subtly and then more openly, that doing something with Mary—touching, holding, playing, or having sex—might be appropriate. If Mary was not available—for example, if they occurred while he was at work—he was asked to keep the feelings alive, "letting them simmer on the back burner," by thinking for a few seconds of what he might do with Mary when he had the opportunity. If the encounter with Mary would not take place for several hours, the feelings could simmer all the while by periodically focusing on them and the thoughts or fantasies that accompanied them for a few seconds or minutes. Bob was shown how he could do this without seriously interfering with his work; it was explained that such activity would help his work by giving him needed breaks to relax and refocus his attention.

As the weeks went by, Bob became more interested in both touching and sex. He started associating these activities with internal stimuli—feelings of restlessness, tension, excitement, and later, warmth—that he had not before considered as sexual or having anything to do with his wife. He began to experience these feelings either as sexual or as indicating a desire to touch or in some other way be with Mary. In a sense, Mary began to loom as a "solution" to these feelings. Bob went about his "keeping the excitement simmering" in his usual compulsive way and sometimes got highly aroused at work. We all knew something was happening when Mary laughingly complained that he had several times "attacked" her as soon as he came in the house, without so much as a hello. By this time, they had broken the bans on intercourse and 15-minute sex.

One of the reasons Bob changed so rapidly was that the sexual experiences were invariably good. Mary was almost the perfect partner for someone who wanted to get more interested in sex. As Bob put it in one of the last sessions, "I can have her anytime, anyplace, anyway. She's always ready to take whatever I can give. I used to see that as a problem but I'm learning it's just the opposite—a real treasure."

The therapist never said much about Bob's obsessive concern with work. The line always taken was that being with Mary, sexually and otherwise, could help the work, that it was a way of relaxing and unwinding which could replenish his energy and powers of concentration. By taking this approach, the therapist avoided confrontations about the importance of work. Since Bob was not put in a position where he had to defend himself in this regard, he felt free in his conversations with Mary, and later with the therapist, to explore its ramifications. Although his commitment to work remains strong, and he still brings home more of it than many other men, by the end of therapy he was able to balance this commitment with another one, to having fun and being together with his wife.

Decreasing Mary's Sexual Desire

Mary reminded us of a woman Peter Benchley wrote about in his novel *The Deep* (1977):

> To Gail, sex was a vehicle for expressing everything—delight, anger, hunger, love, frustration, annoyance, even outrage. As an alcoholic can find any excuse for a drink, so Gail could make anything, from the first fallen leaf of autumn to the anniversary of Richard Nixon's resignation, a reason for making love. (p. 63)

Like Gail, Mary was someone for whom sex filled almost every need and for whom almost every cue, internal or external, elicited a sexual response.

While the therapist was working with Bob to increase his sexual interest, she was also working with Mary to decrease hers. She was asked to assess her feelings after every intimate contact with Bob. The therapist introduced the exercise by saying she was sure Mary did not feel the same after talking, touching, and sex, but it was important to determine just what the different feelings were. Mary had previously maintained that "nothing does it like sex." She was quite surprised to find that sometimes other types of contact served just as well or nearly as well. The therapist at first refused to accept her conclusion, saying there must be some difference and that Mary should attend even more closely to her feelings after nonsexual encounters. The more she attended, the more strongly she maintained that often a "warm talk or a good cuddle" could be almost as satisfying as sex and produced similar feelings of "bondedness" with Bob. Of course, it was doubtful that she would have reached such an understanding had she not been having any sexual activity.

Mary was asked to try to differentiate more carefully between the feelings and cues she thought were sexual. Was it possible that some could be interpreted as indicating desires for closeness, attention, support, or comfort? She observed for several weeks and found that she could make some distinctions. She also discovered that some of the cues she had thought were sexual were actually quite vague, capable of being satisfied either by sex or by some other forms of contact.

Sex was an important pillar of Mary's self-esteem. She knew she was attractive and good at sex, and regular doses of it were required to keep her feeling good about herself. One consequence was that whenever she did not feel confident and strong, she needed sex to lift her spirits. This was a problem because she became almost desperate, which turned Bob off.

Two approaches were taken to this issue. First, Mary was encouraged to change jobs. The one she held did not excite her or give her a sense of satisfaction or accomplishment. She therefore turned frequently to sex for excitement and to feel better about herself. She was in the nursing field and was fortunate in being able to find a more suitable job without much ado. As soon as she started the new job, she heard about a research project at the hospital that grabbed her interest and enthusiasm, but she hesitated about participating because it required work after hours without compensation. The therapist encouraged her to give it a try, reminding her she could quit if it did not work out. She was accepted as a volunteer on the project, a position she loved and one that gave a constructive channel for her tremendous energy and enthusiasm, aside from giving her a strong sense of satisfaction.

Second, she was asked to try new ways of dealing with low moods. Among these were carefully thinking about the causes of her discontent and trying to resolve them when possible; discussing her feelings and the issues with Bob, a system having been worked out whereby she could let him know that she was feeling bad and really needed his attention; or asking Bob to "mother" her. Although Mary's first response to low moods was usually a sexual one, she gradually learned to resist this temptation most of the time and instead to turn to one of the options just presented. A nice twist occurred several times when she told Bob she was feeling bad and wanted to talk to him; he said, "Well, maybe sex would help more than talking. I'm available."

This case was almost entirely successful in achieving its major goals. When therapy ended, after 12 sessions spaced over 17 weeks, both Mary and Bob were content. They were having sex more frequently than ever before in their relationship and also spending more time together doing other things. Bob was no longer as concerned that sex took time away from his work; he now often turned to sex as a work break and enjoyed it immensely. He dealt with Mary's invitations much better and only rarely felt threatened or pressured by them. Mary had learned to meet some of her needs outside of sex, and while she easily could have handled even more sex, she was satisfied with what she had. A phone conversation with the couple 7 months after the end of therapy revealed that the situation remained about the same, with one important exception. Mary was now employed full time on the research project; she said she felt quite confident and secure and rarely needed sex as an ego booster or confidence builder anymore.

One of the main reasons for the success of this case was the strength of the relationship. Mary and Bob both liked and loved each other, and were committed to the marriage and to working out the problems in it. Even though Mary wavered a bit at the beginning of treatment, the commitment was strong enough to carry them both through the frustrations and difficulties created by the therapy. Obviously, not all couples have as much love and commitment, and dealing with them is more difficult.

Neither the therapist nor the couple was able to pinpoint any particular variable as the crucial one. All three thought that everything that was done was necessary and helpful. The therapist, however, did think that her handling of Bob's obsession with work was tricky and could have produced trouble. She believed she had taken the best approach by not confronting it and in fact by encouraging Bob to look upon sex as an aid to doing better work. As it turned out, this allowed Bob himself to think about, discuss, and ultimately decrease the influence of the work-before-pleasure ethic that was such an important part of his personality. The therapist thought that had she attacked Bob's commitment to his work, she would have aroused strong resistance and perhaps lost any chance of helping him change.

A Case of Low Arousal

Tom and Betty were in their late 30s and had been married 14 years. The presenting complaint was decreased frequency of sex in the past several months and increased frequency of arguments about sex and other matters.

Until about 6 months before entering therapy, Betty had regarded herself as "good in bed," because Tom wanted sex often and always enjoyed it, and because she was willing to do whatever he liked. Betty had never had an orgasm, but because she had never thought much about it, she had no complaints. She enjoyed the closeness of sex and certainly did not consider herself to be frustrated or missing anything. She did not lubricate very much, but K-Y Jelly, recommended early in their marriage by her gynecologist, provided an easy solution. Betty regarded sex as a sensuous, pleasurable, loving experience, and she was especially pleased with how well she satisfied her husband.

Then, about 8 months before treatment began, Betty heard some interesting news from a friend who was in a women's sex therapy group. The friend, Sue, talked frequently and at length about how she never got much from sex, but things were changing because she was learning about her sexuality and how to have orgasms. When she had her first orgasm a few weeks later, she rushed over to tell Betty, and Betty heard of all the wonders that attended orgasm ("Sue said it was the most marvelous feeling"). She was fascinated by Sue's report and decided that she, too, should have orgasms. (Why Betty was so strongly influenced by Sue's report is an interesting question for which we have no answer.)

With the guidance of a self-help book and some advice from Sue, Betty started masturbating and in less than a month had her first orgasm. After repeating this experience a number of times, she mustered the courage to ask Tom to stimulate her in the ways she stimulated herself. She was not immediately orgasmic in this manner, but after more than a month of working at it, she had a few orgasms.

The problems arose at about the time Betty started asking Tom to stimulate her, and they steadily got worse. Tom and Betty were more irritable than ever before in their marriage. They argued constantly, often over trivia, stopped intimate conversation, and both lost interest in sex. Their relationship, which had previously been quite satisfactory, seemed on the verge of falling apart. This prospect frightened them enough that they could admit that something was terribly wrong and that they needed help. Their family doctor could not decide if they needed marital counseling or sex therapy and referred them to one of the authors.

The case was confusing at first because Tom and Betty were fighting about so many issues that it was difficult to determine what to focus on. In going over the history of their bickering, it finally became clear that things started to deteriorate when Betty had asked Tom to stimulate her so that she might reach orgasm. Both said they stopped enjoying sex about that time. Betty said sex had become hard work. Reaching orgasm was a long and arduous process for her—whether she did it herself or with Tom's stimulation, she required about 25 to 50 minutes of very careful stimulation, very careful because it became painful if not done very lightly and in the right place. It also took intense concentration; any interference, such as Tom changing position or talking, or a dog barking, was sufficient to turn her off. Of her orgasms, she said, "They feel OK, I like them, but they're not exactly exciting, certainly not what I thought they'd be like after listening to Sue."

Tom's complaint was similar to his wife's. He said he was not against her having orgasms and in fact welcomed her expanded sexual interest ("Being able to give her pleasure turns me on and makes me feel proud"). But, he continued, the idea of having to stimulate her so carefully and for so long, without being able to say anything or change positions or stop to rest for fear of distracting her, was a real bore. And worse, he felt guilty for feeling this way. He did not want to think of himself as a male chauvinist or a selfish person, but he just could not endure what sex had become.

Because sex had become boring and a task, they both withdrew from it, and they stopped touching because they feared touching would lead to sex. The therapist guessed that their frustration and anger from not touching and not having sex, and their concern about what was happening to their marriage, was what led to fights in other areas.

The therapist thought the main problem was that Betty was never highly aroused in sex. This would account for the need for such lengthy stimulation, her distractibility, and the very mild orgasms she had. Increasing her sexual arousal, therefore, became the goal of therapy, with the understanding that heightened arousal would lead to orgasm. Tom and Betty agreed to the plan. While we dealt with arousal, they were allowed to have intercourse in the old way when they felt so inclined. Betty would not try to have orgasms during the first part of therapy. The therapist made a promise to work with her on orgasms after her enjoyment and excitement were enhanced.

To help Betty unwind from the cares and tensions of the day, a number of transition activities were suggested. Some of the more effective ones for her at the beginning of therapy were having a bite to eat after returning home from work; taking a leisurely bath, with or without Tom; having a glass of wine or a cup of coffee, depending on her mood; or lying in bed next to Tom without much activity. These transition activities were viewed simply as ways of giving Betty the space to let go of work and tension so she could be more open to activities designed to increase her sexual arousal.

Betty was taught the method of keeping arousal alive—simmering on the back burner—discussed in the previous section. The problem was that her feelings of sexual arousal were not very intense at any time. It was discovered that two things that did excite her were Tom's orgasms ("When I feel all his tension and power start to let go, I feel a strong warm glow and then a rush of warmth and relaxation") and playing tennis. (She was an avid and skillful player and, as she put it, "Nothing is as exciting as a good set; it's absolutely exhilarating.") Betty knew how to get aroused but was not using this knowledge to her own sexual benefit. Only a few changes seemed necessary to help her take advantage of the feelings she already had.

Betty was repeatedly told, sometimes directly and sometimes indirectly, that she could feel in sex exactly what she felt in tennis—the tightness, the power, the exhilaration—and that the warmth and rush of relaxation she experienced in response to Tom's ejaculations were things she could feel in response to her own sensations. During sessions and at home she was asked to take a few minutes to relax and allow her "unconscious mind" to determine ways of making this come about. While playing tennis, she was to take a few seconds now and then to assess the state of her mind and body: whether she was warm or cold, the feelings in her heart and stomach, the state of her muscular tension, and so on. The same was done regarding her state when Tom ejaculated. In both cases, the constant question was how she could let herself get into a similar state when she was being sexually stimulated.

She discovered that when playing tennis and observing Tom ejaculate, she moved her body quite freely; there was, she said, "a strange mixture of tension and relaxation I really can't describe, but I know there's lots of movement, especially in tennis; I'm constantly moving and tensing and relaxing." In contrast, when she or her husband stimulated her, she was stiff as a board with hardly any movement—because of her forced concentration, she thought—and her breathing was barely noticeable. She was asked to try one volley of tennis with Tom, breathing and moving exactly the way she did in sex. It was a disaster—she could not hit the ball over the net—but she learned something very important in the process. The message was so obvious that the therapist did not even comment on it.

While practicing keeping her arousal alive during the day, Betty was encouraged to move and tense and relax different muscles, especially those in the hips and pelvis, and also to do some breathing exercises. This activity increased the intensity of her feelings. Later, she was asked to recall a particularly strong ejaculation of Tom's as she was fantasizing and moving around. Then she was to alternate this memory of Tom's ejaculation with thoughts about what she wanted him to do to her that would give her pleasure. Her feelings of excitement gradually got stronger and stronger.

Perhaps because of her unhappy experiences with clitoral stimulation or perhaps because of the repeated association of her pleasure with Tom's orgasms, which usually occurred during intercourse, the fantasies she developed of him giving her pleasure almost invariably were of intercourse. While she said a bit of clitoral stimulation might be fine in the beginning, what she really wanted was his penis inside her. This led to an interesting development in therapy, which we discuss later.

Betty always disengaged herself from tennis before having any type of intimate contact with Tom. This, of course, is not unusual.

After exercise, most people try to rid themselves of the by-products—the sweat, heavy breathing, excitement, etc.—before moving on to sensual or sexual activity. While this seems to make good sense, the situation can be beneficially viewed in another way. The exercise produces a state of physiological and psychological activation which is not much different from sexual arousal. This was especially true for Betty, who talked about tennis the way some people talk about sex. The obvious question then becomes, if tennis or dancing or jogging or whatever already has you halfway or more there, why not use the energy rather than discarding it during warm-down and wash-off and then starting from zero activation in sex?

To take advantage of the tennis high, Betty had to do two things. First, whenever possible immediately after playing tennis, she was to engage in sensual/sexual activity with Tom or by herself. If actual activity was precluded, she was to take a few minutes to fantasize what she might do with him. Second, when she had not played tennis but was about to begin some sexual activity with Tom, she should first take a few minutes to swing her racket in the bedroom, exactly as if she were on the court. This practice worked extremely well because Tom found her movements very sexy and made appropriate comments; this helped Betty strengthen the connection between the excitement she was experiencing and sex. Her sexual arousal increased rapidly.

The situation of Betty swinging her racket and Tom commenting from the sidelines is part of another focus of our work—a shared building of arousal. Some people are successful when they forget or tune out their partners and focus exclusively on their own sensations or fantasies. As long as tuning out is effective and as long as the partner does not feel left out, there is much to be said for this method. However, many people do better and their partners feel more included when the development of arousal is shared. This seemed the best approach for Tom and Betty.

As much as possible, Tom was included in Betty's unwinding and arousal activities. He knew about all of them and even when he could not actively participate—for example, there simply was not room for both of them to simulate playing tennis in their bedroom—he was often able to watch and share his growing excitement with Betty, which, in turn, increased her excitement. Tom grew quite proficient in telling her how turned on he felt, something he had not done prior to therapy because it distracted her. Later, Betty started telling him about her feelings, which usually aroused both of them. Both were also encouraged to use teasing techniques—for example, stopping stimulation periodically, regardless of the type of stimulation being done, and saying with a smile something like "You want it so bad, I'm not sure I'm going to give it to you." Teasing is not without risk, especially where there is a lack of trust or other serious relationship difficulty, but in this case it seemed to warrant experimentation after the couple was getting along better. And it worked out well. The teasing and begging that followed it ("But I have to have it; I'll do *anything* if you'll only continue") almost invariably served to increase arousal and playfulness.

After the first two therapy sessions, the word orgasm was used only in reference to Tom. As far as everyone was concerned, we were working on Betty's ability to become as aroused as possible. The therapist thought that given high excitement and some specific means of stimulation, orgasm would take care of itself. Talking about orgasm might put unnecessary pressure on Betty.

As for stimulation, a number of steps were taken. In the beginning, aside from having intercourse the old way, there was a lot of nongenital touching, similar to Masters and Johnson's (1970) sensate focus, but including teasing. Later, genital touching was included, with Betty always stimulating Tom first. This was done to capitalize on Betty's response to Tom's ejaculation. After he was done, he stimulated her. This did not yield any striking results because Betty had become almost phobic about clitoral stimulation that lasted more than a few minutes. So two changes were made. At times, Tom's stimulation of her was nongenital but included the breasts; she was to go as high as possible with this type of stimulation, along with moving around and breathing as in tennis, and stop whenever she desired. At other times, when she requested it, Tom would stimulate her with one or two fingers thrusting in her vagina. He had sometimes done this in the days before she became interested in orgasm. But now, given her much higher arousal, she experienced new sensations and found it much more pleasurable. The therapist thought Betty was close to orgasm but withheld this information and instead asked what would make her feel even better. The reply: "To have his penis inside me."

Although Tom and Betty had continued to have intercourse all the while, these experiences had been primarily for Tom's pleasure and orgasm. What was needed now was a way of making intercourse a vehicle for Betty's pleasure. In preparation for the next step, Tom had been given some advice to help him develop better ejaculatory control. His control was not bad to begin with, but the therapist thought some enhancement would be helpful. Tom developed the needed control when Betty stimulated him and during intercourse, using the subtle adjustment method described by Zilbergeld (1978).

Tom was advised that for the next few weeks, intercourse belonged to Betty. She was to be in absolute control and use his penis as she pleased. The Kegel exercises (1952) had been recommended to her in the second therapy session, and she had practiced them faithfully every day. She had already remarked that her internal sensations during intercourse seemed more intense, which was probably due to the effects of the Kegels and her increased excitement. And Tom had already commented that intercourse seemed "tighter" and more stimulating. The therapist noted that one of the fringe benefits of Betty's greater arousal and increased muscle tone was an increase in internal tumescense that made for a snugger fit during intercourse. Betty was given a number of suggestions for further enhancing internal stimulation, a subject treated in more detail elsewhere (Ellison, in preparation).

Special care was taken to ensure that intercourse did not turn into the kind of labored exercise that clitoral stimulation had. A 15-minute time limit was imposed, and the therapist repeatedly cautioned that they should stop immediately if either partner felt nervous, pressured, or as if he or she were doing hard work. And the only goal mentioned was for Betty to feel as good as possible.

The therapist's concern that intercourse might repeat the path of clitoral stimulation was probably unfounded. Betty and Tom felt differently from before. Tom thoroughly enjoyed the stimulation he received while inside her and was quite proud of the ejaculatory control he could show off regularly. Betty was much more turned on and could easily handle things that before would have distracted her and turned her off. She and Tom both talked and made other sounds during sex, and this was now experienced simply as part of the enjoyment.

It took only 2 weeks for Betty to reach orgasm with the new way of having intercourse. She happily announced at the start of the 10th session that she had had several orgasms that week: "I was a little self-conscious at the end (before orgasm), realizing I had to do certain things to go over the edge, but it was great. It wasn't work, more like going with what's there, and there's plenty there these days. And the orgasms felt so much better, almost like descriptions I've read in novels."

The couple was seen for 2 more visits, spaced over 5 weeks. The time was used to give their new patterns a chance to stabilize and to discuss and role-play dealing with problems that might crop up in the future. This work proceeded without incident. As a bonus, Betty's negative associations to prolonged clitoral stimulation evaporated. She several times had orgasms with only clitoral stimulation in less than 15 minutes. Although they were more intense than the ones she had had this way before therapy, she still preferred orgasms in intercourse.

After the 10th session, Betty no longer swung her tennis racket in the bedroom before sex. She did not need it anymore. During the last visit, she told the therapist about the new wall decoration in the bedroom—the tennis racket. "Just in case I ever need to remind myself," she commented.

Tom and Betty's relationship improved quickly and dramatically during the first few weeks of treatment. As the therapist had assumed, the arguing and distancing were apparently reflections of their sexual problems. As soon as they were working together to deal with these, the rest of the relationship reverted to its earlier and happier state.

Tom and Betty were called a year after the termination of therapy. Though the racket still hangs on the wall, Betty has had no need to "remind herself." They have sex about as often as they did in the days before the problems developed, but both enjoy it more. Betty is proud of her sexual accomplishments and satisfaction, and so is Tom. As he said, "Her pleasure adds a whole new dimension that was missing before. I'm glad I can give her as much as she gives me."

This case, like the preceding one, had the advantage of a strong and committed relationship. While we have worked on desire and arousal problems with couples whose relationships were neither as strong nor as committed, there is no question but that the better the relationship, the quicker and easier the therapy. The fact that Tom and Betty's marriage was in bad shape when they entered treatment, as was Mary and Bob's, does not detract from this conclusion. Our experience indicates that the important issues are the strength of the relationship before the trouble began and the commitment of the partners to each other and to working out the problem together.

The therapist almost made a mistake that could have cost heavily. He assumed that after Betty's arousal had been increased, the proper approach would have been for her to have orgams with clitoral stimulation. When Betty balked at the idea of clitoral stimulation, the therapist at first thought of how to deal with this "resistance." Fortunately, after consultation with the coauthor, he realized that while the current trend of "clitoris first, then vagina if at all" may work for some women, it did not fit for Betty. So he just went along with what Betty suggested, penile thrusting, and circumvented the whole issue of resistance.

We have mentioned several times that after that first two sessions, the word "orgasm" was not used except to refer to Tom. This is consistent with our work with other problems where we rarely mention the goal after the start of therapy; for example, in working with a man with erection difficulties, we rarely talk about erections. We are not presumptuous enough to think that the client forgets about orgasms or erections because we do not mention them. Therapist and client are both aware of what the client hopes to achieve. But we hope to put the goal in the background and substitute some other, more easily attainable standard, for example, meeting one's conditions or feeling as high as possible. The reason for this is that our experience suggests that too much attention to erections and orgasms tends to produce a strained laboring toward the goal, which in itself is counterproductive. Even when the goal is achieved, in the process sex often becomes hard work.

Unsuccessful Treatment in a Case of Low Desire and Low Arousal

Cindy, a 26-year-old woman who had been married 4 years, was referred by her lawyer. Her husband, Larry, from whom she had been separated for a year and a half, was urging her to move back in with him or to make their divorce final.

The relationship had been difficult and strained from the beginning. As she described it, Larry was always finding fault with her and seemed to delight in humiliating her in front of friends; he had also thrown things at her and hit her several times. Cindy was almost constantly angry at him but had not found an effective way of dealing with her feelings except by leaving. She went on at great length and with much bitterness about the way he had treated her. On the other side, she was attracted to what she called his "strength," the fact that he had been her first lover, and to the many interests they had in common. Another reason for staying married was that he shared with her in caring for their 3-year-old son.

Sex with him had been good for her only a few times, just before and for a short while after the wedding. Cindy said Larry wanted sex frequently and had good ejaculatory control, but she invariably felt tense with him and rarely had orgasms. She gradually lost interest in sex with him during their first year of marriage; later, she became almost phobic about his approaches. She would "freeze up" whenever he made a sexual overture and sometimes even when he gave her a friendly hug. Once in a while, she would force herself to have sex with him, but the experiences were not enjoyable for either of them. They had not had sex during their separation, even though they saw each other frequently and he wanted sex. Larry tried to be patient about her reluctance but at times would explode in anger.

Larry had been getting more insistent about the necessity of a decision regarding the future of their marriage. Cindy was unable to move back in with him or to make the divorce final. This upset Larry and even Cindy's lawyer, who had taken an almost fatherly interest in her. Cindy felt the pressure and decided she had to make a choice. The big issue for her was whether she could get sexually interested in Larry again; if she could, she would probably go back to him. If she could not, the marriage would have to end.

There was an important complication. Cindy had started an affair with an older man, Bert, some months before leaving Larry. It was largely due to Bert's encouragement and support that she felt able to leave. Larry knew of the affair and did not like it but had tolerated the situation until recently. With Bert, sex was fine for Cindy: "I feel like a woman with him and he doesn't make me feel like a fool or a bitch." She was still seeing Bert, who was married but estranged from his wife, and seemed to care a great deal for him. But, she said, because of their son it might be better if she could work out the relationship with Larry, and she wanted to see if she could again get turned on to him.

Larry accompanied Cindy to the second session and corroborated most of what she had said a week before. He was apologetic about the way he had treated her in the past and said he was ready to do anything that might get them back together. He was adamant that a decision had to be made soon; he was tired of being neither married nor single. Both agreed to give therapy a chance.

Since Cindy froze up whenever Larry touched her, sex was out of the question. Consequently, a number of assignments involving talking, nonsexual touching, and sleeping together were given in this and the next two sessions. Cindy was to be in complete charge of how much touching there was and could terminate the activity at any time. Larry was warned that he would feel frustrated. He was: He wanted to move much faster but he understood the need for proceeding slowly and was, considering his history, remarkably patient. The exercises did not go smoothly—Cindy would usually get tense rather quickly and want to leave the situation—but there was some progress. In the fourth session Cindy said she was feeling more relaxed with Larry than she had for some time.

A few days later, however, she called to request an appointment for herself. In it, she told the therapist that she had decided to make the divorce final. Several reasons were given. First, she had talked to her mother and sister about Bert, and they were much more understanding and accepting than she had anticipated. This made her feel much better about seeing him. Second, Bert had recently told her that he was going to divorce his wife regardless of what Cindy did. This made possible at least the thought of a "total relationship" with him, which Cindy took as a challenge. She was not sure it could work out but she wanted to give it a try. Since Larry was not willing to share her and was pressing for her to return to him, there was only one way to give the relationship with Bert a fair chance. Third, Cindy kept comparing Larry and Bert, with Larry always coming out on the short end. Even in therapy, everything with him was an effort and a hassle; with Bert, on the other hand, everything seemed to be natural and easy.

Cindy recognized that her encounters with Bert were usually brief and passionate and therefore not truly comparable to those with Larry, but she did not give this thought much weight. Last, the therapy exercises had convinced her that she probably could get turned on again to Larry, although it would take some time. This scared her. It had taken all the strength and courage she could muster, along with Bert's support, to leave Larry. Suppose she went back to him and things returned to the old pattern? She was not sure she would have the strength to leave again.

Concern for her son did not loom large in her decision. When the therapist asked about this, Cindy replied that Larry would probably still want to take an active part in the boy's care and, in any case, she thought the boy would be happy if she was happy.

Therapy did not achieve the goal of helping Cindy regain sexual interest in her husband. One reason was that her commitment to the marriage was ambivalent and was weakened by her relationship with Bert. With him, sex was good, there was no backlog of negative feelings, and neither sex nor the rest of the relationship, as limited as it was, required work. Problems are frequently encountered in cases where one of the partners has a good or at least smoothly flowing outside relationship. Therapy almost always requires effort and self-consciousness and often leads to feelings of frustration and pain, and this is as true of brief, behavioral-oriented therapy as of long-term, insight-oriented treatment. Few clients enjoy the effort or pain, but love and commitment can make the work bearable. Those with outside relationships suffer from the inevitable comparisons. Why work so hard to get what you already have without any effort? In some cases, it has proved beneficial to have the client break off the affair for a given period of time, during which a commitment is made to the primary relationship and the therapy. But this did not seem possible for Cindy. The therapist's probing in the first session strongly suggested that Cindy would not break off with Bert or even reduce the amount of contact with him, no matter what the possible consequences. In retrospect, however, it does seem that the therapist could have done more to alert Cindy to the inevitability of comparing Larry and Bert and to feeling that going with Bert was the simplest solution.

It also seems that the therapist too readily accepted Cindy's idea of what should be worked on in therapy. Her anger, rather than her lack of sexual interest, might have been a better place to begin. It is probable that it was her unexpressed anger at Larry that blocked her sexual interest. If she had been helped to better deal with those feelings, this case might have had a different outcome. One way would have been by criticizing him openly in a way that reduced, rather than increased, her feelings of bitterness and helplessness. Another possibility would have been revenge, getting back at him for what he had done to her in a way that took the charge off of those feelings. (We realize that therapists do not talk much about revenge, but we have found it to be very helpful in a number of cases.) We should mention that we did not think it possible for Cindy to relabel her anger as sexual. It was too pervasive and she, unlike many other people, found anger to be very unsexual.

Some Principles of Working with Desire and Arousal Problems

We start with the belief that there is no such entity as sexual interest or arousal. On the contrary, what we have are various situations and cues to which people attach erotic significance. This view is not new; many have commented on it (Gagnon & Simon, 1973; Rook & Hammen, 1977; Whalen, 1966; Wincze, Hoon, & Hoon, 1977). What has been lacking is appreciation of possible clinical applications.

Let us turn first to the uses and functions of sex. We all learn that sex is appropriate or useful in certain ways, for example, to show affection, to prove one's masculinity or femininity, and to relieve tension. This learning is accompanied by detailed discriminations. For example, a man might believe that a sexual quickie for the purposes of relieving tension is appropriate only with masturbation or prostitutes; with a partner he cares for, a quickie would be in bad taste.

The more functions sex serves, the more cues will be endowed with sexual meaning and, in general, the greater sexual interest will be. Interest can be increased or decreased by changing the number of stimuli to which sexual meaning is attached. In the first case, Tom was helped to increase his sexual appetite by showing him that sex was relevant to his desire to do his work well and also that it was an appropriate way of dealing with his feelings of general excitement, tension, and restlessness. In other words, he found new uses for sex and erotic meaning in cues that hitherto had not had such meaning.

It is unlikely that therapy would have been as successful as it was had he not also been able to change his views about what sex meant. He came to therapy believing that sex was a serious performance which had to be done well and which consumed much time and energy; he learned that sex could also be short, playful, and a way of recharging his psyche.

His wife, Mary, underwent a similar change but in the opposite direction. In the beginning, she attached erotic meaning to a wide variety of stimuli, which is another way of saying that sex served a host of functions for her. She learned that sex was not the only way to feel good about herself, to get attention, to relax, and to feel a sense of bondedness with her mate. Like her husband, she had to learn to make fine distinctions, to determine when sex was the most appropriate "solution" for her needs at a given moment and when other activities were better suited. By the end of therapy, she had narrowed the range of stimuli to which she attached a primarily erotic significance and had expanded the range of cues for which nonsexual activity was an appropriate solution.

One way people use sex deserves special mention. Sex often provides a way of maintaining optimal distance for one or both partners in a relationship. Let us take a woman as an example. Her sexual interest or arousal may be less when she feels she needs to be more distant from her partner; the decreased appetite or lower arousal helps maintain the distance she desires. If too much distance is created, she will become more interested or aroused. Of course, it can work the other way as well. If her partner is not particularly interested in sex or does not like sexy women, increased interest or arousal on her part could push him away.

When maintaining distance through sex leads to desire discrepancies or arousal problems, the issue of distance is what requires consideration because the problems are merely reflections of it. In the interests of brevity, we only mention a few possibilities. The couple or person can learn to maintain the desired distance in areas other than sex; they can learn to better recognize the signs that more (or less) distance is needed and take appropriate action before the need becomes desperate (e.g., in some cases, just taking some time for oneself, away from one's partner and from the home, can take care of the need for more distance); they can learn that having sex and being highly aroused need not necessarily create more closeness than is desired; and sometimes the amount of closeness or distance a person wants can itself be modified, although this is the most difficult of all the options mentioned.

Before attempting to manipulate interest and turn-on, it is important to consider the role of transition activities. The effectiveness of therapy for almost any sexual problem is enhanced to the extent that clients are able to disengage from what might be called negative tension before they turn to sensual or sexual activities.

It is no secret that modern living produces tremendous tension which often inhibits sexual interest, excitement, and performance. Most therapists are at least somewhat aware of this and may remind their clients to choose a relaxed time for doing sexual assignments. But clients often find that they do not have any relaxed times; they do not know how to get rid of negative tension. Many times it is essential to suggest transition activities (Zilbergeld, 1978) for the client's exploration. Several which worked well for Betty were mentioned earlier. The types of transitions employed are of little moment, the important thing being that they help the client move from a tense, pressured state to one which feels more comfortable and in which he or she is more open to sexual stimuli. (It may well be that one of the main reasons for the great effectiveness of Masters and Johnson's therapy is that the whole experience is, in a sense, a transition activity, far away from the cares and pressures of everyday life. Since most of us do not take clients out of their usual environments, we need to help them become more relaxed where they are.)

Transition acitivities can be done alone or with a partner. When done together, they can function as a bridge into a shared building of arousal and enjoyable sexual activity.

One of the most important things we have learned in working with arousal problems is that physical stimulation does not necessarily equal turn-on. Many therapists seem to believe that the more someone is touched and rubbed, the more excited he or she should get. While this is often the case, it does not always hold. One example is the man who can maintain an erection for an hour of intercourse but cannot ejaculate because all that stimulation does not arouse him (Apfelbaum, 1976). Betty was another example; 25 to 50 minutes of clitoral stimulation simply did not excite her much, although it sometimes produced a mild orgasm. Almost everyone can think of times when the same stimulation which on other occasions was quite exciting either failed to have any effect or evoked feelings of annoyance, anger, sadness, and so on. Our own experience and that of people we have questioned about this is that effectiveness of stimulation is very much dependent on the situation (where, when, with whom, and one's mood at the time).

In cases of desire discrepancies or arousal difficulties, an important therapeutic task, therefore, is to arrange situations so that they will be experienced as sexual or sexually arousing. Not only do blocks need to be removed or decreased (by providing for privacy, relaxation, trust, or whatever else the client needs), but usually we also must provide for new ways of viewing arousal and sexuality. Since dealing with obstacles is relatively familiar ground, we discuss only new ways of viewing sex and arousal. Several relevant variables—the functions of sex and the rules that guide sexual conduct—have already been mentioned. Here we discuss two more: dealing with sexual advances and relabeling internal cues.

Many sexual problems are rooted in the way people deal with sexual invitations. It will be recalled that Bob felt very pressured when his wife initiated sex, and this finally led to a complete loss of interest. This is a sex-role reversal of the more traditional situation in which the man almost always initiated, usually in an aroused state, and the woman could not catch up to him—this situation being one of the reasons for the old myth that men are horny and women frigid. The man, as initiator, had an advantage: Before making an overture, he could already be thinking about sex and getting turned on. His partner, on the other hand, might be busy with other things and not thinking about sex, or even about him. If she accepted the overture, she had to disengage from the other activities, make a transition, and get turned on, and do all these things fairly quickly because of the large head start he had. Because this script was frequently paired with another—once the man comes, sex is all over—many women who could not catch up became frustrated and lost interest in sex.

We attempt to help clients make more satisfying responses to invitations. As illustrated in our work with Bob, we ask them to slow down and carefully consider what they want to do each time they receive a sexual advance. Many options are considered: outright refusal, outright acceptance, and counterproposals. If the person is interested in sex but needs more time to make a transition and get aroused, we help him or her find ways of doing this, invariably with the partner's participation. We do not worry much about the initiator getting too excited, for this rarely creates difficulties.

Once a person stops fearing sexual proprosals and realizes that there are many acceptable and satisfying ways of responding to them, optimal desire and arousal are easier to achieve.

Perhaps the most promising method of increasing sexual arousal is the relabeling of internal excitation. A little background material is in order. Physiological activiation is more flexible than has generally been acknowledged. As Kinsey and his associates pointed out years ago,

"Nearly all of the elements of sexual response are found in other situations, particularly in other emotional responses and most particularly in anger" (Kinsey, Pomeroy, Martin, & Gebhard, 1953, p. 704). Kinsey found 14 physiological similarities between anger and sexual response, for example, increased pulse rate, blood pressure, and muscular tension. More recent work has supported Kinsey's observations (Zuckerman, 1971). And in a brilliant series of experiments focused on emotions other than sex, Schachter and Singer (1962) demonstrated that activation of the nervous system resulted in different emotional responses and behavior depending on the context and the subjects' expectations.

We interpret all the above to mean that almost any type of excitation provides energy that is relatively flexible and available for different types of interpretation and behavior. Take a man who feels some excitation. Assume he is nude and in the bedroom with his wife. If she looks appealing to him and seems interested in sex, he may well experience the excitation as sexual and conduct himself accordingly, perhaps by making a sexual advance. Now, the same scene, but this time the man recalls that his wife was not satisfied the last few times they made love. Instead of interpreting his excitation as sexual arousal, he may experience it as annoyance or anger or guilt and act accordingly—by arguing with her, by telling her he's not interested, or by apologizing for his ineptness. Kinsey provided another example: "It not infrequently happens, both in lower mammals and in man, that anger, fighting, and quarrels suddenly turn into sexual response" (Kinsey *et al.,* 1953, p. 704)

If we view excitation as relatively plastic and capable of being channeled and relabeled, some new ways of dealing with arousal present themselves. Most people get very excited about something in their lives, and this can be used to enhance their sexual arousal, as demonstrated in the case of Tom and Betty. Associating sex with the excitement Betty felt while playing tennis, and thus in effect relabeling that excitement, helped her become more sexually aroused so that physical stimulation could have a greater effect on her. We believe that for many clients, this is a far more powerful method than the more common one of trying to increase their arousal by having them use their own sexual fantasies. The fact is that many people's fantasies are not very exciting. Betty's certainly were not. But two things—her husband's orgasms and playing tennis—did turn her on. We simply made use of the excitation that was already there by giving it a sexual connotation.

One thing that excites almost everyone is arguing or fighting. As Kinsey and others have noted, at least in the early stages, anger is almost indistinguishable in physiological terms from sexual response. Staged fights, sometimes including wrestling or hitting with batakas, can be used to facilitate sexual arousal. Of course, there are risks in this method and care must be taken, although for some couples fighting is the norm, and all they are missing is the connection between what they feel when they fight and sexual turn-on. Care must also be taken to find ways of broadening the excitement produced by arguing, so that sexual arousal can be achieved without always using arguments as foreplay.

Lest we be accused of sexual imperialism, we want to make it clear we do not think that every emotion and every stimulus should be labeled as sexual. Relabeling has its dangers. As an example, we saw one couple who frequently fought but never finished the fights because both started feeling sexual just as the screaming reached its peak, and they then made passionate love. This pattern was destructive because the air never got cleared and each lovemaking experience was only the prelude to the next fight. Both partners had complaints they wanted to express and have heard, but the practice of relabeling the anger as sexual excitement prevented this from happening. The therapist stopped the cycle by sitting the couple down and getting them to listen to each other. The experience was painful for both, and it was easy to see why they had always taken the easy way of getting turned on in the middle of their quarrels. There are many times when feelings should be expressed exactly the way they are. If their expression is blocked, they soon come out again, and an ugly cycle is developed in which there is never any peace.

Although the therapist must be careful in suggesting the reinterpretation of experiences, this can be a valuable method of increasing arousal, as we hope we demonstrated in the case of Betty. The question the therapist must constantly ask is: By relabeling certain sensations, feelings, or other stimuli, am I asking the client to siphon off energy from something that is important and should be left as is? We see little objection to using Betty's tennis high as a way of enhancing her sexual excitement. But in cases where anger, sadness, pain, or other feelings are used, there is no substitute for common sense and good clinical judgment.

This brings us to the topic of depression, a condition widely asserted to cause decreased interest and arousal. While there is good reason for thinking these assertions have some validity, there is actually little research on the subject and little understanding of what persons with different types of depression can and cannot do sexually.

Many cases of decreased arousal or desire due to depression require only the passage of time for resolution. Clients who have recently lost a spouse or suffered some other type of severe setback often may need more time to pass for them to have energy available for sexual responses. While we do not want to appear to be saying that therapy is always appropriate (it often is not) or more effective than the passage of time, we do believe that even with serious depression, there are cases when sexual interest and arousal can be enhanced.

Listless or apathetic depression has been the most difficult for us to work with, for there is not much obvious energy or excitation to use. Our method in such cases has focused on the elicitation or provocation of any type of feeling, whether sadness, anger, bitterness, or whatever. These feelings can then be worked with, and perhaps some can be relabeled as sexual. This approach has been successful in a few cases, but it has failed in an equal number; so far, we have no way of predicting when it will be useful. Agitated depression is easier to deal with, because agitation is just another way of saying excitement or energy, which can often be transferred to sex.

Some increase in sexual interest and arousal can be achieved in some cases of depression by changing the client's notion of what sex requires and what functions it can serve. Some depressed clients think they cannot or should not have sex because their interest is not as great as before or because they have less energy or enthusiasm. It can help them to understand that sex does not require a certain level of interest or enthusiasm, that it does not require erection, intercourse, or orgasm, and that it can serve many needs, for example, closeness, support, and comfort. We do not try to sell sex and are content if clients choose not to engage in it (and for some, this is clearly the best choice). But for those who have some interest, we try to divert attention away from performance and toward the fulfilling of needs and gaining some pleasure. A lot of holding and touching is recommended, which is what many depressed people seem to need more than sex. Sometimes this itself leads to sexual activity, which we "allow" but do not push. For those who want to get more into sex but need permission and specific instruction, we recommend genital stimulation that is not intended to produce erection or orgasm, at the same time doing whatever possible to increase arousal. We sometimes also suggest insertion of the flaccid penis into the vagina, again not to produce orgasm or erection, but for the closeness, warmth, or other meaning the client may give such activity. Sometimes a client's interest or arousal is increased by such measures and sometimes not. But the results are usually good in either case.

We believe the ideas and approaches in this chapter offer a start in two areas that have so far proved refractory to most of the traditional methods of sex therapy. But we are aware that they are only a beginning, and like most beginnings, the conceptualizations and methods are primitive and in need of refinement.

References

Apfelbaum, B. *A critique and reformulation of some basic assumptions in sex therapy: The relation between sexual arousal and sexual performance.* Paper presented at Congrès International de Sexologie, Montreal, Canada, October 30, 1976.

Benchley, P. *The deep.* New York: Bantam, 1977.

Ellison, C. Coital orgasms for women. Article in preparation.

Gagnon, W., & Simon, J. H. *Sexual conduct.* Chicago: Aldine, 1973.

Goldberg, M. Absence of sexual desire in men. *Medical Aspects of Human Sexuality,* 1973, *7,* 13–32.

Haley, J. *Advanced techniques of hypnosis and therapy.* New York: Grune & Stratton, 1967.

Haley, J. *Uncommon therapy. The psychiatric techniques of Milton H. Erickson, M.D.* New York: W. W. Norton & Co., 1973.

Heiman, J. R. A psychophysiological exploration of sexual arousal patterns in females and males. *Psychophysiology,* 1977, *14,* 266–274.

Kaplan, H. S. *The new sex therapy.* New York: Brunner/Mazel, 1974.

Kaplan, H. S. Hypoactive sexual desire. *Journal of Sex and Marital Therapy,* 1977, *3,* 3–9.

Kegel, A. Sexual functions of the pubococcygeus muscle. *Western Journal of Surgery,* 1952, *60,* 521–524.

Kinsey, A. C., Pomeroy, W. B., Martin, C. E., & Gebhard, P. H. *Sexual behavior in the human female.* Philadelphia: W. B. Saunders, 1953.

Masters, W. H., & Johnson, V. E. *Human sexual response.* Boston: Little, Brown & Co., 1966.

Masters, W. H., & Johnson, V. E. *Human sexual inadequacy.* Boston: Little, Brown & Co., 1970.

Masters, W. H., & Johnson, V. E. *Human sexuality and sexual dysfunction.* Talk presented at Conference on Human Loving, Palo Alto, Calif., September 29, 1978.

Robinson, P. *The modernization of sex.* New York: Harper & Row, 1976.

Rook, K. S., & Hammen, C. L. A cognitive perspective on the experience of sexual arousal. *Journal of Social Issues,* 1977, *33,* 7–29.

Schacter, S., & Singer, J. E. Cognitive, social, and physiological determinants of emotional state. *Psychological Review,* 1962, *69,* 379–399.

Singer, I. *The goals of human sexuality.* New York: W. W. Norton & Co., 1973.

Watzlawick, P. *The language of change.* New York: Basic Books, 1978.

Watzlawick, P., Weakland, J, & Fisch, R. *Change.* New York: W. W. Norton & Co., 1974.

Whalen, R. E. Sexual motivation. *Psychological Review,* 1966, *73,* 151–163.

Wincze, J. P., Hoon, P., & Hoon, E. F. Sexual arousal in women: A comparison of cognitive and physiological responses by continuous measurement. *Archives of Sexual Behavior,* 1977, *6,* 121–133.

Zilbergeld, B. *Male sexuality.* New York: Bantam, 1978.

Zuckerman, M. Physiological measures of sexual arousal in the human. *Psychological Bulletin,* 1971, *75,* 297–329.

Treatment of Female Sexual Disorders

II

Introduction: Treatment of Female Sexual Disorders

The sad but true state of affairs regarding women and sex is that many women have difficulty enjoying their sexuality. The societal and parental injunctions contributing to female guilt and anxiety about sex are, by now, well documented. The early childhood training many girls receive urging modesty and restraint, passivity and withdrawal are common knowledge. Many adolescent girls are still being told to keep their legs crossed, to avoid touching themselves "down there," to recognize that men are out "for one thing," and that "sex is dirty; save it for the one you love"! The double standards and conflicting messages women have received while growing up are fertile ground for inhibition and suppression of sexual curiosity and exploration. It should come as no surprise then that, despite popular appeals urging women to enjoy, many women have difficulty translating the message into practice.

The feminist movement, the increasing availability of contraception and abortion, the growing equality between men and women, the explicit rewriting of marital vows, and the liberalization of society's views regarding a woman's right to do almost anything she chooses have undeniably helped many women to enjoy their sexuality more. Nevertheless, dilemmas exist for the modern woman:

1. Can she enjoy sex without love and romance? Does she want to?
2. Given increased permission and even injunction to be active in bed and out, how active should she be?
3. Given her right to experience orgasm, how insistent should she be in terms of number and manner received? Is it equally acceptable not to have orgasms? Not to desire them?

There continues to be a lack of clarity in the diagnosis of female sexual disorders. While women are being spared the designation of being too hot or too cold, the variety of orgasmic disorders attrib-

uted to women is ever increasing: primary, secondary, situational, premature, or delayed. Many of the current diagnostic designations generally fail to pay sufficient attention to the quality of pleasure derived from sexuality and focus instead on the ability to progress smoothly through the sexual response cycle.

While treatment of female sexual disorders does not require years on the proverbial couch investigating early trauma and subsequent conflict, the armamentarium of techniques available within the new sex therapies is really quite limited. Systematic desensitization or relaxation training for the reduction of anxiety, masturbation or vibrator training for primary orgasmic dysfunction, sensate focus and massage for the gradual introduction to pleasurable arousal and genital sensation, dilation for vaginismus, and erotic fantasy training and imagery to promote excitement and curb distraction comprise the collection of specific techniques for overcoming female sexual disorders.

In the absence of a greater variety of techniques, and in recognition of the complexities of some of the problems, great skill is demanded of the sex therapist in performing a comprehensive and intelligent assessment of just which factor(s) contribute to and maintain problems and which therapeutic strategies will foster change. Above all, the sex therapist treating female sexual disorders must be a skilled psychotherapist, since many of women's sexual difficulties lay not simply in ignorance of what to do or how to do it, but involve guilt, anxiety, fear and distrust.

By and large, the new sex therapies have been quite successful in reversing primary orgasmic dysfunction, vaginismus, and general arousal deficits. More work is needed in finding effective ways of overcoming situations in which the woman is capable of "performing" without difficulty but derives little or no pleasure from participating in sex. A special challenge exists in fostering the sexuality of the older woman who often finds herself bereft of both a functioning partner and societal sanction for continuing to enjoy her sexuality!

The chapters in this section illustrate some of the problems encountered and some of the methods employed in the treatment of female sexual dysfunctions.

4

Group Treatment of Anorgasmic Women

LONNIE BARBACH

For the Victorian woman, anorgasmia was not a problem since she was not expected to enjoy sex, much less experience orgasm. Today, not only are women expected to have orgasms, they are expected to have multiple orgasms, through a variety of means, in a reasonable period of time, and to enjoy them with pleasure and pride. With all of this emphasis on orgasmic attainment, it is not surprising that orgasmic dysfunction constitutes the largest category of female sexual dysfunction today.

Investigation of the determinants of orgasmic difficulty reveals a host of possible etiological factors, from inhibitions stemming from parental and religious upbringing to lack of mate compatability. Confounding the problem of etiology is the numbers of women who share similarly constrictive upbringings or nonoptimal sexual circumstances who nevertheless experience orgasm without notable difficulty. Despite their theoretical differences, sex therapists agree that orgasmic problems are overwhelmingly psychological rather than physical in origin and that the causative factors are multiple and far from clear.

The diagnosis of orgasmic dysfunction is similarly plagued with confusion. While Masters and Johnson distinguish between primary, situational, and random orgasmic inadequacy, other investigators identify inhibited orgasm and impaired orgasm, which includes premature and incomplete orgasm. Still others speak of orgasmic anesthesia and delayed orgasm, as well as of ability (or lack of it) to enjoy multiple orgasms. A considerable controversy exists concerning whether inability to experience orgasm during intercourse constitutes a sexual dysfunction. There is even debate as to the definition of what constitutes an orgasm and how to identify reliably whether or not a woman is experiencing one.

Despite the confusion in diagnosis and etiology, short-term directive sex therapy has proven quite effective in assisting nonorgasmic women to experience orgasm. Both Masters and Johnson approaches and masturbation training programs have proven successful in overcoming orgasmic difficulties. In addition to these core interventions, a number of variations have been described and used effectively.

For example, group approaches have been employed in the treatment of the preorgasmic and situationally orgasmic woman. An innovator in the use of such women's groups has been Lonnie Barbach, who convincingly demonstrated their efficacy in a careful research program.

In her chapter, Barbach describes one such women's group. The group brings together a number of women from diverse backgrounds and various orgasmic difficulties who nonetheless help themselves and each other through the 15-hour treatment program. Barbach illustrates not only how both motivation and commitment to change are enhanced in the group format, but also how personal growth in areas other than orgasmic attainment is achieved. She employs a variety of interventions to facilitate progress, including the clever use of paradoxical messages to handle control struggles between the group leader and individual women. She also displays the considerable psychotherapeutic sophistication that is necessary of a group leader in this situation—the ability to be not only a good educator, but also a sensitive, skilled clinician. One provocative issue raised in her chapter is the question of who should be the final arbiter of whether ogasmic attainment is achieved—the woman herself, objective physical measurement, or the therapist.

Lonnie Barbach is on the clinical faculty of the Department of Psychiatry, University of California, San Francisco. She is the author of For Yourself: The Fulfillment of Female Sexuality *and* Women Discover Orgasm: A Therapist's Guide to a New Treatment Approach.

Through the years, there have been many competing theories as to the causes of anorgasmia in women. The causes cited range from simple lack of information and faulty socialization to pervasive psychological disturbance. The current understanding seems to be that for most cases, there is no one single cause for orgasmic dysfunction, but rather that a number of interacting factors account for a woman's inability to experience orgasm.

Causes of Anorgasmia

Lack of Information and Misinformation

A popular viewpoint, and one that appears to explain those cases of orgasmic dysfunction which are readily reversed with minimal intervention, is that anorgasmia results from lack of information or from misinformation. The early psychoanalysts, for example, Caprio (1953), Fenichel (1945), and Lorand (1966), and, more recently, Helen Kaplan (1974) refer to sexual ignorance, prudishness, misinformation about normal sex, and inadequate understanding of appropriate stimulation techniques as creating orgasmic dysfunction. The behaviorists, Lazarus

(1963) and Wolpe (1969), among others, blame sexual problems on faulty attitudes, and Masters and Johnson (1966) add that the absence of sexual learning or negative attitudes on the part of one's parents greatly contribute to anorgasmia.

Both men and women can suffer from an informational void or, worse yet, believe erroneous theories and totally inaccurate information. When their own sexual behavior and responses do not fit their false images of normal sexual functioning, anxiety or sexual dissatisfaction frequently result. In addition, being reared in a strictly sexually negative religious environment has been found to affect sexual responsivity adversely (Kinsey, Pomeroy, Martin, & Gebhard, 1953; Masters & Johnson, 1970). Religious teachings frequently lead women to feel that they are bad or abnormal if they experience strong sexual urges. Feelings of shame, and sometimes disgust, toward the genitals and sexual functioning often result from exposure to religious orthodoxy.

The Elusive Vaginal Orgasm
Freud's distinction between a vaginal and a clitoral orgasm, plus women's lack of accurate anatomical and physiological information, have resulted in women feeling abnormal if they do not experience orgasm as the result of the penis thrusting in and out of the vagina. Although Shere Hite (1976) found that 70% of her sample of women required direct clitoral stimulation in order for orgasm to occur, most of them continued to feel abnormal if the vaginal orgasm was not within their grasp.

The repercussions of this viewpoint cannot be overemphasized. Sherfey (1972) states: "Not just the couples with sexual problems and most of the educated public, but almost all psychiatrists and physicians (excepting gynecologists and endocrinologists) are still committed to the belief in the existence of the vaginal orgasm as distinct from the infantile clitoral orgasm and consider the vaginal orgasm to be a vital sign of normal feminine development.... Could many of the sexual neuroses which seem to be almost endemic to women today be, in part, induced by doctors attempting to treat them?" (pp. 27–28).

Belief in a Standard Sexual Response
Each woman's sexual responsivity is as individual as are all other aspects of her functioning. Masters and Johnson (1966) state: "It always should be borne in mind that there is wide individual variation in the duration and intensity of every specific physiologic response to sexual stimulation" (p. 7). For example, some women become sexually aroused very quickly, while others respond more slowly. Some women

require intense and direct clitoral stimulation to reach orgasm, while others react to subtle pressure and indirect clitoral stimulation.

Yet much of the public remains unconvinved by the documentation produced by research (e.g., Hite, 1976) and persistently adheres to some notion of sexual normality. Consequently, if a woman believes that there is only one right way to function sexually, she will try to fit herself into a mold she assumes is "normal" and thus will not attempt to develop lovemaking techniques that will meet her unique needs and enhance her sexual pleasure.

Orgasm Is Learned

The need to learn to be sexual, to learn appropriate techniques for deriving sexual satisfaction, is a relatively revolutionary concept, especially for those women who grew up believing that sex should be a totally spontaneous and natural activity. However, Kinsey's data laid the foundation for the important assumption that orgasm could be considered a learned response for some women and that failure to achieve it was therefore not necessarily a sign of neuroses, but rather due to faulty learning. Further, a learned response reflects certain cultural definitions. Thus, Margaret Mead (1949) points out: "Therefore there seems to be a reasonable basis for assuming that the human female's capacity for orgasm is to be viewed much more as a potentiality that may or may not be developed by a given culture" (p. 217).

Female Role-Scripting

In our society, both men and women are taught that men are the authorities on sex. With no instruction, each man is somehow expected to understand each woman's unique sexuality. This, of course, is presumed to occur without any input from the woman herself, who, if she is decent and respectable, is expected to be innocent and to have no sexual knowledge. The man cannot ask her for information, since he is supposed to know, and not knowing would make him appear less masculine. The woman, on the other hand, cannot tell him, because she is not supposed to know or fears that if she directed him in any way she might hurt his ego.

As a result of the mystical vision of sex that arises out of this mutual lack of information, many women do not learn about themselves sexually and do not accept responsibility for their sexuality, but rather expect their man to awaken them. The research of Nelson (1974) showed that high-orgasmic women were found to be discriminating about their sexual activity and able to tell their partners what they liked and did not like; they were active in initiating sex, concentrated primarily on themselves during lovemaking, and tended to direct lovemaking overtly in order to get what they wanted. Low-orgasmic women, on the other hand, had typically "feminine" attitudes. They did not talk about sex at all, were basically passive and rarely initiated sex, focused selflessly on their lover during lovemaking in an attempt to please him, and amiably went along with whatever happened during lovemaking.

Nelson's research gives further credence to the theory that the way women are trained to behave may in itself contribute to the lack of orgasmic responsivity. The sex-role training of American girls establishes passivity and dependence as desirable female attributes. This training teaches women to approach life from a powerless position. They feel no sense of positive power to attain things for themselves, only to attract a man who will take care of them.

A woman trained to be passive and not to assert herself may give up control over her life to others—a spouse, for example, or the fates. When she does attempt control, it is often in the form of resistance or negative control. Such a woman may deprive herself of the experience of orgasm as a way of punishing her partner for her dissatisfaction with their relationship by making him feel inadequate sexually. This is understandable in light of the fact that in this society, sex is still widely viewed as an activity engaged in for the man's pleasure. Since women use sex as a way to catch a man, they can withhold sex when they are angry. By the same token, a woman may find herself wanting to have orgasms so as to please her partner or make peace in her marriage, rather than as a way of giving herself the pleasure she deserves. Not surprisingly, these kinds of relationship problems generally result in sexual problems.

Fear of Loss of Control
The lack of control that women feel over their lives can be pervasive. Kaplan notes that the fear of losing control over feelings and behavior is very common among women who are preorgasmic and that the resulting defense mechanisms of holding back and overcontrolling are central to the pathogenesis of this disorder. At the intrapsychic level, a feeling of control is intimately related to the individual's sense of ego boundaries, that is, the degree to which she experiences herself as separate and differentiated from others. Having well-defined ego boundaries affords a person a certain sense of control; she feels the power and security of being whole and autonomous. This sense of differentiation affects her experience of orgasm, since most women at the point of orgasm experience a sense of loss of control. For a woman

with no initial sense of control, relinquishing conscious control in experiencing the orgasmic state can be very anxiety-producing. Women with tenuous ego boundaries express the fear that they will dissolve or merge with their partner as the intense sexual sensations rise.

The compensatory overcontrol that affects sexual expression frequently also encompasses the expression of all feelings, including anger as well as caring. Such women do not feel capable of expressing any intense feelings to a limited degree. Without a sense of control over themselves, they experience the world and their options as black or white, all or nothing, with no gradations between the extremes. They are unable to set limits and find themselves either immobilized and unable to approach something new or overwhelmed because they jump in too quickly.

This analysis of the importance of control is somewhat simplified, but I hope the basic premise is clear: Girls are trained to be passive and to relinquish control for their lives. The sense of insufficient control leads to other problems: lack of ego differentiation, inability to express feelings, lack of orgasm. Consequently, if girls are trained to be more assertive and independent and less passive and dependent, one would expect that the incidence of anorgasmia would be greatly reduced in situations in which these dynamics come into play. This premise is substantiated by the findings of anthropologists Ford and Beach (1951):

> The societies that severely restrict adolescent and preadolescent sex play, those that enjoin girls to be modest, retiring, and submissive, appear to produce adult women that are incapable or at least unwilling to be sexually aggressive. The feminine products of such cultural training are likely to remain relatively inactive even during marital intercourse. And, quite often, they do not experience clearcut orgasm. In contrast, the societies which permit or encourage early sex play usually allow females a greater degree of freedom in seeking sexual contacts. Under such circumstances, the sexual performance of the mature woman seems to be characterized by a certain degree of aggression, to include definite and vigorous activity, and to result regularly in complete and satisfactory orgasm. (p. 266)

Other Factors

Certain fears other than loss of control often accompany lack of orgasm. These fears may be based on lack of accurate information, various sexual misconceptions, or other life issues that have somehow become connected to the inability to experience orgasm. The psychoanalysts and the behaviorists refer to fears of pregnancy, childbirth, and venereal disease, among others, as affecting the woman's anxiety level and hence responsiveness during sex.

The psychoanalysts used to believe that a number of other situations resulted in anorgasmia, such as penis envy, the Electra complex, or the prostitution complex. Most of these theories have been either dismissed or reinterpreted. While most of these situations do not generally appear to be linked with orgasmic dysfunction, the notion that deep-seated psychological problems cause orgasmic dysfunction is still held by many psychoanalysts. Although in some rare cases this may be true, cases that do not respond to a brief, more behavioral model and require intensive psychotherapy have been few and far between. Depth interviews by Fisher (1973) seem to indicate that, for the most part, lack of orgasm and psychological disturbance are not correlated: "There are so many things with which orgasm consistently is *not* linked. Particularly noteworthy is the fact that it does not seem related to maladjustment or psychological disturbance. . . . There does not appear to be a relationship between the 'mental health' of a woman and her ability to attain orgasm" (p. 275).

It appears that although the general status of a woman's mental health may not be called into question by her lack of experience of orgasm, many psychological concerns may be linked to the issue of orgasm. Deeper fears frequently become apparent once women directly engage in the behavior of sexually arousing themselves. At this point, women discuss feeling overly vulnerable to their partners. The fear of losing them becomes exaggerated as they imagine the intensity of the intimacy which would occur at the point of orgasm. Or they fear that they will not find their partners attractive once they become orgasmic and hence will have to face the possibility of divorce. Many women fear that by becoming orgasmic, they would have to become more mature or that their lives would in some ways be different. These and other fears tend to go hand in hand with the dynamic of lack of control.

Treatment Approaches for Anorgasmia

Psychoanalytically Oriented Psychotherapy

In the past, if a woman sought help for anorgasmia, she was generally referred to a therapist who was psychoanalytically oriented. The therapist would treat the anorgasmia as a symptom of underlying problems or conflicts and would propose years of psychoanalysis as a solution. Treatment often resulted in the woman being happier with some aspects of her life, but it did not affect her ability to experience orgasm. In a study of 61 partially and totally frigid women treated four times a week for a minimum of 2 years, O'Connor (1972) found that 25% of the cases were cured and an additional 35% showed some improvement.

Behavioral Therapy

The behavioral approach to treatment, with its foundation in learning theory, is based on the notion that orgasm is a learned response and that failure to achieve it could therefore be the result of inadequate learning. It argues that because of learned habits, some women feel intense anxiety as a result of participation in sex. The basic curative mechanism consists of helping the woman to unlearn the primary stimulus configuration and to relearn a more appropriate configuration through the use of systematic desensitization and vicarious learning.

Behavioral therapists Brady (1966), Lazarus (1963), Madsen and Ullmann (1967), and Wolpe (1969) report from 86 to 100% success in the treatment of female orgasmic dysfunction, quite impressive results compared to those of psychoanalysis. However, behavior therapy, while effective in cases in which the manipulation of the behavior alone is sufficient, sometimes ignores important intrapsychic areas.

Conjoint Sex Therapy

Although Masters and Johnson do not call themselves behavioral therapists, their treatment incorporates fundamental behavioral principles. The homework they prescribe is a basic desensitization program to extinguish performance anxiety, and their male/female team of therapists provides vicarious learning by modeling behavior for the clients—a couple—to imitate.

Masters and Johnson (1970, p. 314) report that of a sample of 193 primary nonorgasmic women[1] treated in a 2-week program, 17.6% could be considered to be failures at the 5-year follow-up. Couples with serious marital or psychological difficulties in addition to the sexual problem were not accepted for treatment. Although treating the couple conjointly provides important information regarding the partner relationship, information not easily acquired by seeing only one member, it also is very costly in terms of therapist time and monetary expense to the clients. Also, since the therapy format requires treating the couple, it precludes the treatment of women without partners or of women whose partners are unwilling to participate in treatment.

Masturbation Desensitization

Lobitz and LoPiccolo (1972) developed the following nine-step masturbation desensitization program for women who had never experienced orgasm by any means. The steps proceed after success with the previous step has been achieved.

Step 1: Nude bath examination; genital examination; Kegel exercises (Kegel, 1952).

Step 2: Tactual as well as visual genital exploration with no expectation of arousal.

Step 3: Tactual and visual genital exploration with the goal of locating areas that produce pleasurable feelings when stimulated.

Step 4: Manual masturbation of the areas identified as pleasurable.

Step 5: Increased duration and intensity of masturbation if no orgasm occurred in Step 4.

Step 6: Masturbation with a vibrator if no orgasm occurred as the result of Step 5.

Step 7: After orgasm has occurred through masturbation, the husband observes the wife masturbating.

Step 8: The husband stimulates the wife in the manner she demonstrated in Step 7.

Step 9: Once orgasm occurs in Step 8, the husband stimulates his wife's genitals manually or with a vibator during intercourse.

Lobitz and LoPiccolo developed a coordinated program of working with a woman individually on masturbation while working with the couple conjointly on related sexual and communication issues. They reported 100% success in a sample of only three women, the slowest of whom required 3 months to achieve orgasm through masturbation. This program appeared to have considerable potential; however, they did not make it available to unattached females, and it was as costly as more traditional sex therapy.

The Preorgasmic Group Process

A new approach to the treatment of the anorgasmic woman seemed to be needed—one that could be available to women regardless of their relationship status; one that was brief, relatively inexpensive, and economical in terms of therapist time so that a large number of women could easily benefit; yet one that could be individualized to meet the unique needs of each woman.

The program involves groups of six or seven women who meet together for 10 sessions of 1½ or 2 hours each. The sessions are generally scheduled once or twice weekly. Each woman is required to do an hour a day of assigned sexual and nonsexual tasks at home and to report back to the group at the next meeting on how her "homework" and other relevant concerns are progressing. The initial assignments follow the Lobitz and LoPiccolo nine-step masturbation program. As the women progress, the assignments are tailored to meet each woman's distinctive needs. The therapist works with each woman on an individual basis to design, with her help, assignments that fit her particular problem, personality, and sexual value system.

The theory behind the women's group treatment model, then, combines the premises of various other treatment modalities. It is partially behaviorally oriented, with a graduated desensitization program. It incorporates the tenets of other body-oriented therapies by providing a way for women to explore and learn to be more comfortable with their bodies. This exploration often leads to the uncovering of fears, conflicts, and relationship problems which are examined through individual inquiry within the context of the group. Negative cultural attitudes and role-scripting regarding women's feelings about their sexuality are combatted by giving the explicit message that each woman is unique and therefore is the authority on her own sexuality. The women are told that they are deserving of pleasure—including sexual pleasure—but that it is their responsibility to obtain that pleasure if and when they desire it.

Working with women in a group situation while drawing on the nine-step masturbation program seemed to resolve the major limitations of previous approaches: the requirement of partner participation and the costliness of individual or couple therapy. In addition, the supportive aspects of a women's group actually facilitate the process, thus making women's groups not only easier to conduct than individual therapy, but often more successful in terms of outcome. The nature of the group process makes it almost immediately validating: It eliminates feelings of isolation and abnormality as each woman works with and learns from others like herself.

The original treatment program was designed in California in 1972 by Nancy Carlsen and myself. Since that time, hundreds of groups have been run, and over 90% of the women who had never experienced an orgasm prior to therapy learned to have orgasms with masturbation, with approximately 85% becoming orgasmic with their partners (Barbach, 1974; Heinrich, 1976). Women entering the program being situationally orgasmic had a lower success rate, with approximately 65% becoming orgasmic during sex with their partners, assuming partners were available (Barbach & Flaherty, in press). Success for preorgasmic women was the experience of orgasm through vibrator or manual masturbation. Success in becoming orgasmic with a partner was the experience of orgasm with a partner over 50% of the time that the woman desired the experience of orgasm. Orgasms through manual manipulation, oral sex, intercourse, or intercourse plus additional clitoral stimulation were all considered successful. In other words, orgasm through coitus alone was not the criterion for success, since recent studies show that approximately 70% of the female population require direct clitoral stimulation to orgasm (Hite, 1976).

The following is a case study of one preorgasmic women's group which I conducted in 1978. The group was composed of 7 women who met together for 11 1½-hour sessions. The first 6 sessions were held twice a week for 3 weeks, and the last 4 sessions were held once weekly. A follow-up session was conducted 3 months after the 10th session. This particular group was chosen not only because of its recency, but also because it turned out to be a highly representative group in terms of dysfunction as well as heterogeneity of life-style, age, and background of the women involved. Table 1 presents a brief description of the 7 group members.

Jenny was a 37-year-old single Jewish social worker. Although easily and reliably orgasmic masturbating with manual and vibrator stimulation, she had experienced an orgasm with a partner only once or twice in her life after having smoked marijuana. Before entering the women's group program, she had been in Freudian analysis for 3½ years and continued to participate in this therapy during the course of the group. When asked, in the pregroup screening, how she would sabotage reaching her goals, she replied that she would try to take over as a cotherapist and also feared that her use of humor as a shield for her anxiety would interfere with her progress.

Pamela was 28 years old. She had never experienced an orgasm by any means, although she participated in dance therapy, primal therapy, bioenergetics, and hypnosis prior to entering the group, in addition to a sexuality group led by two therapists in New York for the explicit purpose of enhancing sexuality. At the pregroup interview, Pamela was almost totally hopeless about the outcome of therapy. She said that she would sabotage treatment by believing that it would not happen to her and that she felt she would not be able to put herself in a sexual mood while participating in the homework. When asked why she felt orgasm

TABLE 1
Description of Women

Name	Presenting problem	Age	Marital status	Religious preference	Education	Previous current therapy	Sexual orientation
Jenny	Not orgasmic with partners	37	Single	Jewish	MSW	Yes	Heterosexual
Pamela	Never experienced orgasm	28	Single	Catholic	MA	Yes	Heterosexual
B. J.	Not orgasmic with partners	26	Single	Protestant	Mid-MA	No	Heterosexual
Josephine	Experienced orgasm only once	26	Single	Protestant	High school	No	Lesbian
Maria	Orgasmic only through partner manual and oral stimulation	27	Married	Mexican-American Catholic	Mid-BA	No	Heterosexual
Beverly	Never experienced orgasm	62	Widowed	Protestant	BA	Yes	Heterosexual
Abby	Never experienced orgasm	37	Divorced	Catholic	MA	Yes	Heterosexual

had never occurred, she answered that it was because her head was controlling her, and she was afraid of what might happen if she did have an orgasm, specifically, that she might die.

At this pregroup interview, I assessed Pamela as a typical preorgasmic woman with fears of loss of control. But only later, when I became cognizant that she could use the vibrator directly on her clitoris for hours without experiencing any arousal and stopped only when the sensations became painful, did I begin delving into the complexity of her situation.

B. J. was a 26-year-old single student in a master's program in psychology. Just prior to entering the group, she had become pregnant and required an abortion. This situation had distressed her greatly, and she felt she could no longer trust men. In addition, she had been in a serious automobile accident a few years previously which had resulted in considerable brain damage, making it difficult for her to verbalize some of her thoughts.

Upon entering the group, she had never been orgasmic with a partner, and although she was orgasmic with masturbation, she felt that these orgasms were not sufficiently intense. She felt that she would sabotage the therapy by not completing the homework assignments, a typical response from women entering the group.

Josephine was a 26-year-old self-defined lesbian working as a waitress and living alone in San Francisco. She had no sexual partner at the beginning of therapy and was very shy and soft-spoken.

She had experienced an orgasm once in her life and could not account for any reason why she should not be orgasmic. Two years previously, she had participated in a preorgasmic group but was not successful. For the most part, she had used the Hitachi vibrator to masturbate with, and although she had experienced arousal quite rapidly, had not experienced an orgasm. Like B. J., she felt she would sabotage the therapy by not completing the homework.

Maria was a 27-year-old married Mexican-American woman with two children. At the beginning of the group, Maria was orgasmic infrequently with manual and oral stimulation provided by her partner and was unable to masturbate. In addition to feeling that masturbation and her genitals were disgusting, she had intense fears of loss of control which manifested themselves in fears of exploding with orgasm and concerns of nymphomania.

Maria was a typical example of what I call resistant women. These are women who, due to their lack of sense of control, experience no positive power in the sense of being able to control any of the people or events around them and therefore define their power in withholding.

When asked how she would sabotage her own progress, she answered that she would play to lose and would ultimately give up in the end, the typical experience of someone who has no sense of positive power and of winning.

Beverly was a 62-year-old widow of 4 years who had never experienced an orgasm with her husband of 40 years. She was a perfect example of a woman who was reared with repressive attitudes toward sex and, being sexually ignorant, had little idea of how to achieve her sexual goals. Self-assertion turned out to be a major problem for Beverly, who had considerable difficulty putting herself and her needs first. Consequently, she had difficulty setting aside time to complete her homework, although she lived in a large house by herself. She said that she would sabotage by being so afraid that orgasm would not happen that she would end the group as a failure who did not wholeheartedly try.

Abby was a 37-year-old divorced teacher who had been living with her boyfriend for 1 year before the group began. As the result of 10 sessions of individual sex therapy with a trained sex therapist, she had begun masturbating but had never experienced orgasm. She felt that she would sabotage the therapy by finding things to do other than her homework and, consequently, not putting in the effort required to attain the results.

Through the following session-by-session description of the group, it is interesting to note that, for the most part, the women were aware of their own methods of resistance prior to beginning treatment, which considerably aided me in my approach to working with each of them. (See Table 2 for a summary of what occurred during the 11 sessions.)

Session 1

The first session proceeded as any typical group. The women were initially anxious and, with the exception of Josephine, expressed their anxiety by talking. Typical issues were aired, such as regretting the lack of opportunity to talk to other women openly about sex; anger at their parents and the society for not providing them with information about sexuality, while instilling negative and restrictive attitudes; and anger at men who "got theirs" while they remained frustrated. In addition, since two of the women in the group had been greatly disturbed by recent abortions, this topic was discussed at some length as well. The following are some excerpts taken out of the general discussion to present a flavor of the content covered.

> PAMELA: I feel uncomfortable.... Why am I here? Why do I have to be here? I feel like ... I really don't want to talk about it ...

MARIA: I feel nervous.... I am a pretty nervous person any-way.... I don't know if I can say if it is because of this.

THERAPIST: There is one thing I am realizing.... I know the particulars of all of you, but you don't know each other.... So, maybe we can share our feelings about what it is like not to have orgasms.

PAMELA: Well, I feel a tremendous frustration and also feel like half a person.... I keep going from one place to another thinking someone will be able to help me solve my problem, but it hasn't happened.... Not with the vibrator, not through pot. I always look to the next therapist, or whatever, as being the goal to aim for.... There are a lot of frustrations and anger and turning inward and hating myself for not being able to be a whole person. I don't want to be with men anymore because there is this feeling that I can't have an orgasm, and I am tired of lying about all the time. I would just like to be able to experience whatever I want to feel, even for myself without a man there, just for me...

ABBY: When I was 18, 19, and 20 I think I should have gotten an Academy Award for my last performance ... it was great ...

JENNY: In my 20s, I never lied. I never said I did when I didn't but I rarely initiated it. Most of them were a bunch of dumb clods too, and didn't know the difference.

MARIA: To get married and find the right man and live happily ever after ... the magic penis ... and if you have kids, you have to have orgasm; there is no way out of it.... It's supposed to be the only way to conceive. The only thing that I have trouble with is that I can't masturbate and I get mad at him if he doesn't give me an orgasm.... I am waiting for the "Doc" to come along and give me my orgasm for today, or whatever. It is like I freeze up. I just start getting real stiff.... I like romanticism and if he does everything the way I expect it to be, then I have an orgasm, which is very rare, because usually he does something wrong.... It just blows the whole thing for me.

ABBY: It is like you are cutting yourself off.

JENNY: I think I don't have orgasms because of my upbringing.

B. J.: Is that just an excuse?

ABBY: I didn't know, until I was 18 or 19, that I never even had an orgasm. I never saw my parents touch one another.... But I feel that I had no understanding of the process and that all the books that I would read were on how to please a man. I read them and it was like I should have had an Academy Award nomination. I knew how to do everything, but I didn't know how to ask for anything. It was when I started reading books about my own anatomy and how it may be that just entry into my vagina wasn't enough. I didn't know that something more was needed and I will be hanged, that if at that point I would have asked.... It has only been recently that I have been willing to say, "Hey, I need you to do this." I am really

TABLE 2
Summary of Treatment by Session

Session	Major topics	Assignments
1	Lack of sex education; anger at male sexual partners; feelings of sexual inadequacy; abortion.	Full-length body viewing; tactual body exploration; Kegel exercises.
2	Homework discussion: negative feelings toward body. Maria, Pamela, Josephine, and Abby: fears of loss of control with orgasm. Anatomy of genitals; physiology of orgasm.	Everyone: visual exploration of genitals; drawing of genitals; tactual exploration of genitals; 1 hour of luxuriating.
3	Homework discussion: feelings of disgust engendered by genital assignment; feelings of self-worth engendered by luxuriating assignment. B. J. and Jenny: breakthrough in self-worth and self-assertion. Movie of woman masturbating to orgasm.	Everyone: "yes" and "no" assignment; masturbation, but *not* to orgasm for all except Jenny, who is allowed to have an orgasm.
4	Homework discussion: Maria's resistance to homework and fears of orgasm. Jenny continues assertiveness progress. Discussion of mental erotica.	Everyone: masturbation with addition of concomitant mental stimulation. Maria: role-play an epileptic orgasm. Beverly is out ill.
5	Homework discussion: fifth-session slump—everyone feels discouraged. Pamela: group massage, highly emotional. Jacobson's relaxation exercise is taught.	Everyone: continue masturbation; practice relaxation exercises. Jenny: notice men. Josephine: continue to focus using pornography. Beverly is out ill.
6	Homework discussion: B. J. has first intense orgasm. Maria completes homework and has orgasms. Abby and Beverly: ambivalence. Jenny has met three men.	Everyone: intensify masturbation. Abby and Beverly: fantasize their lives in 1, 5, and 25 years still never having experienced an orgasm. B. J., Abby, Beverly, and Jenny: assertiveness exercises.

TABLE 2 (*continued*)

Session	Major topics	Assignments
7	Homework discussion: Abby has first orgasm. Beverly is depressed—homework backfired. Jenny is taking social risks. Josephine is disconnecting personality change from experience of orgasm.	Everyone: masturbation. B. J. and Jenny: masturbation with fantasy of asserting self sexually with a partner. Maria: inhibit orgasm with partner. Josephine and Beverly: intensify masturbation. Beverly: assertiveness exercises. Pamela: observe patterns of relating to mother.
8	Homework discussion: Maria is assertive with partner. Josephine has first mild orgasm.	Same as last session except Abby: masturbate in front of partner; Pamela: just notice what she feels with partner sex—orgasm still forbidden.
9	Homework discussion: concerns about termination. Psychological issues linked to orgasm for Beverly. Abby has orgasm with partner.	Abby: continue partner exercises. Jenny: ask for or initiate new thing sexually with partner sex. B. J.: practice asserting self sexually with casual partners. Beverly: buy and use a vibrator. Maria is ill. Pamela is on vacation in Mexico.
10	Homework discussion: Abby, B. J., and Josephine stop having orgasms. Beverly has first orgasm. Jenny: relationship problems. Pamela feels sexual feelings with partner.	Maria does not show up and does not cancel. Work on assignments on daily basis.
Follow-up	Pamela is orgasmic. Maria discusses anger and withholding of orgasm. Jenny continues to be more open. Abby and B. J. are orgasmic with partners. Beverly backslides, using orgasm to compensate for other emotional problems.	Josephine cancels—relatives in town. Continue daily individualized assignments.

clumsy at asking. Something you said about feeling disappointed about putting the burden on him, rather than on me,
like you do it to me while I lie back here, because I did it all
these years and to all these other people, so now it is your
turn. I know that's not fair.

PAMELA: I have had trouble asking men to do things for me that
would give me pleasure because I didn't know what was
pleasurable. I used to be very active sexually and really get
into the act, but never into anything where I would be feeling
it. We would get into all kinds of positions. Nothing ever did
it. I am questioning whether it is a problem that is psychological. I don't know. I have the feeling that it could be something
physical. I know I have seen my "clit" and I know I have one.
They talk about the blood rushing to it and feeling something.
I never feel an onrush or a buildup of any kind. . . . I keep
thinking that if it is a physical thing it could be taken care of
with an operation or something.

Before the end of this first session, a sense of group cohesiveness
had formed. The homework assigned was the same for all the women.
They were asked to set aside an hour a day of quiet, private, and
sensual time to explore their bodies. On the first night, they were to
visually explore their bodies by looking at themselves carefully from
different angles and in different positions in front of a full-length mirror. On the second night, they were assigned to explore their bodies
tactually from two vantage points. First, they were to notice what their
bodies felt like to their hands, as if they were someone else touching
their bodies, and to notice what their skin, muscle, fat, etc., felt like.
Second, they were to massage themselves with different types of touch
to see which kinds of touching were most pleasurable to the different
areas of their bodies. In addition, Kegel exercises were assigned to
strengthen the pubococcygeus muscle. No ban was put on intercourse,
but the women were explicitly warned not to try to have orgasms while
interacting sexually with their partners.

Session 2

None of the women in this group had unusually negative feelings about
her body, and in doing the homework, all were generally pleased with
the process. The following brief transcript is typical of the women's
responses to the body looking and touching assignment.

JOSEPHINE: I think it was the time. . . . I don't think I've looked at
my body for an hour enough . . . and I did start getting a bit
bored. I felt I tried all the positions possible and still 15 more
minutes (*Laughter*) . . . it was kind of different, because before, I would look vainly in the mirror and then go away and

come back and look when I felt like it. Plus, I didn't feel like I was the only one looking at my body. I knew that we would all be looking at our bodies.

BEVERLY: The one part I think I mentioned last week that I didn't like was my stomach.... But when I looked at myself and leaned completely over and looked under my legs, I thought, "My breasts are saggy." How could I have the nerve to say that? There's no muscle there. There really isn't.... Then I looked at myself more; I would just remind myself... that I did life drawing and I used to like to do life drawing if somebody had a big bottom, so you could really get into it. And that's just exactly what I looked like. (*Laughter*) I was... big, and full.

The rest of the second group session was spent discussing their attitudes toward sex and how these attitudes were instilled by their parents. The other important issue addressed in this session concerned Maria and Pamela and, to a lesser extent, Josephine and Abby. These women experienced some of the typical fears of dying, exploding, and having epileptic fits as sexual arousal mounted, all of which symbolize a fear of loss of control over their body boundaries.

MARIA: Just after I was 18 and I wasn't a virgin anymore, I asked this older woman, "How does it feel to have an orgasm?" And she said, "Oh, it's like an explosion. Your whole body explodes." And I think that must've made an impression on me, 'cause I think something's going to happen to me. I'm going to PSHEW!!...

THERAPIST: Explode?

MARIA: Explode. And I'm scared of that.

PAMELA: But you've had orgasms, though, you said.

MARIA: Yeah.

PAMELA: And do you explode?

MARIA: I don't explode.

PAMELA: So then your body knows that you won't explode... 'cause I'm afraid I'll die... if it happens. I'll lose such control and that'll be the end of it. But also, I feel pain with the vibrator only because I'd press it down sometimes real hard to make me come. And it doesn't happen. You know, I get mad at it.

ABBY: I'm scared of shaking and looking like I'm in an epileptic fit. That's what I'm scared of. I'm also scared of not being able to hold my urine at a certain point because that happened to me a couple of times.

In working with these women, I was formulating the first stage in approaching their orgasm, which was to enable them to take small steps and very gradually become accustomed to the sensations of arousal with the safety of knowing that they were not to push themselves to experience orgasm until they felt secure in doing so. Taking a gradual approach allows the women to learn that they have the control in their hands. They can discontinue arousing themselves when they feel frightened or uncomfortable, rather than holding back and fighting the intense sensations. In this way, they slowly become more familiar and comfortable with the intense feelings.

During this second session, the women were taught about the anatomy of their genitals and the physiology of their sexual response. Their homework was twofold. During their special daily hour, they were to visually and tactually explore their genitals. They were assigned to draw a picture of their genitals to aid in desensitizing them to that part of their bodies. The tactual exploration was designed to prepare them for the following session's assignment of masturbation. In addition, the women were assigned an hour of purposeful luxuriating. This could be carried out in any manner they desired. The assignment to luxuriate provides the initial step in enabling the women to take time for themselves. This is important, because if the women do not feel that they have a right to pleasure, the right to be selfish, which forms the foundation for believing they are worth the time and effort spent on receiving pleasure, they will not experience orgasm, particularly when a partner is involved.

Session 3

Most women experienced negative feelings and an underlying sense of disgust in doing the genital looking and touching assignment, as indicated by Abby's response. However, none of the women in this particular group was overly phobic.

> ABBY: I must say something. I had a lot of resistance to doing this and I saved it for today to do, knowing I had to do it. I wasn't going to come to class without a picture ... and then I started drawing, and I drew one picture and then I started looking and I thought, "This isn't right." And then I started doing it again. And then I got absolutely intrigued, and I kept looking and looking, seeing more things to draw. And I forgot about being hung up on doing it.

Abby's response is typical: initial anxiety which diminishes once action is taken to confront the anxiety-producing situation.

The third session formed the turning point for Jenny and B. J. The major problem for both lay in lack of self-worth and consequent inability to assert themselves. The most difficult issue for most women who have difficulty experiencing orgasm is feeling worthy of the time spent on themselves and the pleasure experienced.

Jenny's response to the luxuriating assignment illustrates this difficulty in receiving from others.

> JENNY: It feels too good to allow myself to luxuriate. I'm geared more to do things for other people rather than to do things for me.... My profession.... I'm a social worker.... I have a Yiddish mama, who taught me very early to wait on my husband, who's still waiting out there. (*Laughter*)... Probably, about 8 or 10 years ago, I had a group of people over to my house and I was serving something and I picked up a coffee cup and handed it to the first man that was sitting next to me. He said if I had lived in Japan, I would have made one hell of a geisha girl. I said, "What do you mean?" He said, "This is America, you serve the women first." I was just used to serving men first. My father was always served first, my uncles, and grandfather. I always served the men first.

Jenny set the example for the group as she took time for herself to make and eat a sensual meal in a sensual atmosphere and arrived with legs shaved, hair styled, and dressed carefully and attractively, a noticeable difference in appearance from the first two sessions. To foster the development of self-worth further, the women were assigned to say "no" to three things that they did not want to do anyway but would usually agree to do. In addition, they were instructed to ask for or let themselves have three things they wanted but would generally deny themselves.

The remainder of the session was spent watching and discussing a short film, *Reaching Orgasm* (C.O.R.T., 1975), which shows a woman masturbating to orgasm. The film is used to desensitize the women to the assignment of masturbation and to demystify the process of orgasm. Since most of the women had never seen a sexually explicit film before, some were noticeably upset by this experience, and again, the sense of disgust with being openly sexual arose.

In addition to the "yes" and "no" assignment described above, the women were assigned to get into a sensual mood and to masturbate for an hour each day. In order to afford the safety for those women who required it, the women were explicitly instructed *not* to have an orgasm.

The initial sign of a budding group norm arose, consisting of the women's premature concern about success. This sense of fear that the group program would not be successful permeated the rest of this particular group. I pointed out the process that they were already feeling like failures, and yet the assignment to masturbate had just been made.

Session 4

Everyone seemed to be progressing a little, possibly because the pressure to perform had been dealt with during the previous session. As a result, the women began reporting small advances. Abby found that she could get highly aroused in minutes but would have to stop masturbating or let the tension decrease because the intensity was experienced as discomfort.

Even Pamela was experiencing some minor progress as she described sensations of arousal which occurred at times and at places which prohibited acting on the feelings.

Jenny was progressing. She was doing more things for herself and felt as if she deserved them. She was practicing being more assertive and was gaining comfort in looking attractive.

As the group moved into the middle sessions, the women's resistance to attaining orgasm came to the fore. Maria declared that she had been avoiding the homework, and, with further questioning, it turned out that the avoidance was particularly predominant when she experienced pleasure with the masturbation.

MARIA: The first night, I went home and I used my hand like you said and I became more aware of my body than I'd ever been before.... And then it was taking just so long then that I didn't want to go on with my hand anymore. I got the vibrator and I used the vibrator and I thought, "She told us not to have an orgasm, but damn it, I'm gonna have an orgasm anyway." And that pretty much blew it.... But I did, I must say, did get to a higher point than I've ever gotten before. I could take it further, to a higher point than pain, so to speak.... I thought for sure the orgasm was coming, then I found I was just getting so worked up into having it, pretty much because I would be resisting what you had asked, so then I decided I shouldn't go on any more and I stopped... and then, the next night, I got so caught up in work and stuff and didn't take the time out, nor did I have time today...

THERAPIST: And now that you've gotten pretty turned on, you haven't done the homework.

MARIA: Yeah... gets me so mad... walking around with the same level of tension that I feel at that point and I just walk away from it like.... It's like building up to such a crescendo that you know my fear of looking epileptic (*Laughter*)...

THERAPIST: Is that what your fear is, that you'll be epileptic?

MARIA: Right... at the point of orgasm. And so now it's (*Shuddery noise*)... all the time.

THERAPIST: I'd like you to try something, OK? With the homework ... and that is that as you get up to about an 8, 7 or a 6, whatever it is, as you are feeling a little bit turned on, I'd like you to role-play an epileptic orgasm. I want you to get used to whatever that fantasy is. I want you to act that out, that epileptic, all those things that you think will happen... OK?

MARIA: Oh, God.

THERAPIST: That's a tough one for you. If it's too soon, then wait another session before you do it.

Maria's initial statement confirmed my sense that she was withholding in addition to being afraid: therefore, I used a *paradoxical approach* and by doing so accounted for both fear and resistance. Telling her to role-play the epileptic orgasm would provide a sense of safety once she saw that she could fabricate the fit without having one. And if she were resisting, it afforded the opportunity for her to disobey my directions and succeed in her own way.

Since the touching alone is insufficient without concomitant mental arousal, a discussion of erotic enhancements ended the session, and the women were assigned to add mental stimulation to the physical stimulation by utilizing fantasy or pornography or by focusing carefully on the kinesthetic sensations.

Session 5

Beginning with this session, each woman's homework was individualized to take into account the unique issues and pace of each woman. Beverly was out ill this session with a bad flu. The group norm which had been beginning in the third session was now fully blown, and everyone appeared to be feeling stuck and depressed. Since most groups experience a slump, with the women feeling discouraged and hopeless in the sixth session, I reframed the group's depression to indicate that they were moving quickly, since they were experiencing the sixth-session slump in the fifth session. After this, the majority of the session was spent on Pamela, who began to deal with some of her feelings of isolation, fear, and frustration with her inability to change herself into a more caring, feeling, and open person.

PAMELA: I'm about ready to give up, I think it's hopeless. I'm just staying in my apartment. I'm not reaching out, I'm not doing anything.

THERAPIST: I'm trying to figure out where you learned to block so well.

PAMELA: It's dead, everything is dead inside. I can sit here forever and not feel anything; empty, nothingness. It's like my chest caves in, it stops my breathing. My shoulders, like everything is going to come down. Heaviness just goes through.

THERAPIST: I'd like to try something. Would you lie down over here? This will take about 5 minutes. Will everyone come down here? Each of you just take a section and give Pamela a massage.

PAMELA: (*Crying*)

THERAPIST: It's OK, just lie there and cry. It's OK. Keep breathing ...

PAMELA: It scares me. I can't handle it. (*Crying*) Knowing you care. I feel vulnerable ... I don't deserve it ... but I want it ... I need it ... it's nice. (*Crying louder and biting fist*) I won't let my mother comfort me. I'm so angry at her, so angry I won't let her know I exist.... It is so much easier to hold myself than let it out. I hold my breath so I don't let anything out. (*Screaming, crying*)

THERAPIST: (*Comforting words*)

PAMELA: I'd rather destroy myself than let it come out.

This continued, and as the feelings subsided the group stopped the massage.

THERAPIST: You can see how tight you are holding on, and somehow you will have to learn to let go.

PAMELA: But I don't know how to.... But it doesn't have anything to do with sex.

THERAPIST: You can't expect to feel anything with sex either if you're holding everything inside. How are you feeling?

PAMELA: I feel better.

As the transcript shows, the experience was highly emotional for Pamela, and the group members' identification with her provided a breakthrough for each of them in terms of experiencing emotion and opening themselves up to being vulnerable. It also established a very strong sense of group cohesiveness.

Finally, I demonstrated Jacobson's relaxation technique and instructed the women to practice the relaxation before masturbating.

Session 6

The emotional breakthrough of the fifth session led to another breakthrough, as B. J. experienced her first intense orgasm during the previous day's homework, and the motto "just keep at it," which was to be repeated again and again by different members throughout the sessions, was born. In typical fashion, the other group members responded with mixed feelings of jealousy and happiness.

It appeared that the fourth session's paradox had worked with Maria as she completed the masturbation homework for the first time and experienced orgasms. By not confronting her or trying to force her to fulfill the homework, she was free to respond to the progress being made by the other group members. I made a mental note to continue this stance with Maria, realizing that she fought by withholding and that she would attain her goals more easily if I kept telling her not to push herself and assigned homework that was too easy for her to fulfill so she could defeat me by doing more.

The major therapeutic work in this session concerned Abby and, to a lesser extent, Beverly. Abby was thwarting herself by not fully committing herself to working on the homework. Her ambivalence was getting in the way. It is not possible to circumvent ambivalence by focusing on the positive; however, it is possible to do so by focusing on the negative.

ABBY: What I'm experiencing and you picked it up before, and I've known about it. Like, it's not gonna work, but I'll keep trying. I've had to be in the city every day and I just haven't felt like masturbating, but I know I could have found the time if I wanted to, if it had been a top priority. So, what I think I'm doing is repeating an old recurring pattern of not following through.

THERAPIST: Remember what you said in the first session about how you would sabotage?

ABBY: No.

THERAPIST: Would you like to hear it in your own words?

ABBY: Sure.

THERAPIST: Not making an effort, finding other things to do. . . . Would you close your eyes for just a second? Imagine yourself getting older, going through the years, visualize yourself getting older, imagine what is going on in your life. Imagine yourself not having orgasms. Getting older and still not having orgasms. What is it like? (*Silence*) . . .

ABBY: I see two things. I feel one part of me is very used to being like that. It is a comfortable way to be. It doesn't feel bad, because I don't have the other side of it to know how good it could be.

THERAPIST: So it is comfortable?

ABBY: No, it's a kind of ambivalence. The conflict is not knowing what the other one is about.

THERAPIST: Maybe that is how your life is going to be for you.

ABBY: O-o-oh. I don't want to live through that part of me.

THERAPIST: I think it is important to get in touch with the fact that that may be the way your life is going to be. It has been true for you up until now.

ABBY: What I may be saying is that I don't find it very helpful to be told that this is maybe the way I'm going to live my life.

THERAPIST: But that is a real possibility and it is really important for you to look at it. For homework, I would like you to go home and fantasize what it would be like to never have an orgasm. To experience it again and again, to experience that side, to really feel what that side is like. Obviously you can do for your homework whatever you want to do, but that is what I would assign you to do.

ABBY: It's difficult to do.

The paradox I had created enabled Abby to fight me and not wait 35 years to experience an orgasm. A similar issue to Abby's existed with Beverly, who was constantly hopeful and, consequently, was never in the present. She was already considering which therapist she could see or which book she could read if the group were not successful.

BEVERLY: I've worked too hard at it and thought about it too long to do that. I've been hopeful all my life that it was going to happen.

THERAPIST: And you can keep being hopeful, until the end. There is a state called being hopeful and you can just continue to be hopeful. And it will be very upsetting for you to think about what I'm telling you to think about, but being hopeful won't make it go away. The resistance is very strong, and it could win.

Consequently, I gave her the same assignment as Abby, but, as will be seen in the next session, the results of the assignment were quite different for the two women.

Meanwhile, Josephine was moving along slowly and quietly, and Jenny had met three potentially interesting men after having been assigned in the previous session to notice men.

With the exception of some additional assertiveness exercises for Abby, Beverly, Jenny, and B. J., the group members were extending their masturbation by intensifying what was already working with the expectation that orgasm would naturally result if they continued to concentrate on the buildup of pleasure.

Session 7

Jenny was enjoying herself and taking more risks, which appeared to be enhancing her self-esteem. In addition, she was becoming aware of her rigid life patterns and was taking enormous personal risks in reevaluating the current state of her life.

The other major breakthrough for this session was with Josephine, who was finally feeling secure enough in the group to speak up. The following transcript shows how Josephine had the experience of orgasm tied to a whole personality change and how I tried to disconnect the two.

THERAPIST: Any sense if you did become orgasmic, how would your life be different?

JOSEPHINE: Hopefully my sex life would improve a little bit . . .

THERAPIST: How would it improve?

JOSEPHINE: I would probably go out with more women . . . and not be as shy. . . . I don't know if that's really the reason I'm shy and nonaggressive . . .

THERAPIST: So you wouldn't be so shy and unaggressive. You would be less shy and more aggressive. . . . Just by having an orgasm. . . . Would you like to be less shy and more aggressive?

JOSEPHINE: Yeah . . .

THERAPIST: You would . . .

JOSEPHINE: Not necessarily with sex. . . . Just overall. . .

THERAPIST: You really think that just somehow by having an orgasm that it will change your whole personality?

JOSEPHINE: Well, perhaps.

THERAPIST: How shy and unaggressive do you feel in here?

JOSEPHINE: The same as always . . .

THERAPIST: I would like you to say a sentence of how you feel about each of us . . .

JOSEPHINE: Unclear . . .

THERAPIST: It's hard I know. . . . So's having orgasms . . .

JOSEPHINE: I feel something different about everybody . . .

THERAPIST: Well, try . . .

JOSEPHINE: I admire you, Jenny, because you are older and you're still so nice. . . . I'm glad you keep on telling me to keep at it, I need that . . .

JENNY: Thank you.

JOSEPHINE: I'm glad you had an orgasm. You worked hard for it.

B. J.: Thank you.

JOSEPHINE: I admire you because of your age and you still are working on improving yourself.

BEVERLY: Thank you.

JOSEPHINE: (*Similar messages to Pamela and Abby and then silence*)

THERAPIST: How are you feeling now?

JOSEPHINE: I feel really . . . still feel nervous . . .

THERAPIST: Because you realize it's almost like with the masturbation. You go almost all the way. . . . Then, just before the end you give up—there is still Maria and me left.

JOSEPHINE: Do I have to do the rest?

THERAPIST: It might be nice for you to follow through to the end.

JOSEPHINE: (*Finishes*)

My instructing Josephine to go around the circle and tell each of the women what she appreciated about them was an attempt to show her that she was assertive enough to accomplish the task now, indicating that the orgasm was separate. In the process of completing the task,

Josephine stopped with two women left unacknowledged. I could not resist pointing out the similarity of her stopping just short of completion in both this process and her masturbation. Since I felt that Josephine could complete the exercise, I waited until she felt comfortable to continue, and she did succeed and felt very good, although very nervous at the end.

The results of the paradoxical assignment of really getting in touch with what it would be like to never experience orgasm had interesting results, as it proved successful for Abby and backfired with Beverly.

THERAPIST: How are you feeling about me now?

BEVERLY: I was either going to achieve it or if I didn't I wasn't going to put it all on you.... I would fight back... Because nobody else is responsible.... And the feeling I got from you last week was to look at the possibility that it would never happen and that was a pretty final one.

THERAPIST: So you thought that I was saying that it probably won't happen to you...

BEVERLY: That you have to do it. Be well prepared that it will very likely, not probably, but very likely will not happen...

THERAPIST: How are you feeling now?

BEVERLY: Well, I'm just feeling that it may and it may not. I haven't made any further plans. I'll just leave myself open. But I won't refuse to do the homework. But I'm not feeling as confident as I might.... And that's important...

THERAPIST: Yeah, and I'm feeling really badly.

BEVERLY: You are?

THERAPIST: Oh, yeah. Because I feel like what I did backfired. ... What I was trying to do and what generally happens with what I was doing with you is to get someone to really get into that opposite place so they can give it up. I was trying to get you angry enough to really sit down and start working on it... that was what I was doing consciously.... I have had no concern about you having orgasms since you came into the group.... But now I'm getting a little concerned about it.... But my feeling is if you continue to do the homework and continue to work at it, then it will work. Where I was really getting stuck was where you already were on the next therapy program. And you were already thinking about how you were going to handle it when this didn't work... you weren't with the moment.... You weren't with the feelings at the time.... You weren't really looking at it for right now.... And I was doing something that my hope was would get you into that place.... It didn't work...

ABBY: It worked with me...

THERAPIST: What happened with you?

ABBY: I went away and thought of a couple of things. I went through the fantasy of being that woman out in the desert. I

thought for a long time, "Who was this person that I'm so willing to be?" Suddenly, I realized that it wasn't even me. It was my mother. That was my mother who just checked out of sex and was very scholarly and all this. . . . So the exercise was good for me. Meanwhile I had two orgasms . . .

PAMELA: Great.

ABBY: I have to thank you because I was doing this and I thought that this was getting hard and I thought about what B. J. said, "When it gets difficult, I have to keep on." . . . I kept on remembering your face. . . . But I did have something weird happen. . . . The second time I had one I . . . shook, I guess and I pissed all over everything. . . . And then I had to piss every 20 minutes for the rest of the night. . . . And then D_____ came home and we made love.

I began to concentrate on assertiveness with Beverly, teaching her to satisfy her own needs first rather than constantly giving to others and ending up feeling unappreciated and resentful.

Maria, meanwhile, had had a few orgasms with masturbation, but was now resisting partner work. Since a paradoxical approach had worked with her in the past, I assigned Maria to do exactly what she had been doing the previous week: to purposely inhibit her orgasm with her partner and, unless absolutely necessary, to avoid sexually interacting with him.

Pamela's mother was coming to town, and she was worrying about how she would deal with the visit. I foresaw that if Pamela changed *any* of her patterns of relating to her mother, a significant difference might result in her sexual growth. Meanwhile, Pamela was experiencing emotional highs and lows rather than numbness.

B. J.'s orgasms continued, and she decided that she felt good enough about them to practice masturbating while fantasizing about being with a partner as a bridge to partner work. All the other women assigned themselves the masturbation homework with the focus on developing their responsivity further.

Session 8

The most impressive progress in this session was by Maria and Josephine. As usual, Maria took the opportunity to do the opposite of what I prescribed and became more sexually assertive with her partner. In addition, she continued to experience orgasm with him a greater percentage of the time than pregroup, although not on all occasions.

As a result of the work in the previous session, Josephine experienced her first orgasm, although quite mild in intensity. Her homework was to continue with the masturbation. In an attempt to intensify the experience, she was instructed to arouse herself close to the point of orgasm and then reduce the stimulation, reinstating effective stimulation again and reducing it again once high levels of arousal were reached.

Pamela was still feeling more emotionally open and was not only talking to her mother about sex, but was also aware of more physical touching between the two of them than ever before. Beverly continued to struggle with asserting herself, and was reassigned to say "no" to three things that she did not want to do anyway but would not usually say "no" to, as well as to ask for and let herself have three things she wanted but usually would not ask for or let herself have.

Abby felt ready to begin partner work and decided to masturbate in front of her partner as her next assignment. B. J. had no new partner, and some of the session was devoted to the social skills involved in meeting and developing relationships, which was of concern not only to B. J. and Jenny, but to Josephine and Pamela as well. Jenny, meanwhile, went out on dates with two of the men she had met the previous week and especially liked one of them.

Session 9

Concerns about termination arose in this session. Although all of the women except for Beverly had experienced substantial progress in their enjoyment of sex and experience of orgasm, they were not yet ready to have the group end. After dealing with the women's feelings about termination, most of the session was spent on Beverly. In the following transcript, we not only see the psychological issues which were linked to orgasm for Beverly, but we also witness the effectiveness of the group process as she was confronted in a caring manner by a number of women, most notably, Abby. As a result, Beverly allowed the tears to come and finally asked each of the group members for a hug, an indication that as the result of a strengthened sense of self-worth, she was beginning to take a risk by allowing herself to directly ask others for what she wanted—namely, some caring.

THERAPIST: I'm still confused about why you're not orgasmic.
BEVERLY: When I get way up there, I feel stimulated the rest of the day...
THERAPIST: ... and that's why you should do your homework the next day or later on that day again. You didn't get a vibrator?
BEVERLY: I'll have to...
ABBY: That comment you made about doing it enough to make up for three days. It's like you don't need to do it but a little bit each day...
BEVERLY: I want to feel this release aside from feeling that I'm close to it.

THERAPIST: Who's going to give you the answer?

BEVERLY: Nobody...

THERAPIST: Because I have a feeling, and I could be wrong, that you feel you will have to have a partner, it's going to be in a book, a therapist will give you the answer to it, if you just breathe deeply, and... what you are not quite doing enough of is spending the time with yourself and, when you do it, when you spend the time with yourself you really do progress. And then you wait a whole other week, before you really do it again.... I have a question. Do you really think you have a right to this?

BEVERLY: It's not having a right.... I don't deserve things.... I put myself last...

THERAPIST: Right.... You put yourself last...

BEVERLY: I know that. With people I've gone to as therapists, they've said part of what you're saying.... Part of it has to do with my age, too. You know I don't have that much time to achieve or accomplish these things...

THERAPIST: Are you willing to relax into it? It doesn't have to happen tomorrow. There's another day... Are you willing to do a second group?... How are other people feeling listening to Beverly?

ABBY: I'm feeling a little, partly strained with you. I feel like you are making a lot of excuses. The *no's* that need to be said, a lot of them have been around having people being in your house...

BEVERLY: I recognize that...

THERAPIST: Well, what do you think would be different? What would be different if you had an orgasm?

BEVERLY: Well, whatever you're supposed to experience as a woman in life, satisfaction as a woman...

THERAPIST: How is an orgasm tied up with feeling like a woman? I mean an orgasm could make you feel like a man, what difference does it make?

BEVERLY: I think that all the years when I didn't have them, I was wondering if I was a frigid person. But I was told that I wasn't. I knew I wasn't frigid because my emotions were warm...

THERAPIST: But you don't *quite* know things.... If you had an orgasm, then you'd *really* know...

BEVERLY: Well, I think that would prove it...

THERAPIST: I see. So, this would prove that you are not a... this will be a total validation of Beverly. If you are orgasmic that means in some sense that you're OK...

BEVERLY: No, I mean in this one sense of being a completed woman, yes.... Not in the rest of my life...

Abby experienced an orgasm with her partner and was continuing with partner exercises. Josephine was pleased that her orgasms were getting stronger. Jenny was very excited about the new man in her life, but in discussing him with the group, became aware of being concerned that he was not as interested in her as she was in him. B. J. was enjoying her orgasms on her own but was concerned about getting sexually involved with a partner even though there were two available. She was looking for a meaningful relationship that would meet her needs but, meanwhile, was being encouraged to practice on the more casual relationships if that fit within her value system. Maria called in ill, and Pamela was on vacation with an old boyfriend in Mexico.

Session 10

In typical fashion, the anxiety generated by the ending of the group resulted in three women not having orgasms between the 9th and the 10th sessions. However, this situation presented a good opportunity to put expectations into perspective, since we have found that maintaining sexual changes is, in part, due to the client's expectation of success. If she expects to have an orgasm every time she has sex, she will panic when job, family, or other stress inhibits both her sexual desire and her sexual response. The realistic position that sexuality fluctuates with other factors in one's life allows for periods of low sexual interest and response without the woman feeling as if all the gains she has made have been lost. She realizes that once the stress lessens and she attends to the factors necessary for her sexual responsivity, orgasm will return.

> THERAPIST: You're upset.... They just stopped.... Miraculously, on the last session your orgasms have stopped.... Anybody else's orgasms stop? (*Two others*) This is indicative of last sessions...
>
> B. J.: Is this common?
>
> THERAPIST: Unfortunately, yes... very common.... I don't know what's going on with you, but... all I know is that in many groups there's a couple things that happen.... One is the sixth-session slump, which you all had in the fifth session.... And then around the ninth or tenth session, women will come in and all of a sudden their successes will have all turned into failures. Orgasms have stopped and everything...
>
> B. J.: But why?
>
> THERAPIST: I'm not really worried about it.... As far as the long-term is concerned... I've just never known anybody to get to a place and all of a sudden totally lose it.... If you were different from who you are, I might be able to believe it's true.... But I'm not worried about it coming back.... It's a short group... and everybody's anxieties come out at the end... which is like, "Oh my God, the group's not going to be here. Now what? I've lost everything." It's very common...
>
> B. J.: I just freak out. I start labeling myself as being nonorgasmic.

JENNY: I see a lot of things that are ups and downs, so why should sex be any different?

Beverly could hardly contain herself during this discussion. She had had her first orgasm, which occurred just under the wire, 2 hours before the session, and everyone was elated.

BEVERLY: I had an orgasm.... At 3 p.m., reading *Fanny Hill*. It was good. I'm still on page 94.... I'm embarrassed a little.... All you people standing around me.... Everybody had something to say last week to me.... Everybody was very supportive last week.... I listened to what everybody had said: "Do your homework, and don't expect it.... Don't." ... So I didn't ...

THERAPIST: What was it like? Were you using your hands or a vibrator?

BEVERLY: I was using a ... not the plain battery vibrator which hadn't been too successful, but the new one, so I was using that ... but the position for me was different. It was the way Abby had described it.... Your legs up against the wall and I was turning the book.... Well, I had to turn the page.... And kept getting more stimulated and I thought, "No, no, no, turn it off, turn it off" ... and all of a sudden I felt a flooding and I thought to myself, "I hope this is different." ... This *is* different and I just put the book down ...

PAMELA: Where did you feel it?

BEVERLY: I felt it very definitely in the genital area.... Very strongly. There was like an electric current all the way through up to your face.... I felt it very strongly.... I would say it was the way I anticipated it, but didn't think it would be as uncontrollable.... I thought that I would have control over it ...

THERAPIST: Did that scare you?

BEVERLY: A little, but not enough to make me stop.... I couldn't have stopped it really.... You couldn't really stop it.... It seemed to go on for a long time ...

THERAPIST: Now, what was the difference? What allowed it to happen this time and it hadn't in the past?

BEVERLY: I don't know. I have felt as close to it before.... I have felt the pressure ... the narrow margin of difference ... I think the position made the difference ...

It was important to go over the details of Beverly's orgasm because some women who have not become orgasmic will say that they have so that they do not feel like failures or that they have let down the other group members or therapist.

Jenny, meanwhile, was having some basic problems in her new-found relationship. Her partner informed her that although he wanted to remain friends, he was no longer interested in being lovers. She was also contemplating taking off a year to travel. She was aware that she was not feeling quite the need for security that she had in the past and felt more confident in her own ability to survive no matter what she decided to do.

Maria missed the 10th session in addition to the 9th and this time did not call to cancel. When I called her, she said that she forgot because she was on vacation and that the lack of routine resulted in her forgetting. Although she said that there was nothing else bothering her when I inquired, I felt that something was interfering with her attending the group. However, knowing that Maria would resist anything I would say, I chose to inquire no further and simply apprised her of the date of the follow-up group.

Pamela's week in Mexico with her partner clearly opened up a lot for her, and although she was not yet having orgasms, she was feeling sexual pleasure and allowing herself to relax enough to focus on and enjoy the sexual feelings.

I fully expected that Pamela would have to join another group in order to become orgasmic and was not prepared for her results in the follow-up session.

Follow-Up

The group had its follow-up reunion 3 months after the 10th session. This presented the opportunity not only for me to see how the sexual and nonsexual changes had been maintained, but also for the women to share any new occurrences with each other.

The biggest surprise of all was Pamela, who reported that she had agreed to be a research subject for Hartman and Fithian in Long Beach, California, where she had been hooked up to a number of machines that measured her physiological responses during masturbation with her vibrator. They announced, as the result of the research, that she was not only clearly orgasmic, but multiply orgasmic. Pamela was finding this hard to believe, since her experience of orgasm did not match up to her expectations.

> PAMELA: But, I'm still not convinced that it is an orgasm.
> THERAPIST: I gathered that.... And you know there's no more proof. You got final proof from Hartman and Fithian and you still won't accept it...
> PAMELA: The machine showed me and they showed me ... the charts of women who didn't experience what I've been experiencing...
> THERAPIST: What do you have invested in not believing them?
> PAMELA: I didn't feel that thing!
> THERAPIST: What?

PAMELA: I don't know.... You tell me you have it ...

THERAPIST: You have it ...

PAMELA: I get up there ... like this and then I go down ...

THERAPIST: Do you remember what an orgasm was? It's the release of a buildup of tension. What would be happening if you really had an orgasm?

PAMELA: Something traumatic ... something that is different than you can feel ... the contractions, I don't feel those contractions ...

THERAPIST: There are lots of women who don't ...

JENNY: One of the things I've gotten out of this group is hearing the whole variety of things that happen to different people. ... What happens to me, happens to me ... and it may not happen to other people and it may happen to some.... What happens to you happens to you.

PAMELA: But I think that I'm controlling it.... I'm not controlling that buildup because I feel that it is really happening ... and my body's tensing up and ... I get to this point and then I stop it and it goes down.... But I'm controlling it.... It's not like when you have an orgasm and it builds up and you don't control it any more ...

THERAPIST: So you expect it to be this thing that will just take over your body ...

PAMELA: Beverly, you experienced something like these muscle spasms.... Well, I'm waiting for that ...

THERAPIST: Well, I have something different. Are you going to wait for mine, too? And she's got something different too, are you going to wait for that one also? I think you are having an orgasm.... Obviously, you are if it is registering on the machines that strongly.... You might be able to relax more while you are doing it.... It's not necessarily the thing that is going to take you off into the cosmos, which is what I think you are waiting for.... You're waiting for this incredible, mind-shattering, LSD trip.

PAMELA: Something is going to happen.... I'm waiting for something to happen.... It's so intense ... strong feeling through me ...

THERAPIST: Does it feel good?

PAMELA: Not necessarily ...

THERAPIST: What does it feel like?

PAMELA: It feels.

THERAPIST: Does it feel like you want it to stop?

PAMELA: No. I want more.... Because I want it.

THERAPIST: You want more of something that feels terrible?

PAMELA: Yeah, because I'm waiting for that peak ...

THERAPIST: If there's nothing else over there.... Would you still continue doing it?

PAMELA: (*Sheepishly*) Well, it gets more exciting when it builds up.

THERAPIST: Oh, it does?

ABBY: When I saw you the other day, and you talked about other things you were experiencing, I said to you, you've got to be having them. . . . Remember?

PAMELA: I agree with you. Things have happened. It's so different than when I started in February. . . . I was feeling nothing . . .

THERAPIST: There's one thing that you can do and that is to slow down the arousal process. . . . When you get to that point of your excitement, don't keep working really hard, let it go down and build up again, and then let it go down and build up again some more. . . . Just to see what experiences you have with that, that's all. . . . Instead of just pushing all the way through the intensity. It's experiencing intensity a little bit differently. And experiencing it at the moment, not where it's going to take you.

Pamela was delighted to have her experience of orgasm confirmed by us. At that point, she brought out a bottle of wine to celebrate. She said that although she was not certain that she was orgasmic, she wanted to be prepared to celebrate just in case she really was.

Maria surprised me by showing up for the follow-up session, during which she discussed some of her feelings about the group and why she had avoided the previous two sessions.

MARIA: I did cop out in not coming because I felt the group wasn't what I expected. . . . And that's why I didn't show up. . . . I did expect more. . . . I think we touched upon it this evening . . . that with sexual orgasms and all I thought that personalities would change. . . . I thought that's why I wasn't having orgasms . . . because I expected a whole personality transformation. . . . I'm afraid of my emotions, and I'm seeing lately that I have a terrible time confronting people, and therefore groups. . . . I'm always afraid that if I allow myself further confrontation, that I would get overly emotional. . . . I'm just scared of all those emotions. I don't want to feel that. . . . I want to be calm, collected, analytical, controlled, detached, observant. . . . I don't want to be overly emotional . . . or lose myself in any way. . . . For me it's easier to go back . . . until I could handle it. I couldn't handle it the two times I missed . . .

Through discussing this, Maria realized how little she confronted others when she was not getting what she wanted, and this led to the following discussion of how she withheld orgasm when angry at her partner.

MARIA: I felt that he has an orgasm every time we have sex, so why shouldn't I . . . why should I be deprived of having an orgasm every time . . .

THERAPIST: It's probably not possible every single time . . . but most of the time if you wanted. . . . But meanwhile, what's the difference between the times when you do have an orgasm and the times when you don't?

MARIA: I probably go into it thinking, I'd better have an orgasm or I'm going to be mad ...

THERAPIST: And then you do or you don't?

MARIA: And then I don't ...

THERAPIST: OK, so you set it up.... Anything else you notice about the times you don't have orgasms?

MARIA: How can I say it? Like if I felt that I was hassled in the day with cleaning or cooking or something ... he comes and he's reading.... How dare he sit and read when I've been doing all those things? ... I feel ... that that is my way of getting even.... This is just coming to me now.... And then the days where he assists me with the dishes or something everything's fine.... It's all very simple ...

THERAPIST: So when you're angry enough ... instead of just being angry, you just don't have an orgasm ... and then you can really be angry, right? A good legitimate reason ...

MARIA: Yeah. Except I'm hurting myself ...

THERAPIST: Anyhow, in addition he doesn't know what you're angry about ...

MARIA: That puts a lot of pressure on him.... That's the other thing I was thinking about ... is that when I don't have an orgasm he feels that I don't love him.... And then he gets more desperately into pleasing me ...

THERAPIST: That's a great payoff in addition ...

MARIA: There's another game that I have.... I can fantasize about being with someone else.... That if I don't have an orgasm, there's someone else better.... But I know that it would be just the same so I'm not going to do that ...

THERAPIST: You do that especially when you're angry?

MARIA: Yeah.... Because fighting is hard for me.... We never fight ...

THERAPIST: So you have a whole new opportunity to learn how to be angry directly ...

MARIA: How? When I'm making love with him, do I say I'm angry?

THERAPIST: Wait a second.... You know before you get into bed?

MARIA: So, I shouldn't get into it ... when I have that feeling ...

THERAPIST: That's one way.... You know the way it will end if you do ...

This follow-up session was the most useful for Maria, who began to understand the interplay between her inability to express her feelings, particularly anger, and her inability to have orgasms. She reported that she knew she had to come back to the group and knew that she would discover something very important about herself but was unwilling to do so earlier. Now that she felt more self-confidence, she was willing to take the risk. For me, this was further validation of Maria's withholding stance. Fear of loss of control, emotionally, resulted in the withholding of feelings and withholding of orgasm.

Jenny was very excited about her forthcoming trip and reported that she was continuing to allow herself to be more vulnerable to others by asking more for what she wanted and not agreeing to do things that she did not want to do.

Abby was reliably orgasmic with her partner and was enjoying sex more than ever. B. J. had had a few sexual encounters since the 10th session and had had an orgasm during one of them. She was feeling very optimistic about her ability to be orgasmic with a partner if she could find herself a partner with whom she could have an intimate relationship.

Beverly was backsliding a bit as she described spending hours trying to have an orgasm. She had resorted back to wanting to have the release of the orgasm to compensate for the other emotional releases she was not having in her life due to problems with her children. We had to reiterate that an orgasm was merely an orgasm and would occur when she felt sexually turned on, but it might not occur when she was not aroused and certainly would not if she were using the orgasm to free her from other problems. I suggested further therapy to assist her with her other concerns and referred her to a therapist near her home.

Josephine called in to say that she would miss the session because she had relatives in town and could not get away. She felt very good about her orgasms but was still unhappy about not finding a woman with whom she could have a serious and intimate relationship.

Summary
The results of this group are typical. All of the women became orgasmic with masturbation. Generally, preorgasmic women learn to have orgasms in the 10 sessions when treated in a group setting. Sometimes, women who are withholding, who exhibit a negative resistance like Maria, become orgasmic after the group has ended. In my experience, a few women have required a bit more time and have had orgasms by the follow-up. Some women who try to move too quickly and who become frightened by the intensity of the sexual feelings may require a second group in order to slow down and begin again at a more relaxed pace.

Also typically, the women in regular sexual relationships of a fairly short history began experiencing orgasms with their partners at least a good portion of the time. Women in longer-term relationships lasting over 3 years seem to exhibit mixed results. If they complete the partner homework assignments, they tend to become orgasmic within their sexual relationships, but they make no progress if the assignments are not carried out. This may occur because negative sexual practices are so ingrained that direct treatment of both partners may be necessary to effect change or because the secondary gains of not being orgasmic outweigh the momentary experience of sexual pleasure.

Also in typical fashion, the women without regular sexual partners either had a few experiences of orgasm with partners or felt that once they were in steady sexual relationships they would be able to communicate or do the necessary things in order to experience orgasm. These women were less likely to involve themselves in sexual relationships that were only meeting the needs of their partners now that they felt they deserved more for themselves and were better able to tolerate their loneliness during periods when good relationships were not available.

NOTE

1. A primary nonorgasmic woman, according to Masters and Johnson (1970, p. 227), is one who has never achieved orgasm by any means. A situationally nonorgasmic woman has experienced at least one orgasm but is anorgasmic either with masturbation or with coitus or is infrequently and inconsistently orgasmic by these means.

References

Barbach, L. Group treatment of preorgasmic women. *Journal of Sex and Marital Therapy*, 1974, *1*, 139–145.

Barbach, L., & Flaherty, M. Group treatment of situationally orgasmic women. *Journal of Sex and Marital Therapy*, in press.

Brady, J. P. Brevital relaxation treatment of frigidity. *Behaviour Research and Therapy*, 1966, *4*, 71–77.

Caprio, F. *The sexually adequate female*. New York: Citadel Press, 1953.

C.O.R.T. (Producer). *Reaching orgasm*. San Francisco: University of California, 1975. (Film)

Fenichel, O. *The psychoanalytic theory of neurosis*. New York: W. W. Norton & Co., 1945.

Fisher, S. *The female orgasm*. New York: Basic Books, 1973.

Ford, C., & Beach, F. A. *Patterns of sexual behavior*. New York: Harper & Row, 1951.

Heinrich, A. G. *The effect of group and self-directed behavioral–educational treatment of primary orgasmic dysfunction in females treated without their partners*. Unpublished doctoral dissertation, University of Colorado, 1976.

Hite, S. *The Hite report*. New York: MacMillan & Co., 1976.

Kaplan, H. S. *The new sex therapy*. New York: Brunner/Mazel, 1974.

Kegel, A. H. Sexual functions of the pubococcygeus muscle. *Western Journal of Surgery*, 1952, *60*, 521–524.

Kinsey, A. C., Pomeroy, W. B., Martin, C. E., & Gebhard, P. H. *Sexual behavior in the human female*. New York: Pocket Book, Simon & Schuster, 1953.

Lazarus, A. A. The treatment of chronic frigidity by systematic desensitization. *Journal of Nervous and Mental Disease,* 1963, *136,* 272–278.

Lobitz, W. C., & LoPiccolo, J. The role of masturbation in the treatment of orgasmic dysfunction. *Archives of Sexual Behavior,* 1972, *2* 163–171.

Lorand, S. Contribution to the problem of vaginal orgasm. In H. Ruitenbeck (Ed.), *Psychoanalysis and female sexuality.* New Haven, Conn.: College & University Press, 1966.

Madsen, C. H., Jr., & Ullmann, L. P. Innovations in the desensitization of frigidity. *Behaviour Research and Therapy,* 1967, *5,* 67–68.

Masters, W. H., & Johnson, V. E. *Human sexual response.* Boston: Little, Brown & Co., 1966.

Masters, W. H., & Johnson, V. E. *Human sexual inadequacy.* Boston: Little, Brown & Co., 1970.

Mead, M. *Male and female: A study of the sexes in a changing world.* New York: Laurel Editions, Dell, 1949.

Nelson, A. *Personality attributes of female orgasmic consistency (or, romance makes you frigid).* Unpublished master's thesis, University of California, Berkeley, 1974.

O'Connor, J. F., & Stern, L. O. Results of treatment in functional sexual disorders. *New York State Journal of Medicine,* 1972, *72*(15), 1927–1934.

Sherfey, M. J. *The nature and evolution of female sexuality.* New York: Vintage Books, Random House, 1972.

Wolpe, J. *The practice of behavior therapy.* New York: Pergamon Press, 1969.

5

Psychological Treatment of Dyspareunia

ARNOLD A. LAZARUS

The complaint of dyspareunia is most commonly heard by the gynecologist who often identifies a physical cause for sensations of pain or discomfort during intercourse. It is only when physical factors have been treated, or found absent, that psychological factors are implicated as the cause of the problem. It is then that the woman appears for sexual therapy.

The actual incidence of dyspareunia is unknown, since many women are willing to endure some amount of pain or discomfort in the mistaken belief that sex, at best, is a conjugal duty that must be endured. More recently, with the emphasis on sexual equality and the conviction that women can, and should, derive pleasure from sexual encounters, many more women are appearing at sex therapy clinics with the complaint of dyspareunia, in some cases of long-standing duration.

Although much has been written about other female dysfunctions, and even about dyspareunia stemming from physical causes, little attention has been directed to the treatment of psychological dyspareunia. In part, this may stem from the fact that dyspareunia per se may not totally preclude either arousal or orgasm, although it can interfere with each and result in sexual disinterest. If dyspareunia results from too little lubrication, an arousal dysfunction may be the prime diagnosis and treatment will be directed at methods of enhancing arousal. If no physical factor can be identified, and the complaint of discomfort persists, dyspareunia of psychological origin must be diagnosed.

Lazarus, the originator of multimodal therapy, identifies three general classes of factors that may contribute to psychological dyspareunia: developmental, traumatic, and relational. However, he warns that whatever class of factors appears to be the precipitating cause, caution is necessary. Psychological difficulties, of whatever nature, have multiple antecedents, and one-to-one relationships between an outstanding event(s) and subsequent difficulty are rare. Hence, Lazarus recommends a comprehensive multimodal assessment of the BASIC ID (behavior, affect, sensation, imagery, cognition, interpersonal relations, and drugs) to arrive at a realistic understanding of the factors contributing to and maintaining dyspareunia. The results of that assessment are used to determine treatment. As will be seen in his chapter, Lazarus is not wedded to one particular treatment technique; he intervenes in many modalities with a variety of methods, from relaxation to imagery rehearsal. In addition, Lazarus raises the provocative question of whether sexual mismatches between mates may be a prime consideration in psychological dyspareunia rather than specific traumatic or developmental events. And if so, what are the ethical and treatment implications?

Arnold A. Lazarus is Professor of Psychology at the Graduate School of Applied and Professional Psychology, Rutgers University, and the author of many books in psychology, including Behavior Therapy and Beyond, Multimodal Behavior Therapy, *and* In the Mind's Eye.

Introduction

"Dys-" is a prefix used to signify ill, bad, difficult, painful, or disordered. "Pareunia" is derived from Greek and refers to "lying beside in bed." Hence, "dyspareunia" denotes painful intercourse or coital discomfort. The pain or discomfort may be described in terms of "pressure," "aching," "tearing," or "burning," and may have a wide range of individual intensity and duration. Regardless of whether the experience consists of momentary sharp pains or prolonged and intense discomfort, it is usually upsetting for both partners. Consequently, sex becomes a stressful act, a chore to be avoided or curtailed.

Perhaps the first question to ask a patient who complains of dyspareunia is whether a medical (usually gynecological and/or urological) examination has ruled out organic pathology. Pain or discomfort during sexual arousal and activity may signify anatomical defects (such as congenital and structural abnormalities) as well as a variety of pathological factors (such as infections of the genitourinary tract, diseases of the urethra and bladder, or illnesses that reduce or erase sexual desire). Various lesions, ranging from growths to postpartum or postoperative scarring of the genital tract or adjacent areas, may also cause coital discomfort.

Given that competent physicians have ruled out organic reasons, dyspareunia may be considered psychological and treated accordingly.[1] Psychological factors fall into three main categories: developmental, traumatic, and relational. Examples of *developmental* factors include an upbringing that invested sex with guilt and shame, misinformation that engendered anxiety and tension, or religious taboos that aroused ambivalence and confusion. *Traumatic* factors refer to fears that were precipitated by previously painful coital experiences such as violent defloration, a clumsy lover, or the aftermath of rape. *Relational* factors may include situational events (e.g., inadequate foreplay contributing to lack of arousal, fears of being overheard, anxiety that children may wander into the room, and various minor upsets and annoyances), but the major component in the context of relational factors involves the enduring and fundamental feelings and attitudes between the sexual partners.

It is remarkable that relatively little has been written about the psychological treatment of dyspareunia. Apart from scattered case histories, the literature on sex therapy and psychotherapy has tended to gloss over the numerous strategic and tactical factors for overcoming this distressing condition. The chapter on dyspareunia in Masters and Johnson (1970) covers 29 pages and deals almost entirely with organic factors—infection, endometriosis, postsurgical complications, tumors, cysts, and so forth. Similarly, in the book edited by LoPiccolo and LoPiccolo (1978), the chapter on "Diagnosis and Treatment of Coital Discomfort" by A. R. Abarbanel lists more than 100 diseases and disorders of the genitourinary tract and the reproductive organs that can produce dyspareunia. Psychological factors and treatments are mentioned only *en passant*.

As mentioned in other chapters of this volume, problems of sexual dysfunction have not responded impressively to traditional psychodynamic, Rogerian, or other conventional psychotherapies. The advent of sex therapy was a reaction to the need for problem-focused, reeducative methods that did not relegate sexual problems to the bottom of the heap of intrapsychic forces. This does not imply a mechanical, superficial, or simplistic approach. The psychological treatment of sexual problems in general, and dyspareunia in particular, cannot afford to overlook the subtle network of interpersonal processes, the impact of imagery and cognition, and the associated range of affective, sensory, and behavioral responses. Hence, a broad-spectrum or multimodal approach will be advocated. The psychological orientation outlined in this chapter is in marked contrast to O'Connor's (1976) view that female dyspareunia "is a hysteric disorder which generally can be traced to childhood trauma" (p. 76).

Comprehensive Assessment

Dyspareunia that stems from a fear of pregnancy in a woman who is medically unable to take contraceptive pills or to use an IUD is clearly a very different entity from coital discomfort based on sexual guilt and shame. Similarly, a traumatic etiology calls for a different treatment process than would be the case with a couple in whom painful intercourse was the product of marital strife. All clinicians tend to agree that it is unwise to fit patients to treatments and that effective therapy requires one to fit the treatment to the patient. The latter calls for a thorough and comprehensive assessment.

From a multimodal standpoint (Lazarus, 1976), history-taking and evaluation would cover seven parameters:

1. *Behavior.* Are there deficits and shortcomings in sexual technique?
2. *Affect.* Is guilt, anger, fear, or shame a primary or contributary factor? Are feelings of love and physical attraction conspicuously present or absent?
3. *Sensation.* Since dyspareunia presents as a sensory complaint, this modality requires a detailed initial assessment (see below).
4. *Imagery.* Are there intrusive images (negative mental pictures) that disrupt sexual enjoyment? Is there a poor or distorted body image?
5. *Cognition.* Do negative self-statements, irrational self-talk, and erroneous notions play a significant role in undermining the client's sexual participation?
6. *Interpersonal.* What basic interaction and personal climate exists between the partners in sexual and nonsexual settings?
7. *Drugs (biological).* Is the patient on any medication, especially antihypertensive drugs, tranquilizers, or sedatives? Is there evidence of improper hygiene?

It is necessary to pinpoint the frequency, intensity, and duration of pain and discomfort in order to appreciate the level of sexual and relational disruption.[2] The sensory modality is explored by obtaining answers to the following questions: Does the pain or discomfort occur before, during, or after arousal? Is the onset gradual or sudden? Is the discomfort mild, moderate, or severe? Is the pain persistent or is it in the form of twinges? How often does it occur? Is most of the discomfort felt only at intromission? Does pain increase with deeper penetration? Is orgasm a trigger for pain? Does any coital position help or aggravate the situation? Is the discomfort always in the same place? Where exactly does it occur? Does a lubricant tend to reduce the discomfort?

Dyspareunia is not a unitary or monosymptomatic problem. A woman who suffers coital pain because erotic stimuli are invested in her mind with guilt and shame is very different from an emancipated feminist who has excessive performance anxieties. Certain inept or self-appointed "sex therapists" are improperly trained to ferret out the

subtle network of antecedents, ongoing behaviors, and their consequences in each area of malfunction. The subjectivity of pain is a personal and individual matter which may arise from diverse objective factors. Those clinicians who advocate push-button panaceas need to learn that virtually every presenting complaint may be dissected into clusters of specific problems that call for a multitude of specific treatments. The following is a case in point.

The Case of C. S.

C. S., a 29-year-old married female computer programmer, experienced painful intercourse on her honeymoon. Premarital intercourse with a former fiancé had occasioned no difficulties. Her husband insisted on waiting until after the wedding for religious reasons, although they frequently engaged in mutual masturbation to orgasm. Her discomfort during sexual intercourse grew more severe and prolonged ("Sometimes I would feel sore and sensitive for days afterwards!"), and over the previous 2 years their sexual practices had consisted only of oral–genital stimulation.

Gynecological and other medical examinations revealed no pathology, but an iatrogenic problem arose when a physician questioned her too pointedly about possible lesbian tendencies. She obsessed over the idea and finally consulted a psychiatrist who managed to reassure her, and who also led her to conclude that her problems were not based on any generalized underlying hostility toward men. Nevertheless, the psychiatrist did proclaim that she resented her husband for adopting complete premarital control by refusing to consummate their relationship before marriage ("It seems that I am punishing him now by refusing to let him enter my body").

C. S. and her husband were referred to a "sex clinic" where they were seen by a male and female cotherapy team who prescribed a graduated sensate focus (Masters & Johnson, 1970). Despite verbal disclaimers from the therapists, the couple experienced this treatment as an implicit demand to conform and perform, and they emerged feeling like "foolish failures." A family friend recommended the Multimodal Therapy Institute in Kingston, New Jersey, and I agreed to see C. S. for a consultation.

Initially, there was a paucity of relevant information in each modality. The main behavior was avoidance; her affect included some frustration, anxiety, and guilt; in the sensory mode, she alluded to sharp pains during and throughout intromission; but as we explored imagery, a slew of significant facts came to light.

THERAPIST: I want you to close your eyes, relax, and imagine as vividly as you can that you and your husband are having intercourse and that you feel no pain. [It is often informative to begin with a picture of the avowed treatment goal.]

PATIENT: Do I feel *anything?*

THERAPIST: That's up to you.

PATIENT: (*Closes her eyes for about 30 seconds*) I see it happening and I feel nothing.

THERAPIST: Now try to imagine that you do feel good sexual feelings. There's no discomfort but a very pleasant massaging and erotic pleasure.

PATIENT: (*Opens her eyes after about 10 seconds*) No I can't picture that. Right off, I got the idea "That's dangerous!" "Keep away!" I can picture that with other men, but not with my husband. I can masturbate to images of being in bed with other men.... It's got something to do with my husband.

THERAPIST: How about imagining that you are not yet married to him. It is premarital sex you are having with him. Can you picture that and allow yourself to experience pleasant sexual feelings?

PATIENT: You want me to try that fantasy now?

THERAPIST: Would you mind?

PATIENT: Oh, no, I don't mind. (*Closes her eyes for about 30 seconds*) That's amazing! (*Opens her eyes*) That's really peculiar. I can do it. I can see it. It was really strange. I had no problem.... As long as we're not married it's alright.

THERAPIST: I wonder what there is about being married that makes such a tremendous difference?

PATIENT: I don't know.... Perhaps it's all connected to trust.

As we explored this issue more fully, an interesting superstition emerged, one that is at variance with a common cultural norm. Like many women, C. S. believed that men often leave after a sexual seduction or "conquest" ("My mother would say that the way to keep a man is not to give in to him sexually"). Some women believe that if they submit sexually before marriage they will lose their partner, but after marriage, sex cements the bond. C. S., however, seemed to have the opposite point of view. "I know it's completely irrational," she protested. Yet every image involving the scene of coital activity with her husband invariably elicited a theme of rejection and abandonment.

The foregoing information was obtained during an initial 90-minute consultation. C. S. and I had established good rapport, and we decided to continue working together. Given her pervasive and specific fears of rejection and abandonment, and in view of her penchant for mental imagery, I decided to embark on a course of therapy using coping imagery and images of mastery (Lazarus, 1978). The *coping imagery* involved a series of vignettes in which her husband left her but she could, nonetheless, picture herself coping with the desertion, the loneliness, and the humiliation. It took about eight weekly therapy sessions, reinforced with homework assignments in applying coping-imagery exercises, before she was able to picture the "rejection-from-husband scenes" without feeling devastated. Throughout these same sessions, *images of mastery* involved specific pictures in which she saw herself meeting other men, taking the initiative, dating, and finding specific outlets to offset the loneliness and abandonment. The rationale is that if one has no options, no alternatives, the risk factor is overwhelming. The terror of attachment and loss is somewhat mitigated by the image of personal survival even under such adverse circumstances. One is then more likely to take the chance of entering into a deeply intimate, nondefensive relationship.

Therapy also dealt with numerous irrational cognitions along the lines of Ellis and Harper (1975). For example, C. S. oversubscribed to the idea that approval from significant others was a dire necessity, that divorce was an insurmountable stigma, and that marriage was a form of ownership. These ideas were parsed, challenged, and thoroughly disputed. During the therapy, I had requested to meet with C. S.'s husband in order to gain an appreciation of the dyadic factors in their marriage. He had refused to see me and insisted that he had no need or desire for therapy. But after some 3½ months of treatment, when C. S. suggested that they might attempt to have "proper intercourse," her husband was impotent. I met with him alone for two sessions and then saw the couple together for two sessions.

After the initial failure with a prostitute about a year before meeting C. S., her husband developed performance anxieties. This was part of the reason he insisted on postponing sex and only consummating their relationship after marriage. As he became more comfortable with C. S. during their courtship, his anxieties abated, and on their honeymoon he had no sexual difficulties. C. S., however, complained of pain and discomfort, and gradually he found his potency becoming affected by her lack of ardor and by his own guilt for inflicting pain on her. Their mutual decision to avoid intromission and to focus exclusively on oral–genital sex while C. S. sought medical and psychological treatment restored his potency. My assessment of the husband revealed no untoward psychopathology or immediate problems other than those outlined above. Consequently, I saw the couple together and described a sensate-focus regimen that they could practice at home in their own time, at their own pace. I emphasized the critical importance of avoiding any sort of performance demands. He was not to pressure her and vice versa. Since I detected some reluctance and ambivalence in both parties, I decided to "side with the resistance" and commented that it would probably take at least 6 months before they would have potent and pain-free sexual relations. C. S. promised to inform me "if and when we succeed" and to consider returning for additional therapy if more than 6 months elapsed.

About 3 weeks later, she called to say that they had been avoiding all sexual contact. We had a three-way telephone conversation, and I decided to apply the usual paradoxical procedure of promoting the desired response by prohibiting it (Fay, 1978): "May I suggest that you start practicing the sensate-focus exercises, but do not even attempt intercourse until you double-check with me and I give you the go ahead." Less than a month later, C. S. called to report that they had "screwed" twice in one day. When her husband first moved into position for possible insertion, C. S. had said, "Wait! Arnie told us that we have to check with him first." Her husband answered, "To hell with Arnie!"

Minor setbacks and temporary relapses occurred during the course of the next several months, and a few "booster sessions" were administered. These consisted mainly of some "pep talks" that reinforced the nondemanding aura of sexual togetherness. A specific follow-up inquiry 18 months later revealed a sustained and satisfactory level of sexual, social, and interpersonal adjustment.

Commentary

The foregoing case shows that singularity of thought is a great impediment to learning and therapeutic progress. Human processes are multileveled and multilayered. The need for pluralism cannot be overstated. Even in C. S., a woman whose problems were relatively straightforward, a person without undue guilt, raging conflict, or traumatic upheavals, the problem of dyspareunia was clearly a product of several convoluted factors. The multimodal assessment showed that her problems were not merely the upshot of an allegedly punitive attitude toward her husband, together with some general sensual anxieties. Nor was it "all connected to trust." Instead, even this rather uncomplicated case revealed a coalescent mixture of some of the foregoing factors in addition to superstitions, fears of rejection and abandonment, response deficits, irrational ideas, elements of countercontrol (Davison, 1973), and performance fears. Imagine trying to treat these same features in a borderline personality with a history of religious indoctrination plus the aftermath of incest and more than a tinge of paranoia! Instead of searching for a panacea or hoping for unimodal answers and unitary constructs, a new awareness of the multifaceted nature of psychological problems encompasses (1) specification of goals and problems; (2) specification of treatment techniques to achieve these goals and remedy these problems; and (3) systematic measurement of the relative success of these techniques.

A brief elaboration of the techniques of coping imagery and images of mastery might lend substance to this commentary. The use of these imagery methods is based on a fundamental assumption, namely, *that we are unable to perform in reality that which we cannot achieve in fantasy.* A person, for instance, who wishes to quit smoking and says, "I can't picture myself stopping!" will, in all probability, remain unable to give up the habit. An impotent man who is unable to imagine himself obtaining and maintaining an erection in the presence of a sexual partner needs to achieve this mental picture before he can hope to effect a satisfactory real-life adjustment. In the foregoing case, given C. S.'s overwhelming vulnerability to rejection and abandonment, especially from her husband, it was necessary to replace her parasitic attachment with a mature and self-sufficient response pattern. To achieve realistic mental pictures of oneself coping rather than disintegrating in the face of abandonment and aloneness is an essential precursor to the emotional risk-taking that comes with any deep attachment.

The words "I can't," together with the defeatist images that accompany this proclamation, are responsible for a great deal of human limitation and suffering. When C. S. stated, "I can't make it in life without my husband," it was necessary for her to acquire a repertoire of mental pictures depicting herself coping with or without him. In her case, the view of her husband as "emotional oxygen" was undermining her capacity to relax and enjoy having sexual intercourse with him. I introduced the coping-imagery procedure in the following way:

> Let's imagine that a UFO lands from a galaxy outside our solar system and whisks away your husband. You will never see him again. We can but hope that he will have a happy life wherever he is headed, but here you are on earth without him. Now you can decide to kill yourself because your life support is gone. But don't do that. Instead, let's see how you can manage to cope and survive and even end up smiling again and being happy.

I elicited from her a series of images where she saw herself leaning on friends, keeping very busy, and eventually recovering from the loss. Thereafter, in subsequent sessions, I introduced more realistic pictures of rejection (e.g., "Imagine that he has found another woman!"), and we worked through a similar series of coping reactions.

Images of mastery pave the way for various skills that add confidence to the probability that one will cope in the face of adversity. In the case of C. S., she had to see herself mastering the art of meeting new men, dating, conversing, and relating. At first, she pictured herself being awkward, inept, shy, making stupid remarks, and failing to impress. Gradually, this gave way to images where she could see herself being charming, seductive, witty, and relaxed. The assumption behind these tactics is that a healthy or happy marriage is not based on desperate, last-chance, clinging attachments. In a worthwhile marriage, one remains with one's spouse not because one has to but because one desires to. An awareness of one another's "high market value" vis-à-vis members of the opposite sex engenders self-respect and mutual respect.

Again, it must be emphasized that C. S.'s successful sexual and interpersonal adjustment called for a broad range of interventions. Let us now turn to some prevalent unimodal conceptions that serve to underscore the need for a multimodal approach to the treatment of dyspareunia.

Multimodal Factors

Recently, I was consulted by a woman suffering from dyspareunia who was firmly convinced that her basic problem was a fear of erotic stimuli. She attributed this to a misguided nun who had instilled the belief that "genital pleasures pave the way to hell." She had seen a psychiatrist who felt that she had fully rejected these ideas "intellectually," but that a "conditioned response" nevertheless persisted which signaled guilt and fear whenever she felt herself becoming aroused. After drawing up a Modality Profile of her BASIC ID (*B*ehavior, *A*ffect, *S*ensations, *I*mages, *C*ognitions, *I*nterpersonal relationships, and *D* rugs or biological factors), the simple-minded conditioned-reflex hypothesis gave way to a matrix of specific problems:

Behavior. There was evidence of constricted reactions in sexual and nonsexual settings. For example, she absolutely refused to use a lubricant to try and ease her coital discomfort, and she assiduously avoided all situations that might draw public attention to her (crowds, restaurants, dinner parties, sports, games, and so forth).

Affect. She tended to bottle up her feelings, but admitted feeling "annoyed and frustrated much of the time," and kept it well under control.

Sensation. Dyspareunia was present during any form of penile insertion ("It's just very uncomfortable rather than truly painful").

Most of the discomfort was localized around the labia minora and the vaginal outlet. She also reported feeling generally tense and often had headaches. She was completely nonorgasmic. Dysmenorrhea also constituted a problem, and she was often bedridden during the first 8 hours of her menstruation.

Imagery. Loss of control was a central theme in this modality. She had memories of a film depicting inmates of a mental institution losing control during sexual frenzies.

Cognition. Perfectionism and a host of categorical imperatives ("shoulds" and "musts") tended to characterize much of her thinking.

Interpersonal. She was much more of a "taker" than a "giver." A girlish rather than womanish quality rendered her uncomfortable in adult-to-adult interactions. Her husband was inclined toward paternalistic overprotection.

Drugs (biological). Medical examinations revealed no organic pathology except for a mild and labile, anxiety-related hypertension.

This woman is presently in treatment and is proving to be a difficult and resistant case. My reason for presenting her here is to underscore the need for adequate assessment procedures. Catch-all terms—conditioned response, fear of losing control, passive–aggressive personality, Oedipal conflicts, etc.—are too often used as central explanatory constructs by mental health practitioners. These labels need to be broken down into their component parts if the victims of emotional suffering are to achieve successful and durable outcomes (cf. Halleck, 1978).

Relationship Factors

In the field of psychotherapy, it is very easy to leap to unfounded conclusions. The fallacy of arguing from a temporal sequence to a causal relationship is particularly widespread. Two events may coexist, be correlated, but they need not be causally related. A case history may reveal that a patient with dyspareunia had experienced no discomfort prior to an extramarital relationship. To assume that there has to be a causal connection between the love affair and the subsequent dyspareunia is fallacious. The extramarital liaison may have contributed substantially, moderately, or insignificantly to the development of later coital discomfort. If psychotherapists would remain extremely cautious and tentative about ascribing causes to various antecedent events, less biased and more accurate assessments might be forthcoming. The following is a case in point.

The Case of S. J.

S. J., a 24-year-old woman, was married for 2 years. A bright and extremely attractive law student, she had dated many men prior to marriage, but she was a virgin until her engagement. Sexual intercourse was always uncomfortable at best and often extremely painful. The pains were described as "pressure, at times a throbbing like a tooth-ache, and sometimes a sort of cutting sensation as if something is tearing inside." She could not localize the discomfort, and lubricating jellies were of little help. She was prone to cystitis, but there were no other medical problems according to her gynecologist, who added that while her vagina was "small and tight," it was nevertheless within normal limits.

I met with S. J. and her husband, a young, hard-driving and al-ready successful accountant. He seemed to be a considerate and profi-cient lover, a fact that S. J. confirmed. "We have a fabulous relation-ship," she stated, "but sex has never been good." S. J. sometimes climaxed with prolonged clitoral stimulation. "Even with a vibrator it takes me about 15 minutes to come!" she complained.

Her history, however, was replete with psychological trauma and conflict. An only child, she was aware that her father "played around," and she witnessed bitter scenes between her parents, which eventually culminated in an acrimonious divorce when she was 10 years of age. Her father had not contacted her in the ensuing 14 years, and she did not know if he was alive or dead. Her reaction to this abandonment involved a good deal of self-recrimination. She felt that she must have disappointed him in some fundamental way.

After the divorce, her mother had a succession of boyfriends, one of whom persuaded the patient to perform fellatio when she was 12 years old. She informed her mother, who blamed her and punished her for being too seductive. This incident was related with considerable emotion, a mixture of confusion, self-blame, and resentment toward her mother. In general, S. J. lacked the level of self-acceptance and self-worth that one would like to see. She was prone to guilt and far too ready for self-downing and self-abnegation.

What bearing did these specific factors have on her current sexual performance and lack of enjoyment? Theorists of many different per-suasions could readily create a mosaic in which her dyspareunia would be an obvious manifestation of these background factors. In the ab-sence of further data, I assumed that the psychic scars left by paternal abandonment, plus the father's own sexual indiscretions, had probably colored her own present sexual outlook. In addition, I theorized that the unsatisfactory mother–daughter relationship (poor modeling, ambivalent identification, unexpressed hostility) also played a role. And she reported feeling "terrified when that man made me suck him."

Therapy was focused on a cognitive and affective reevaluation of each event. I challenged her catastrophic self-talk, searched for benign hypotheses to account for some of the variance (e.g., "What other reason, apart from your own shortcomings and failures as a child and as a daughter, could have led your father to keep away from you?"), and I pointed out several irrational and syllogistic errors in her reasoning. This formed the main basis of the cognitive interventions. The affective modality was tackled mainly through an analysis of specific feelings surrounding each area of distress, by means of desensitization. ("Let's picture a scene going back in time. . . . You are about 7 or 8 and your parents are arguing. . . . Picture that scene vividly, relax, and try to feel calm and indifferent.") We also used the empty-chair technique. ("Imagine that those two chairs next to you are not empty but that your mother and father are sitting in them. Now I want you to try and really see them, imagine they really are there. . . . What do you want to say to either one or both of them?")

From time to time, S. J.'s husband came to the sessions. He was supportive and sympathetic to our therapeutic endeavors, but he did ask to see me alone and confided that he had decided to have an affair with his receptionist. At one session when S. J.'s husband was present, he expressed impatience with the therapy. S. J. erupted into atypical anger at him, and a heated argument followed. This led me to explore the basic feelings between them much more closely, but S. J. insisted that apart from minor annoyances that sometimes flared up into heated arguments, the basic tenor of their relationship was one of love, caring, and mutual respect.

About 6 months later, after some 24 sessions, we had made considerable headway concerning S. J.'s self-blame, self-confidence, and self-acceptance, but no improvement was evident in her sexual responses. Once or twice she reported feeling "less discomfort," but no sustained carry-over came into effect. On one occasion, a prolonged sensate-focus interaction followed by cunnilingus produced two orgasms within a few minutes of each other, but intromission was only "less painful" rather than truly pleasurable.

I began to question if the physicians who examined her had overlooked some medical disorder. The usual psychological factors associated with dyspareunia were not present—there were no religious conflicts, no apparent fears of rejection, no undue guilt, no heightened fear of pain or erotic stimuli, no specific fear of failure, no sexual myths or fallacies—and she had come to terms with many affect-laden issues out of her past. It was about this time that a perplexed S. J. confessed that she had gone to bed with one of her classmates, "a dynamic, Aryan-looking young man" for whom she had felt "a sneaking attraction" since first seeing him. "It really was an impulse," she explained. "We had kidded around for a couple of months, and lately he started coming on strong. . . . I really decided to go along with it out of curiossity." For the first time ever, S. J. reported having experienced vigorous penile thrusting *without any pain or discomfort whatsoever.* During a "repeat performance" the following day, S. J. claimed to have achieved "an intense orgasm."

It transpired that while S. J. loved her husband, she had never felt *physically* attracted to him, a fact that she tended to downplay, ignore, and deny. During our initial assessment interview, she claimed to be "turned on to him." There was nothing about her husband's appearance that displeased her. She considered him "pleasant to look at, well built, masculine, and cuddly," but she had never experienced a "surge of excitement" or an autonomic thrill as was true in response to some other men. ("I guess deep down I've always known that there is a lack of chemistry, but I hated admitting it to myself or to anyone else. . . . I thought it might develop with time because I truly love him.") She ventured that due to being "small and tight inside," perhaps she had to be fully aroused in order to avoid discomfort.

At this juncture, therapy seemed to provide a crutch that enabled S. J. to experiment. She had sexual relations with the senior partner of a law firm where she had worked during the summer and enjoyed it without discomfort, but coitus with a different classmate proved unsatisfactory and painful. "I'm in touch with a definite pattern," S. J. declared. "For me, sexual chemistry means a certain look that's difficult to put into words, but physically it seems that the guy must be tall and slimly built, with blue eyes and light-colored hair and skin. I'm just not the Burt Reynolds type." S. J.'s husband was relatively tall and slim, but his eyes were brown and he had a medium complexion with dark hair.

Earlier in the therapy, I had asked her to conjure up erotic fantasies during sex to determine whether this would decrease coital discomfort, but she reported no success with this method. Since pursuing her extramarital activities, however, she found herself able to have pain-free intercourse with her husband "when I really get into imagining that he is somebody else." She has been extremely careful to prevent her husband from discovering any of her affairs, and he, in turn, has been most discreet about his own extramarital activities. The present status of the therapy is that I am seeing them individually to examine the viability of their marriage.

Commentary

The case of S. J. raises many issues—procedural, professional, and ethical. But my reason for describing this case was mainly to emphasize how readily one may be misled into assuming that causal links exist, when, in fact, only tenuous connections may be present. When S. J. described the type of man to whom she felt sexually attracted, my first question was, "Do you recall how your father looked and how he was built?" She remembered her father as "pleasant-looking, average height and build with curly reddish-brown hair, and grey-green eyes, I think." But what conclusion could we draw if her father had been tall, slim, blond and blue-eyed, or short, fat, and dark? It seems far too glib and fatuous to infer that she is embroiled in a secret search for her father figure or that there is some "reaction formation" at work!

Perhaps the most parsimonious explanation is that S. J.'s background factors rendered her deficient in self-esteem and failed to provide her with subjective security and a sense of autonomy. Consequently, her marriage choice was predicated more on matters of security, dependency, and protection than on attraction, male–female involvement, sexual compatability, and mature emotional reciprocity. Thus, while the various antecedent events may have contributed indirectly to the dyspareunia per se, none of them could be regarded as specific causal agents. Was she incapable of marrying a nurturant man who would provide love and security as well as sexual and erotic pleasures? Did her background predispose her to select a mate whom she found physically nonerotic, or was this aspect fortuitous? We have no answers for these questions, only speculations.

It is simplistic and rather puerile to conclude that S. J.'s marital sexual discomfort is entirely a function of insufficient or inadequate sexual attraction or arousal. It remains to be seen, for instance, if marriage per se tends to generate coital displeasure, since nearly all her sexual pleasures have resided outside the confines of engagement or marriage. But whatever the case, the various antecedent events and their particular roles and consequences remain open-ended. Nevertheless, therapeutic progress ensued by dwelling on a variety of situational and specific problems rather than searching for underlying and cohesive causal themes.

The Use of Systematic Desensitization

Many years ago (Lazarus, 1963), I had pointed out that "where specific or reasonably clear-cut fears inhibit sexual pleasure, systematic desensitization is the method of choice." While this statement, in my present judgment, is probably accurate, over the years I have found relatively few cases in whom specific clear-cut fears were present without a variety of secondary anxieties and interpersonal difficulties. Nevertheless, as some of the cases in this chapter have shown, some form of habituation or desensitization through imagery may play an important role in the treatment of dyspareunia. There are instances that seem to call for more elaborate, precise, and systematic desensitization tactics. A typical example of this formal technique (taken from my 1963 article) appears below:

Mrs. A., aged 24 years, had been married for 2½ years, during which time she claimed to have had coitus on less than two dozen occasions. She always experienced violent dyspareunia during intercourse as well as "disgust and anxiety at the whole messy business." She could tolerate casual kissing and caressing without anxiety and at times found these experiences "mildly pleasant." The background to her problem was clearly one of puritanical upbringing, in which much emphasis was placed on the sinful qualities of carnal desire. Mrs. A.'s husband had endeavored to solve their difficulties by providing his wife with books on sex techniques and practices. Mrs. A. had obligingly read these works, but her emotional reactions remained unchanged. She sought treatment of her own accord when she suspected that her husband had developed an extramarital attachment.

After diagnostic interviews and psychometric tests, systematic desensitization was administered according to the following hierarchy (the most disturbing items being at the head of the list):

1. Having intercourse in the nude while sitting on husband's lap.
2. Changing positions during intercourse.
3. Having coitus in the nude in a dining room or living room.
4. Having intercourse in the nude on top of a bed.
5. Having intercourse in the nude under the bed covers.
6. Manual stimulation of the clitoris.
7. Husband's fingers being inserted into the vagina during precoital love play.
8. Caressing husband's genitals.
9. Oral stimulation of the breasts.
10. Naked breasts being caressed.
11. Breasts being caressed while fully clothed.

12. Embracing while semiclothed, being aware of husband's erection and his desire for sex.

13. Contact of tongues while kissing.

14. Having buttocks and thighs caressed.

15. Shoulders and back being caressed.

16. Husband caressing hair and face.

17. Husband kissing neck and ears.

18. Sitting on husband's lap, both fully dressed.

19. Being kissed on lips.

20. Being kissed on cheeks and forehead.

21. Dancing with and embracing husband while both fully clothed.

Variations in the brightness of lighting played a prominent part in determining the patient's reactions. After 4 desensitization sessions, for instance, she was able to visualize item 14 (having her buttocks and thighs caressed) without anxiety if this was occurring in the dark. It required several additional treatments before she was able to tolerate this imagined intimacy under conditions of ordinary lighting.

The therapist asked Mrs. A.'s husband to make no sexual overtures to his wife during the period of treatment (to avoid resensitization). Mrs. A. was desensitized 3 times a week over a period of less than 3 months.

When item 17 on the hierarchy had been successfully visualized without anxiety, Mrs. A. "seduced" her husband one evening and found the entire episode "disgustingly pleasant." Thereafter, progress was extremely rapid, although the first 2 items were slightly troublesome, and each required over 20 presentations before the criterion (a 30-second exposure without signaling) was reached. A year later, Mr. and Mrs. A. both said that the results of therapy had remained "spectacularly effective."

Commentary

Where specific fears or feelings of guilt are predominant, systematic desensitization is probably one of the most effective techniques. Generally, this procedure is only one element in a broad-spectrum treatment regimen. Most cases require assertiveness training, social skills training, and some form of marriage therapy. It is important to draw a distinction between those women who suffer from coital distress and who genuinely wish to overcome the problem and those who use real or imagined painful intercourse as a manipulative and controlling device. In several dysfunctional marriages I have known women who complained of pain during sex as an excuse to avoid frequent or further contact with their husbands. In these instances of *pseudodyspareunia*, the mainstay of therapy is to unravel the games and to teach authenticity in place of passive–aggressive tactics.

In reviewing my last 10 cases of female dyspareunia, I was curious to determine how many of these women attributed their sexual problems to *developmental* factors (a background that invested sex with guilt, sin, shame, and fear) as opposed to a history of *traumatic* events (rape, incest, illnesses) and how many cases reflected specific *relationship* difficulties. Of these 10 cases, only 1 revealed a truly traumatic etiology (she had been molested as a child), 2 came from puritanical homes with mothers who viewed sex in a highly pejorative light, and another 2 cases were basically homosexual (which constitutes a separate descriptive category, and one that is not necessarily problematic). The remaining 5 were all in unhappy and unsatisfactory relationships. I wonder if these figures compare with statistics for the population at large. I am unaware of any large-scale data on the incidence of dyspareunia or on the basic personal and interpersonal factors that underlie this condition. It would not surprise me if it were true that after ruling out organic factors, at least half the women who suffer from dyspareunia are having sexual intercourse with the wrong man!

In terms of treatment outcomes, the woman who had been molested as a child was treated mainly with an elaborate desensitization procedure that extended over 86 items. Cognitive restructuring and social skills training also became an integral part of her therapy. After 2 years of treatment, she was considered "moderately improved" insofar as she could tolerate sexual intercourse but seldom desired it.

By contrast, the 2 cases whose puritanical upbringings seemed mainly responsible for their respective problems of coital discomfort, both responded rapidly and gratifyingly to a regimen of cognitive disputation, desensitization, relaxation training, and allied methods. One of the women was seen 22 times over the course of 5 months, and the other required only 9 sessions over 2½ months.

The two homosexual women were entirely different from one another. The only similarity was that both were married and both tended to experience sexual intercourse with their husbands as painful and nonerotic. While the one had enjoyed several lesbian attachments, the other merely had active dreams and fantasies about lesbian relationships, but she refused to "give in to these disgusting ideas." My attempts to enable her to accept her homosexual feelings led her to terminate therapy and to enter psychoanalysis with a view to achieving a heterosexual adjustment. The other woman expressed interest in achieving a bisexual capacity, but she fell in love with a woman, divorced her husband, and terminated therapy before we could commence.

The 5 cases who were embroiled in unhappy or untenable relationships were also very different from one another. Three obtained divorces and established satisfactory sexual relationships with other men. One woman whose passive–dependent behaviors rendered her less mature than a typical 10-year-old proved refractory to my ministrations. Her husband was even more seriously disturbed (he was hospitalized with a diagnosis of acute schizophrenia on 2 occasions), and the problem of dyspareunia played an insignificant role in an encrusted dyadic interaction replete with symbiotic attachments and elements of folie à deux. The other case involved a somewhat psychopathic woman who elected to remain married for financial reasons but whose sexual pleasures outside of marriage were quite extensive before and after therapy. She requested hypnosis so that she could learn to "switch off" and tolerate sex with her husband. I taught her a method of self-hypnosis and relaxation over 4 sessions, which she claimed helped her achieve her objectives.

What emerges most clearly is that dyspareunia is not a unitary disturbance but, like most psychological problems, involves a broad spectrum of personalistic and idiosyncratic variables. As Halleck (1978) underscores:

> We are too restricted by the parochial teachings of our own past to have learned to use effectively all dimensions of treatment. . . . We will achieve the goal of multidimensional treatment more quickly to the extent that we approach our patients with open minds and a relentless commitment to study and confront the complexities of human behavior. (p. 501)

ACKNOWLEDGMENT

My genuine thanks to Drs. Allen Fay, Sandy Leiblum, and Larry Pervin for their helpful comments on the initial draft of this chapter.

NOTES

1. Males who complain of coital discomfort—painful erections, painful ejaculations, postcoital hypersensitivity—almost invariably have a medical problem. Venereal infections and nonspecific prostatitis are perhaps among the most common. Purely functional dyspareunia in the male is rare, and this chapter will therefore deal with the treatment of female dyspareunia.
2. The difference between vaginismus and dyspareunia is that intromission is generally painful in the latter condition but impossible in vaginismic

women because the vaginal entrance remains tightly clamped due to an involuntary spasm of the vaginal sphincter (see Chapter 6).

References

Davison, G. C. Counter-control in behavior modification. In L. A. Hamerlynk, L. C. Handy, & E. J. Mash (Eds.), *Behavior change: Methodology, concepts, and practice.* Champaign, Ill.: Research Press, 1973.

Ellis, A., & Harper, R. A. *A new guide to rational living.* Englewood Cliffs, N.J.: Prentice-Hall, 1975.

Fay, A. *Making things better by making them worse.* New York: Hawthorn Books, 1978.

Halleck, S. L. *The treatment of emotional disorders.* New York: Jason Aronson, 1978.

Lazarus, A. A. The treatment of chronic frigidity by systematic desensitization. *Journal of Nervous and Mental Disease,* 1963, *136,* 272–278.

Lazarus, A. A. *Multimodal behavior therapy.* New York: Springer, 1976.

Lazarus, A. A. *In the mind's eye.* New York: Rawson, 1978.

LoPiccolo, J., & LoPiccolo, L. (Eds.). *Handbook of sex therapy.* New York: Plenum Press, 1978.

Masters, W. H., & Johnson, V. E. *Human sexual inadequacy.* Boston: Little, Brown & Co., 1970.

O'Connor, J. F. Sexual problems, therapy, and prognostic factors. In J. K. Meyer (Ed.), *Clinical management of sexual disorders.* Baltimore: Williams & Wilkins, 1976.

6

The Treatment of Vaginismus: Success and Failure

SANDRA R. LEIBLUM, LAWRENCE A. PERVIN, AND ENID H. CAMPBELL

While many of the chapters in this book attest to the diversity of theoretical approaches available for intervening in sexual disorders, most sex therapists approach the treatment of vaginismus in a similar fashion. The major goal of treatment is the elimination of the spasmodic reflexive contraction of the muscles controlling the vaginal entrance, and the treatment typically proceeds in a step-by-step fashion with the insertion of objects (dilators or fingers) of increasing size.

Despite the high degree of agreement concerning treatment approach, and the high reported incidence of success generally found, treatment is not effective for all women with this condition. Determining which factors predict success and failure is important, especially since failure can be profoundly discouraging for the woman and her partner. In this chapter, Leiblum, Pervin, and Campbell report on the treatment of three cases, with varying outcomes. What stands out is the diversity of women, partner relationships, and sexual enjoyment characteristic of women with vaginismus. The factor most predictive of successful outcome appears to be the nature of the supportive factors that permit the overcoming of the anxiety about change—both the motivation within the woman and in the interpersonal environment, as well as the nature of the alliance formed with the therapist. The implication for sex therapy generally is that the most effective techniques available can prove futile in the face of ambivalent motivation and support for change and a noncongruent patient–therapist relationship.

Sandra R. Leiblum is Director of the Sexual Counseling Service at the College of Medicine and Dentistry of New Jersey–Rutgers Medical School and Clinical Associate Professor of Psychiatry. Lawrence A. Pervin is Professor of Psychology at Rutgers University. Enid H. Campbell is Professor of Psychology at Trenton State College.

Introduction

Vaginismus is a perplexing and frustrating problem. The woman who experiences the involuntary, spasmodic contraction of the pubococcygeus and related muscles controlling the vaginal opening is unable to have intercourse but may be quite capable of becoming sexually aroused, lubricating, and experiencing multiple orgasms. Virgin wives and their partners often report a rich sexual repertorie. However, once the wife senses or fears that her vagina is going to be "penetrated," the muscles are tightened so that intercourse is impossible. Whether because of ambivalence about resolving the problem or otherwise, what is striking in so many of these cases is the number of years that go by before the couple actively considers treatment. Indeed, often it is the desire to have children that forces these couples to seek help. Although vaginismus is considered to be relatively rare, it is likely that it is present to a far greater degree than is statistically reported. In addition to cases in which vaginismus has precluded intercourse are the many cases in which women experience partial vaginismus on intermittent sexual occasions. Often such difficulties seriously interfere with sexual pleasure but are not considered sufficiently disturbing to warrant treatment.

A brief review of four studies on vaginismus published since 1970 may serve to highlight current thinking and issues relevant to incidence, etiology, treatment, and prognosis. Masters and Johnson describe vaginismus as an involuntary reflex "due to imagined, anticipated, or real attempt at vaginal penetration" (1970, p. 250) and refer to it as a psychosomatic illness. They discuss a variety of etiological factors, including a response to male sexual dysfunction, the psychosexually inhibiting influence of religious orthodoxy, a prior sexual trauma, a response to a homosexual identification, and a secondary response to dyspareunia. Etiological factors are considered to be important in the treatment, and particular attention is paid to the contribution of the male partner: "Interestingly, the syndrome has a high percentage of association with primary impotence in the male partner, providing still further clinical evidence to support procedural demand for simultaneous evaluation and treatment of both marital partners" (p. 252). In treating both partners, Masters and Johnson start with a demonstration of the existence of the involuntary nature of the vaginal spasm or contraction. It is considered important that both partners understand that the response is involuntary and reflexive rather than intentional. Beyond this, the main element of treatment is the use of Hegar dilators in graduated sizes to enable the woman to allow penetration by an object the size of a penis. The use of the dilators is initiated and conducted by the husband with the wife's physical control over verbal direction of the exercises. Masters and Johnson report that they have seen 29 cases in 11 years and have had success in the treatment of every case once the cooperation of the partners in the dilation therapy had been obtained.

Ellison (1972) reports on the treatment of 100 cases of vaginismus in which less than one-fifth first complained directly of a sexual disability. While no incidence figures are given, the suggestion is made that vaginismus is a much more common complaint than people think. He, too, refers to vaginismus as a psychosomatic problem, though, in contrast to Masters and Johnson, he places greater stress on the underlying psychodynamic pattern, in particular, guilt caused by an underlying sexual conflict and fear of punishment. In one case, he describes a woman who feared that her vaginal opening was too small and that excruciating pain and torrential bleeding would result from intercourse. Ellison also emphasizes the role of the partner and describes the husbands as frequently "timid, gentle, over permissive men who have either overt or hidden anxieties about their own sexual role and potency" (1972, p. 45). He suggests that both partners fear the fundamental aggressiveness of sexual activity and for this reason both must be part of the treatment. However, unlike Masters and Johnson, Ellison suggests that treatment begin by working alone with the woman to establish rapport and allay her anxieties. After a pelvic examination, where a female physician is seen as having an undoubted advantage, information is given to correct misinformation, and then behavior therapy in the form of systematic desensitization is begun. The use of graduated glass vaginal dilators is also suggested to decondition the woman's reflexive contraction to anticipated pain. While generally optimistic about treatment results, Ellison suggests that patients who associate sex with excretion and see it as dirty and revolting have a poorer prognosis than do patients who experienced a physical trauma at an early age. The suggestion appears to be that when the vaginismus is more clearly associated with a conditioned response to a traumatic event, there is a better prognosis than when the vaginismus is part of a more general psychodynamic conflict and personality problem. The suggestion also is made that the prognosis is better for those women who are able to have an orgasm than for those who cannot.

In the third study, Fuchs, Hoch, Paldi, Abramovici, Brandes, Timor-Tritsch, and Kleinhaus (1973) describe vaginismus as a phobic process associated with a fear of penetration, not only of intercourse but of gynecological examination as well. They suggest that psychoanalytic treatment can be successful but is time-consuming. Instead they recommend the use of systematic desensitization in the context of therapy as a medical emergency. Hypnosis is used in conjunction with systematic desensitization for relaxation and for imagery production. A graduated series of *prelubricated* Hegar dilators is also employed, and the authors suggested that the doctor–patient–husband relationship is critical for success. In neither this paper nor the one by Ellison (1972) is sensate focus mentioned as a part of the treatment. In a note added to their reprinting of the paper by Fuchs and associates, LoPiccolo and LoPiccolo (1978) suggest that the use of dilators, with or without hypnosis, is the method of choice for vaginismus and that in some cases a gynecological examination is possible though intercourse is not.

In the final study to be considered, Helen Kaplan (1974) describes vaginismus as a conditioned response generally associated with a phobic response to coitus and vaginal penetration. The phobic avoidance response is seen as distinct from the conditioned spasmic response and as antedating the vaginismus or being secondary to it. General sexual inhibition and orgasmic inhibition may or may not be associated with the vaginismus. In terms of incidence, Kaplan suggests that vaginismus is a relatively rare disorder, though no precise statistics are given. In terms of etiology, Kaplan discusses and rejects the psychoanalytic view of vaginismus as a conversion symptom expressive of the woman's hostility toward men and her unconscious wish to castrate them in revenge for her own castration (Fenichel, 1945, p. 174). Instead, Kaplan suggests a multicausal concept of vaginismus as a conditioned response to any adverse stimulus associated with intercourse or vaginal entry: "Vaginismus occurs when a negative contingency becomes associated with the act or fantasy of vaginal penetration" (1974, p. 417). The aim of treatment, then, is the extinction of the conditioned vaginal response. This is accompanied through the insertion of graduated rubber or glass catheters until a catheter the size of an erect penis is inserted without pain or discomfort. Often the patient's or partner's finger is used rather than a catheter. Then the woman is instructed to guide her husband's penis into the vaginal opening with her remaining in control throughout. Where the phobic element remains strong, it is treated through the use of systematic desensitization. Here, the patient repeatedly imagines the feared stimuli while deeply relaxed. In sum, the conditioned vaginismic response is treated through the insertion exercises, and the phobic element is treated through the use of systematic desensitization. The essential therapeutic ingredient is seen as the repeated exposure of the woman, in imagery and in actuality, to the feared situation while trying to keep anxiety at a minimum and reassurance at a maximum. No specific recommendations are made concerning the woman's partner since this depends upon the particular dynamics of the case. Finally, Kaplan suggests that the outcome is successful in virtually 100% of the cases, though on some occasions, success is followed by the husband having difficulties with impotence or premature ejaculation.

The following points emerge from these four studies:

1. There is obvious agreement concerning the structure of the vaginismic response but it is alternatively described as a psychosomatic disorder, a phobia, a conditioned response, and a conversion reaction.

2. There are no statistical figures concerning incidence. Most authors view it as rare, though one author suggests that it is more common than people might think.

3. Varieties of possible etiological factors have been considered, ranging from a specific traumatic event to an underlying psychodynamic conflict. In most cases the role of the husband is seen as an important contributing factor in the maintenance, if not the cause, of the vaginismus.

4. Regardless of the etiological hypothesis, the authors agree that the treatment method of choice is the gradual insertion into the vagina of objects (i.e., fingers, tampons, dilators) of increasing size under conditions of relaxation and patient control. Systematic desensitization also is often used, particularly in the treatment of the phobic elements. Views concerning the participation of the husband vary from recommending full involvement at each stage of the treatment, to inclusion once the wife has begun to make progress, to a varied response depending on the dynamics of the case.

5. All of the authors view the prognosis as very good. For the most part, failures do not occur, are not reported, or are not discussed. Perhaps it is because of the high rate of success that so little attention is given to factors contributing to complete success, partial success, and failure in the treatment of vaginismus.

In the following sections three case histories will be reported. These range from complete success, to partial success, to failure. We will then discuss some of the patient and treatment characteristics that may contribute to such varying degrees of success in the treatment of vaginismus.

Case 1: Success

The first case involves a white couple in their mid-20s. The intake evaluation indicated a severe penetration phobia and vaginismus. She reported having been in psychotherapy for over a year, with little benefit concerning the vaginismus problem. Though the couple had an active sex life and she was able to have orgasms through masturbation and oral sex, intercourse had not occurred during the 4 years of their marriage. The specific reason for contacting the Sexual Counseling Service at Rutgers Medical School at this time was the wish to begin a family. A discussion of the treatment program follows, with a summary of major techniques and events presented in Table 1.

In the first session with a cotherapy team, the couple appeared to be friendly, nervous, highly motivated, and very affectionate toward one another. The wife was girlish, immature, and somewhat hysterical. The husband was more realistic in describing their problems and was protective (almost paternal) toward his wife. He tended to make decisions for both of them, and she instinctively turned to him for advice and decisions. At the time they came for help, she was unemployed and experienced acute gastrointestinal symptoms without any discernible physical cause. The husband believed it would be good for her to have a child to keep her occupied. Very early in the discussion, the wife centered attention on a new source of anxiety and a new obsession. Each was given a confidential questionnaire to be completed at home, and before mailing out her husband's questionnaire, she looked at the section on extramarital affairs and was distressed to read that her husband had had extramarital intercourse once, a number of years ago, with someone he met in a bar after drinking heavily. Though he had otherwise been devoted and faithful, her preoccupation with and distress over this event led to severe sleeping and eating difficulties. While there was some brief discussion of her background and the couple's marital relationship, her anxiety about what had happened and fear that her obsession would remain with her for the rest of her life dominated the initial session.

TABLE 1

Case 1: Treatment Sessions and Progress

Session	*Techniques employed and progress noted*
1–3	History-taking.
4–12 (6 joint sessions and 3 individual sessions with wife and female cotherapist)	Emphasis on relaxation, desensitization, self-control: Kegel exercises, progressive relaxation training, fantasy exercises, finger insertion, viewing of film of intercourse, interpretation of defensive nature of obsession, scheduling of gynecological exam. Husband is able to insert his finger into wife's vagina.
13–15	Discussion of gynecological exam, successful intercourse experiences, and issues of contraception and pregnancy.
16	Follow-up session. Intercourse and general sexual relationship are reported to be very satisfactory. Wife is pregnant.

The sex history was taken in an individual session with the female cotherapist. The wife again began with her current upset and obsession. She was having problems of diarrhea, vomiting, and general agitation. In terms of background, she was the elder of two sisters. Mother was described as insecure, dependent, and fearful of her husband. She would not get a job because menstrual difficulties led her to spend one week a month in bed. Father was described as a large, strict, strong man with a booming voice. Though never hit by him, she was terrified of him. Father and mother had to marry because mother was pregnant. The patient received a Catholic upbringing but attended public schools. Sex was not talked about at home, and what she learned about sex came from friends. At age 7, she and a friend were molested by the uncle of a neighborhood friend. She could not recall any of the details except that her father raged about it and threatened to tear the man apart. Growing up, she was generally fearful and felt that father put her down in everything she did. The patient's family was critical of "trashy" people in the neighborhood who were sexually active. Generally, the patient tried to please the parents, father in particular, and related to her husband in a similar fashion. At age 14, she inserted a tampon against her mother's advice and was so anxious about it that she had to go to a physician to have it removed. She reported that while sex (other than intercourse) with her husband was generally pleasurable, she had fears during oral sex that her husband's tongue would rip her apart. She felt that her vagina was not big enough and that his penis was huge.

The male cotherapist met with the husband individually to get some of the details of his background and to determine his perception of the problem. He was the eldest of three children, with a younger brother and sister. He was raised in a Catholic family and attended parochial school until high school. His parents were described in positive terms, and he reported feeling closer to his mother than his father. Sex was discussed openly in his home. He started masturbating at age 14 and reported no feelings of guilt about it. He had limited sexual experience prior to meeting his wife but reported no earlier difficulties. He contrasted his home and himself with his wife's family and her personality. He viewed his wife as overly attached to her father. When they were first married, she was reluctant to move away and defended her father strongly whenever anything critical was said about him. He saw his wife's father as "an animal" with enormous arms and hands who was idealized and feared by his daughter. She would never smoke in his presence or be seen having any physical contact with a boy, including holding hands. He described great love for his wife and wondered whether part of the problem was that he had never tried hard enough to have intercourse. He avoided this because of fears of hurting her, particularly in terms of tearing some of her muscles of her hymen. He was puzzled about why his wife had this problem, particularly since her unmarried sister was sexually active. He wondered whether perhaps her difficulties were related to her trauma at age 7, and noted that the girl she was with at the time, who also was molested, was now a lesbian.

The early sessions tended to focus on the wife's obsession with her husband's extramarital experience. Despite much support by the therapists and repeated reassurances by her husband that he had been otherwise faithful and did not feel that this would occur in the future, she continued to be preoccupied with this episode. This was about where things stood after three sessions with them as a couple and a session with each individually. At this time, it was decided to have her begin Kegel exercises and relaxation training. Additionally, some individual sessions with the wife and female cotherapist were scheduled to avoid going along with the possible defensive–avoidance aspects of her obsession while still giving her considerable support and reassurance.

The next five sessions consisted of three joint sessions and two individual sessions limited to the female cotherapist and wife. The results were mixed, but there was evidence of some progress. For example, she continued to do the Kegel exercises but often found it easier to tighten her pelvic muscle than to relax it. She followed the directions concerning the progressive relaxation training but continued to find that thoughts of her husband's sexual experience intruded. In the individual sessions, the therapist interpreted her obsession as a way of distracting herself so that she would not fully experience her fear concerning intercourse. In addition, there was discussion of her fears of pregnancy and of her almost complete dependence on her husband. While she hoped to have a family, the main initiative in this area was coming from her husband. She did not feel ready for the responsibility of parenthood and did not want to make the mistakes with her children that she felt had been made with her. No decision had been reached concerning contraceptive devices, so that this was another source of anxiety for her. The therapist helped her to recognize her right to determine when she was ready to be a mother and which kind of contraceptive device was preferable.

Three other developments of significance took place during these five sessions. First, after the therapist suggested that *she* try inserting her finger into her vagina, she asked her husband to do so. At first, she felt a tightening of her vaginal and abdominal muscles as he approached. The importance of relaxation, lubrication, some sexual arousal, and her control over when and how far his finger was inserted was emphasized. Again, her own responsibility in this area was stressed. Progress began to be made, and during one of these efforts she recalled the details of the traumatic molestation at age 7. The event involved the man putting his finger into her vagina and it hurting her. She felt relief about being able to recall this experience. The second significant incident involved the couple viewing the film *Free* demonstrating intercourse. Her response to the film was that it looked like fun, but she was not sure that she could feel that way herself. There was some discussion of her tendency to be pessimistic and to put herself down. The third development involved scheduling an appointment to see a gynecologist. The goal was to better familiarize both of them with her vagina and to discuss various contraceptive alternatives.

The 11th and 12th sessions consisted of one joint session and one individual session with the wife. During these sessions, she began to look more at her family's attitude toward sex and how often sex was negatively valued. Also, fantasy exercises were practiced in conjunction with relaxation. In the course of one fantasy exercise, she reported feeling aroused when imagining having intercourse with her husband while his friends watched. The fantasy exercises were also used to prepare and desensitize her for the upcoming gynecological examination. Finally, she received considerable support in handling pressures from her husband to move toward intercourse and to avoid using contraceptives.

She arrived for the 13th session excited to report that following the gynecological examination, her husband had been able to insert his penis almost completely. While not in pain, she told him to stop since she was afraid. When he withdrew, he noticed some blood and was reluctant to continue. She felt very aroused and wanted to resume their efforts, but her husband's anxieties prevailed. She reported being pleased but disappointed that her husband's response was not more enthusiastic. At this session, she also reported that the examination with the gynecologist had gone extremely well. The gynecologist, who had been contacted by the sex therapists and was sensitive to the patient's difficulties, took great care to explain everything that we would be doing. His supportive manner, perhaps in conjunction with the preparatory fantasy exercises, permitted a full pelvic examination, which had previously been impossible. The gynecologist reported that her hymen was still intact but that there was no need for him to perforate it since it would not be a barrier to intercourse.

In the course of the next two sessions, the couple reported striking progress. They succeeded in having intercourse three times and felt very optimistic. The husband ejaculated quickly the first time but reported no subsequent difficulties. While still somewhat apprehensive, she was delighted with her progress. They were not using any birth control devices, since he was against them and she was unable to assert herself in this area. For the most part, she remained quite dependent on him. She found herself occasionally bothered by the idea of her husband's extramarital experience, but the idea was slowly fading into the background. Since they were quite delighted with their progress and optimistic about the future, therapy was terminated after the 15th session, with a follow-up visit scheduled for a month later.

In the follow-up visit, they reported continued pleasure in their progress. They were enjoying intercourse approximately three times weekly. They were not using contraceptive devices and, while she hoped that she would not become pregnant immediately, she was receptive to the possibility. She volunteered to help other women with this problem. While clearly pleased with the outcome, both husband and wife were uncertain about the factors that were critical to the success of the treatment. A follow-up call 8 months later found the couple to be getting along well and the wife pregnant. She said she was pleased and was particularly happy that she had experienced no nausea or other physical discomfort in the first 5 months of her pregnancy. Their sexual relationship was described as excellent, though recently the husband had become concerned that the fetus might be injured during intercourse. She was not worried, and, in fact, was able to reassure him.

Case 2: Partial Success

The second case involves another white couple in their mid-20s, married for 5 years, with a child 2 years old, and the problem of vaginismus since marriage. A summary of the treatment program for this case is presented in Table 2.

The wife was first seen at a community mental health center. She came for treatment at the insistence of her husband, who threatened to leave unless she got some help with her problem. Although she resented his labeling her as the problem, and believed that his lack of warmth contributed to it, she felt pressure to comply with his ultimatum. She was seen for four sessions at the mental health center prior to being referred to the Sexual Counseling Service. These sessions focused mainly on educational matters and included an individual session with the husband. The wife appeared to have great difficulty in

TABLE 2

Case 2: Treatment Sessions and Progress

Session	Techniques employed and progress noted
1–3	History-taking.
4	Discussion of treatment plan; husband refuses participation.
5–12	Kegel exercises, genital self-examination, guided fantasy exercises with relaxation, her control over insertion of husband's finger and penis. Partial penetration is possible, but full intercourse is problematic.
13	Session with couple to discuss sensate focus.
14–16	Husband refuses sensate focus and further participation. Wife continues Kegel exercises, fantasy with overcorrection; dilators of increasing size are utilized. Success at intercourse is erratic. Patient feels that vaginismus problem is gone and that problem now is husband's attitude and differing sexual desires.
17	10-week follow-up. Situation remains unchanged. Wife is pleased with results; husband is moderately satisfied.

talking about herself and failed to complete a body-exploration assignment because she was reluctant to touch herself. The husband left his session early to attend a sporting event. He felt that it was his wife's problem, though he might "consider" joint therapy sessions if it would be of help.

At the Sexual Counseling Service, the treatment program was conducted by a male therapist. The husband behaved in a hostile and denigrating manner during the sessions, while the wife seemed frightened, timid, and depressed. The husband felt frustrated and disgusted and reported that she seemed indifferent to sex and influenced by "some religious thing." He felt angry at himself for putting up with her for so long, that he had "wasted" five years of his life and "was not about to waste five more." She cried during the initial session and felt embarrassed, mistreated, and misunderstood. Apparently, their child had been conceived through some semen entering her vagina during an attempt at intercourse without penetration. There were frequent arguments and little communication or understanding. He felt that there must be something wrong with her vagina, which he compared to a "nostril," and that the chances of therapy working were about zero. She was not sure what was wrong and gave therapy a 50–50 chance for success.

In the individual history-taking session with the wife, she had difficulty talking about herself and had to be repeatedly prompted for what little history could be obtained. She came from a close-knit, religious family of four. Her father had almost become a priest, and was described as quiet and generous. Her mother was strict and outspoken. Sex was not discussed at home. She went to public schools except for 2 years at parochical school which she described as uneventful. She had no premarital sex experience. She enjoyed kissing but not anything else and had relatively little contact with men prior to meeting her husband at age 16. She did not masturbate until after the birth of her child. She recalled having had gynecological exminations during her pregnancy but did not associate them with pain. She also recalled the doctor telling her that she was a virgin. She recalled little about childhood and could identify no significant experiences that might relate to her current difficulties. At present, she felt that sex was a chore and that she could do without intercourse, though she did enjoy closeness and physical warmth. She had no difficulty lubricating and had orgasms easily during occasional masturbation and foreplay. Her only explanation of her vaginismus problem was that someone must have told her that it hurts because she had such a fear of pain. In addition, she noted that while she could insert her small finger into her vagina, her husband's penis seemed "so big and I'm so small."

In the individual history-taking session with the husband, he reported that he was not sure that he still loved his wife, that she had humiliated him by taking him for a fool, and that now she was being a phony in being nice to him. He was the eldest child in a family of six. Father was an alcoholic who was nasty and punishing—"like a sergeant in the army." Mother was described as religious and a martyr type—"I'll slave so you can do this." Sex was taboo at home, and he recalled his father cutting a picture of a nude woman out of the newspaper so that the children would not see it. He started masturbating at age 15 but stopped, for unknown reasons, at age 16. He had little experience with girls and felt awkward in making sexual advances. He met his wife when he was 17 and felt attracted to her. They had little sexual contact prior to marriage, and the difficulties became apparent immediately after the wedding. He reported no erectile or ejaculatory difficulties. He felt that extramarital affairs were "allright" but had not had any. He felt that his wife should have become a nun and that the only things keeping him home were the child and the cost of separation and divorce. While ascribing the problem to his wife, he acknowledged some "hang-ups" and expressed a fear that intercourse might cause physical pain to his wife.

In addition to these evaluation sessions, therapy consisted of 13 sessions and a follow-up visit 10 weeks after termination. In the first conjoint therapy session, treatment possibilities were discussed. Despite an explanation of the involuntary nature of his wife's response, the husband continued to feel bitter and duped, suggesting that treatment proceed without him. There was discussion of the bind he was putting his wife in by giving her an ultimatum and then telling her that if she made progress it did not mean much because she only wanted his paycheck. He continued to be unwilling to become involved in the sensate-focus exercises, since he felt that they would be giving her what she wanted—physical closeness but no "sex." While distressed by his anger, the wife was willing to work independently on the problem.

The early sessions focused on the use of the Kegel exercises, genital self-examination, insertion of penile-shaped objects into her vagina, and fantasy exercises to reduce anxiety and associate pleasure with intercourse. Her initial efforts at the Kegel exercises were half-hearted, but once she was asked to keep a record of them, she did them faithfully and dutifully brought in her detailed record each week. She had a great deal of initial difficulty in examining her genitals with a mirror. She reported feeling tense and fearful of self-injury. She perceived her genitals as "ugly" and recalled her mother telling her that the body is ugly. The patient realized that she communicated the same message when she told her daughter that it is dirty to touch her genitals. She also had a great deal of difficulty inserting her finger into her vagina. She was tense, inserted her finger briefly, and quickly retracted it. If she rotated her finger at all, she experienced pain and found it much easier to rotate her body while leaving her finger stationary. Gradually, she began to feel more comfortable and reported experiencing an orgasm when removing her finger, but little real pleasure. In order to develop the association between having an object in the vagina and pleasurable sensations, she was asked to insert her finger into her vagina during masturbation. At this point, she began inserting a lubricated tampon. This was a new experience for her, since she had never used a tampon except once in adolescence, when she inserted one and then had difficulty removing it. Finally, desensitization was begun, in which she would imagine inserting her finger, a tampon, and then her husband's penis. She had difficulty in developing fantasies generally but especially with imagining inserting her husband's penis.

Despite the therapist's recommendation that they refrain from attempting intercourse, such efforts were continued at the husband's insistence. By the end of 4 weeks of exercise, he was able to achieve partial penetration and he felt that she was making some progress. This pleased her, but she continued to want him to ejaculate quickly and also continued to fear that his large penis could not entirely fit into her vagina.

During the next four sessions, she continued her Kegel and insertion exercises. She was surprised when she had an orgasm with her husband's finger inside her vagina. She continued her fantasy exercises in conjunction with relaxation both during the sessions and at home on her own. She found that her revulsion was diminishing. Efforts at intercourse, however, remained problematic. Only partial penetration was possible, and she would insert his penis at the point of ejaculation "to get it over with." She discussed the possibility of sensate-focus exercises with him, but he continued to refuse to participate.

The husband was invited to attend another session to maintain contact with him and to secure his perceptions of his wife's progress. He reported an improvement in their sexual relationship—his penis could now enter about halfway and on one occasion entered completely. The possibility of sensate-focus exercises was again recommended as a means of satisfying his wife's needs for greater warmth and communication. Despite the fact that he was only interested in full penetration and increasing the frequency of intercourse, he agreed to attempt these exercises. Since they felt that they had little privacy, there was discussion of putting their child to bed earlier so as to have more evening time to spend together.

The efforts at sensate focus proved to be a failure since the husband resisted all attempts to become involved. One positive outcome of this effort, however, was that it became apparent that they could arrange to be in bed together when their relationship was going well. During the final three sessions, she continued her Kegel and fantasy exercises and began using dilators of increasing size. In the fantasy exercises during the therapy sessions, an effort was made to overcorrect for her fears that her vagina was too small for her husband's large penis; that is, she was asked to imagine herself as possessing an almost cavernous vagina which could incorporate a penis without any difficulty whatsoever. She was gradually able to insert a dilator the size of a penis, though her efforts were erratic. Success at intercourse also remained erratic. At one point, she felt that her husband just wanted to "jump in" and she tightened up. He felt that she had no interest in sex and again threatened to leave. Just prior to the final session, they attempted intercourse with almost complete entry and with some pleasure for her. Interestingly enough, as she made more of an effort to initiate intercourse, she found that her husband was "tired" and not really interested in daily intercourse after all. At the time of termination, she felt that while full penetration was not routine, the vaginismus problem itself was gone and that what remained was the problem of his attitude and their differing sexual desires.

At the follow-up session 10 weeks later, the situation remained fairly stable. They reported having intercourse two to three times weekly, occasionally with full penetration and at times with approximately two-thirds penetration. He felt that this was satisfactory, although he desired sex more frequently and wanted to engage in oral sex. She felt that things were fine, although she still objected to oral sex. He continued to be denigrating toward her, comparing her unfavorably with a television actress, and she continued to tolerate his hostility and her own resentment. She reported to be quite pleased with treatment, while he was "somewhat satisfied." The wife was contacted by phone 6 months after termination and reported that the situation had remained relatively the same as at termination and, at times, better.

This case may be viewed as an illustration of partial success, both because of continued difficulties with consistent full penetration and because of the continued difficulties in working out a mutually satisfactory sexual and marital relationship.

Case 3: Failure

The third case represents a complete *treatment* failure. The patient, a 25-year-old black social worker, had been separated from her husband for 18 months. Although she and her husband had been married for 5 years, penetration had never been accomplished, and she remained a virgin. At the time she sought assistance, she was dating an older man who was gentle and caring toward her. She felt hopeless about her condition and feared his discovering that, although she had been married, she was still a virgin. It was under this impetus that she went to the local health maintenance organization and requested a hymenectomy. Since her fear of intercourse and penetration was so pervasive that she could not even tolerate a gynecological examination, they referred her for psychotherapy. Disappointed with their decision, she reluctantly called the Sexual Counseling Service.

During the first session, she displayed considerable anxiety and despair about her condition. She related with detachment to the female clinician and provided minimal information. The patient was the elder of two sisters and grew up in a lower-middle-class family. She described her mother as unaffectionate and cold, saying that her mother also had sexual difficulties. In fact, according to the patient, her mother also had vaginismus and had difficulty tolerating full penetration to the

present day. Her mother gave her and her sister repeated warnings
about maintaining one's virginity at all costs; the stigma of being an
unwed mother was posed as a constant threat. She began menses at age
12 without difficulty but was not told the facts of reproduction until she
was 14 years old. She recalled that her sex-education teacher warned
the girls that intercourse "would hurt" and that her girlfriends substantiated this message. The patient said that she always feared intercourse, expecting to experience great pain.

She met her husband-to-be when she was a freshman in college.
He was the first person she dated, and she went out with him for 4
years until their marriage. Although her husband dropped out and she
had academic difficulties, she continued and graduated from college.
Both her husband and his parents resented the fact that she succeeded
in school while he did not. Although the couple attempted sex on
numerous occasions, it was always unsuccessful. She enjoyed foreplay
and affectionate closeness but panicked whenever he attempted penetration. Eventually, he gave up trying. The marriage was punctuated by
a host of difficulties, both financial and interpersonal, and her husband
alternated between anger at her and depression. It was he who finally
decided to leave the marriage, which he did without much warning. She
reacted to her husband's departure with considerable despondency,
feeling responsible for the marital breakup.

During a second history-taking session, she reported that she had
attempted masturbation only a few times during her adolescence. She
did this by rubbing a blanket between her legs but felt so guilty that she
ceased. She also reported that on the few occasions when she went for
a gynecological examination, she became so anxious that she broke
into tears and would not allow an internal examination. In view of her
enormous anxiety, a relaxation program was started. She was instructed in the method of progressive relaxation and asked to practice
it twice daily. Further, she was told that following her relaxation exercises, she should take a hand mirror and visually explore her genitals.

On the third session, she reported that she felt "silly" doing the
relaxation exercises and had not practiced them. She also reported
feeling "hopeless" about overcoming her problem. She had seen her
boyfriend several times during the week and, although she enjoyed his
company, she refrained from becoming physically involved with him
since she could not bear the humiliation of his discovering that she was
a virgin. In order to secure his cooperation and support for the rest of
treatment, the therapist advised that the boyfriend be told directly of
the patient's fears of intercourse. She refused, saying that it was "impossible." The rationale of practicing self-stimulation was explained to

her, and it was emphasized that with her self-stimulation exercises, she would have total control over her body and need continue only as far as she felt comfortable. The various myths and fallacies regarding masturbation were discussed, and she agreed to experiment with tactual exploration at home.

She returned the following week, saying that she could not complete the assignment. She had, however, become involved in "necking" with her boyfriend and felt more relaxed with him. She again expressed concern about going further, since he would *then* discover that she was a married virgin. In light of her refusal to share her sexual concerns with him, and her wish that she might have a hymenectomy, the pros and cons of such a procedure were explored. The therapist agreed to speak with her gynecologist and to recommend surgical removal of the hymen. The patient was told to contact her gynecologist directly for an appointment. She refrained from doing so for 2 weeks following the referral and, when she did, the doctor said that it was not necessary. Following that visit, she was successful in inserting her small finger into her vagina.

During the fifth session, she reported this success, but expressed discouragement about treatment. She did not view her ability to insert her finger into her vagina as indicative of improvement, had ceased masturbating, and had not told her boyfriend of her sexual fears. Further, she had attempted intercourse with him unsuccessfully and her panic about penetration was fully reinstated. The therapist pointed out to her that she was sabotaging her treatment program by not following therapeutic instructions—she did not practice relaxation or masturbation at home but went ahead with an activity that the therapist had explicitly told her she was not ready to attempt. The patient agreed, saying that she had given up most activities soon after she started, and rationalized her lack of commitment to treatment by saying, "It's very difficult." She asked whether hypnosis might be used to overcome her problem. The therapist pointed out that her wish to have the problem hypnotized away might reflect her unwillingness to take responsibility for touching her own body. She reluctantly agreed with this interpretation.

The patient missed the next two sessions and, when she reappeared, said that she had not made any progress. Her tone indicated that she blamed the therapist for this. She felt that the therapist, who was white, failed to understand her cultural inhibitions against sexual activities such as masturbation or oral sex, and said that she was worried about the confidentiality of her sessions. She was reassured on the latter point, and the session was devoted to working on the transfer-

ence issues. At the end of the session, she was invited to join a women's sexual-enhancement group as an adjunct to her treatment. She
refused, saying that she could not discuss her problems in a group. The
therapist urged her to continue the relaxation exercises, provided reassurance that she was not alone in her problem, and indicated that her
problem could be resolved if she would commit herself to the treatment
effort. Since she was still dating her boyfriend, the possibility of using
his penis as a substitute for her own fingers was discussed. She indicated that she preferred this to masturbation and was instructed to
guide his penis around her clitoris and labia minora as a means of erotic
arousal.

She returned to the next (seventh) session and indicated that she
did not want to continue treatment. She had not followed through on
any of the suggestions from the previous sessions and felt that improvement was hopeless. Termination was mutually agreed upon, with
an open invitation to recontact the Sexual Counseling Service in the
future.

Although the formal therapy effort was a total *treatment* failure,
the patient was, in fact, successful in resolving the vaginismus problem! Ten months after treatment had been terminated, the patient was
contacted as part of a standard follow-up from the Sexual Counseling
Service. The patient indicated that she had overcome the problem with
the assistance of her boyfriend 4 months after therapy had been terminated. She eventually told him that she was a virgin, and "much to my
surprise, just as you predicted, he did not view it as a major problem."
Together, they continued penetration efforts and currently were enjoying intercourse about four times weekly without difficulty. When asked
what had enabled her to finally overcome her phobia, she replied, "I
wanted to love him in a total and complete way." She indicated that
she felt secure and cared for in the relationship and had finally recov-
ered from her attachment to and depression over the loss of her first
husband. She added that she "had no idea" of why she could "let it
happen within this relationship" and not in her first. The patient still
does not masturbate ("I don't need to and don't care to"), although she
now finds masturbation acceptable for others.

Discussion

We shall now return to some of the issues raised in the Introduction
and review them in light of these three case illustrations as well as
observations from other cases. In proceeding with this discussion, it
may be useful to focus on three questions:

1. What are these women and their partners like?
2. What factors seem to be important in the etiology of vaginismus?
3. What factors play a role in the success or failure of treatment?

The Women and Their Partners

Beyond the common symptomatology, it is clear that there is great diversity among these women and their relationships to their partners. Even in terms of the problem itself, one sees considerable heterogeneity. A pelvic examination is possible with some and not with others; in the second case, the woman had even experienced the birth of a child.[1] Despite this experience, she viewed her vagina as too small for her husband's penis and, until therapeutic intervention, found intercourse impossible because of the tightening of her vaginal muscles. The three cases presented also illustrate the wide diversity of other aspects of the sexual experience. In the first case, the couple was able to engage in and enjoy a wide variety of sexual practices other than intercourse. This was not true for the other two cases. Two of the women were able to experience arousal and orgasm with little difficulty, whereas the third was quite sexually inhibited.

TABLE 3

Patient Characteristics

Case	Age (yr)	Religion	Years married	Educational level	Previous psychotherapy	Referral source
1	Wife: 24	Roman Catholic	4	High school graduate	18 mo individual psychotherapy (wife)	Gynecologist
	Husband: 25	Roman Catholic		High school graduate		
2	Wife: 25	Roman Catholic	5	High school graduate	None	Social worker
	Husband: 25	Methodist		High school graduate	None	
3	Wife: 25	Episcopalian	3[a]	High school graduate	None	Gynecologist

[a] Patient had been divorced for 18 months when seen for treatment.

Table 3 presents relevant patient characteristics. In addition, one can note the strong dependency that existed in the first two women and that is frequently seen in others. Both women preferred to stay at home and both relied heavily on their husbands and/or parents to make decisions. While almost nothing is known about the husband in the third case, the husbands in the first two cases provide some interesting contrasts. Both husbands were somewhat naive sexually, though neither had a specific sexual dysfunction. Both husbands showed a fear of injuring or causing pain to their wives and demonstrated a remarkable tolerance for abstinence from intercourse, though each responded quite differently to the wife's difficulty and efforts at change. Fertel (1977) has commented on the observation that husbands of "virgin wives" are often overly considerate, weak, and passive–dependent. Their lack of persistence in insisting that their spouse attempt to overcome the phobic avoidance of intercourse is said to express their own fears abut the aggressiveness of sex and serves as an unconscious collusion in maintaining the problem. While there is some evidence to support such an interpretation in the first two cases (e.g., the sexual naiveté and fears of injury to the spouse), they also were quite different in their individual histories and reported attitudes toward sex.

In sum, amid some similarities is striking diversity in the nature of the women, the nature of their husbands, and the relationships between them.

Factors Important in the Etiology of Vaginismus
The etiology of vaginismus remains a perplexing question. The literature reports a wide variety of factors contributing to vaginismus, including past sexual trauma, psychological and social factors in the family of origin, physical pain (dyspareunia), and conditions in the present such as the partner's impotence or the woman's hostility toward her partner. A specific childhood sexual trauma was found only in the first case, in which the wife was molested by a man at age 7. From her description, the trauma was at least equally a result of her father's reponse to the event as it was a result of the event itself.

Religious orthodoxy was not a consistent theme in these three cases, though in each case there was considerable evidence that sex was treated as a taboo area. More striking than religious orthodoxy were the rigid and restrictive attitudes toward sex in all three families of origin. The disgrace and dishonor of an out-of-wedlock pregnancy was an important theme. Perhaps of even greater significance was the fact that all three women reported that their mothers were sexually anxious and inhibited. While such a pattern appears striking, it is equally obvious that many women with such backgrounds do not develop this problem. Indeed, the ability of the sisters in all three cases to have intercourse clearly indicates that other factors must also be involved.

One problem in understanding the etiological factors involved in cases of vaginismus seen in sex therapy is the brevity of treatment and minimal detail obtained concerning varied aspects of the individual's psychological functioning. As in behavior therapy in general, sex therapy tends to be problem-centered and pragmatic. Therefore, much of the richness of detail obtained in long-term, dynamic psychotherapy is not available for consideration. For example, in the cases presented, little is known about the women's feelings toward their bodies other than their difficulty in touching and examining their genitals. This can be contrasted with the material gained from two other patients seen in individual psychotherapy. Both experienced frequent situational vaginismus and inhibition in touching and examining their genitals. Beyond this, however, there was considerable additional material indicating strong negative feelings, at times including revulsion, toward their vaginas. One patient talked of feeling that she was damaged, incomplete, and had a hollow, empty space inside her. Both reported fantasies of the vagina functioning similar to a mouth and also reported early feeding difficulties in which they would shut their mouths tight and prevent feeding as a means of expressing rage and gaining control.

To summarize, the cases presented fit with the impressions of other clinicians that many factors play a role in the development of vaginismus and that no single etiological pattern emerges as definitive. Thus, the etiology of vaginismus remains somewhat of a mystery, fortunately one that is not necessary to solve to be of help to most patients with this sexual dysfunction.

Factors Influencing the Course of Treatment

In this section, we come to what is perhaps the most critical concern of this chapter: an explanation for the varying degrees of success among the three cases. In accounting for the differences, we can consider aspects of the patients such as motivation to change, quality of the partner relationship, and general sexual comfort, as well as relationship factors. Discussion of each of these variables follows. A summary of these factors in relation to each of the patients is presented in Table 4.

All of the women displayed considerable ambivalence about confronting their problem and, as has been noted, each came to treatment because of some external pressure. Of the three, the first woman stood to gain the most from achieving successful intercourse. She enjoyed a stable, loving relationship with her husband, found other sexual activi-

TABLE 4

Patient Characteristics Relevant to Treatment Progress

Case	Marital satisfaction (Locke–Wallace score)[a]	Ability to masturbate to orgasm	Sexual repertoire Non-coital sex with partner	Previous trauma	Other symptoms	Completion of assignments	Treatment outcome
1	Wife: 127 Husband: 116	Yes	Oral–genital, mutual masturbation	Yes	Gastro-intestinal, obsession	High	Success
2	Wife: 97 Husband: 63	Yes	Mutual masturbation	No	Headaches, depression	Moderate	Partial success
3	Divorced	No	Non-genital caressing	No	Depression	Very low	Failure

[a] High score = marital satisfaction.

ties enjoyable, and, while experiencing somewhat conflicting feelings, did wish to become a mother. In the second case, sex generally was devalued, and she found the rewards of motherhood mixed. In the last case, there was little motivation to conquer the vaginismus throughout her marriage, and she entered treatment more out of humiliation at being a divorced virgin wife than out of a wish to enjoy sexual or interpersonal intimacy.

Motivation to change clearly involves both the quality of the relationship with the partner and more general potential for meaningful interpersonal relationships. In the three cases, there appears to be a positive relationship between degree of improvement, marital satisfaction, and generally satisfactory interpersonal relationships. For example, on the Locke–Wallace Marital Adjustment Test (Locke & Wallace, 1959), the husband and wife in the first case had scores of 116 and 127, respectively, while the corresponding scores for the second case were 63 and 97 (low score = high dissatisfaction). The first couple enjoyed an affectionate and mutually caring relationship (albeit one of dependency on her part and overprotectiveness on his), whereas the second couple was locked into a hostile, withholding marriage. The husband's refusal to attempt the sensate-focus exercises because they would give his wife what she desired is indicative of the hostility he expressed toward, and perhaps engendered from, his wife. Although the third woman had a caring male friend, she was fearful of intimacy generally and during therapy refused even to tell him of the treatment effort. Since she was still in the early phases of her relationship with her boyfriend, she still felt distrustful and dubious about making a complete therapeutic commitment.

Finally, in relation to patient characteristics, let us consider general sexual comfort. The three cases presented suggest that the extent to which the vaginismus is part of a more generalized sexual inhibition is relevant for predicting the outcome of treatment. In the first two cases, both women were able to masturbate to orgasm and were orgasmic with partner stimulation as well. The third woman, on the other hand, was inhibited sexually in all respects. Comparing the first two women, it is clear that the first was able to engage in a greater variety of sexual practices with greater pleasure. These varying degrees of general sexual comfort and discomfort were important not only because they were associated with other aspects of the partner relationship but also because they were related to the ease with which the patient could undertake the various assigned exercises.

Turning to the treatment process itself, the cases presented would appear to support the view that the deconditioning of the reflexive vaginal response is an important therapeutic ingredient. In the first case, dilators were not used, but there were successful efforts on the part of the husband to insert his finger into his wife's vagina. Additionally, the skillful handling of the gynecological examination was followed by a significant improvement in tolerating penetration.[2] The relaxation training and fantasy exercises also appeared to be critical ingredients in the successful treatment of this case, which began with such difficulty. In the second case, the gradual insertion into the vagina of objects of increasing size under relaxing conditions and the supplementary use of fantasy were also instrumental in treatment success. In this case, the Kegel exercises seemed useful in directing the patient's attention to self-control and in heightening her awareness of bodily sensations. In both the first and second cases, the observation of films and encouragement of fantasy appeared to serve a permission-giving and guilt-reducing function.

While these treatment techniques clearly are important, they occur in the context of a patient–therapist relationship. All of the procedures emphasized above require the active cooperation of the patient. The patient's attitudes toward herself and her difficulty, toward her partner, and toward the therapist thus become important aspects of the treatment. In other words, in sex therapy we must be sensitive to the issues of transference and resistance. In short-term therapy, the therapist relies on the positive feelings of the patient to give weight and credence to the educational and prescriptive program and to overcome minor resistances. These positive feelings appeared to be present in the first two cases but absent in the third.

In all three cases, there was evidence of resistance to treatment and change. The nature of the resistance and the extent to which it interfered with treatment varied. In the first case, resistance primarily took the form of psychosomatic symptoms and the obsession with the one occasion of marital infidelity. In the second case, there were periodic failures to comply with homework exercises. In the third case, resistance took a general form of rebellion and aggressive withdrawal—appointments were missed, exercises were skipped, and intercourse was attempted despite the therapist's advice. The basis for the resistance in terms of the avoidance of anxiety and maintenance of the status quo was apparent in all three cases. What appeared to be different were the supportive factors that would permit the overcoming of the resistance. We are speaking here of the positive feelings toward the therapist and the relationship factors operating to increase motivation for change. In the third case, the therapist was, perhaps, insufficiently understanding of the patient's need to move more slowly and to gain greater trust in her relationship with her boyfriend before complying with therapeutic instructions. Although her accusations that the therapist failed to accept her sociocultural inhibitions against masturbation may be seen, in part, as a resistance against assuming responsibility for her sexual satisfaction, they also underscore the need for the therapist to be fully cognizant of the patient's fears and worries about "giving up" a dysfunction. In retrospect, it seems obvious that both the patient's distrust of "psychotherapy" from the professional establishment and her lack of security in her relationship with her new boyfriend contributed to the treatment failure.

We have come full circle in discussing the factors contributing to varying degrees of success in the treatment of vaginismus. These factors involve motivational inducements for change coming from within the person and from the surrounding interpersonal environment, as well as the quality of the alliance that is formed with the therapist and the ways in which resistances are met and handled. While related to one another, they form distinctive elements that contribute toward the final outcome.

Conclusion

Most therapists report good success in treating vaginismus. For the woman who has succeeded in overcoming her anxieties, there is an affirmation of herself as an adult woman, relief from long-standing feelings of shame, and freedom to decide on motherhood. Where the marital relationship is good, both partners are jubilant that they no longer have a shameful secret that makes them seem different from others. It would appear, however, that sex therapy is not always completely successful in the treatment of vaginismus and that many cases never come to the attention of sex therapists. As we have seen, partial success may occur in some cases and complete failure in others. We have tried to understand the reasons for these varying degrees of success, and more work remains to be done in this area. Beyond this are the cases in which improvement in the partner with the presenting problem is followed by the development of a problem in the spouse. There have been reports of such developments, but they did not occur in the two successful cases presented, and the frequency with which they do occur remains to be determined. Finally, while discussion has focused on the treatment of primary vaginismus in what have been called "virgin wives," they may represent only a small proportion of the population with difficulties. While vaginismus as generally seen in sex therapy may be a relatively rare phenomenon, many more women report having had similar experiences during periods of stress and marital difficulty. When viewed in this broader context, vaginismus may be found to be much more common than previously reported in the literature.

NOTES

1. Other cases of such impregnation with only shallow penetration have been reported in relation to the problem of vaginismus (Fertel, 1977).
2. In addition to a preliminary gynecological examination being essential, at times, such a visit during treatment can be useful in desensitizing patient anxieties, in increasing patient sophistication regarding the anatomy of the vagina, and in remedying any medical problem that may have developed during the course of treatment (e.g., infection).

References

Ellison, C. Vaginismus. *Medical Aspects of Human Sexuality*, 1972, *8*, 34–54.

Fenichel, O. *The psychoanalytic theory of neurosis*. New York: W. W. Norton & Co., 1945.

Fertel, N. Vaginismus: A review. *Journal of Sex and Marital Therapy*, 1977, *3*, 113–121.

Fuchs, K., Hoch, Z., Paldi, E., Abramovici, H., Brandes, J. M., Timor-Tritsch, I., & Kleinhaus, M. Hypnodesensitization therapy of vaginismus: *In vitro* and *in vivo* methods. *International Journal of Clinical and Experimental Hypnosis*, 1973, *21*, 144–156.

Kaplan, H. S. *The new sex therapy*. New York: Brunner/Mazel, 1974.

Locke, H. J., & Wallace, K. M. Short marital adjustment and prediction tests: Their reliability and validity. *Marriage and Family Living*, 1959, *21*, 251–255.

LoPiccolo, J., & LoPiccolo, L. (Eds.). *Handbook of sex therapy*. New York: Plenum Press, 1978.

Masters, W. H., & Johnson, V. E. *Human sexual inadequacy*. Boston: Little, Brown & Co., 1970.

Treatment of Male Sexual Disorders

III

Introduction: Treatment of Male Sexual Disorders

It is the view of some, perhaps many, that historically men have had things "pretty good" sexually. Comparisons are made with women indicating that men traditionally have been permitted greater sexual freedom and generally have been perceived to be more entitled to sexual pleasure. While such details are perhaps useful in comparing the plight of men and women, they may interfere with a more complete understanding of male sexual functioning. First, such comparisons may suggest that men have not had sexual problems, whereas obviously this is not the case. The fact that the preponderance of transvestites are male to female, and that the majority of sexual deviants and sexual offenders are male, should give pause to those who would envy the situation of men relative to women. Second, such comparisons may have in them an implicit assumption that the sexual experiences and pleasures of the male somehow are independent of the feelings of his partner. While social and individual values and preferences enter in here, one could argue that limitations in the female's sexual freedom and pleasure potentially detract from the male's sexual freedom and pleasure. In sum, rather than asking who has had it better (or worse!), perhaps we should be asking about the effects of biological changes and social mores on the sexual lives of both men and women.

Since accurate comparative statistics are difficult to obtain, it is hard to know whether men in current Western society experience greater or less sexual difficulty than men in past times or in other societies. As was noted in the introductory chapter, what professionals define as illness, what people themselves define as illness, and the license for admitting illness and seeking treatment vary so much over time and across cultures that meaningful comparisons are difficult, if not impossible. Whatever the record of the past, the record of the present indicates that many men suffer either from some specific sexual dysfunction or from some inhibition in sexual enjoyment and pleasure. If being told "Keep your legs crossed" as a little girl set the stage for damaging effects on female sexuality, being told that one's masculinity depended on "scoring" was hardly much better for male sexuality. The double standard presented many problems for women, but the associated sexual attitude also presented problems for men who had to live with a division between "good girls" and "bad girls," or the old Madonna–prostitute complex. The attitudes toward sex of the past generation, and even the present generation, have been broadly damaging to members of both sexes. While changes in societal attitudes have, for the most part, been beneficial, serious problems remain, and some changes have been mixed blessings.

For now, then, we are left with an appreciation of some of the consequences of these problems: the disruption of sexual functioning and sexual enjoyment and the efforts of sex therapists to remedy the situation. Probably the single greatest increase in sexual anxiety for the male concerns his "ability to perform" and satisfy his partner. This "performance anxiety" can be expressed in various aspects of the sexual process and becomes manifest in the problems of premature ejaculation, erectile dysfunction, and retarded ejaculation. While performance anxiety need not be the only, or even the major, psychological aspect of these dysfunctions, it almost invariably enters in. Males are becoming increasingly interested in what excites women, not just in terms of giving women greater pleasure but also in terms of "performing" better. In addition to these anxieties, other concerns about aggression, control, and intimacy can and do interfere with trouble-free sexual functioning.

As in the case of the treatment of female sexual dysfunctions, the treatment of male sexual dysfunctions relies on the efficacy of a limited number of techniques. While in some cases the treatment is straightforward, and the therapist and patient can look forward to success with relative assurance, in many cases the problem is more complicated, and the therapist must use considerable judgment concerning which techniques to use, the rate at which to proceed, and the additional relationship factors that need to be considered as part of the treatment. The sensitivity of sexual functioning to such a wide array of biological and psychological factors is what so often makes sex therapy both fascinating and difficult.

The chapters that follow cover the major male sexual difficulties that come to the attention of sex therapists. While not all therapeutic approaches are represented, the chapters cover a range of orientations to the understanding and treatment of male sexual dysfunctions. As with the chapters on female sexual dysfunctions, the psychoanalytic view is not represented because the approach is sub-stantially altered in the context of sex therapy. On the other hand, it should be noted that many dynamically oriented therapists treat sexual dysfunctions within the context of sex therapy and, as em-phasized by Kaplan, emphasize insight as an adjunct to the basic sex therapy techniques. Finally, the chapters give a clear picture of the many paths that therapy can take and the difficult questions concerning success and failure faced by all sex therapists.

7

Treatment of Premature Ejaculation

MICHAEL A. PERELMAN

Of the major male sexual dysfunctions, premature or early ejaculation ranks with erectile disorders as the most common. Since there is a strong subjective component in the assessment of premature ejaculation, it presents diagnostic problems and issues not unrelated to those concerning orgasmic dysfunctions in women. Interestingly enough, it appears that one consequence of the increased emphasis on orgasms in women has been an inclination on the part of some women to label their partners as "premature" if they themselves require extensive penile thrusting in order to achieve orgasm during intercourse or if they regard penile stimulation as the only acceptable source of genital stimulation. As norms and sexual expectations change, there are new kinds of performance pressures with consequent changes in what is viewed as a sexual problem.

Fortunately, there exists a variety of effective treatment programs. While Masters and Johnson rely on the cooperation of the partners to go through sensate-focus and "squeeze" exercises, other approaches emphasize masturbation training in developing ejaculatory control. Still other approaches emphasize rewriting the couple's sexual script so that ejaculation is not considered to be the end of the sexual experience, but rather a point along the way. Such an approach can be particularly effective with young males in whom the refractory period between ejaculations is relatively brief. However, it can be equally effective with older males who are able to enjoy other methods of stimulation with their partners. In sum, effective treatment programs include working with the couple or the individual in developing a mutually satisfying sexual script as well as working on the early ejaculation problem itself.

Following the discovery of short-term directive treatment approaches to achieving ejaculatory control, a number of investigators reported success in treating men in groups. In this chapter, Perelman reviews the variety of approaches employed in the treatment of premature ejaculation and the relative efficacy of each. He describes his own method of time-limited group treatment, citing cases involving men seen in both male-only groups and couples groups. Perelman emphasizes that despite the specific techniques employed, successful treatment inevitably involves the skillful handling of resistance to treatment. Finally, he raises this important question: When must mari-

199

tal or relationship therapy take precedence over sex therapy if treatment is to be effective?

Michael A. Perelman is Director of Research at the Human Sexuality Program, Payne Whitney Clinic, Cornell–New York Hospital Medical Center. He is Chief of Training at the Institute for Behavior Therapy, and is engaged in the private practice of sex therapy in New York City.

———————

This chapter will review the sex therapy of premature ejaculation (PE). The author's model for sex therapy has been adapted from Kaplan (Kaplan & Perelman, 1979), but treatment is conceptualized within a cognitive-behavioral framework. Cognitive-behavioral theory is a newly emerging therapeutic orientation, derived from social learning theory (Bandura, 1969). Many of the general principles have been explicated elsewhere (Mahoney, 1974; Meichenbaum, 1977). Suffice it to say, these approaches are directive and primarily address problems as they exist in current life situations. Treatment procedures interact at all spheres of an individual's functioning, that is, the cognitive, behavioral, and emotional modalities.

Definition and Diagnosis

There is considerable disagreement about the criteria used to diagnose PE (ejaculatio praecox) when a man does not ejaculate ante portal or immediately upon intromission. Labeling a male as "premature" has depended not only on the length of coitus, but also on the sexual attitudes of both partners, which vary with sociocultural background. Earlier researchers attempted to quantify the criterion for defining PE in terms of time (ranging from 30 seconds to 2 minutes) or number of thrusts. Recently, and perhaps in response to growing consciousness concerning female sexuality, prematurity was defined in terms of female-partner requirements. Masters and Johnson (1970) advocated this approach and defined a premature ejaculator as a man who cannot delay his ejaculatory reflex for sufficient time during intercourse to satisfy a responsive partner during 50% of their coital experiences. Although this criterion appeared to be a useful innovation, the variability of orgasmic speed and ability among women severely limits its utility. The Masters and Johnson view can be contrasted with Kinsey (Kinsey, Pomeroy, & Martin, 1948), who viewed rapid ejaculation as a superior biological response, "however inconvenient and unfortunate his qualities may be from the standpoint of his wife" (p. 580).

The critical factor in PE is the lack of a learned ability to delay orgasm, once sexually aroused, regardless of time. Control, however, exists when a man is able to discriminate high levels of arousal or premonitory sensations (PS) from ejaculatory inevitability (EI) and can respond accordingly, depending on whether he wishes to delay or experience his orgasm. Tactics vary among individuals, but often include relaxation, slowing down, or changing position. While men with the problem of PE vary in many characteristics, a single learning deficit does characterize them all to some extent. They are men who have not learned to discriminate adequately varying levels of sexual arousal and subsequently are unable to act in order to delay their orgasm. A few are so "out of touch" that orgasm is almost complete before they are cognizant of its occurrence. Most often, these men only become aware of impending ejaculation during emission, when delaying tactics are ineffective. The treatment of PE must then incorporate concepts of recognition of sensation and subsequent mind/body adjustments in order to delay orgasm.

Regardless of the definition used, researchers agree that PE is a prevalent and serious problem. Men who are premature ejaculators question their own masculinity and often have a reduced sense of self-worth. Their sexual partners typically feel angry and "used," leading them to seek professional guidance, to seek another lover, or to avoid sex. Avoidance of sex is particularly deleterious, since it tends to exacerbate the PE. Couples might try other forms of sexual stimulation but often report viewing them as second best. Concern over PE can cause partners to adopt a "spectator role" during sex, which increases the likelihood of PE and occasionally causes the male to develop secondary impotence (Masters & Johnson, 1970). In fact, at one time PE was labeled impotence, although the mechanisms of ejaculation and erection are physiologically distinct.

Causes of PE

As indicated, the inability to tolerate high levels of arousal without rapid ejaculation characterizes the psychophysiological syndrome of premature ejaculation. The degree to which physical as opposed to psychological factors are involved in maintaining the disorder has not yet been established. There is some preliminary laboratory evidence that premature ejaculators orgasm at a lower level of sexual arousal than do other men (Spiess, 1977). The implications of this research for coital duration time capacity or a physiological predisposition to prematurity require further investigation.

Although PE generally has been regarded as having psychological causes, there are some rare instances in which it is caused by disease. Oliven (1974) has presented a good general review of organic causes of male potency disorders. For instance, in the elderly, disorganization of the ejaculatory response can by symptomatic of diffuse arteriosclerosis. Shapiro (1943) described a 2% incidence of abnormal shortness of the preputial frenulum, which has been confirmed by surgical cure.

Whereas in the cases cited above both masturbation and intercourse are affected, in the vast majority of cases the problem is specific to coitus, and it is this fact that gives testimony to the importance of psychological factors. Psychoanalytic literature on PE primarily concerned itself with theoretical discussions about the dynamics of PE, rather than its treatment. Authors discussed the prevailing psychosexual concepts of their time, beginning with Abraham's (1917/1949) view that PE was a reproduction of childhood enuresis. Shapiro (1943), who reviewed 1130 cases of premature ejaculation, found only 8% to have a childhood history of enuresis. Generally, the analysts postulated that PE was an expression of unconscious conflicts toward women which symbolically defiled and denied pleasure to them. Regarding the numerous negative personality attributes postulated by the analysts about the premature ejaculator, no significant correlation between PE and psychopathology, degree of sexual conflict, marital disharmony, or socioeconomic level seems to exist. The diversity found among premature ejaculators defies classification beyond the PE itself. In fact, clinical experience suggests that some loving men were unnecessarily burdened by guilt subsequent to their reading psychoanalytic explanations of their disorder.

The systems approach views PE as a tool used to play out a couple's power struggle. Marital therapy, however, seems to have minimal effect upon this symptom, even if considerable improvement in the relationship is obtained. Early behavior therapists viewed anxiety surrounding sexual functioning as the primary cause of the dysfunction. However, efforts to treat the dysfunction by reducing anxiety through relaxation strategies, systematic desensitization (SD), and assertiveness training have generally led to negative results (Lazarus, 1971, pp. 141–162). This lack of success in improving ejaculatory control with techniques which have been highly effective in ameliorating anxiety generally may have two explanations. First, when anxiety is the consequence of PE rather than its antecedent, techniques designed to ameliorate the anxiety will be ineffective (Lazarus, 1973). Second, although SD can diminish the anxiety that interferes with the patient's

(1975) and Perelman (1976), while also preferring the original Semans approach, emphasize the benefit of first teaching the procedure during masturbation.

While all researchers agree about the success of the Semans approach, theoretical differences persist as to why it works. Semans (1956) postulated that the premature ejaculator's reflex mechanism was "abnormally rapid" and felt that this treatment altered the neuromuscular response mechanism. Masters and Johnson (1970) felt that their treatment diminished performance anxiety by providing a context in which gradual improvement in control, not speed, is being reinforced. In this manner, the patient is conditioned to tolerate extensive stimulation without immediate ejaculation. Kaplan felt that "anxiety about sexual expression" distracted the man from perceiving PS, concluding: "Treatment of premature ejaculation is then based on the assumption that sensory feedback of sensations of preorgastic sexual arousal will result in ejaculatory continence, without necessitating any special effort on the patient's part to control orgasm" (1974, p. 302). This erroneously implies that the very experience of focusing on sensations is sufficient to provide control. It is necessary, but not sufficient.

A number of factors, both immediate and remote, may combine to interfere with a man learning to identify and respond to his PS (Perelman, 1976). Over time, such proprioceptive insensitivity becomes conditioned, regardless of initial antecedents. Treatment teaches both "focusing in" and body adjustment. Whereas initially, a man is required to stop completely, with practice only subtle body maneuvers become necessary (Perelman, 1976). I would concur with Zilbergeld's (1978) assessment that all men make such adjustments during lovemaking, whether conscious or not. Typically, such reactions become automatic in much the same manner that other complex fine motor skills are learned, for example, driving an automobile. Therefore, men successfully treated for PE would be indistinguishable from normals in their sexual demeanor.

A Cognitive-Behavioral Model for Sex Therapy

This chapter emphasizes the utility of a cognitive-behavioral perspective in the treatment of sexual disorders generally and the treatment of PE specifically. Cognitive-behavioral theory permits both the conceptualization of strategies for implementing change techniques as well as a means of understanding and managing resistance. Resistance is used here to indicate any thought, feeling, or behavior which interferes with the primary objective of symptomatic improvement.

The primary objective of sex therapy basically is limited to the relief of the sexual symptom. The cognitive-behavioral sex therapist intervenes *directly* to modify the immediate obstacles to successful sexual functioning. The immediate obstacles are initially presumed to be functionally autonomous of possible remote causes of the dysfunction. While appreciating the existence of remote obstacles, they are explored therapeutically only as they are proven to be the next line of defense maintaining the dysfunction. In this manner, cognitive-behavioral sex therapy is distinguished from more global forms of therapy such as psychoanalysis or rational-emotive therapy (RET). The therapist provides a permissive, educative environment and prescribes sexual and communication tasks which the patients conduct at home. These tasks provide new sexual experiences in small discrete steps so that anxiety is minimized and new learning can occur. This aspect of treatment is essentially education and counseling and sometimes, although increasingly less often, is a sufficient treatment in and of itself.

More often, resistance is encountered during the course of treatment. It is the management of resistance that distinguishes therapy from counseling and education. All sex therapy, at some point, requires patients to confront the secondary gains they may derive from their difficulties and to tolerate uncomfortable levels of anxiety necessary for change. The duration of therapy is functionally related to the number of intermediate and remote obstacles encountered in treatment.

Sex therapy, in fact, is somewhat uniquely standardized, with most therapists using similar exercises as the key ingredient to enhancing the patient's functioning. The similarities of the immediate obstacles to success both between and within the sexual dysfunctions account for this standardization. This is especially true of PE, where reliance on a variation of the Semans procedure is almost universal. Sex therapists are differentiated by the manner in which they conceptualize the patient's unsuccessful attempt at the sexual task and how this "failure" is managed.

To elaborate further, resistance to the sex therapy process almost invariably emerges during the course of treatment. Identification and resolution of resistance is crucial to therapeutic success. Emerging resistance(s) reveal the varying levels of factors which maintain the couple's sexual problem. Appreciation of this concept does not imply, however, that sex therapy requires the integration of behavioral tasks within a psychoanalytic theoretical model, as postulated by Kaplan (1974). Cognitive-behavioral therapists are not surprised by the emergence of resistance; it merely sharpens their understanding of the disorder's etiology. Then the therapist refines the hypotheses generated during the evaluation session to determine the content of the psychotherapeutic sessions. Resistance may be seen in the symptomatic client or in the partner. For instance, a spouse may realistically or irrationally expect that improvement in her partner's PE will lead to him abandoning her for a more attractive partner once he is cured. She will then seek to avoid doing any exercise which may result in a personal calamity for her. Avoidance of the prescribed experience is probably the most common resistance in sex therapy.

To illustrate, a premature ejaculator might sabotage his own treatment by not performing the Semans exercise properly. When asked to concentrate on his penile sensations, he might instead worry that "her hand is tired," thus creating an interfering anxiety. Exploration of this resistance might illuminate the following layering of obstacles to effective ejaculatory control:

1. He is unaware of PS.
2. His mind is focused elsewhere: "Is her hand tired?"
3. He wishes to please his wife and is therefore concerned with her fatigue.
4. This leads to anxiety, which further interferes with ability to observe PS.
5. His desire to please his wife is based on his irrational belief that it is his responsibility to make his wife consistently happy.
6. This might stem from an irrational overgeneralized desire to please all important women in his life (beginning with mother) in order to avoid abandonment.

Intervention, however, would initially begin on levels 1–4, with an attempt to bypass (Apfelbaum, 1977; Kaplan, 1974) his abandonment anxiety (levels 5 and 6). Bypassing means that no direct attempt is made to change or challenge the basic underlying irrational belief system which may be maintaining the dysfunction. The therapist would simplistically request the wife to reassure the husband that it will please her if he concentrates on his PS. This redefinition of "pleasing" utilizes his irrational desire to facilitate therapeutic progress. If the bypassing is unsuccessful, then RET (Ellis, 1978) might be used to effect the necessary attitudinal changes at levels 5 and 6. In this manner, treatment can hopefully proceed with as few interventions as possible and, subsequently, in the briefest time possible.

There are a number of techniques in the therapist's armamentarium which are used to manage resistance: repetition of sexual tasks;

reconceptualization of failures into successes; paradoxical intention; self-disclosure (Kaplan, 1974; Munjack & Oziel, 1978). The therapist can use the transactional technique of marital therapy while confronting the patient within the supporitve warmth of the therapeutic environment. Humor can be an exceedingly effective tool in the management of obstacles to treatment success. One patient from an old colonial South African family informed the author that as a "Hamilton," all the townspeople expected him to be superb at everthing. He was therefore unwilling to date, for fear of subjecting himself to humiliation because of his PE. The therapist kiddingly suggested that Robert place the following ad in the local newspaper:

> Public announcement: Robert Hamilton is a severe premature ejaculator. Any parties still interested may contact him at his exchange.

This intervention held great significance for him, and he was able to use it to allow himself to experiment with being less perfectionistic, thereby enabling him to date. The point here is a simple one: Therapists must find ways that are meaningful to the patient to get them to do therapeutic tasks they would otherwise avoid.

In order to implement the preceding objectives, patients are seen without a cotherapist on a once-weekly basis in conjoint or individual counseling. Sex therapy is considered complete when the immediate obstacles to sexual functioning have been resolved and when the patient seems to have sufficient understanding of both the causes and the cure of the dysfunction so that relapse is unlikely. In treating PE, the time required for such a result varies from two visits (education) to 18 months (multidysfunctional patients), with a median of 12 sessions.

Improving Therapeutic Efficiency

The reportedly high incidence of PE and the widespread publicity concerning the effectiveness of sex therapy programs have produced considerable demand for these services. Despite this pressure, treatment for PE and other sexual dysfunctions was not being made available to the public at large due to a limited number of professionals adequately trained to provide service. Awareness of this problem has led to a growing interest among professionals in improving the cost/effectiveness ratio of sex therapy by manipulating treatment formats. These efforts can be placed into two overlapping categories: self-administered programs and group treatments. The self-administered programs contain audiovisual and/or written components which are either therapy adjuncts or complete treatment packages.

Lowe and Mikulas (1975) reported improvement in ejaculatory control for five couples who used a self-administered booklet supplemented by weekly phone calls. Commercial films have been produced which depict various aspects of sex therapy including PE, but no clinical evaluation of their effectiveness has been published. Videotapes have also been used as adjuncts to sex therapy (Hartman & Fithian, 1972). Recently, a number of books have been published which advocate a "treat yourself" philosophy of no therapist involvement (Altman, 1976; Barbach, 1975; Kass & Strauss, 1975; Zilbergeld, 1978). While no information as to the efficacy of these approaches is available, clinical experience indicates that some can be useful adjuncts to the therapy session (Perelman, 1978). Others, however, are misleading in both their advertising and content.

In reviewing cases of PE who presented for treatment following unsuccessful attempts at utilizing either self-help books or sex therapy texts, two problems consistently emerge. First, these men usually ignore the authors' instructions and rush through the exercises indiscriminately. Second, they do not interrupt stimulation when first experiencing PS, but instead prolong it until it is invariably too late. They describe it as a test, and such attempts are clearly counterproductive to learning the necessary skill. Unfortunately, their previous exposure to these techniques often makes them more resistant to sex therapy procedures when they do come for treatment.

The impressive results obtained by sex therapy have prompted an interest in experimenting with group treatment formats. Group therapy, which reduces the therapist's time per patient and provides additional therapeutic advantages, remains the most researched format for improving efficiency. Barbach (1974) and Schneidman and McGuire (1976) successfully integrated sex therapy and group process to treat anorgasmic women. Groups have also been used for sexual enhancement of "normal couples" (Hartman & Fithian, 1972; LoPiccolo & Miller, 1975), dysfunctional couples (Leiblum, 1978; Leiblum, Rosen, & Pierce, 1976) and elderly couples (Rowland & Haynes, 1978). Kaplan, Kohl, Pomeroy, Offit, and Hogan (1974) described a pilot investigation into the treatment of couples with PE by group sex therapy. Zilbergeld (1975) and Perelman (1978) adapted this model for the treatment of PE in men without partners.

Perelman (1977) has researched the efficacy of two different group models in the treatment of PE: a couples group and a men's group (consisting of male partners only).[1] Four cases taken from two of these groups will be presented to illustrate the specificity of success for PE. The first case describes how an alternative to traditional sex therapy procedures, a men's group, was successfully utilized in treating PE. The remaining three cases, while incidentally demonstrating group formats, were included to illustrate how treatment can result in failure or only partial success. Table 1 summarizes the essentially identical procedure used in both group formats.

TABLE 1

Summary of Treatment by Session

Session	Major topics[a]	Assignments
1	Group exercise to learn names; synonyms to a sexual word list are discussed as a disinhibition experience. Cohesiveness and supportiveness develop via clients writing anonymous lists of sexual hopes and fears which are discussed. Topics included: impotence; performance demand; "natural" spontaneous sex vs. skill-building; and initial ban on coitus.	Bathe together and discuss early sexual experiences. Sensate focus I (nongenital).
2	Clients describe earlier experiences with PE. Therapist explains etiology and definitions of PE. Masturbation and making time for sex are also discussed.	Sexological exam. Sensate focus I. Simultaneous masturbation (optional).
3	After clients discuss previous homework, therapist describes and answers questions regarding male and female physiology; premonitory sensations (PS); ejaculatory inevitabililty (EI); Semans technique; and concept of "pleasure, not prowess." Clients describe unsuccessful techniques previously used.	Male masturbation to learn awareness of PS and EI. Sensate focus II (genital). Pubococcygeal muscle exercises.
4	Individual client resistances become clearer, leading to discussion of castration	Sensate focus II. Semans exercise: Manual stimulation (stop/start) of

TABLE 1 (*continued*)

Session	Major Topics[a]	Assignments
	anxieties; orgasm-as-goal orientation to sex; and sexual initiation and refusal. Therapist reiterates concept of Semans technique, and clients discuss variations in PS.	penis by partner without a lubricant or lotion.
5	Assignment results in discussion of artificiality of Semans technique and nonspontaneity of exercises. Therapist stresses training concept. Relationship problems are discussed to bypass actual and potential resistance.	Sensate focus II. Manual Semans with lubricant. Fellatio (optional) using stop/start.
6	Therapist leads discussion on effect of varying coital positions and artificial lubricants on PS and control. Training and practice concepts are reemphasized during explanation of passive intravaginal containment ("stuffing" and "quiet vagina").	Sensate focus II. "Stuffing" and "quiet vagina" in female-superior position[b] using stop/start.
7	Clients' failures with different exercises are reconceptualized into positive learning experiences. More discussion on perceiving PS. Therapist uses dolls to show coital positions while describing relative merits.	Foreplay based on knowledge gained from sensate focus II. Stop/start using lateral-scissors coital position.
8	Previous exercise leads to discussion of fear of failure; clients' expectations of perfect control already; clinical nature of exercises; and variation in progress among clients. Therapist encourages more male passivity during sex; practice/conditioning model of change; use of manual clitoral stimulation during coitus; and	Foreplay. Stop/start using female-superior coitus.

TABLE 1 (*continued*)

Session	Major Topics[a]	Assignments
	varying coital motions to affect control.	
9	Therapist solves individual problems relating to issues mentioned in previous four sessions. A termination process is begun with no new technical information offered.	Foreplay. Stop/start using female-superior or lateral-scissors coital positions.
10	Clients share feelings regarding termination and review key program concepts. Therapist discusses integrating Semans technique into a less structured sex life and solves individual problems. Clients express feelings of accomplishment and growth.	Practice using Semans procedure with different coital positions.

[a] Previous assignment always discussed.
[b] Hartman and Fithian (1974).

Clinical Examples

Cases 1 and 3 participated in a men's ("husbands") group ($n = 6$), while cases 2 and 4 were in a five-dyad couples group. In both groups, therapy was twice weekly, in 1½-hour sessions, over a 5-week period. Additionally, each dyad was seen for two pretreatment assessment sessions. The groups provided a structured forum for the dissemination of key concepts and for conveying homework instructions. Transactions among members were interpreted solely to facilitate improvement in sexual functioning or communication and were not analyzed to resolve underlying conflict or to produce personality changes. Supportiveness among members was maximized, while confrontation between members was generally discouraged. Self-disclosure by the therapist created an atmosphere conducive to openness and helped to reduce performance anxiety associated with public discussion of sexual behavior and attitudes. The major difference between the two groups was the omission of the women from the actual therapy sessions in the husbands group. The wives were provided (via the husbands) with summaries of educational information discussed in the group and copies of the homework assignments to facilitate the transmission of information. All the couples were seen for a follow-up session.

Case 1: Beverly and Allen (Husbands Group)²

Background Information

Allen was a 25-year-old self-employed musician, with a 7-year history of PE. He had been involved in a 3-year relationship with Beverly, a 20-year-old manager of a retail fabric shop. Allen was successes oriented and had become involved with his career to the exclusion of Beverly. She felt that between his career and his overprotective mother, there was no place for her in his life. Beverly felt unappreciated by Allen and was considering terminating the relationship because of the poor quality of their sex life. She viewed sex with Allen as "unexciting" and avoided it because she so often felt "cheated." Beverly's sexual rejection of Allen exacerbated his PE and indirectly helped to maintain his focus on his career rather than his relationship. Beverly had defensively increased her time commitment to her job, leaving only one evening a week to be together. They had developed an avoidance pattern typical of cases of sexual dysfunction, with their sexual frequency diminishing from daily at the beginning of their relationship to less than once a month. Beverly summarized their relationship in response to the following question:

> THERAPIST: Do you still find your partner attractive?
> BEVERLY: Yes, except when I'm frustrated [sexually]; then I feel even hate.... We used to satisfy each other pretty well by other means but as time went on we both fully realized the problems; we just couldn't face it so we didn't touch each other after awhile.

Allen was raised by "wonderful, but old-fashioned Italian Catholic" parents. However, both he and Beverly indicated that his mother was overly intrusive in his life. There was minimal discussion of sex in the home. He became aware of sexual impulses at age 10 and began masturbating in his early teens. During masturbation, Allen would typically bring himself to orgasm quickly. He experienced PE in all of his sexual encounters, regardless of partner or the type or amount of stimulation.

Beverly also came from a middle-class Italian-American home, but her parents had married and divorced each other twice. She reported no discussion of sex in the home, but love was emphasized. Beverly had never masturbated. She was orgasmic with manual stimulation from Allen, but was anorgasmic during coitus. Beverly was very depressed about her present and past relationships. Her first lover died of cancer, and her second partner deceived her frequently. She entered her present relationship with some of the defensiveness characteristic of unrequited love. She summarized her relationships in the following manner:

> *The one who loved me—died.*
> *The one who didn't—lied.*
> *The one who couldn't—tried.*

Formulation

While Allen was concerned with pleasing Beverly, he also felt resentful toward her. He regarded his career as his first and only major accomplishment: It was all that nourished his fragile sense of self-esteem. In part, his involvement in his career grew out of a desire to impress Beverly so that she would not abandon him. The effect of this was decidedly opposite, since she was feeling abandoned herself and was close to terminating the relationship. Allen's conflicts may have stemmed from troubled early childhood relationships, for example, the aforementioned negative interactions with his mother. One might speculate that his sexual problem developed as a result of unresolved unconscious anger at women and fear of abandonment by significant females. We may presume that a psychoanalyst would seek to foster ejaculatory control by helping Allen gain insight into and resolve these oedipal conflicts. In contrast, an interpersonally oriented therapist would attempt to identify and rectify the couple's destructive relationship interactions which might be indirectly maintaining Allen's dysfunction. This position could easily be justified when considering the seemingly poor quality of their relationship. Allen felt ambivalently toward Beverly and believed that she criticized his manner, career, family, and friends much too frequently. This anger often went unexpressed directly, instead manifesting itself as passive–aggressive avoidance of Beverly. Moreover, Beverly's fears that if her boyfriend were to function well sexually he would abandon her for one of the concert-hall "groupies" also adversly affected their relationship. Illumination and resolution of these transactional conflicts would be considered a necessity by a marital therapist.

The sex therapist, on the other hand, would attempt to intervene directly to rectify the immediate obstacle to ejaculatory control. Allen and Beverly would be taught the Semans procedure early in treatment so that he would be aware of PS and subsequent body adjustments necessary for good control. The transactional and intrapsychic problems discussed above would be addressed only to the extent that they presented an immediate obstacle to therapeutic progress. In other words, an educational/counseling approach would be pursued until a resistance arose which required therapeutic management. At this time, the therapist was interested in investigating methods of improving therapeutic efficiency. In order to meet these objectives, Allen was referred to the husbands-group format previously described.

Treatment

The husbands-group program included two conjoint pretreatment assessment sessions, followed by 10 men-only group meetings during a 5-week period. During the first assessment session, Allen's avoidance of Beverly was confronted since it presented a direct obstacle to time for homework exercises in addition to having a deleterious effect on the relationship. Allen was instructed to practice making time available for the twice-weekly coitus he wanted in the future. It was explained to him that their once-a-month intercourse frequency was low enough to cause PE in the most skillful of lovers. During the second session, this theme was elaborated upon further. Allen was asked to make a choice: Was he willing to spend less time with his musical career for at least the next month in order to become a successful lover? He was assured that while the program was likely to help him, it would require two after- noons per week for sessions, as well as a number of evenings to do the exercises. Additionally, the therapist felt that Allen needed to spend other time with Beverly so that she would not feel that he was merely using her to get help with ejaculatory control. This was said in front of her to circumvent her feeling used and so that she would see the therapist as an ally. This was especially important, since the therapist was not scheduled to meet with them together again until the group was concluded. They both readily agreed to these conditions, and Beverly in fact indicated Allen's greater availability to her since the first as- sessment session. The couple was told the specifics of the group pro- gram, which was to begin in 10 days.

A possible obstacle to treatment surfaced before the group even began. Three days after the second evaluation session, the therapist received a letter from Beverly which reiterated her negative feelings and presented an ultimatum. Allen was unaware of the letter, parts of which are reprinted below:

> As I sat in your office I found it so hard to release my true feelings. Not because I don't think my complaints are valid, but because I think your [sic] getting him to really try for the first time. . . . However, I see a very spoiled child. He's used to his way. His promises have been nothing more than words to stop my complaints—I consider those promises lies. He's selfish. I'll tell you this I've decided to give this whole thing till February [4 months]. If he doesn't live up to all or at least try to live up to his promises, this girl is leaving him. There comes a point where try-

ing and giving in becomes a foolish thing to do to ones [sic] own person and nobody's fool will I be.

On the surface, the letter indicates a willingness to try and make the relationship work for at least 4 months. As such, the content does not imply any immediate obstacle to treatment which would require a response. However, the transparent message of anger, hurt, and disappointment was all too clear. Such an ultimatum usually indicates a very poor prognosis for sex therapy, which seemed even worse considering the "husbands" format was to be used. While ostensibly compliant, Beverly seemed to be lying in wait to pounce on Allen's first insensitivity or broken appointment, thus completing their version of the "I gotcha game" (Berne, 1972). Therefore, a choice point arose for the therapist:

1. Acknowledge the note very briefly and indicate appreciation of Beverly's willingness to proceed with the program. In other words, continue as planned, but realize that a possible crisis may emerge—for example, she breaks up with him (which had occurred in the past) the moment he regresses to his earlier inconsideration. Should such a crisis occur, the couple could be seen for conjoint counseling and Allen's group participation could be reevaluated.

2. View the letter as a request from Beverly for more contact with the therapist and therefore refer the couple for conjoint therapy where relationship issues as well as the Semans technique could be addressed directly.

3. Develop a treatment plan that balances the concept of minimal intervention at the immediate–obstacle level against the likelihood of an emerging crisis.

The therapist chose the third option, feeling that a judicious intervention might circumvent the potential crisis and thus provide a more humane as well as efficient treatment. The plan was to bypass her emerging resistance through a brief telephone consultation. On the telephone, Beverly initially became more adamant, saying that she saw the future as bleak. The therapist attempted to manage this obstacle with two maneuvers. First, he joined her resistance, allowing that Allen was probably the culprit she painted him, but indicating that this could only be established if she would do her utmost to be available for the exercises—to show him up. In this manner, the therapist attempted to mobilize her competitive feelings in the service of the treatment program. Second, and most important for this couple, she was reassured that Allen's avoidance was due to anxiety about sex and fear of failure and not to lack of caring. In an almost conspiratorial tone, the therapist helped Beverly reconceptualize Allen's interest in music as an attraction to feelings of mastery rather than a rejection of her. The therapist predicted that if she could help Allen develop feelings of adequacy as a lover, by reinforcing all the subtle improvements, he would progressively invest greater energy in their relationship. This reconceptualization and reassurance allowed her to invest herself more fully in the therapy, which was successful from that moment on. Each responded very positively to the exercises, which allowed them to commmunicate more and spend more time together sexually.

The group itself seemed to provide an interesting mechanism for bypassing some of their relationship problems. The group provided Allen with a support system similar to the musician friends whom she disliked. This had an unexpected effect. Spending some time socializing with group members, he would go home and discuss them rather than the musicians. This helped to structure the conversations away from areas she had been negatively sensitized to, resulting in a more warm, reinforcing reaction. These conversations, in addition to the exercises themselves, allowed for more intimate time together in 5 weeks than in the previous 5 months. He progressively became a more interested and proficient lover and surprised her with a vibrator and her first cunnilingus experience. In turn, she became less critical and demanding of him, as well as helping him learn from the exercises. Allen was confused by an initial coital failure with the Semans procedure, and it was Beverly who observed that he had slight thrusting movements even when he felt that he was lying perfectly still. Allen brought this to the other men's attention by beginning the following session with: "I'm always rubbing my dick somewhere—always rubbing."

They learned to understand each other's sexual and emotional needs. Their sex life became mutually fulfilling, and Allen's control greatly improved. Their sexual successes generalized to other aspects of their lives. Beverly reported, "My new knowledge and awareness made me a much more confident woman... never a raving maniac anymore." Allen stated, "The program has made me a more tolerant, level-headed, and rational person.... I never thought it would be as awesome a turnaround as it was." Two-year follow-up indicated that Allen's ejaculatory control had remained stable and that Beverly had learned to orgasm during coitus. The couple had a "big Italian wedding" a few months earlier and seemed reasonably content.

This case is somewhat atypical. Frequently, dysfunctional patients can be relieved of their symptoms, but changes in basic personality structure or in the fundamental dynamics of the marital relationship is not the norm. Typically, there is a specificity of outcome, which will be illustrated in the next two cases.

Case 2: Mr. X. and Ms. Y.—Symptom Resolution with Relationship Disruption (Couples Group)

Background Information

Mr. X., a 30-year-old writer, had lived with Ms. Y., a 31-year-old schoolteacher, for the past 2½ years. Mr. X. described himself as "a rock-hearted German, tending to be self-righteous although I would like to be more flexible." Both were intelligent, attractive, and articulate, although Ms. Y., while talkative, tended to be a particularly passive, unassertive woman. She viewed herself as dominated by Mr. X. but indicated, "I suffer in silence." They seemed relatively happy with their relationship, although both independently indicated a feeling that Mr. X. was desirous of other sexual partners. He did, in fact, have one brief affair of which Ms. Y. was unaware.

Mr. X. first became aware of his sexual impulses at age 10, when he would fantasize about girls. When Mr. X. was 12, his father discussed reproduction with him for the first and last time. Mr. X. described his father and mother as strict Roman Catholics who were very inhibited about sex. Mr. X. masturbated throughout high school and college but felt very guilty about it. Occasionally he would stop masturbating when he felt PS but would not climax. He felt that this was a less evil sin, and, interestingly, this early experience allowed him to progress more quickly with the Semans technique during therapy. His early sexual experiences were very limited, and Mr. X. did not first kiss until age 20. His first intercourse experience was with a Mexican prostitute when he was in the Peace Corps. He ejaculated prematurely and had done so during all other coital experiences, including two other extended relationships.

Ms. Y. was anorgasmic during coitus with Mr. X., as she had been with all her previous sexual partners. She described herself as going through a "promiscuous period," but had had three sequential monogamous relationships during the past 5 years. She first became aware of her sexuality at age 14, when she developed "crushes on boys in class, and wanted to hold hands and dance close." Her parents were affectionate with one another, and her father, a schoolteacher, stressed the importance of communication. In sex, Ms. Y. felt that a woman should be more subtle than a man, who should be the initiator and aggressor.

Response to Treatment

Mr. X. and Ms. Y. had a positive response to treatment. Both enjoyed the couples-group exerience and looked forward to the sessions. Mr. X. became more relaxed in his sexual behavior and learned to control his ejaculatory response. Ms. Y. became more sexually assertive and active. She was now occasionally coitally orgasmic, and both indicated that communication between them was much improved. Despite this, Mr. X. and Ms. Y. separated between the last group session and the posttreatment assessment session.

Following the last group session, Mr. X. had spent a week alone in California at a convention, where he was able to interact with other women. When he returned, they decided to separate, feeling there were irreconcilable differences. Ms. Y. desired a monogamous marriage and wanted a child shortly. She had wanted to marry Mr. X. but preferred to find a man who shared her desire for a monogamous commitment and intimate sharing. Ms. Y. stated, "He's attracted to the idea of getting married and having children in the abstract, while I'm concrete—this is what I want." Both Mr. X. and Ms. Y. felt that their desire to separate was not a function of their mutually improved sexuality but of their improved communication. Each was previously minimally aware of the other's views on commitment, which they only briefly discussed before on vacation. They had been afraid to discuss it subsequently, but during the program they became much more open with each other. While they viewed the situation as growth-producing, their mutual discomfort during the posttreatment assessment was evident.

Thirty-Month Follow-Up

Mr. X. felt that the program was a success for him, and he continued to use the concepts he learned: "It's more fun when you do—it lasts longer and you know it's better." Generally, he reported being more sexually confident, but had not developed a more intimate relationship at present. He had gone with one woman for 8 months during the previous year but then broke it off. He continued to distance himself from people and was actively planning an extended trip to the South American jungles. Interestingly, he reported seeing Ms. Y. on a weekly basis for the last few months. He went through a period where he considered marrying her, but stated, "I was ready, but she wasn't." Sex was fine between them, but their future, unlike his trip, was uncertain.

Case 3: Mr. and Mrs. W.—Symptomatic Improvement, Further Therapy Necessary (Husbands Group)

Background Information

Mr. W. was a 30-year-old self-employed financial consultant. He had come to New York from Milan 4 years before to attend graduate school in business administration. Two years later, he married Mrs. W., a 41-year-old divorced businesswoman, who had moved to New York from the Midwest. While initially comfortable with one another, their relationship became characterized by severe marital discord, hostility, and tension. Mr. and Mrs. W. engaged in mutual recrimination, blaming each other for sexual, marital, and business problems. Mr. W. was always a premature ejaculator, but his problem became more severe as their relationship deteriorated. Mrs. W. was anorgasmic during coitus and was becoming increasingly more anxious during their infrequent sexual encounters. Both often resorted to intellectualizing and each felt that the other was afraid of intimacy. Initially, marital therapy was recommended, but the author was later persuaded by their persistent pleas to allow them into the group program.

Mr. W. had always been anxious about his sexual potency. He felt guilty about masturbating as an adolescent and had avoided relationships with women before coming to America. He had two brief homosexual affairs in Italy and one in the United States. The latter was precipitated by an anxiety reaction to a business failure. He was intermittently impotent in the few coital experiences he had before marriage. His performance anxiety was not limited to his sexual functioning, and he was very demanding with regard to his new business. Mr. W. had a low sense of self-esteem and typically was very anxious.

Mrs. W. was raised a Southern Baptist and reported learning from her mother that sex was for the man's pleasure. She indicated being sexually molested by her mother's stepbrother at age 9. Mrs. W. was first married at 18 and divorced within 4 years. She had a son by this first marriage, who was 17 years old at the time. She had had a 10-year affair with a married physician with whom she learned to be multiply orgasmic. Mrs. W. felt that Mr. W. needed to learn to be more sensual as well as more physically attentive to her. She criticized him in a highly dramatic manner and was generally a hysteric who described herself as "fiercely independent."

Response to Treatment

Throughout the therapy, Mr. and Mrs. W. tended to talk instead of doing the exercises. Their resistance was initially bypassed by the investigator informing them that termination was imminent if the exercises were not done. Mr. W. especially did not want to be dropped from the program because he found the group so reassuring and supportive. Mrs. W. enjoyed the physical closeness provided by the exercises, but their progress was interrupted by a week-long visit from her sister and her son.

Unbeknownst to the therapist, Mr. W. was attending "aesthetic realism" classes while engaged in the therapy program. Mr. W. gave Mrs. W. a recording of a class following an argument over Mr. W.'s hostility toward Mrs. W.'s sister and son. On the tape, Mr. W. discussed his lack of love for his wife and how the marriage was merely a convenience. Resenting the message and the way in which it was communicated, Mrs. W. left home for the Y.W.C.A.

An individual-couple therapy session was scheduled to deal with this crisis. Mr. W. felt that Mrs. W. overextended herself to her family at his expense. Mrs. W. saw Mr. W. as "radiating hate and jealousy." The therapist recommended terminating sex therapy and beginning marital or divorce counseling. Beneath the bickering, both seemed afraid of commitment. Mrs. W. agreed with an interpretation that she was afraid Mr. W. would leave her for a younger woman if he became more sexually adept. He denied this and reassured her of his positive feelings for her. They requested to be allowed to continue the program in case they decided to remain married. The therapist agreed and suggested they try "behaving themselves into a different way of thinking and feeling."

Following the individual session, they became more communicative and appreciative of each other. Although Mrs. W. slept on the couch, their sex life improved appreciably. Mr. W. improved his ejaculatory control and Mrs. W. became fully orgasmic, reportedly feeling "much freer sexually." Mr. W. stated, "I have acquired a better understanding and control of my sexuality—a more open and effective attitude ... this has contributed to a greater respect for myself." While each reported greater satisfaction with the relationship, they both remained unhappy with their marriage. In order for sex to be good, they had to feign lack of emotional involvement. By remaining distant, they were able to enjoy each other sexually, yet both were emotionally unsatisfied. This case was a particularly good example of how sexual functioning can be improved without the quality of life also getting better. The couple was referred for further marital counseling.

Two-Year Follow-Up

While no longer experiencing erectile difficulty, Mr. W.'s ejaculatory control was poor. He reported an urgency to ejaculate during intercourse, which he correctly attributed to their low coital frequency. Only when tension between them was low did they have sex, which resulted in a half-dozen encounters in 2 years. In retrospect, he reported no longer viewing sex as the problem: "We were focusing on the sex, but that was not the problem. It was a screen. It was a gesture of good will on both our parts to go for help for sex."

They never pursued the referral for marital counseling, preferring to "do a very slow gradual separation from each other." He no longer found her attractive, with the 12-year age differential becoming a focus for his resentment. Additionally, he felt that he should have married an Italian woman from a similar background, who could more easily understand his family. They both described this as a period of transition in which they spent time with their careers rather than with each other. While both saw the marriage as precarious, offers of another marital therapy referral were declined.

Case 4: Nancy and David—Sabotage of Therapy Due to Relationship Instability (Couples Group)

Background Information

David was a 21-year-old college graduate who, despite ambivalent feelings, was planning to postpone his entrance into Yale Law School until the following year. He was delaying school in order to try living with Nancy, whom he had been dating for 7 months. Nancy was a 23-year-old assistant editor who preferred living and working in New York. Except for the PE and a difference in frequency preference, David and Nancy felt that their sex life was excellent. This positive view of their sexuality distinguished them from most other couples. Their Sexual Interaction Inventory scores were the least pathological of any couple in their group and were healthier than "normal." Their Locke–Wallace Marital Adjustment Scores were high, and they were complimentary of each other during the pretherapy assessment interviews. In short, their youth, motivation, and intelligence suggested to the therapist that they would be excellent candidates for sex therapy.

Response to Treatment

During the early therapy sessions, it became clear to the therapist that both David and Nancy held overidealized images of each other. They used the sexual dysfunction as a screen for other relationship problems which they wanted to ignore. Both were very controlling, and their sexual-frequency incompatibility became the focus for other conflicts. In spite of this, they made progress sexually until the seventh session. David had received a letter from law school indicating that he would have to enroll in the fall or lose his admission. He intended to enroll and was very disappointed when Nancy indicated that she would not accompany him. This began a period of mutual hostility and resentment. In order to deal with the imminent separation, each chose to deprecate the other in order to minimize their sense of loss. Their mutual bitterness and inflexibility was severe: "He should change to be a better human being or no one will want him." They continued to live together because of convenience, but their communication became increasingly vitriolic. They completed the treatment program, but Nancy was uncooperative with regard to the exercises. While they continued intermittently to have sex together, they rarely followed the program suggestions. David had previously been so invested in seeing himself as sexually knowledgeable that it was difficult for him to accept an externally imposed structure. Given their mutual hostility, he became more resistant. Surprisingly, there was a slight increase in coital duration time, but therapy was a failure.

The university's letter forced the couple to examine their commitment to each other, and they found it to be lacking. This occurrence in the middle of sex therapy was counterproductive to any further progress. The effect on the therapy was adequately summarized by Nancy:

> A relationship has to be stable for this not to be a pain in the ass—we're not that stable, though we thought we were. It takes a lot of commitment to go through with this. I think the women are doing the men a favor and they have to care about them a real lot unquestionably. We weren't close enough for me to feel it was *our* problem.

Both David and Nancy felt that their breakup had nothing to do with sex or the therapy program. Rather, they attributed their problems to their unfulfilled expectations of each other. These issues were all discussed during the posttreatment session, in which they seemed to develop a somewhat increased acceptance rather than resentment of each other's views. The therapist met briefly with both of them to help them obtain a more balanced perspective of the previous month's experiences.

No follow-up information is available.

Discussion

The cases presented indicate some of the range of responses that patients have to sex therapy procedures. The same behavioral changes will be appreciated in a diversity of ways by different patients. While almost all men treated for PE improved their coital duration time, their evaluations of their differing degrees of improvement varied markedly. The popularity of and publicity about sex therapy in recent years seem to have given rise to a growing number of misconceptions among the public concerning the breadth and impact of successful treatment. Sex therapy for PE can provide patients with a structure which will enable them to obtain the knowledge necessary to learn ejaculatory control, yet some patients were disappointed with that admittedly specific skill. Despite pretherapy cautions and explanations of probable treatment outcome, many individuals were diappointed at not becoming "studs" or "femmes fatales" in bed. Some of this disappointment seemed irrelevant to the degree of control actually obtained, but was related to conscious and/or unconscious desires which were often initially hidden from the therapist. The degree of nonsymptomatic change which was experienced as a result of treatment seemed to be related to a number of variables which will be discussed below. These gains or lack of them need to be considered beyond their importance as outcome criteria, as there are strong indications that the maintenance of symptomatic improvement may be a function of the nonsymptomatic changes in the dyad, for example, Case 3. The cases presented will be discussed below in terms of factors accounting for differential improvement, with special attention given to relationship harmony and stability.

Specificity of Treatment Outcome

The first two cases presented demonstrate how PE can be successfully treated by two different theme-centered and time-limited group therapies. Both cases illustrate how these group treatments improved general sexual functioning. Additionally, Case 1 indicates how a treatment group comprised only of male partners significantly improved relationship harmony. The success of that group strongly implies that the conjoint therapy model advocated by Masters and Johnson (1970) is not a prerequisite for the resolution of PE. However, all four cases demonstrate that there are many levels of "cures" produced by group sex therapy, which is also true of sex therapy generally. Sex therapy is not a panacea for all patients who complain of PE, marital discord, and other problems in living. While the cases reflect a variety of differential responses of couples to treatment, a fuller illumination of these differences could only be appreciated by listening to many patients evaluate their success or failure. The conclusion to be drawn from an analysis of statements of premature ejaculators and their partners on inventories, and particulary during interviewing, is that sex therapy has a limited and specific effect.

While most couples can improve ejaculatory control and general sexual functioning, the impact of therapy on marital harmony is typically marginal and may be disruptive. Sager (1974) sees such specificity of treatment effect as common and as not reflecting poor therapy, but rather as indicating that pretherapy differences in marital harmony have a greater effect on outcome than does treatment. He identified three categories of marital discord and their relation to sexual functioning which are useful in understanding the results of the four cases presented: (1) sexual dysfunction which produces secondary marital discord; (2) some degree of marital discord which impairs sexual functioning; and (3) severe marital discord and basic hostility which prevents the cooperation necessary for adequate sexual functioning or effective therapy. Sager recommended sex therapy for couples in the first two categories and marital or divorce counseling for those in the last. The results of the four cases presented indicate that improvement in marital harmony varies directly with the couple's placement in these categories: The greatest improvement was seen in the couple in the first category, and the least improvement in those in the third category.

The one exception to this classification system was the couple (Case 2) whose relationship was indirectly being maintained by the sexual dysfunction. Kaplan (1974) predicted that "permanent disruption of the marital system as a result of successful sexual therapy tends to occur primarily in relationships which frustrate the basic needs of one or the other partner" (p. 452). Mr. X. had a strong desire to experience sex with other women, yet he feared "humiliating himself" in front of them. When Mr. X. was more confident of his sexual prowess, he was no longer afraid to act on his desire to seek out other female partners. His sexual success with them was consistent with this author's clinical experience. Learning ejaculatory control with one partner will frequently generalize to other women as well. This result is contrary to those of Yulis (1976), who suggested that concomitant assertiveness training might be required to achieve generalization with a nontreatment partner. However, Mr. X. and Ms. Y.'s experience is a particularly interesting example of treatment specificity, as it demonstrates the critical difference between improved communication and improved harmony. While communication was improved, as was ejaculatory control and sexual functioning, the relationship was disrupted. This result is very dissimilar from the undifferentiated success reported in Case 1.

Case 1 (Beverly and Allen) demonstrates the large global improvements which can be obtained when much of the relationship disturbance is secondary to the ejaculatory incontinence (Sager's first category). Although Beverly's pretreatment Locke–Wallace relationship harmony score was extraordinarily low, much of her unhappiness was being indirectly maintained by Allen's dysfunction. Concomitant with improved control, the more confident Allen became highly attentive to Beverly, and at posttreatment assessment, her Locke–Wallace score had almost doubled to well within the mean for satisfied couples. The critical intervention in their case was probably the telephone call to Beverly which mobilized her motivation for cooperation and successfully bypassed her resistance (her justifiable anger and resentment). While the intervention was necessary, it was, of course, insufficient in and of itself to produce a cure. There are three factors which resulted in effective treatment for them, as well as for other individuals treated for PE. These will be briefly summarized below.

Group Treatment Sessions

Discussions of sexuality are frequently fraught with dishonesty and tension in our culture. Such an atmosphere contrasts dramatically with the honest, warm, open, therapeutic environment of group sessions. Three essential curative ingredients of the group format described by Barbach (1974) seem particularly salient: (1) the supportive nature of the group; (2) permission-giving aspects; (3) therapist variables. A high level of supportiveness existed throughout the program, with members spontaneously applauding one another's successes. Receiving permission from a respected authority to change maladaptive sexual responses has been viewed as particularly important in sex therapy (Peck, 1975). The permission to give and accept pleasure was even greater in the group formats because of the added encouragement of the other group members.

The therapist modeled sexually competent behavior (via self-disclosure techniques) and a calm, relaxed attitude toward sexual matters. In addition, he facilitated rapid improvement in sexual functioning by helping Allen confront his resistance to progress. The therapist's role as a demystifier of sexual physiology and clarifier of sexual misconception contributed to the reeducative component of the therapy process. The group enhanced this reeducative effect, as therapeutic discussions with one patient almost inevitably clarified problems for others.

Sensate-Focus and Communication Exercises

Beverly and Allen had a very positive response to the general sexual-skill-enhancing exercises. While their therapeutic value has been previously reviewed, the curative effect of these exercises upon this couple was profound. Allen's ineffective techniques were often replaced for the first time by caresses genuinely appreciated by Beverly. The sensate-focus exercises did not precipitate the anxiety reaction described by Kaplan (1974); the advantages outweighed the minimal resistances encountered. These exercises also served a valuable continuous-assessment function. They were particularly useful indicators of the type of resistance the couple would manifest when presented with the Semans technique.

The Semans Technique

The Semans technique was the primary component used to systematically improve Allen's ejaculatory control. Using the procedure, Allen gradually developed a sense of performance reliability which complemented his improved control and sexual functioning. The systematic, gradual presentation of this procedure was an important aspect of its success, as mere awareness of its intent typically would not have been sufficient to produce improved ejaculatory control. Allen, as many other patients, had unsuccessfully attempted to use a Semans-type procedure on his own. His lack of success seemed to be caused by the rapid rate at which he, as many others, attempted to progress through the training process. It seems likely that a growing number of individuals who apply for sex therapy services in the future will have failed using some type of self-administered program previously.

Experience dictates that PE can sometimes be treated successfully regardless of concomitant psychopathology (Tanner, 1973), marital discord (Kaplan, 1974), and sundry additional problems in living (Perelman, 1976). However, success is very unlikely when the PE is merely a symbol for and often secondary to an array of serious relationship problems (Sager's third category). Mr. and Mrs. W.'s (Case 3) marital difficulties indicated successful resolution of Mr. W.'s PE to be unlikely, but their surprisingly high degree of motivation and promises of mutual cooperation seduced the willing author to accept them for treatment. While treatment for ejaculatory control was eventually successful and sexual functioning was improved, no changes in the destructive marital interactions were obtained. In such a situation, either the couple will separate or the sexual improvement will deteriorate.

While initially successful in bypassing the couple's intermediate obstacles to controlled coitus, such therapeutic dexterity was not in the couple's best interest. The therapist was colluding with the couple in making a secondary issue primary. The literature is not particularly helpful in making such decisions; recommending marital therapy preceding sex therapy is offered as standard procedure (Kaplan, 1974; Sager, 1974). The reader will remember, however, that such a referral was both offered and refused. In retrospect, a superior treatment plan would have utilized the desire for sex therapy as leverage in order to engage the couple in marital therapy. One general problem with the group therapy project into which they sought entrance is its implicit presumption that patients will be responsive and amenable to the particular techniques being investigated, regardless of pretherapy differences on symptomatic and nonsymptomatic measures. The minimal-therapist-intervention concept could have been maintained by allowing Mr. W. to join the husbands group, but making participation contingent upon the couple participating in concurrent conjoint marital therapy. His high motivation for the men's group probably would have overcome their mutual reluctance for marital therapy. Over the course of the 5-week program, three or four conjoint sessions might have sufficed to develop a therapeutic alliance with the couple, which would have allowed them to accept a redefinition of their problem. Presumably, their participation in marital therapy could have then continued past the termination of the sex therapy group. Perhaps at that point, a referral for continued marital counseling could have effectively been made and the groundwork for such an approach developed. Although preferable, longer-term marital counseling by the sex therapist was not possible under the administrative structure of the hospital. Their self-referral for sex therapy aside, all of the actions cited above presume that the couple desired (if minimally) a less strife-ridden marriage or calmer separation than what they seemed intent on carrying out, regardless of therapeutic maneuverings.

Finally, it is often difficult to diagnose whether a couple's relationship discord is too severe to allow for the cooperation necessary for sex therapy. Although preferable, the format used in the cases presented did not allow for a behavioral prescription to be used as a probe to aid in diagnosing the level of pathology (Chassin, Perelman, & Weinberger, 1974; Kaplan, 1974). While many couples were appropriately rejected from these groups and referred for marital counseling, some couples were accepted when further assessment would have been preferable. Leiblum, Rosen, and Pierce (1976) recommended a Locke–Wallace Marital Adjustment score of 80 as a minimum screening cutoff point when using a group format. This would have correctly resulted in

Mr. and Mrs. W. being rejected, but Beverly and Allen also would have been rejected, and David and Nancy would have been accepted.

Case 4, as many other failures in sex therapy, was an example of inadequate diagnosis. Although not evident during the pretherapy assessment, David and Nancy were, in fact, a poor risk for sex therapy. The only warning was the possibility that the differences in frequency preferences were symptomatic of other relationship problems. Retrospectively, the following statement of Nancy's on an assessment form seems significant: "For some reason I (we) haven't been in the mood recently. However, in our outside lives there have been difficulties. Also we're just getting over the initial "honeymoon" when people first meet—it's getting very *real* and *complicated* with each other." Although asked about the remark during the second evaluation session, Nancy dismissed it casually as reflecting the previous week's mood; the therapist pursued it no further until the issue reemerged as resistance weeks later. Their response to the law school letter then created an unmanageable crisis in their relationship. The primary difference in managing the case today, besides a hopefully more astute diagnosis, would be in not recommending the couples group for David and Nancy. The couples group, more than the male-only group model, is not well suited to unmarried individuals with relatively recent relationships (theirs was 7 months old). The couples group can increase pressure on a relationship due to the female partner's direct, continuous participation. More is required of her than of a woman in the husbands group in terms of time commitment to the therapy program. The greater pressure might, in turn, cause couples to reevaluate their commitment to the relationship. The therapy may become a focus of or intensify other hostility, for example, "What have you done for me lately?" While this is, of course, true of individual-couple conjoint counseling, the group dramatically heightens such pressure. Today, I would proceed with the couple conjointly and focus on the issues of commitment and stability more rapidly, should they emerge, rather than pursue the sex therapy directly. If a separation did occur, David would be encouraged to pursue a very brief therapy to treat the PE before going away to law school.

The potential use of groups for increasing the availabiity of sex therapy requires additional research regarding its effectiveness as compared to individual-couple approaches. Outcome research investigating the optimal balance between the patient's involvement with a therapist and exposure to sexual information and exercises via film or video is also necessary. However, there must be concurrent research into the effect of patient variables on the outcome of sex therapy. The cases presented strongly indicate that there is an interaction between patient characteristics (both psychopathology and marital discord) and the therapy process. This interaction would be a critical factor in determining the level of minimal therapist involvement. There is some preliminary evidence which seems to indicate a shift toward a more pathological patient population applying for sex therapy service. The publicity surrounding sex therapy might be making it an "easier" chief complaint than other problem areas.

Strikingly, a cursory review of requests of the past 2 years for sexual counseling at New York Hospital indicated some changing epidemiological factors. The proportion of patients seeking treatment for PE was no longer higher than that for other male dysfunctions, which had been the case when Kaplan *et al.* (1974) began to experiment with group treatment. Additionally, those presenting with PE were less likely to have an encapsulated problem and were more likely to have a number of intermediate and remote obstacles maintaining their dysfunctions.

While these changes might be idiosyncratic to New York Hospital, an alternative explanation will be examined. A similar shift toward concomitant pathology was observed by Klein, Dittman, Parloff, and Gill (1969) in patients seeking behavioral treatment for phobias, which were formerly viewed as a primarily encapsulated symptom. It seems unlikely that such shifts document early analytic theories that these problems are always symptomatic of underlying conflicts which must be resolved before symptomatic relief can be obtained. Rather, the shifts might reflect the degree to which healthier people are independently improving their own sex lives. A reasonably intelligent and psychologically healthy couple might well make use of the plethora of materials currently available on improving sexual function to remedy their dysfunction without professional help. At least they might be able to improve their sexual functioning to the point where it would not be noxious enough to require expensive, time-consuming therapy. Patients seeking sex therapy would then, in increasing proportions, be individuals lacking in marital resources, having additional psychopathology and complex multifaceted sexual complaints. This would, of course, present us with a very different population from that of Masters and Johnson (1970), who reported that "the majority of the marital units contending with sexual dysfunction do not evidence psychiatric problems other than the specific symptoms of sexual dysfunction" (p. 21). Such a shift might well be expected to affect treatment outcome regardless of our increasing therapeutic skill in managing resistance.

There is a general paucity of follow-up in psychotherapy treatment outcome research. Unfortunately, sex therapy is no exception. Almost a decade has passed since Masters and Johnson reported a five-year follow-up failure rate of 2.2% in treating PE. Whether or not we are currently treating this dysfunction with such success remains to be seen. The four cases were offered not to suggest a 50% failure rate, but to call attention to the manner in which intermediate obstacles (relationship discord) can interfere with treatment success. This author's current failure rate is approximately 10% in working with couples and single men. In summary, although PE is very treatable by the methods described, it is hoped that expectations will be tempered regarding outcome and that attention to potential therapeutic pitfalls will be increased.

ACKNOWLEDGMENT

The author acknowledges the helpful suggestions of Steven T. Fishman, who reviewed an earlier draft of this chapter.

NOTES

1. Perelman (1977) indicated that couples in both couples and men-only groups significantly improved ejaculatory control and overall level of sexual functioning. All the dyads in the husbands group improved their level of marital harmony, while some dyads in the couples and control groups did so. These results cast doubt on the Masters and Johnson (1970) dictum which mandated a conjoint therapy format when treating sexual dysfunction. Two-year follow-up, however, indicated that the treatment program was less efficacious than originally indicated. Eight of the 10 men maintained their improved ejaculatory control, but improvement of marital harmony was not consistently maintained; some relationships deteriorated to pretherapy levels or worse.
2. Brief excerpts of this case appeared in *Psychiatry in General Medical Practice,* edited by G. Usdin and J. Lewis. Copyright 1979 by McGraw-Hill, Inc. Reproduced by permission.

References

Abraham, K. Ejaculatio praecox. In E. Jones (Ed.), *the International psychoanalytical library* (No. 13). London: Hogarth Press, 1949. (Originally published, 1917.)

Altman, C. *You can be your own sex therapist.* New York: G. P. Putnam's Sons, 1976.

Apfelbaum, B. A contribution to the development of the behavioral–analytic sex therapy model. *Journal of Sex and Marital Therapy,* 1977, *3*(2), 128–138.

Bandura, A. *Principles of behavior modification.* New York: Holt, Rinehart & Winston, 1969.

Barbach, L. Group treatment of preorgasmic women. *Journal of Sex and Marital Therapy,* 1974, *1*(2), 139–145.

Barbach, L. G. *For yourself.* New York: Doubleday, 1975.

Bennet, D. Treatment of ejaculatio praecox with monoamine-oxidase inhibitors. *The Lancet,* 1961, *2* (December) 1309.

Berne, E. *What do you say after you say hello?* New York: Grove Press, 1972.

Chassin, L., Perelman, M., & Weinberger, G. Reducing parental resistance to examining family relationships: The therapeutic use of a child management task. *Psychotherapy: Theory, Research and Practice,* 1974, *11*, 387–390.

Ellis, A. The rational-emotive approach to sex therapy. In A. Ellis & R. Greiger (Eds.), *Handbook of rational-emotive therapy.* New York: Springer, 1978.

Hartman, W. E., & Fithian, M. A. *Treatment of sexual dysfunction: A bio-psycho-social approach.* New York: Aronson, 1974.

Hastings, D. W. *Impotence and frigidity.* Boston: Little, Brown & Co., 1963.

Johnson, V. E., & Masters, W. H. A team approach to the rapid diagnosis and treatment of sexual incompatibility. *Western Journal of Surgery, Obstetrics and Gynecology,* 1964, *72*(6), 371–375.

Kaplan, H. S. *The new sex therapy.* New York: Brunner/Mazel, 1974.

Kaplan, H. S., Kohl, R. N., Pomeroy, W. B., Offit, A. K., & Hogan, B. Group treatment of premature ejaculation. *Archives of Sexual Behavior,* 1974, *3*(5), 443–452.

Kaplan, H. S., & Perelman, M. A. The physician and the treatment of sexual dysfunction. In G. Usdin & J. Lewis (Eds.), *Psychiatry in general medical practice,* New York: McGraw-Hill, 1979.

Kass, J., & Strauss, F. *Sex therapy at home.* New York: Simon & Schuster, 1975.

Kinsey, A. C., Pomeroy, W. B., & Martin, C. E. *Sexual behavior in the human male.* Philadelphia: W. B. Saunders, 1948.

Klein, M. H., Dittman, A. T., Parloff, M. B., & Gill, M. M. Behavior therapy: Observations and reflections. *Journal of Consulting and Clinical Psychology,* 1969, *33*, 259–266.

Lazarus, A. A. *Behavior therapy and beyond.* New York: McGraw-Hill, 1971.

Lazarus, A. A. Multimodal behavior therapy: Treating the BASIC ID. *Journal of Nervous and Mental Disease,* 1973, *156*, 404–411.

Leiblum, S. *Group therapy of sexual dysfunction.* Paper presented at the meeting of the Eastern Association for Sex Therapy, New York, March, 1978.

Leiblum, S. R., & Rosen, R. C. The use of behavior modification techniques in sexual counseling. *The Journal of Perth Amboy General Hospital,* 1974, *3*(3), 12–19.

Leiblum, S., Rosen, R., & Pierce, D. Group treatment format: Mixed sexual dysfunctions. *Archives of Sexual Behavior,* 1976, *5*(4), 313–322.

LoPiccolo, J., & Miller, H. A program for enhancing the sexual relationship of normal couples. *The Counseling Psychologist,* 1975, *5*(1), 41–45.

Lowe, J., & Mikulas, W. Use of written material in learning self-control of premature ejaculation. *Psychological Reports,* 1975, *37*, 295–298.

Mahoney, M. J. *Cognition and behavior modification.* Cambridge: Ballinger, 1974.

Masters, W. H., & Johnson, V. E. *Human sexual response.* Boston: Little, Brown & Co., 1966.

Masters, W. H., & Johnson, V. E. *Human sexual inadequacy.* Boston: Little, Brown & Co., 1970.

Meichenbaum, D. *Cognitive-behavior modification*. New York: Plenum Press, 1977.

Mellgren, A. Treatment of ejaculatio praecox with Thioridazine. *Psychotherapy and Psychosomatics*, 1967, *15*, 51–52.

Munjack, D., & Oziel, J. Resistance in the behavioral treatment of sexual dysfunctions. *Journal of Sex and Marital Therapy*, 1978, *4*(2), 122–139.

Oliven, J. F. *Clinical sexuality (3rd ed.)*. Philadelphia and Toronto: J. B. Lippincott, 1974.

Peck, H. B. *A transactional analysis perspective on the new treatment approaches to the sexual dysfunctions*. Paper presented at the meeting of the International Transactional Analysis Association, San Francisco, August, 1975.

Perelman, M. A. The treatment of premature ejaculation by time-limited, group sex therapy (Doctoral dissertation, Columbia University, 1976). *Dissertation Abstracts International*, 1977, *37*, 5369B. (University Microfilms No. 77-8262, 218)

Perelman, M. A. *Group treatment of premature ejaculation, two years later: Success or failure*. Paper presented at the meeting of the Association for the Advancement of Behavior Therapy, Atlanta, December, 1977.

Perelman, M. A. *Adjunctive group therapy: Mixed male sexual dysfunctions*. Paper presented at the meeting of the Eastern Association for Sex Therapy, New York, March, 1978.

Rowland, K., & Haynes, S. A sexual enrichment program for elderly couples. *Journal of Sex and Marital Therapy*, 1978, *4*(2), 91–114.

Sager, C. J. Sexual dysfunctions and marital discord. In H. S. Kaplan, *The new sex therapy*. New York: Brunner/Mazel, 1974.

Schneidman, B., & McGuire, L. Group therapy for nonorgasmic women: Two age levels. *Archives of Sexual Behavior*, 1976, *5*(3), 239–247.

Semans, J. H. Premature ejaculation: A new approach. *Southern Medical Journal*, 1956, *49*, 353–358.

Shapiro, B. Premature ejaculation: Review of 1130 cases. *Journal of Urology*, 1943, *50*, 374–379.

Spiess, W. The psycho-physiology of premature ejaculation: Some factors related to ejaculatory latency. (Doctoral dissertation, State University of New York at Stony Brook, 1977). *Dissertation Abstracts International*, 1977, *38*, 1424B. (University Microfilms No. 77-20,036,203)

Tanner, B. Two case reports on the modification of the ejaculatory response with the squeeze technique. *Psychotherapy: Theory, Research and Practice*, 1973, *10*(4), 297–300.

Wolpe, J., & Lazarus, A. A. *Behavior therapy techniques*. New York: Pergamon, 1966.

Yulis, S. Generalization of therapeutic gain in the treatment of premature ejaculation. *Behavior Therapy*, 1976, *7*, 355–358.

Zilbergeld, B. Group treatment of sexual dysfunction in men without partners. *Journal of Sex and Marital Therapy*, 1975, *1*(3), 204–214.

Zilbergeld, B. *Male sexuality*, Boston: Little, Brown & Co., 1978.

8

Treatment of Erectile Dysfunction

ALBERT ELLIS

Erectile disorders constitute the most distressing class of sexual dys-
functions common to males. Viewed objectively, erection is not
synonymous with ability to have or enjoy sex, but almost all men
regard the loss of erection not only as signaling the end of their sex life,
but also as an emasculating slur on their manhood. In part, the undue
emphasis on erection as the prerequisite for sex is a result of our
society's emphasis on performance rather than pleasure, on the goal
rather than the process of physical intimacy. Most men (and their
partners!) do not realize that they do not need to have an ejaculation or
orgasm during each sexual encounter, and this contributes to the
enormous pressure placed on the ability to have and sustain long erec-
tions.

Various approaches have been employed throughout the years to
overcome erectile failure. By and large, most investigators agree that
psychodynamic-depth approaches are not useful. Other options in-
clude a variety of behavioral interventions, ranging from systematic
desensitization to in vivo *sensual exercises. Masters and Johnson*
methods have been found to be quite effective, particularly with the
male who has a caring and cooperative partner. For single males,
treatment approaches may take a number of paths, from masturbation
training to relaxation and hypnotic therapies.

While the elimination of performance anxiety is widely regarded as
an essential component of treatment, it constitutes but one aspect of
the problem. Many sexologists are now aware that unrealistic sexual
expectations, insufficient arousal, absence of the proper setting condi-
tions for sex, and too great a premium placed on erection are all con-
tributing factors.

A proper diagnosis to distinguish physical from psychogenic erec-
tile difficulties is of critical importance, although, as Ellis points out in
his chapter, psychogenic causes are by far the most common. What is
particularly important is an adequate assessment to identify all of the
causes and maintaining conditions of the difficulty.

In his chapter on the treatment of erectile disorders, Ellis clearly
and persuasively shows that erectile dysfunction would not be as de-
vastating as it is for most men were it not for their interpretation and
subsequent self-defeating conditions regarding the experience. He illus-
trates how a rational-emotive approach to treatment identifies the mul-

tiple cognitive, emotional, and behavioral antecedents of the problem and how interventions must often occur in all three areas to ensure success. His emphasis on disputing irrational beliefs is particularly important for both the male and his partner and provides a realistic way of dealing with occasions in which erectile failure does occur. Ellis' endorsement and illustration of a variety of intervention methods for the treatment of erectile failure is reflective of the new sex therapies generally. Given the imprecise state of knowledge regarding the causes and treatment of sexual disorders currently available, the sex therapist must have available a variety of treatment methods and the skill to implement them. Ellis clearly does.

*Albert Ellis is Executive Director of the Institute for Rational-Emotive Therapy in New York. He is the author of numerous books (*Sex without Guilt, Sex and the Liberated Man, A New Guide to Rational Living*) and hundreds of articles on rational-emotive therapy in general and sex therapy in particular.*

———————

A great deal has been written about the treatment of sexual inadequacy in the male, but much of this material is about "premature ejaculation" or what might more properly be called "fast ejaculation" (Ellis, 1960, 1975a, 1976; Hartman & Fithian, 1972; Kaplan, 1974; Masters & Johnson, 1970; Semans, 1956). This chapter will only consider "primary sexual dysfunction," or "erectile dysfunction," which means a male's inability to get a full erection under almost any conditions and/or his easily losing erection; when the term "impotence" is used in this chapter, it will mean only this form of sexual malfunctioning.

Masters and Johnson (1970) define primary impotence as a male's never being "able to achieve and/or maintain an erection quality sufficient to accomplish successful coital connection" (p. 137). Out of 277 males whom they saw with sexual problems, only 12% had this disorder; and of the more than 1000 men I have seen with various forms of "impotence" during the past 35 years, only 10% had serious erectile dysfunction.

Diagnosis of Erectile Dysfunction

As has been noted in the literature for almost a hundred years, almost all forms of impotence are largely of psychological rather than physiological origin (H. Ellis, 1928). To differentiate organic from psychological deficits accurately, sex therapists often take a long sex history and insist on a full medical examination; but a few direct questions may serve equally well, since if it is ascertained that the client sometimes achieves erection in intercourse, usually does so during masturbation, has little trouble during petting, and often has good erections while asleep, it is fairly certain that his problems are of psychological origin.

Organic Causes of Erectile Dysfunction

Many physiological causes of erectile dysfunction exist, including diseases (e.g., diabetes and multiple sclerosis), glandular deficiencies, vascular disorders, drug abuse, surgical trauma, and dietary deficiencies (Ansari, 1975; Comfort, 1978; Ellenberg, 1978; Ellis, 1960; Kaplan, 1974, 1977; Meyer, 1976; Prasad, 1978; Weiss, 1972). Some physical problems do not directly cause this problem but result in relatively low sex drive that indirectly leads to poor erection (Apfelbaum, 1977a, 1977b; Schumacher & Lloyd, 1974). Some males not only have a degree of low sexuality or mild physical blocks to functioning, but they also refuse to try to overcome this handicap and to work hard to bypass it; consequently, they have a combined physical and psychological cause for their lack of "ability." Their anxiety and their low frustration tolerance about their primary disability lead them to wind up with a much greater degree of malfunctioning than they would "naturally" have (Ellis, 1957, 1976, 1978b, 1979b; Ellis & Abrahms, 1978).

Definitive diagnosis of the role of organic contributions in erectile dysfunction can be aided by a lengthy interview, a comprehensive physical examination, and by a detailed questionnaire to be filled out by clients (Annon, 1974, 1975; Derogatis, Meyer, & Dupkin, 1976; Hartman & Fithian, 1972; Kaplan, 1974; LoPiccolo & Steger, 1978; Masters & Johnson, 1970). Devices that directly measure daytime and nocturnal penile tumescence can also be employed (Geer, 1975; Gonick, Kenepp, Ficher, & Martin, 1978; Heiman, 1978; Karacan, 1978; Schiavi, 1976). Good clinicians, however, as noted above, can usually differentiate organic from psychological origin of poor erection by asking a few simple questions about the conditions under which the male usually functions.

Psychogenic Etiology of Erectile Dysfunction

Psychodynamic and psychoanalytic theories hypothesize that lack of erectile ability arises from severe complexes, especially the Oedipus complex, stemming from traumatic childhood experiences (Freud, 1965), but these theories have little evidence to support them (Hogan, 1978; Masters & Johnson, 1970). A much better validated theory is that of rational-emotive therapy (RET) and other cognitive-behavior therapies. This view states that sexual arousal depends on the male's concentrating on exciting stimuli and is easily blocked when he focuses on something nonsexual or antisexual (such as business problems or the idea that he *has* to succeed at sex and it is *awful* if he does not). If he brings about performance anxiety by spying on himself during sex and concluding that he is an incompetent person for failing, he will often interfere with his getting and/or sustaining an erection (Annon, 1974, 1975; Ellis, 1954, 1960, 1962, 1971, 1975b, 1976; Kaplan, 1974; Masters & Johnson, 1970, 1976a, 1976b; McCarthy, 1978; Zilbergeld, 1978).

In RET terms, at point A (Activating Experience or Activating Event), a male has the opportunity to have sex, and at point C (emotional and behavioral Consequence), he feels anxious and fails to get an erection. He (and, alas, some of his therapists!) wrongly believe that A causes C—that the pressure of going to bed with a desirable partner "causes" him to feel anxious and to fail. Actually, the more direct and "real" cause is B—his Belief System about what happens at A. At B, he tells himself two Beliefs: One of these is a set of rational Beliefs (rBs): "I don't like failing. How frustrating if I don't maintain an erection! My partner may disapprove of me for failing, and that would be highly unfortunate." These Beliefs are rational because his desires or goals are to succeed and please himself and his partner, and sex failure would sabotage such goals. If he stayed *only* with these rBs, he would merely feel sorry, frustrated, and annoyed—but *not* anxious at point C (Consequence).

But this male also thinks and "feels" a set of irrational Beliefs (iBs): "I *must* not fail and disappoint my partner! It would be *awful* if I did! I *can't stand* failing and am a *rotten person* who is doomed to fail in the future!" This set of Beliefs is irrational because it helps sabotage his desires, and it includes assumptions and conclusions that are not empirically confirmable and that go beyond reality.

To make things worse, once this male has erectile dysfunction, he frequently develops a set of iBs and inappropriate feelings (Consequences) *about* failing and thereby develops a secondary symptom of disturbance: anxiety about his anxiety. First, he creates ego anxiety about his failing with these iBs: "I *must* not feel anxious and *should* not have made myself fail! How terrible! I am *no good* for producing this anxiety and failure!"

Second, he creates discomfort anxiety about his failing and about his initial anxiety: "I *must* not feel anxious and have so much of a hassle about sex! It's *too* hard for me to succeed and feel good! What a horrible world this is, considering my difficulties in feeling anxious and in enjoying myself sexually!'' Ego anxiety involves a male's viewing himself as an incompetent, worthless *person*, and discomfort anxiety involves his seeing life as *too difficult to bear* when he fails and feels primary anxiety (Ellis, 1978b, 1979b, 1979c). From clinical experience, I would say that few men who have long histories of the primary symptom of erectile dysfunction avoid creating a second-level symptom of both ego anxiety (self-downing) and discomfort anxiety (low frustration tolerance and self-pity) about their primary disturbance.

In addition to performance anxiety, there may be several other etiological factors in erectile malfunctioning, such as the following.

Partnership Problems. As Masters and Johnson (1970), Zussman and Zussman (1977), and other authorities point out, relationship or partnership problems often contribute significantly to erectile dysfunction. These may be of many kinds:

1. Some women insist that their mates *have to* satisfy them sexually and put undue pressure on their partners.

2. Males who once found their mates originally attractive and arousing may lose sexual interest later (Kaplan, 1977).

3. Some women are not keen on sex and avoid having it or properly exciting their partners when they do have it (Ellis, 1960, 1976).

4. A man may not communicate adequately with his mate and may not show her how to arouse and satisfy him (Ellis, 1960; Kaplan, 1974; Masters & Johnson, 1970). A male may have strong desires for novelty and variety and may only be fully excitable if he has several partners simultaneously or serially.

5. A man may be consciously or unconsciously homosexual, and therefore "unable" to respond with a female.

6. Hostility between mates may block erectile functioning.

7. Ignorance may interfere with partners using sex acts and positions that would help a male get and maintain good erections (Ellis, 1960, 1976; Hartman & Fithian, 1972; Masters & Johnson, 1970, 1976a).

General Emotional Disturbance. Although psychoanalytic theory posits that general emotional disturbances frequently stem from basic sex problems, the reverse is generally true: Men who have general feelings of anxiety, depression, worthlessness, self-pity, and hostility are more likely to suffer from erectile dysfunction than those who are emotionally healthier (Apfelbaum, 1977a, 1977b; Ellis, 1954, 1960, 1976; Kinder & Blakeney, 1977; Levay & Kagle, 1977). This does not mean that they require intensive psychoanalysis, which will frequently do much more harm than good and is contraindicated (Reynolds, 1977), but it does mean that their underlying disturbances had better be recognized and dealt with along with their specific sex problems (Ellis & Grieger, 1977).

External Pressure to Succeed. Many commentators have pointed out that erectile dysfunctioning correlates highly with external or socially inculcated pressure on a "liberated" male to succeed at satisfying his female partners with his penis (Ellis, 1976; Ginsberg, Frosch, & Shapiro, 1972; Nobile, 1972; Zilbergeld, 1978). This is partly true, but we had better remember that it is not really the Activating Event (social pressure) at A that causes males to fail sexually at C (Consequence); instead, it more importantly is their iBs: "I *must* accede to these pressures and show my partner (and everyone else) what a great lover I am; otherwise I am no damned good!"

Puritanism and Guilt. When I first started practicing sex therapy some 35 years ago, many of my clients made themselves sexually inadequate by feeling guilty about their sex practices (Ellis, 1954, 1958). This is much less true today, but there are still some men who believe that sex is "wrong" or "wicked," or who believe that because of their nonsexual "immoralities" they are "undeserving" of sexual pleasure. Not many, but some.

Ignorance. In the old days, again, a large percentage of my sexually inadequate male and female clients were profoundly ignorant of what to do to satisfy themselves and their partners. This is much less true today, but some males still block their sexual functioning by believing such myths as that a man must have a fairly large penis and last a long time in intercourse to satisfy almost any female, and that petting is all right, but sex must end up in intercourse to be "good" and "legitimate" (Ellis, 1960; McCary, 1967, 1971; Pomeroy, 1977).

Methods of Overcoming Erectile Dysfunction

I shall now outline the most effective and frequently used methods in RET for overcoming erectile dysfunction and briefly list some non-RET methods that can also be employed. RET is consciously cognitive, emotive, and behavioral, and it invariably tries to reveal to clients and help them overcome their general and sexual difficulties. Its main techniques follow.

Cognitive Methods

RET sex therapy uses about a dozen major cognitive methods, each of which has from 10 to 20 subheadings (Ellis, 1978a). Some of the main cognitive headings are described below.

Disputing Irrational Beliefs

The main and most important RET method is that of showing clients that they have iBs or "*must*urbatory" ideas that create and sustain their erectile inadequacy, and helping them to see these Beliefs clearly and then actively dispute and surrender them, both during the therapy sessions and in the course of steady homework assignments. The three main iBs are as follows: (1) "I *must* perform well sexually; it is *awful* when I don't; I can't stand my sexual inadequacy, and I am an *incompetent person* for having it." This Belief creates anxiety, depression, and feelings of worthlessness. (2) "You *must* help me sexually and lovingly; it is *terrible* when you don't; I *can't bear* your unfairness and inconsiderateness; you are a *rotten person* for treating me in this manner!" This Belief creates anger, hostility, rage, resentment, and overrebellion. (3) "The conditions under which I live *must* be easy and gratifying and provide me with sex–love comfort without any undue hassles; it is *horrible* when they aren't this way; I *can't tolerate* sex frustration; life is hardly worth living in such a miserably uncomfortable world!" This Belief results in low frustration tolerance, self-pity, depression, and withdrawal from difficult sex relationships.

In RET, clients are shown how to Dispute these Bs (Beliefs) after first noting their Cs (emotional and behavioral Consequences or symptoms) and As (Activating Experiences) that occur just before they have erectile dysfunction or anxiety about it. Disputing is equivalent to the scientific method (Ellis, 1962, 1977, 1979b; Ellis & Grieger, 1977; Mahoney, 1977, 1979). Clients learn to use this method to ask themselves logicoempirical questions, such as: "Where is the evidence that I *must* succeed sexually and be approved by my partner? What makes it *awful* or *horrible* if I fail? Why *can't I* stand failing or my anxiety about failing? Where is it writ that I am a *rotten person* if I fail sexually or am anxious about failing?"

If clients learn to correctly think through (not merely parrot!) the answers to these Disputes, they arrive at E, a new Effect, which is in three parts: (1) A cognitive Effect (cE) or new philosophy: "There is no evidence that I *have to* succeed sexually and be approved by my partner, though it would be highly desirable if I did. It is never *awful* or *horrible* if I fail—only damned inconvenient! I definitely *can* stand failing and *can* bear being anxious, even though I'll never like it! I am not (nor is any human) a *rotten person* for having ineffectual *behavior;* I am merely a fallible human who will always make many mistakes but can live happily in spite of them." (2) An emotive Effect (eE)—that is, an appropriate feeling of disappointment, sorrow, and annoyance rather than an inappropriate feeling of anxiety or depression. (3) A behavioral Effect (bE)—a determination to keep experimenting and learning sexually, to improve performance; and action that backs up this determination: the clients' forcing themselves, however uncomfortably, to have more rather than less sex, and thereby to overcome their resistance to having it.

While being highly cognitive in the form of Disputing (as well as in other ways about to be listed below), RET always includes several emotive and behavioral techniques of sex therapy, which will be outlined later. It is never *merely* cognitive but is a comprehensive system of personality change in general and sex therapy in particular.

Information-Giving

Males with erectile dysfunctioning (as well as their partners) are informed about how erection normally takes place and how people interfere with it. They may be told, for example, that their disorder is functional rather than physical; that spontaneous erection at the sight of their partner is not necessary; that worrying about performance will block rather than enhance it; and that withdrawing from sex will usually make things worse rather than better (Ellis, 1960; Lazarus, 1971a, 1971b).

Myth-Attacking

Males who believe cultural or other myths about sex are disabused of these myths and taught, for example, that various "wrong" or "abnormal" sex acts—such as oral or anal relations—are permissible and "right"; that most women do *not* demand intercourse to have full sex satisfaction; that they do not have to have a large penis to satisfy their partners; that simultaneous orgasm may well be an unrealistic goal; and that they can begin to have sex even when they are unaroused and unerect (Ellis, 1960; McCary, 1971; Masters & Johnson, 1970).

Antipuritanical Teachings

If clients and their partners are blocked by puritanical sex views, they are disabused of them by various kinds of teachings: individual instruction by a therapist, group therapy interactions, bibliotherapy, audiovisual loosening up, sex-attitude-restructuring workshops, etc. They are shown that sex covers a wide variety of "proper" acts and attitudes, as long as they have the full cooperation of their partners (Comfort, 1972, 1975; Ellis, 1954, 1960, 1976, 1979a; LoPiccolo & Miller, 1978).

Cognitive Distraction

Males with erectile dysfunction frequently block arousal and orgasm by focusing on antisexual things, such as business or other nonsexual problems, or on the horror of failing. If, instead, they distract themselves and focus on something pleasurable or neutral, they often function adequately (Masters & Johnson, 1970). Some of the better forms of cognitive distraction include (1) sensate focus, or deliberate concentration on sensual pleasuring of oneself and one's partner (Masters & Johnson, 1970); (2) relaxation procedures, such as progressive muscle relaxation; (3) meditation procedures; (4) yoga, taoistic, and other oriental methods of focusing on nonsexual things while engaging in sex; (5) methods of body massage; and (6) intense awareness, satori, or gestalt therapy techniques.

Imaging Methods

Although, as Masters and Johnson (1970) have emphasized, many males spontaneously achieve erection when they are not spying on themselves and worrying that they will fail, many (especially older males) do not. With the latter, it has been found that sexual arousal *can* be "willed" or unspontaneously incited by thinking highly sexual thoughts or engaging in arousing imagery (Heiman, 1977; Kelly, 1976; Lazarus, 1978; Nims, 1975; Rubin & Henson, 1975). In RET sex therapy, males are often trained to imagine exciting sex acts and to use fantasies and even fetishes so that they can unashamedly help themselves get and sustain erections. The use of erotic and pornographic materials is sometimes valuable in this respect (Mann, Berkowitz, Sidman, Starr, & West, 1974).

Sexual Focusing

In sensate focus (Masters & Johnson, 1970), the partners concentrate on their own and on the other's body sensations. Sexual focusing can be, as noted immediately above, on imaginative material, or it can be on physical experiences and excitements during sex acts: on genital and nongenital sensations, on one's partner's satisfactions, on amative feelings, etc. However, as Myers (1974) has noted, the closer people get to orgasm, the less involved with their partner and the more involved with their own physical and mental feelings they tend to be. Consequently, some males with erectile dysfunction had better learn to focus more on their own sensations during sex—and then, after they have functioned satisfactorily and pleasurably, to ensure that their partners are satisfied as well.

Partner Education

Masters and Johnson (1970) and their followers (Zussman & Zussman, 1977) emphasize the necessity of couple therapy for problems of erection, since a man's partner may often contribute to his sexual "disability." I have found couple sex therapy to be quite unnecessary and often even undesirable, since if a man is helped to succeed with only one specific cooperative partner, he may make a minor improvement and may easily start failing again with a new mate. But couple therapy also has its distinct advantages, and a male may often be quickly helped to achieve and sustain erection if his partner is shown that she need not pressure him into believing that only prolonged intercourse with a firm penis will satisfy her sexually.

In one case, for example, I merely had a 5-minute talk with the wife of a man who almost always failed to maintain his erection, explaining, "Look. Your husband is not in the least impotent physically, since he can easily get erections when he is by himself, masturbating, or when he is sleeping and not worrying about performing. But he thinks he *has to* get a stiff erection and to maintain it for 20 minutes of intercourse to satisfy *you*. Therefore, he doesn't focus on his own pleasure but only on your potential *dis*pleasure; and he blames himself mercilessly in case you don't get an orgasm during intercourse. Now, if you can show him—on many different occasions—that you enjoy *all* kinds of sex, that you can come without intercourse, and that even if you don't come you can still enjoy physical contact, that will help considerably to get him to take off the pressure that he wrongly thinks you are putting on him. If you go out of your way to show him that this pressure is *not* coming from you, he will in all probability have much better erections." This wife got my point and put it into practice, and from that day onward, her husband had little difficulty in maintaining an erection almost every time they had intercourse.

Bibliotherapy and Audiovisual Aids

The use of self-help manuals has been a notable part of sex therapy since the early part of this century, and it is conceivable that more people have been helped to overcome their sex problems through the use of bibliotherapy and audiovisual therapy during the last 50 years than have been aided by all kinds of psychotherapists combined (Annon & Robinson, 1978; Ellis, 1975a, 1975b, 1978c; Hartman & Fithian, 1972; Heiman, LoPiccolo, & LoPiccolo, 1976; LoPiccolo & Miller, 1978; Lowe & Mikulas, 1978). In the treatment of males with erectile dysfunction, the use of pamphlets and books can now be effectively implemented with filmed, videotaped, audio, and graphic materials which are now distributed by several leading producers, including EDCOA productions, Focus International, and Multi Media Resource Center.

Other Cognitive Methods

A good many other cognitive methods of sex therapy are applicable to the treatment of erectile dysfunction, including biofeedback and hypnotic techniques. Psychoanalysis may also be employed, but in my own practice as a psychoanalyst, I found it not only virtually useless in treating male and female sex inadequacies, but often iatrogenic (Ellis, 1962, 1971); and that is one of the main reasons why I abandoned it as a method of psychotherapy and created RET. Other investigators of the efficacy of psychoanalytic and psychodynamic treatment of erectile dysfunction have also strongly concluded that it is virtually useless as compared to the directive, nonpsychodynamic approaches now available (Cooper, 1978; Reynolds, 1977; Wright, Perreault, & Mathieu, 1977). Cooper is particularly vehement in this regard: "Classical analysis, which may take up to three years to complete, should not even be entertained for potency-disordered males.... Dogmatic statements as to its efficacy abound, but hard data are lacking. Accordingly, the case for its usefulness at this time remains unproven" (1978, pp. 325–327).

Emotive Methods

Some of the main emotive, dramatic, and evocative methods that are used in RET to treat problems of erectile dysfunction include the following.

Unconditional Acceptance

Males with erectile dysfunction not only observe and condemn their ineffectual *behavior* but also severely castigate *themselves* for performing inadequately. This kind of self-denigration can be ameliorated by their having a therapist with a fully accepting attitude. In one of my earliest sex cases, soon after I began practicing in 1943, I helped a 34-year-old male with a long history of erectile malfunctioning largely by having a few relaxed talks with him about several other men (who actually were friends of mine and not clients) who had similar problems. He could see, by the tone of my voice and my accepting manner, that I did not in the least despise these "disabled" males but actually had a great deal of respect for them. He was so impressed by this that he was significantly helped to accept himself with his "terrible" sex problem. In this kind of accepting atmosphere, he was able to listen better to the sexual information and attitudes that I was feeding him.

Reassurance and Support

Reassurance has distinct limitations in regular psychotherapy, since it may encourage dependency; but many men with erectile dysfunction may be encouraged to give up some of their performance anxiety if a therapist convincingly tells them that they have nothing to worry about and that there is nothing seriously wrong with them (Cooper, 1972; Masters & Johnson, 1970, 1976a). Using techniques of attentive listening and emotional support, Finkle (1977) found that urologists could do successful therapy of males with erectile problems within three sessions at weekly intervals—a shorter time than it takes with other sex therapy methods.

Shame-Attacking Exercises

Many males with erectile malfunctioning feel shame or embarrassment about their lack of potency. A man whom I saw recently felt ashamed if he did not immediately get an erection when a woman fondled his penis, if he lost his stiffness during intercourse, and if his male friends knew that he could only bring his woman friend to orgasm with his fingers and tongue.

In RET sex therapy, clients are often given shame-attacking exercises to show themselves that no act is in itself "shameful" or "humiliating" and is only made so through the individual's self-downing attitude. They do nonsexual exercises, such as wearing outlandish clothes or refusing to tip an obnoxious waiter, and they also do sex-related shame-attacking exercises, such as asking a member of the other sex to go to bed with them on short notice or asking for oral–genital or other forms of sex that they feel ashamed to ask for. Once they inure themselves to doing these "embarrassing" things and to not feeling ashamed, they find it much easier to fail at getting or maintaining erections without severely downing themselves for failing.

Risk-Taking Exercises

Risk-taking exercises are another emotive method used in RET as another form of the shame-attacking technique, because the main "risks" people take are those of looking foolish to or being considered "crazy" by others. To help himself overcome his "horrible" fears of losing an erection, a man may agree to go to a singles' place and try to make a date with five attractive women, or to openly tell some of the details of his sex life to a group of friends or strangers.

Rational-Emotive Imagery

Rational-emotive imagery (REI) is a technique created by Maxie C. Maultsby, Jr. (1975) in the course of which a male suffering from poor erections imagines the worst thing that can happen to him—such as having a partner flay him unmercifully when he fails to get an erection—and gets in touch with his own feelings of anxiety, depression, or worthlessness as he intensely imagines this happening. Then he is asked to work directly on his feelings and make himself feel *only* disappointed or sorry rather than depressed. When he does so, he is asked *how* he changed his feeling from an inappropriate to an appropriate one, and he begins to realize that he did so by changing a central cognition (e.g., "How horrible for this to happen! What a schmuck I am for failing!") to a more sensible or rational cognition (e.g., "Too bad that this happened. But it is hardly the end of the world!"). He then practices, every day for a month or so, this same exercise, until he naturally and automatically tends to feel disappointed or sorry, rather than depressed or inadequate, when he imagines himself failing sexually.

Emotive Self-Verbalizations

Cognitive-behavior therapists often teach clients rational or coping self-statements, in addition to Disputing of iBs (Beck, 1976; Ellis, 1962, 1977, 1979b; Goldfried & Davison, 1976; Mahoney, 1978, 1979; Maultsby, 1975; Meichenbaum, 1977). But such statements may be repeated by the client by rote, in a namby-pamby way, and may therefore prove ineffective. To compensate for this, males with erectile dysfunction can be shown how to say to themselves very vigorously and dramatically such self-statements as: "If I fail to get an erection, I *only* lose pleasure and never lose myself!" "I hope my partner finds me satisfying, but if she doesn't, she doesn't! Tough!" "I would like to have a ball in bed; but I don't *need* what I want and can live happily without it!"

Group Procedures

Group methods of treating males with penile dysfunction may be more effective than individual therapy because these males see other people similarly afflicted, see that others can publicly face their difficulties and talk about them openly, and often get help and good ideas from other group members (Baker & Nagata, 1978; Blakeney, Kinder, Creson, Powell, & Sutton, 1976; Leiblum, Rosen, & Pierce, 1976).

Group procedures can also give dysfunctional males feedback, so that they can see how they come across to other people, particularly to members of the other sex.

Behavioral Methods

Sex therapy has almost always included behavioral assignments, particularly *in vivo* homework assignments. Some of the main behavioral methods used in RET include the following.

Activity Homework Assignments

Unless males with erectile dysfunction take the risk of having sex, they continually reindoctrinate themselves, by avoiding such risks, with such ideas as: "It *would be* terrible if I tried and failed!" and "I *am* a worm for failing!" One of the main treatments for this condition, then, is activity homework assignments in the course of which the male, gradually or cold turkey, keeps trying "risky" or "dangerous" sex acts (David & Blight, 1977; Dengrove, 1971; Ellis, 1962, 1975a, 1975b; Lobitz & LoPiccolo, 1972; Schmidt, Nederlander, & Drake, 1976).

In Vivo Flooding

If clients are willing to carry them out, *in vivo* flooding assignments are often more effective than graduated ones, because the more often a male takes the risk of failing at sex, the more quickly he may see that nothing "horrible" or "terrible" happens and that he may quickly learn some procedures that help him succeed (Ellis, 1977, 1978b, 1979b).

In using flooding, I encourage males with erectile dysfunction to have sex, if they can arrange it, practically every day for 2 or 3 weeks in a row. I induced one of my clients who had not been able to get an erection with his wife for a period of 2 years, and who consequently avoided sex, to try to have intercourse with her every day for a month. For the first several days, he failed completely; from the 5th to the 10th days, he achieved good erections but quickly lost them; on the 11th day, he achieved and maintained a full erection—and had no difficulty from then onward. He became so desensitized to his performance anxiety as he forced himself to pet heavily and to try to copulate with his wife that it soon vanished and did not return even though, on a few subsequent occasions, he failed to get an erection. As he remarked at the end of the month-long *in vivo* desensitization: "I now *know* I can get and hold my erection. So even when I don't do so, I *know* that I can do so again. Voilà!—no more anxiety!"

A method of *in vivo* flooding that I outline in *Sex and the Liberated Man* (Ellis, 1976) and that I have especially used with single men with erectile dysfunction who avoid sex consists of their finding a suitable partner and telling her, quite clearly, that they have an erection problem. They then arrange to go to bed with her, say, on Friday night and literally stay there until Monday morning. I find that few of them can be in bed with an attractive partner for a protracted length of time without becoming less anxious and without beginning to get firm erections as they and their partner intermittently talk and make love.

On one occasion, I suggested this method for a 28-year-old man who had virtually never maintained a firm erection in a 5-year marriage and who never got solid erections in the half-dozen times he had tried with different women since his divorce a year before I saw him. He improved on my suggestion by going to bed with his womanfriend, whom he had only known a few weeks and had so far failed with sexually, on a Thursday instead of a Friday night. Although he had no erection on Thursday night, all day Friday, and Friday night, by 2:00 a.m. on Saturday morning his penis suddenly sprang to life, and by the time Monday morning arrived he had copulated with his partner about ten times and had four rousing orgasms! End of erectile dysfunction!

Operant Conditioning

As in the case of individuals with other problems, males with erectile problems can be shown how to reward or reinforce themselves when they perform onerous or "dangerous" tasks and to penalize themselves when they fail to carry out the tasks they agree to do. One of my 37-year-old clients, who achieved five to ten orgasms a week with masturbation but who refused to carry through on his agreed-upon homework assignments of making love to his wife twice a week to overcome his problem of erectile dysfunction, accepted the reward of playing ball with his children whenever he did carry out the assignment and the penalty of cleaning the bathroom and toilet when he did not carry it out. Within 2 weeks, he did his homework without fail, and 6 weeks later he achieved full erections almost every time he made love to his wife.

Skill Training and Assertion Training

Males with erectile dysfunction are often trained in RET sex therapy to acquire specific encountering, communication, petting, coital, and other skills. To this end, they are taught, coached, given *in vivo* exercises, and instructed through role-playing to practice sex–love performances that will help them gain and sustain erections. Sensate focus and assertion training are the two most common skills that are imparted, but various other competencies may be taught and assigned for practice as well (Dengrove, 1967; Ellis, 1960, 1962, 1975b; Lobitz & LoPiccolo, 1972; Masters & Johnson, 1970; Semans, 1956).

Other Behavioral Methods

Several other behavioral methods of sex therapy may be employed with males with erectile dysfunction. Systematic desensitization has often been found useful, but Kockett, Dittman, and Nusselt (1975) found this method to be significantly less effective than *in vivo* desensitization using sensate focus.

Various mechanical splints have been devised, such as the Loewenstein (1947) coitus-training apparatus, which fit over the limp penis and enable it to engage in active copulation. Once a man knows that this will actually work, he sometimes loses his performance anxiety and achieves full erection.

When used in small quantities, drugs such as alcohol, marijuana, and tranquilizers often facilitate male arousal—possibly because they have something of a placebo effect (Dengrove, 1971). When used in larger quantities, they have serious liabilities, especially those of alcoholism and drug addiction (Farkas & Rosen, 1976).

Penile implants may be used in cases of organic impotence. The Scott prosthesis is an inflatable implant in the penis that employs a hydraulic system to enable a male, through compressing a bulb in his scrotum when he desires an erection, to give himself one. The Small–Carrion prosthesis is a silicone device surgically implanted in each corpora cavernosa, the two bodies of the penis which normally fill with blood when the male has an erection. It gives a permanent erection while leaving the penis flexible enough to be inconspicuous under clothing. In cases in which males become impotent from an insufficient blood flow to the penis, an operation similar to the coronary bypass procedure used on heart patients can be used to treat males with this kind of erectile dysfunction.

One solution to the problem of erectile dysfunction is that of varietism or open marriage, because some males with strong varietist inclinations tend to become less arousable once they become acclimated to almost any single partner. One 26-year-old male I saw for sex therapy a number of years ago could not get full erections with either his wife or his mistress, although he had been quite potent with both of them during the first few months after he started having sex. When he experimented with a few other partners, his full potency was almost immediately restored. Whenever he tried a new partner, he got full erections with her and with his wife or mistress, but after a short while he felt "bored" with the new woman and his erectile ability diminished. Obviously, some males can better their sexual performances if they have a variety of partners or engage in unusual kinds of activities, such as threesomes or orgies. But this kind of "solution" has its distinct limitations and dangers, and is not often to be recommended.

Masters and Johnson (1970) at first used sex surrogates to help train males with erectile dysfunction and had some distinct success with this unorthodox technique. Most sex therapists who have discussed this method, however, point out its various legal, ethical, and practical limitations and tend to recommend it only in a highly hesitant and restricted way (Wolfe, 1978).

Treatment of a Case of Erectile Dysfunction

Juan R., a 48-year-old factory foreman of Puerto Rican background, married for the second time to a 23-year-old attractive office manager, came to sex therapy because he began to lose his erections a year after marriage and became so upset about this that he could not even become erect during masturbation or with other partners. He had previously been a "stud" with his first wife and with several other women with whom he had had extramarital affairs and had been an unofficial counselor to many of his less adept male friends when they had sex problems. He also felt guilty about leaving his first wife and his two young sons.

Cognitive Methods of Treatment

I quickly concluded that Juan's problem was psychological, because he had full nocturnal erections and could easily get aroused when petting with his wife or other women when there was no possibility of having intercourse but lost his erection as soon as they went to bed. Since he was ashamed of his sex failures, I started to use RET with his secondary problem first. At A (Activating Experience), he observed, "I see that I function poorly." At rBs about A, he told himself, "This is highly unpleasant! I hope I don't continue to behave this way! Let me see what I can do to improve my condition." At aC (appropriate Consequence), he felt annoyed and concerned about his poor functioning. At iBs about A, he told himself: "I *must* not function poorly! How *awful* if I continue to do so! I *can't stand* this condition! I am an *incompetent person* if I don't overcome it!" And at iC (inappropriate Consequence), he felt very ashamed of his erectile dysfunction and withdrew from almost all sex, for fear of failing again and of feeling humiliated about failing.

During the very first session with Juan, I started to do active RET Disputing (D) of his iBs: (1) "Why *must* you function well sexually?" (2) "In what way is it *awful* if you don't?" (3) "Even if you always keep failing, where is the evidence that you *can't stand* it?" (4) "Assuming that you keep failing, how does that make you an *incompetent person?*"

Almost immediately, by forcing him to think about and answer these Disputing questions, I helped Juan see, though at first lightly, that he did not *have to* function well sexually; that it was *only* disadvantageous and *not* awful if he remained dysfunctional; that he *could* stand this unlikable state; and that he never had to put himself down as an *incompetent person* when he failed in any important *area*. "You know," he said toward the end of the first session, "I'm beginning to see what you mean: I can still accept *myself* even if I hate my sexual failures."

Once Juan began to accept *himself* with his poor sexual *behavior*, I returned to his primary symptom: his erectile dysfunction. At A, he would go to bed with his wife or mistress. At rBs, he would tell himself, "I hope I succeed! How unfortunate if I fail!" At aC, he would feel concerned about failing. At iBs, he would say to himself, "I *must* succeed, else my partner will think I'm a slob! I *can't bear* this! How *horrible!* She's right: I *am* no good if I fail!" At iC, he almost always failed to maintain a stiff erection and felt anxious and depressed about this.

During the next several sessions, I helped Juan to see his Bs that created his sex failure and self-downing (shame), and I taught him how to go on to D, Disputing his iBs in the logicoempirical manner that is taught to all RET clients who are capable of doing this kind of scientific Disputing. In spite of his only having a high school education, he was able to do this and to say, during the fourth session, "I'm beginning to see that I'm never a good or bad person; only a person who does good or bad things—or things that help me live and enjoy or that hinder me."

Juan also had some corollary iBs that I helped him challenge and surrender: (1) "Because both my wife and mistress are so beautiful and would turn on almost any man, I *have to* succeed with them sexually and am not a real man if I don't!" (2) Because I have always been a great *macho* lover and have helped my male friends with their sex problems, it would be utterly disgraceful if they discovered I was inadequate!" (3) Because I had no really good reason for leaving my first wife and only did so because I was infatuated with my present one, I *need* to justify this move by having great sex with this second wife!"

Juan also made himself hostile with the irrational idea, "My wife *should be* more sexually initiating and active and *must* respond more quickly to my overtures; and isn't it *terrible* when she does not!" And he created self-pity and low frustration tolerance with another iB: "The conditions of my life *should be* easier and I *have to* be as potent as I was years ago, when I had no difficulty getting and maintaining erections. It's *too hard* to succeed now!" When he started to Dispute and surrender these irrationalities, he lost his hostility and developed higher frustration tolerance.

Along with Disputing of iBs, I used several other RET cognitive methods with Juan. I showed him how to focus on the "sexy" qualities of his wife and his mistress and how to use erotic fantasies when he was having sexual relations. He also was taught to use sensate focus by concentrating on arousing and satisfying his partners with his fingers and tongue rather than with his penis; and when he distracted himself, with this kind of focusing, from his self-blaming thoughts and feelings, he found that he usually achieved "spontaneous" erection. When he was very anxious, I also showed him how to use cognitive distraction by imagining a peaceful scene at the seashore and simultaneously letting his muscles relax. I also got him to use RET Disputing with his friends, thereby learning better how to apply it to himself.

Emotive–Expressive Methods of Treatment
As is usual in RET sex therapy, I used several emotive–expressive methods to help Juan overcome his erectile dysfunction. I first gave him *unconditional acceptance* by showing him, with my manner and words, that I could undamningly accept him *with* his poor behavior, including his failing to do some of his homework assignments (e.g., saying he would attempt to have sex several times a week, then copping out and not trying). I sometimes *reassured* him, though not effusively or unqualifiedly, that his impotence was functional rather than organic and that, if he kept working at changing his thinking and his actions, there was a near certainty that he could overcome it.

I gave Juan the *shame-attacking exercises* of letting several of his male friends know he was having erectile problems and of bringing himself to erection when he was in bed with his wife by tapping his penis and thinking sexy thoughts in case she did not arouse him with her lovemaking. Another shame-attacking and risk-taking exercise was telling a new woman about his sex problem and then trying to induce her to have sex with him. I showed him how he could do these "shameful" things without downing himself.

Using *rational-emotive imagery,* I got Juan to fantasize failing with his wife and having her criticize him for this failure. When he felt depressed with this imagery, he was able to change his feeling to one of disappointment by telling himself, "All right. It *is* too bad that I'm not succeeding and that she hates me for failing. But this doesn't mean that I'll *never* succeed. And even if I never do, the world won't come to an end!" After practicing rational-emotive imagery for a month, he began to feel spontaneously disappointed rather than depressed every time he thought about his possibly failing sexually.

After seeing Juan for 12 sessions of individual RET treatment, I used *group therapy* by placing him in one of my regular therapy groups, which he attended for the next 6 months. In the group, he openly discussed his erectile problems and was able to feel quite free in doing so—especially when he discovered that almost all the other males in the group at times had some kind of sex problem. He also worked on his feelings of inadequacy in nonsexual areas, such as his being too much of a "nice guy" in his work as a foreman and failing to discipline the workers under him for fear of losing their approval.

Behavioral Methods of Treatment

As again is routine in RET, I used several behavioral therapy techniques with Juan. Employing *in vivo* desensitization, I encouraged him to take the activity homework assignment of having sex with his wife at least three times a week—not of *succeeding* but merely of *trying.* Soon after he forced himself, against his fears, to do this, his performance anxiety and self-downing appreciably diminished. In addition to some gradually escalated shame-attacking exercises, Juan used flooding techniques by approaching several prospective sex partners in rapid succession and immediately telling them about his sex problem.

I taught Juan the principles of *operant conditioning* by having him allow himself to play paddleball every time he risked having sex with his wife and accept the penalty of cleaning the bathroom for an hour or burning a 20-dollar bill every time he avoided it. We found that the enactment of stiff immediate penalties particularly helped him do the assignments.

Skill training was used by talking about sex positions and showing Juan that he could enter his wife's vagina from the rear, when she was lying on her back, so as to increase the sensual and sexual sensations that aroused him. Since his wife had a small vaginal orifice that was often difficult to penetrate, it was recommended that he use a lubricant such as K-Y Jelly when he tried to make entry.

Outcome

As a result of this RET cognitive–emotive–behavioral approach, Juan improved significantly during the first six sessions, began to have sex two or three times a week, and succeeded in getting and maintaining an erection in about 65% of the times he tried. When he did not become fully erect, he still aroused his partner and brought her to orgasm, so that his relationship with both his wife and mistress significantly improved. His wife, who had threatened to leave him, was immensely pleased and gave up all ideas of separation.

By the time the 12th session arrived and Juan switched to group therapy, he was really accepting the fact that he did not *have to* get and maintain a stiff erection and that his worth as a person was not involved when he failed. He also started to become a much firmer and more efficient foreman, and he started to look for ways that he could borrow capital to open his own business. At the present writing, 6 years after he finished therapy, he comes to my Friday-night public workshops in New York City several times a year, usually with his wife, and he continues to report that even though he is now in his mid-50s, his sex drive is better than ever and he only occasionally fails to get or maintain an erection. And when failure occurs, he easily takes it in his stride.

Contraindications and Limitations of Treatment

Not all cases of erectile dysfunction prove equally treatable, and some respond to one kind of technique while others do not. In general, the most common blocks to successful therapy that I find are the following: (1) The unwillingness of the client to work and to persist at working to help himself improve; (2) the powerful iB, which the client refuses to surrender, that he is unable to overcome his anxiety and that he *can not* change; (3) the mistaken belief that the client has already worked very hard and *done everything* to change and that therefore nothing will be effective; (4) low intelligence and educational status, which interfere with the client's understanding what he has to do to improve and follow the therapist's recommendations; (5) serious general emotional disturbance, such as borderline states and psychosis, which interferes with the client's listening and learning processes; (6) organic problems that have not been properly diagnosed and eliminated along with attempts at psychotherapy; and (7) a moderate or mild degree of physiological impairment (such as low sexuality) that would require great effort for the client to overcome by psychological means, and low frustration tolerance that interferes with his making efforts to bypass and overcome his physical handicaps (Apfelbaum, 1977a, 1977b).

On the part of the therapist, the most common impediments to successful treatment include these: (1) The therapist's rigidly adhering to a theory of causation and of therapy, such as psychoanalytic theory, that has little evidence to support it and that is often iatrogenic; (2) the therapist's low frustration tolerance that blocks his/her vigorously persisting with therapeutic strategies in spite of the strong resistance of the client; (3) the therapist's utilizing only one or a few methods, such as sensate focus or Disputing iBs, which may in themselves usually be effective but which somehow are not working with a specific client, instead of the therapist's having available a variety of cognitive, emotive, and behavioral methods and using different ones if the original ones do not work; (4) the therapist's engaging in sex therapy in a namby-pamby, passive way instead of vigorously getting after clients, checking on their homework assignments, and otherwise being quite active–directive; and (5) the therapist's own emotional blocks about certain areas of sexuality or of human disturbance and his/her refusal to deal with these adequately because of these blocks.

As an example of a case in which insufficient progress was achieved, I saw a 30-year-old male who could only get full erections when he had sex with prostitutes or "bad" women but could not succeed with "nice" women for whom he cared. I ascertained that he was mainly telling himself the iB, "I *must* not show a woman I care for that I may fail sexually because then she would think me a weakling, and she would be right!" With prostitutes or other women he did not care for, he did not have this idea and therefore succeeded with them.

I persuaded him to Dispute this idea philosophically and to agree that he did not *have to* win a woman's approval, even if he cared for her; and as a homework assignment, I got him to go with several women he did care for and to risk having sex with them, although at first he was extremely afraid to do so. Within 2 months, he began improving significantly and soon did so well sexually that he formed a lasting relationship with a woman he considered to be very desirable; with her, he had no potency problems. I saw him occasionally thereafter, mainly to work on his putting himself down for failing at business, and he made some amount of progress in this connection and began to do better economically.

However, 2 years later, his womanfriend fell in love with someone else and left him; he then felt severely depressed and began to be unable again to get and maintain an erection with new partners. I ascertained that he had really had false confidence with his previous mate, and had had it mainly because she accepted him with his original sex disability, just as the prostitutes and "bad" women had done. But when she ended their relationship again, and he started going with women who were critical of him when he failed sexually, he reverted to his iB that he *must* not fail with a desirable partner, and he became dysfunctional again.

I realized that I had made the mistake, in his case, of seeing him for a while with his previous partner and, in the course of couple therapy, helping her fully accept him even when he was unable to get an erection. This worked a little "too" well because he could then lose his anxiety *wth her* but not *in general*. When he returned for therapy after this partner left him, I worked with him on accepting himself unconditionally, with *any* partner, *whether or not* he succeeded sexually; and with this new and more general "antiawfulizing" and "anti*must*urbatory" approach, he was able to refuse to put himself down with several new partners, even when he distinctly failed to get an erection and when some of them were critical of him. At this point, he was *fully* accepting of himself *with* his sexual deficiencies, and he then began to have erectile success with a variety of different women. This case tends to show that even when males tend to make *something* of a philosophic change in their attitudes toward sex failure, a thoroughgoing attitude reassessment may be lacking and retrogession may easily occur.

Treatment of erectile dysfunction is often difficult, requires thoroughgoing philosophic change in many instances, and is almost impossible without repeated *in vivo* desensitization. It may also lead to highly dramatic but short-lasting "cures." Persistence and vigorous active–directive, cognitive, emotive, and behavioral treatment is often required for lasting results.

References

Annon, J. S. *The behavioral treatment of sexual problems* (Vol. 1). Honolulu: Enabling Systems, 1974, & New York: Harper & Row, 1977.

Annon, J. S. *The behavioral treatment of sexual problems* (Vol. 2). Honolulu: Enabling Systems, 1975.

Annon, J. S., & Robinson, C. H. The use of vicarious learning in the treatment of sexual concern. In J. LoPiccolo & L. LoPiccolo (Eds.), *Handbook of sex therapy*. New York: Plenum Press, 1978.

Ansari, J. J. A study of 65 impotent males. *British Journal of Psychiatry*, 1975, *127*, 337–341.

Apfelbaum, B. A contribution to the development of the behavioral–analytic sex therapy model. *Journal of Sex and Marital Therapy*, 1977, *3*, 128–138. (a)

Apfelbaum, B. On the etiology of sexual dysfunction. *Journal of Sex and Marital Therapy*, 1977, *3*, 50–62. (b)

Baker, L. D., & Nagata, F. S. A group treatment approach to the treatment of heterosexual couples with sexual dissatisfactions. *Journal of Sex Education and Therapy,* 1978, *4*(1), 15–18.

Beck, A. T. *Cognitive therapy and the emotional disorders.* New York: International Universities Press, 1976.

Blakeney, P., Kinder, B. N., Creson, D., Powell, L. C., & Sutton, C. A short-term, intensive workshop approach for the treatment of human sexual inadequacy. *Journal of Sex and Marital Therapy,* 1976, *2*, 124–129.

Comfort, A. *The joy of sex.* New York: Crown, 1972.

Comfort, A. *More joy.* New York: Crown, 1975.

Comfort, A. (Ed.). *Sexual consequences of disability.* Philadelphia: Stickley, 1978.

Cooper, A. J. The cause and management of impotence. *Postgraduate Medical Journal,* 1972, *98*, 548–556.

Cooper, A. J. Treatments of male potency: The present status. In J. LoPiccolo & L. LoPiccolo (Eds.), *Handbook of sex therapy.* New York: Plenum Press, 1978.

David, J. R., & Blight, E. M. Interdisciplinary treatment of male sexual dysfunction in a military health care setting. *Journal of Sex and Marital Therapy,* 1977, *4*, 29–34.

Dengrove, E. Behavior therapy of the sexual disorders. *Journal of Sex Research,* 1967, *3*, 49–61.

Dengrove, E. Therapeutic approaches of impotence in the male. III. Behavior therapy of impotence. *Journal of Sex Research,* 1971, *7*, 177–183.

Derogatis, L. R., Meyer, J. K., & Dupkin, C. N. Discrimination of organic versus psychogenic impotence with the DSFI. *Journal of Sex and Marital Therapy,* 1976, *2*, 229–240.

Ellenberg, M. Impotence: What it is. *Diabetes Forecast,* 1978, *31*(1), 36–37.

Ellis, A. *The American sexual tragedy.* New York: Twayne, 1954. (Rev. ed., New York: Lyle Stuart & Grove Press, 1961.)

Ellis, A. *How to live with a "neurotic."* New York: Crown, 1957. (Rev. ed., New York: Crown, 1975.)

Ellis, A. *Sex without guilt.* New York: Lyle Stuart, 1958. (Rev. ed., New York: Lyle Stuart, & Hollywood: Wilshire Books, 1965.)

Ellis, A. *The art and science of love.* New York: Lyle Stuart, 1960. (Rev. ed., New York: Lyle Stuart & Bantam Books, 1969.)

Ellis, A. *Reason and emotion in psychotherapy.* New York: Lyle Stuart, 1962. (Paperback ed., New York: Citadel, 1977.)

Ellis, A. Rational-emotive treatment of impotence, frigidity and other sexual problems. *Professional Psychology,* 1971, *2*, 346–349.

Ellis, A. An informal history of sex therapy. *Counseling Psychologist,* 1975, *5*, 9–13. (a)

Ellis, A. The rational-emotive approach to sex therapy. *Counseling Psychologist,* 1975, *5*, 14–21. (b)

Ellis, A. *Sex and the liberated man.* New York: Lyle Stuart, 1976.

Ellis, A. Rational-emotive therapy: Research data that support the clinical and personality hypotheses of RET and other modes of cognitive-behavior therapy. *Counseling Psychologist,* 1977, *7*(1), 2–43.

Ellis, A. Certification for sex therapists. In R. Gemme & C. C. Wheeler (Eds.), *Progress in sexology.* New York: Plenum Press, 1978. (a)

Ellis, A. *Discomfort anxiety: A new cognitive-behavioral construct.* Invited address to the Association for the Advancement of Behavior Therapy Annual Convention, Chicago, November, 1978. (b)

Ellis, A. Rational-emotive therapy and self-help therapy. *Rational Living,* 1978, *13*(1), 1–9. (c)

Ellis, A. *The intelligent woman's guide to dating and mating.* New York: Lyle Stuart, 1979. (a)

Ellis, A. *Theoretical and empirical foundations of rational-emotive therapy.* Monterey, Calif.: Brooks/Cole, 1979. (b)

Ellis, A. Note on the treatment of agoraphobics by *in vivo* desensitization. *Behaviour Research and Therapy,* 1979, *17,* 161–162. (c)

Ellis, A., & Abrahms, E. *Brief psychotherapy in medical and health practice.* New York: Springer, 1978.

Ellis, A., & Grieger, R. *Handbook of rational-emotive therapy.* New York: Springer, 1977.

Ellis, H. *Studies in the psychology of sex.* Philadelphia: Davis, 1928.

Farkas, G. M., & Rosen, R. C. Effect of alcohol on elicited male sexual response. *Journal of Studies on Alcohol,* 1976, *37,* 265–272.

Finkle, A. L. Sexual psychodynamics of aging: Urologic perspectives. *Journal of the American Geriatrics Society,* 1977, *25,* 393–395.

Freud, S. *Standard edition of the complete psychological works of Sigmund Freud.* London: Hogarth, 1965.

Geer, J. H. Direct measurements of genital responding. *American Psychologist,* 1975, *30,* 415–418.

Ginsberg, F. L., Frosch, W. A., & Shapiro, T. The new impotence. *Archives of General Psychiatry,* 1972, *26,* 218–220.

Goldfried, M. R., & Davison, G. *Clinical behavior therapy.* New York: Holt, Rinehart & Winston, 1976.

Gonick, P., Kenepp, D., Ficher, I., & Martin, K. *Home monitor for nocturnal penile tumescence recording.* Paper presented at the American Urological Association Meetings, Seattle, July, 1978.

Hartman, W. E., & Fithian, M. A. *Treatment of sexual dysfunction.* Long Beach, Calif.: Center for Marital & Sexual Studies, 1972.

Heiman, J. R. A psychophysiological exploration of sexual arousal patterns in females and males. *Psychophysiology,* 1977, *14,* 266–274.

Heiman, J. R. Uses of psychophysiology in the assessment and treatment of sexual dysfunction. In J. LoPiccolo & L. LoPiccolo (Eds.), *Handbook of sex therapy.* New York: Plenum Press, 1978.

Heiman, J. R., LoPiccolo, L., & LoPiccolo, J. *Becoming orgasmic.* Englewood Cliffs, N.J.: Prentice-Hall, 1976.

Hogan, D. R. The effectiveness of sex therapy: A review of the literature. In J. LoPiccolo & L. LoPiccolo (Eds.), *Handbook of sex therapy.* New York: Plenum Press, 1978.

Kaplan, H. *The new sex therapy.* New York: Brunner/Mazel, 1974.

Kaplan, H. S. Hypoactive sexual desire. *Journal of Sex and Marital Therapy,* 1977, *5,* 3–9.

Karacan, I. Advances in the psychophysiological evaluation of male erectile impotence. In J. LoPiccolo & L. LoPiccolo (Eds.), *Handbook of sex therapy.* New York: Plenum Press, 1978.

Kelly, G. F. Multiphasic therapy for a severe sexual dysfunction. *Psychotherapy,* 1976, *13,* 40–43.

Kinder, B. N., & Blakeney, P. Treatment of sexual dysfunction: A review of outcome studies. *Journal of Clinical Psychology,* 1977, *33,* 523–530.

Kockett, G., Dittman, F., & Nusselt, L. Systematic desensitization of erectile impotence: A controlled study. *Archives of Sexual Behavior,* 1975, *4,* 493–500.

Lazarus, A. A. *Behavior therapy and beyond*. New York: McGraw-Hill, 1971, (a)

Lazarus, A. A. Behavior therapy of sexual problems. *Professional Psychology*, 1971, *2*, 349–353. (b)

Lazarus, A. A. *In the mind's eye*. New York: Rawson, 1978.

Leiblum, S. R., Rosen, R. C., & Pierce, D. Group treatment format: Mixed sexual dysfunctions. *Archives of Sexual Behavior*, 1976, *5*, 313–322.

Levay, A. N., & Kagle, S. Ego deficiencies in the areas of pleasure, intimacy and cooperation. *Journal of Sex and Marital Therapy*, 1977, *3*, 10–18.

Lobitz, W. C., & LoPiccolo, J. New methods in the behavioral treatment of sexual dysfunction. *Journal of Behavior Therapy and Experimental Psychiatry*, 1972, *3*, 23–30.

Loewenstein, J. *Treatment of impotence with special reference to mechanotherapy*. London: Hamilton, 1947.

LoPiccolo, J., & Miller, V. H. A program for enhancing the sexual relationship of normal couples. In J. LoPiccolo & L. LoPiccolo (Eds.), *Handbook of sex therapy*. New York: Plenum Press, 1978.

LoPiccolo, J., & Steger, J. The Sexual Interaction Inventory: A new instrument for assessment of sexual dysfunctions. *Archives of Sexual Behavior*, 1974, *3*, 585–595.

Lowe, J. C., & Mikulas, W. L. Use of written material in learning self-control of premature ejaculation. In J. LoPiccolo & L. LoPiccolo (Eds.), *Handbook of sex therapy*. New York: Plenum Press, 1978.

Mahoney, M. J. Personal science: A cognitive learning theory. In A. Ellis & R. Grieger (Eds.), *Handbook of rational-emotive therapy*. New York: Springer, 1977.

Mahoney, M. J. *Self-change: Strategies for solving personal problems*. New York: Norton, 1979.

Mann, J., Berkowitz, L., Sidman, J., Starr, S., & West, S. Satiation of the transient stimulating effect of erotic films. *Journal of Personality and Social Psychology*, 1974, *30*, 729–735.

Masters, W. H., & Johnson, V. E. *Human sexual inadequacy*. Boston: Little, Brown & Co., 1970.

Masters, W. H., & Johnson, V. E. *The pleasure bond*. New York: Bantam, 1976. (a)

Masters, W. H., & Johnson, V. E. Principles of the new sex therapy. *American Journal of Psychiatry*, 1976, *133*, 548–554. (b)

Maultsby, M. C., Jr. *Help yourself to happiness*. New York: Institute for Rational Living, 1975.

McCarthy, B. Male sex function and dysfunction. *Journal of Sex Education and Therapy*, 1978, *4*(1), 37–39.

McCary, J. L. *Human sexuality*. Princeton: Van Nostrand, 1967.

McCary, J. L. *Sexual myths and fallacies*. New York: Van Nostrand, 1971.

Meichenbaum, D. *Cognitive-behavior modification*. New York: Plenum Press, 1977.

Meyer, J. K. (Ed.). *Clinical management of sexual disorders*. Baltimore: Williams & Wilkins, 1976.

Myers, L. *Sex therapy and women's problems*. Paper presented at Conference on Treatment of Sex Problems, Institute for Rational-Emotive Therapy, New York City, April, 1974.

Nims, J. P. Imagery, shaping and orgasm. *Journal of Sex and Marital Therapy*, 1975, *1*, 198–203.

Nobile, P. What is the new impotence, and who's got it? *Esquire*, October, 1972, pp. 95–98; 218.

Pomeroy, W. B. The new sexual myths of the 1970s. *Siecus Report,* 1977, *5*(6), 1; 14–15.

Prasad, A. Zinc supplementation: A new therapy for erectile failure? *Sexual Medicine Today,* 1978, *2*(11), 14–17.

Reynolds, B. S. Psychological treatment models and outcome results for erectile dysfunction: A critical review. *Psychological Bulletin,* 1977, *84,* 1218–1238.

Rubin, H. B., & Henson, D. E. Voluntary enhancement of penile erection. *Bulletin of the Psychonomic Society,* 1975, *6,* 158–160.

Schiavi, R. C. Sex therapy and psychophysiological research. *American Journal of Psychiatry,* 1976, *133,* 562–566.

Schmidt, G., Nederlander, C., & Drake, L. Non-surrogate single sex therapy in treatment of primary impotence. *Journal of Sex Education and Therapy,* 1976, *2*(1), 16–20.

Schumacher, S. S., & Lloyd, C. W. *Interdisciplinatry treatment and study of sexual distress.* Paper presented at International Congress of Medical Sexology, Paris, July, 1974.

Semans, J. H. Premature ejaculation: A new approach. *Southern Medical Journal,* 1956, *49,* 353–358.

Weiss, H. D. The physiology of human penile erection. *Annals of Internal Medicine,* 1972, *76,* 793–799.

Wolfe, L. The question of surrogates in sex therapy. In J. LoPiccolo & L. LoPiccolo (Eds.), *Handbook of sex therapy.* New York: Plenum Press, 1978.

Wright, J., Perreault, R., & Mathieu, M. The treatment of sexual dysfunction. *Archives of General Psychiatry,* 1977, *34,* 881–890.

Zilbergeld, B. *Male sexuality.* Boston: Little, Brown & Co., 1978.

Zussman, L., & Zussman, S. The treatment of sexual dysfunction: Some theoretical considerations. *Journal of Contemporary Psychotherapy,* 1977, *8,* 83–90.

9

The Diagnosis and Treatment of Retarded Ejaculation

Bernard Apfelbaum

Retarded ejaculation (RE) is commonly defined as a difficulty in ejaculating during intercourse or an inability to do so. While the comparable phenomenon in women, coital anorgasmia, is quite common, the male counterpart tends to be rare. There are, as yet, no satisfying explanations for the startling difference in incidence rates for men and women or even why the male retarded ejaculator can sustain unusually long-lasting erections during sexual activities with a partner.

Most sex therapists have regarded ejaculatory inability as representing an inhibition of the orgasmic reflex, and treatment recommendations usually involve the application of highly intense stimulation to the penis before intercourse by a cooperative partner. It is believed that once having overcome the ejaculatory inhibition and having successfully achieved intravaginal ejaculation, most men will be able to enjoy intercourse with ejaculation on subsequent occasions.

In his chapter, Bernard Apfelbaum takes sharp issue with these conceptualizations and presents an intriguing new formulation of both the phenomenon of RE and its treatment. He suggests that most sex therapists, as their clients, erroneously regard erection as a surefire sign of arousal and intercourse as an activity that is positively valued. While these assumptions may be true for the majority of men, they are not true of the retarded ejaculator. For him erection is by no means a sign of arousal. In fact, Apfelbaum suggests that the retarded ejaculator's ability to develop and sustain erections in the absence of desire or arousal is one of the characteristic features of the disorder. Further, the man with this disorder derives little or no pleasure in intercourse. He may regard it as aversive, disgusting, or, at best, a chore that must be endured because society and his partner(s) insist on it. Apfelbaum views the retarded ejaculator as possessing an autosexual orientation. The key diagnostic sign of RE is the fact that only the patient's own touch is erotically arousing. He is inhibited by the touch of a partner and with her his penis is relatively insensate or numb. Apfelbaum suggests that the low success rates typically achieved in the standard treatment of ejaculatory inability are due, in part, to the failure to view RE not only as a performance dysfunction but also, more importantly, as a desire disorder. The desire disorder is specific to the partner and appears especially obvious during coitus, since intercourse is the single activity in which the retarded ejaculator most totally loses the opportunity for self-stimulation.

Apfelbaum's recommendation for overcoming coital ejaculatory inability follows from his view of RE as the male analogue of female coital anorgasmia. Treatment involves both the elimination of performance anxiety (the demand that the male must ejaculate intravaginally and enjoy it) and the prescription to become erotically aroused (that is, subjectively *aroused) before intercourse. A considerable amount of relabeling and cognitive reappraisal accompanies treatment, so that the male can change his view of himself as a "withholding individual" and see himself instead as having learned to give compulsively, albeit without desire, arousal, or pleasure. The reconceptualization of the retarded ejaculator as the "workhorse of sex, doing the work of ten," enables the patient to understand more accurately his own reactions during sex with women and to deal more honestly with his partner.*

Apfelbaum is not only a creative theorist in the field of sex therapy; he is an innovator in the practice of sex therapy. The Berkeley Sex Therapy Group, of which Apfelbaum is the director, is one of the very few centers in the United States that actively utilizes body-work therapists in the treatment of single individuals. The body-work therapist is a paraprofessional staff member who functions both as a cotherapist in the treatment and as a body-work specialist in private sessions with the client. While there has been much discussion about the pros and cons of "surrogates" in sex therapy, Apfelbaum and his colleagues have found trained body-work therapists to be a useful adjunct to treatment.

Bernard Apfelbaum is a Diplomate in Clinical Psychology, the author of numerous articles on sex therapy, and Director of the Berkeley Sex Therapy Group.

Introduction

At one time, all the sexual disorders were thought of as symptoms of deep-seated personality disturbances. With the development of the field of sex therapy, this diagnostic assessment has been revised for most of the sexual disorders. The most conspicuous exception is retarded ejaculation (RE). Although behavioral strategies are used to treat it, most sex therapists are pessimistic about the outcome.

As I see it, RE may be as responsive to brief sex therapy as are the other sexual disorders. This hypothesis is difficult to confirm with certainty because of the clinical rarity of this condition (1–2% of most clinical populations). Although some clinicians believe that the actual incidence of RE far exceeds its clinical incidence, no one has reported an extensive treatment series. Masters and Johnson's (1970) sample of 17 is the largest reported; our sample is 12, with 10 of these being treated cases; Kaplan (1974) states that her sample size was too insignificant to report.

Thus the evidence for my hypothesis that RE may be a less intractable and less deep-seated condition than is currently thought does not have an extensive empirical base. Instead, my supporting evidence is based largely on a critique of current diagnostic and therapeutic assumptions about RE, with case material being used to illustrate alternative assumptions. I will argue that RE is still seen as symptomatic of more deep-seated personality disturbances because the most immediate causes of RE have been overlooked. I will also argue that the generally accepted treatment approach to RE uniquely exposes the limitations of the "dysfunction" conception.

The dysfunction conception leads the clinician to expect that the most rapid treatment results will be gained if performance problems are taken as the therapeutic point of entry. In fact, until recently it was thought that the only cases suitable for the new sex therapy were those with performance symptoms. Desire disorders were, as RE, usually considered to be more suitable for "psychotherapy" than for "sex therapy." As I see it, what makes RE difficult to grasp is its peculiar combination of a performance symptom and an underlying desire disorder. Since the treatment of RE raises so many diagnostic and therapeutic issues, I will begin with a discussion of the issues before taking them up in detail.

Diagnostic Issues

What Is Retarded Ejaculation?

A clue to diagnostic ambiguities in the current conception of RE is to be found in the diagnosis itself. It is intended to refer to the inability to have "intravaginal" (that is, coital) orgasms, but it refers neither to orgasms nor to coitus. The same condition in women is clearly labeled as coital orgasmic dysfunction or coital anorgasmia.

A more serious ambiguity arises from the way this diagnosis is applied. All men who have no erectile problems but who are unable to have coital orgasms are diagnosed as retarded ejaculators. This seems straightforward enough until we recognize the range of cases that this includes. At one end of the range are men who have orgasms easily outside of coitus and for whom the absence of orgasm is specific to coitus. It may even be specific to coitus with one particular partner. At the other end of the range are men who have never had an orgasm of any kind.

Despite this diversity, all current causal conceptions and treatment strategies are directed only at the inability to have specifically coital orgasms. How does this make sense in the case of men for whom the absence of coital orgasms is only a small part of their problem of having any kind of orgasm? Conceivably, these can be seen as different degrees of the same disorder. The idea would be that RE is found in a graduated series, with coital orgasms, the most difficult to reach, at one end and masturbatory orgasms, the easiest to reach, at the other end.

However plausible this idea may be, it does not fit the way RE is thought of and treated, not only by sex therapists, but by depth therapists as well. They focus exclusively on these patients' response to intravaginal containment. What we are forced to conclude is that those cases in which the orgasmic difficulty is more general are mentioned in descriptions of the syndrome but then ignored in diagnostic and therapeutic formulations.

It seems to me that the reason for this is that there are two separate syndromes called RE. What we might call "true" or "specific" RE attracts all the clinical attention because such patients are likely to have partners who bring them to treatment. As I perceive this syndrome, it is not on a continuum with masturbatory anorgasmia. Quite the contrary: The true retarded ejaculator has orgasms easily and enjoys them in masturbation.

The second syndrome might best be called "masturbatory anorgasmia." What we find in this group are cases of partial arousal with erections but neither sufficient libido nor sufficient motivation to work at having orgasms. Of course, we also find cases in this group whose sexual experience is so limited that all we know is that they do not have masturbatory orgasms. There is no way to know whether they also have erectile problems. In other words, I am suggesting that masturbatory anorgasmia is best thought of as a desire disorder.

Since there has been no place to put desire disorders, masturbatory anorgasmia has been included under RE. This practice parallels Masters and Johnson's (1970) inclusion of "random orgasmic inadequacy" (in women) under female orgasmic dysfunction. It is clearly defined as a desire disorder, but their classification was by performance symptoms and so these cases had to be included under orgasmic dysfunction.

I will follow the de facto precedent of ignoring masturbatory anorgasmia, on the basis that it should be classified as a desire disorder. Once masturbatory anorgasmia is removed from consideration, the features of RE, that is, of specifically coital anorgasmia, stand out more clearly. If masturbatory anorgasmia is included, it is harder to recognize what I take to be the key diagnostic sign of RE: Only the patient's *own* touch is erotically arousing, and his basic sexual orientation is "autosexual" (masturbatory), rather than homosexual or heterosexual. As I see it, there is no continuum from coital to masturbatory anorgasmia. The retarded ejaculator could never develop masturbatory anorgasmia, so to group RE with masturbatory anorgasmia confounds what are two contrasting conditions.

Retarded Ejaculation as a Coitus-Specific Desire Disorder
Once the retarded ejaculator's masturbatory facility and enjoyment is appreciated, we can then more easily detect an underlying desire disorder. It is specific to the partner and especially to coitus, the intravaginal context being one in which the retarded ejaculator most completely loses the opportunity for self-stimulation.

I asserted earlier that what makes RE difficult to grasp is its peculiar combination of a performance symptom and an underlying desire disorder. The retarded ejaculator's aversion to a partner is masked by the presence of facile and sustained erections. We are accustomed to thinking that any loss of desire or erotic arousal would be reflected by a loss of erection. The retarded ejaculator does not lose his erections. A hitherto underemphasized feature of this condition is the presence of erections that almost suggest priapism. They are sustained far beyond the ordinary range, but, strangely enough, this almost seems to be a consequence of *lack* of erotic arousal rather than of a high level of arousal.

This quasi priapism helps account for the repeated and rather startling finding that the retarded ejaculator's partners are coitally multiorgasmic despite his coital anorgasmia. Still more surprising, this is found even when the patient admits feeling sexually repelled by or angry at his partner.

I have no adequate explanation for this phenomenon, although sexual functioning at low levels of arousal or even accompanied by aversion is clinically familiar, if theoretically unaccounted for as yet. It is as if the retarded ejaculator's excitement (erection)-phase functioning is out of phase or out of "sync" with his level of desire and erotic arousal.

Performance Implies Arousal
Although the relation between sexual performance and sexual arousal has not been discussed as it bears on RE, my impression is that the clinician considers the retarded ejaculator to be aroused even when the patient admits being repelled by the partner because there is, as yet, no other explanation for his sustained erections. If it were not for the presence of these sustained erections, why else would partner-specific RE be considered a clinical condition? If a patient has *erectile*

problems with one particular partner and not with others, it will most likely be assumed that the stimulus conditions are inadequate. But if the patient has sustained erections and is merely coitally anorgasmic with one particular partner, this is generally taken to indicate that the stimulus conditions are adequate and that the patient is a retarded ejaculator with that partner.

The clinician may also be influenced by the fact that although "no man can will an erection," in Masters and Johnson's famous phrase, most men (and women) can will orgasms. An orgasm can be produced by heavy and sustained friction despite the total absence of erection or even erotic arousal, as in men who suffer from severe chronic impotence.

The Retarded Ejaculator as a Malingerer

Thus, it is easy to assume that the retarded ejaculator is aroused and should be able to have coital orgasms. As a result, he is seen either as severely disturbed or as a kind of malingerer. What makes this an almost unavoidable impression is that the retarded ejaculator often *acts* like a malingerer. He may privately admit that he is unwilling to impregnate his partner even though he has entered treatment on his partner's initiative to find a way to conceive. He may admit that he is repulsed by his partner and enjoys denying her the satisfaction of seeing him have coital orgasms.

Both sex therapists and depth therapists recognize that the retarded ejaculator experiences coitus as traumatic, or at least as unpleasant. Although the patient's aversion to coitus is central to all causal conceptions of RE, no one asks why the patient does not avoid coitus, or at least complain about it. Also, if he is angry at his partner and wants to frustrate her, why does he choose such a surreptitious means? If almost any other kind of activity were under consideration, these might be the first questions one would ask.

Thus, the clinician does not think of helping the retarded ejaculator to be more overt in expressing his complaints about the partner and about not enjoying coitus. Here the clinician appears to be caught in a normative bias, the same one the patient is caught in: Coitus and coital orgasms *should* be enjoyable. This bias leads to the automatic expectation that the patient needs help, not to refuse coitus but to enjoy it. Thus, those patients who we are told have admitted not wanting to have coital orgasms or to impregnate their wives and who admit being repelled by them are just as energetically pushed by the clinician into having coital orgasms as are those patients whose avoidance is less deliberate.

Treatment Issues

The retarded ejaculator is the object of what is by far the most aggressive attack on a symptom to be found in the field of sex therapy. The use of a coercive strategy with RE has even gone so far as to include such an unceremonious procedure as electroejaculation by electrical stimulation of the prostate with an anal probe (as yet unreported in the literature but attributed to British behaviorists). However, the generally accepted procedure for treating the retarded ejaculator is to use a demand strategy in which the partner is required to stimulate his penis in an aggressive and forceful way, suddenly switching to intromission near the point of ejaculatory inevitability.

The idea behind this strategy is that the orgasm reflex has been inhibited and that heavy stimulation will break the "spell." No attempt is made to reconcile this formulation with the picture of the retarded ejaculator as a kind of malingerer, and, as I noted, the same treatment is used even when the patient is believed to be consciously withholding orgasm from his partner.

Although Masters and Johnson use this high-pressure, performance-demand strategy with RE (male coital anorgasmia), with female coital anorgasmia they place special stress on the need to avoid all performance demands. The assumption appears to be that the men are aroused and the women are not, perhaps another example of the impression created by the retarded ejaculator's sustained erections. In contrast, the treatment for RE that I advocate is entirely consistent with Masters and Johnson's treatment of *female* coital anorgasmia. This reflects the fact that I consider the diagnostic similarities to be much greater than the differences between male and female coital anorgasmia.

Beyond Dysfunction

Automatic Erections

The automatic erections that I have claimed are pathognomonic of RE are evident from our own cases, but I will begin with case illustrations taken from Masters and Johnson (1970) and Kaplan (1974) to demonstrate that the evidence for this diagnostic cue has been there all along, though its significance has been overlooked.

Masters and Johnson note in passing that "the incompetent ejaculator [their diagnostic term] can maintain an erection indefinitely during coital sex play, with mounting, and not infrequently for a continuum of 30 to 60 minutes of intravaginal penile containment" (1970,

p. 128). They might well have added that he can maintain an erection even under extremely adverse conditions: They report that one patient was married to a woman he found totally objectionable physically. "He was able to perform coitally with his wife from an erective point of view, but after penetration he was repulsed rather than stimulated by her demanding pelvic thrusting." In another case, "the husband was so physically repulsed by his wife that, *although erections were maintained,* he rarely reached sufficient levels of sexual tension to approach ejaculation [italics added]" (Masters & Johnson, 1970, p. 120ff.). In both cases, we find what amounts to a prescription for impotence, but instead we find extraordinary "potency."

These men are good sexual performers, what I (1977c) have called "bypassers." Evidence for their sustained erections comes from the fact that, as Masters and Johnson also note, the partners of retarded ejaculators tend not only to be multiorgasmic (p. 132), but to respond this way despite feeling rejected and despite what Masters and Johnson (1970) call "levels of pychosexual frustration . . . beyond comprehension":

> Most of these women, despite a real concept of personal rejection, have known many occasions of multiorgasmic response during their marriages. Even those wives rejected by their husbands as physically unappealing occasionally were multiorgasmic during their coital opportunities. (p. 127)

Here we have a prescription for coital anorgasmia, but find orgasmic facility instead. It seems apparent that these women must have been responding to physical and not psychological stimulation. I cite this here primarily as evidence for the retarded ejaculator's almost priapic erections: He is the workhorse of sexual relationships.

One of our patients said that he hated this workhorse role but felt that with a sustained full erection he could not gracefully decline to go on to penetration. He seemed to genuinely dread these erections and puzzled over why they were so persistent since he dreaded having them. Another RE patient said that after extended periods of thrusting, his back gave out before his erection did. I (1977d) have reported on one RE case in which during the treatment the patient learned to urinate through his erect penis. His erection was unaffected.

I should note here that we do not find evidence of automatic functioning in every published case of RE. However, this variable has not been assessed in each case, and the examples given of automatic functioning by retarded ejaculators are among the most dramatic examples of this response style to be found in the literature. Further, all of the seven cases seen by us in individual body-work sex therapy (see below) have shown this characteristic. Three other cases seen by us in couple sex therapy also seemed to be of this type. In two additional cases, seen for only one counseling session each, there was insufficient evidence to evaluate them on this dimension. There are some published cases in which the patient was also diagnosed as impotent (Razani, 1977), and Masters and Johnson reported that some of their RE patients eventually did become impotent. I take these to be mixed conditions.

Case 1: An Automatic Performer

One of the three cases presented by Kaplan (1974, pp. 321–323) provides a striking example of the retarded ejaculator as a good performer. This patient had suffered a spinal cord injury that badly impaired the sensitivity of his penile skin. He was afraid his wife would leave him if she knew he could not reach coital orgasms, and so he faked it for the first 4 months of his marriage. Sexual contact left him "very frustrated and upset," ending in his secretly masturbating. "He was frantic in his attempts to overcome his dysfunction and tried to have intercourse at least once every day." Later in the marriage "he had continued to insist compulsively on daily sex." Evidence for his continuing to have sustained erections despite his fear of failure and lack of desire is the fact that in the "system of lovemaking" they had worked out, "they would have intercourse until she climaxed," and then "she would stimulate him to orgasm manually" even though "stimulation was often very prolonged and tedious." Here is the prescription for impotence, and again the opposite is the case.

Autosexuality

The case cited above is of interest because the numbing of this patient's penile skin mimics the condition that I have proposed is present in the intact retarded ejaculator. In other words, here we have a case of demonstrable penile numbness leading to RE. This may also be a case in which the RE patient's autosexuality has been overlooked, making his organic impairment appear to be the sole cause of his RE. A close reading of the case report indicates that despite his organic impairment, he may have been a true retarded ejaculator by my definition. His penile numbness may have affected him only when he was with his wife. We are not told whether this patient had equal difficulty masturbating. We only know that "he would wait for her to fall asleep, at which point he would masturbate in the bathroom" (p. 322). This appears to suggest that even this patient could masturbate relatively easily. Only manual stimulation by his wife is described as "often very prolonged and tedious." In other words, it may only have been with his wife that he needed the additional sensitivity he had lost because of his injury.

Case 2: Trying to Include the Partner

The retarded ejaculator is much more responsive to his own hand than to his partner's. This is a dramatic phenomenon and deserves more attention than it can be given here. One couple, married 4 years, can serve to illustrate what the retarded ejaculator goes through when trying to include a partner. The husband was able to masturbate easily in his wife's presence. He could also reach orgasm, although with some difficulty, through manual stimulation by his wife, but only if he held his testicles himself. In couple sex therapy they were encouraged to see whether he could taper off self-stimulation while increasing his wife's participation. He was unable to reach orgasm unless he used at least three fingers of his own, while the maximum number of his wife's fingers that could be simultaneously included was two. If this ratio were reversed, with her fingers outnumbering his, his erection was unaffected, but he was unable to reach orgasm. Unfortunately, our information stopped there since this was a failure case (largely a consequence of a conflict between the cotherapists).

The Autosexual Orientation

It is as if this patient's genitals were numb to his wife's touch, though not to his own. In this regard, I think that the retarded ejaculator falls at one end of a continuum. Suppose a survey were to be done and men were asked how they ranked penile stimulation by their partner's hand (heterosexual and/or homosexual) versus their own hand. My prediction is that we would find two rather distinct groups, each having a clear preference for one hand or the other—and each assuming that all men are like themselves. This prediction is based on the finding that in our body-work therapy (see below) about 35% of the patients say that they prefer manual stimulation by their own hand rather than the body-work therapist's. Of course, we do not often find the rigid exclusiveness characteristic of the retarded ejaculator, but the difference is clear in these men's minds. They will often say, as if it goes without saying, "How could anyone else know how to do it better than I? After all, I've been doing it for years."

It is evident that this is just what a retarded ejaculator such as the husband just described would say if he could. He cannot because he feels so totally discredited. He just feels that he should enjoy his partner more. The RE patient will rarely say how much he enjoys masturbation in contrast to heterosexuality and/or homosexuality. However, if Women's Lib and Gay Lib were to be followed by Masturbators' Lib, he might go on at length extolling the relative joys of masturbation—how you are completely freed from the hassle of a demanding partner, free to enjoy yourself in any way you want, free to lose yourself totally, as by devoting yourself to your favorite fantasy. Of course, there is no Masturbators' Lib; there is only the new freedom to masturbate, *not* to prefer masturbation to sex with a partner. And the retarded ejaculator appears to be the least of the liberated in this regard. His position is typically wholly undermined, and he can only doggedly pursue the coital orgasm or, at best, he can reap whatever rewards are his due as the workhorse of sexual relationships.

His position is so undermined that he has no way to report it to the clinician, and the clinician is not predisposed to recognize a masturbatory sexual orientation. Thus, Masters and Johnson (1970) only note that for 14 of their RE cases, "masturbation had been the major form of sexual tension release." Kaplan (1974) does not even provide such a summary statement. However, it is clear that in each of her case examples, perhaps even in her one case of organic impairment, the patient at least had no difficulty in masturbation. In the case of RE, it seems easy for the clinician to take masturbatory facility for granted. It is as if the clinician removes from consideration any sexual response that is not "dysfunctional."

To offer a perspective on those with an autosexual orientation, I should note that retarded ejaculators must be only a small part of this group, since many of those whose primary orientation is autosexual will not have automatic erections, while others may, but probably escape being retarded ejaculators because they have automatic orgasms or orgasms-with-effort as well. Of course, the largest group of autosexuals may be those who make no effort to have an orgasm with a partner, including those who avoid partners altogether to simply pursue their solitary masturbatory ways.

Causal Conceptions of Retarded Ejaculation

My Own View

My own explanation of RE begins with the observation that, for reasons yet unknown, some people are highly reactive genitally even when erotic feeling is minimal or absent. Just as there are men who have automatic erections, there are women who lubricate easily, even copiously, when they have hardly begun to experience passion. There also are those who are bored by orgasms, though they still have them, and even those who are sexually aversive but still respond with erection or lubrication and orgasm.

I think of the retarded ejaculator as being a member of this genitally reactive group. He is inhibited by the touch of a partner, but this is easy to avoid, and, like many men, he may turn himself on by handling his penis himself, shutting out the partner mentally and going on to intromission. However, he cannot continue to stimulate himself and inevitably must experience partner (vaginal) stimulation of his penis during penetration and thrusting. This automatically orients him to his partner, and he experiences a compulsion to satisfy her and a detachment from himself that blocks orgasm. This is exactly what happens to women in coitus who feel compelled to monitor and cater to the male ego.

In the presence of a partner, the retarded ejaculator's erect penis is relatively insensate or numb because it is out of phase with his level of erotic arousal. If we think of arousal as accelerating over the course of the response cycle, the RE patient's sexual response to a partner does not show this interdependency of erotic and physical reactions. In this sense, he has what might be called "premature" erections. If the standard view is that the retarded ejaculator should have coital orgasms, my view is that he should be impotent. Thus, the retarded ejaculator's erect penis with a partner is like a flaccid one: Since the typically correlated erotic feelings are absent or minimal, his erect penis does not amplify sensation in the usual way. This is why he cannot have coital orgasms. During intromission, he is less able to stimulate himself, and he does not get enough stimulation from his partner. His situation is exactly analogous to that of women who, as has recently been recognized, do not necessarily experience adequate physical stimulation during coitus, but need focused and reliable manual or oral stimulation.

How does this analysis jibe with the interpretation that the retarded ejaculator is angry at women and wants to sabotage his sexual encounters? Some patients do report feelings of hostility, and many also recognize that they can feel pleased at the way their unresponsiveness is frustrating to their partners. But what they seem much less aware of is their compulsion to *satisfy* their partners.

The necessity to satisfy a partner can be so taken for granted by the patient that what he is aware of is only the times when he inwardly balks. Any hesitation to devote himself to the partner's satisfaction can seem to him like a serious transgression. Thus, Masters and Johnson report that, of the 14 men suffering from RE who came to treatment with their wives, "three men offered dislike, rejection, open enmity for their wives as sufficient reason for failure to ejaculate intravaginally" (1970, p. 120). Withholding one's own orgasm must be seen as a rather mild form of "rejection" or "open enmity," especially considering that this rebellion never includes refusing or even shortening coitus, much less denying the partner her multiple orgasms. We have to take account of the scale of values by which such a subtle deprivation is considered to be an indication of rejection or open enmity. It seems to me that the retarded ejaculator's exaggerated view of his negative reactions is a measure of the yoke of conscientiousness under which he labors.

It also seems to me that it is this compulsion to please the partner that creates the resentment and impulse toward sexual sabotage that some retarded ejaculators acknowledge. The RE patient's compulsive, genitally focused style can force the partner into a passive role and make her feel that there is nothing she can do for him. Since he would have no sense of consciously choosing this style, his experience of sex is of a continuous demand for performance. This can create a potential for feeling used, but he typically takes his role so much for granted that he has no way to feel entitled to experience himself as being used. Instead, he has flashes of disgust and/or hatred toward his partner.

He also feels disgusted at his own ejaculate, as expressed by his fear of soiling his partner with it. I take this as a sign of his turned-off state. When people are in a sexual situation but not aroused, they often have disgust reactions that disappear when they are aroused.

As for the fear of impregnating the partner, I consider this to be a consequence of the retarded ejaculator's experience of absolute lack of choice in the matter, just as is true for him about coitus itself.

Depth Explanations

Fenichel (1945, p. 172ff.) offers a one-sentence comment on RE that can still serve to summarize the psychoanalytic view: "It may express unconscious fears about dangers supposed to be connected with the ejaculation (castration, death), or strivings, anal (retaining) or oral (denial of giving) sadistic or masochistic in character." In other words, Fenichel here summarizes two causes of RE: (1) a fear that ejaculation will mean castration or death and (2) an unwillingness to "give" (anal retentiveness, oral sadomasochism).

The first causal conception is based on the symbolic implications of a coital orgasm. Thus, Ovesey's (1971) conception of RE is as follows:

[It] results from the patient's misconception of sexual intercourse as an act of masculine aggression in which the penis becomes a weapon of destruction. The patient then fears murderous retaliation from the woman, just as he does from men.

[Retaliation from men is a feared consequence because] successful completion of the act is unconsciously equated with victory over male competitors in which the defeated male is killed, castrated, and homosexually subjugated. (p. 121)

In short, the retarded ejaculator appears to believe that no one wants him to have a coital orgasm. If this is so, why then does he not simply choose to not have coital orgasms? Why, instead, can he not be a thankful *non*ejaculator? Or, better put, why does Ovesey not consider this question?

Ovesey's answer would be that the retarded ejaculator does not choose to avoid coital orgasms because his catastrophic expectations are *repressed,* and he does not *know* that he thinks the vagina has teeth. (Ovesey also mentions vagina dentata fantasies.) My response to this explanation is that it is Ovesey who misses the significance of repression. What repression means is that the retarded ejaculator *cannot* be afraid of having coital orgasms. He cannot dislike it. A fear or a wish is distorted as a consequence of repression and transformed into a symptom only when you *cannot* have it and *cannot* act on it (Apfelbaum, 1977a). This is what id-analytic thinkers like Ovesey miss. They misunderstand the repression model, seeing repressed fantasies as simply representing what the person *really* thinks and feels, rather than as representing what he cannot let himself think or feel.

As I see it, these repressed fantasies are generated by the retarded ejaculator's compulsion to enter into coitus. His penis is, in effect, not his own: He loses it. He has no way to conceptualize this, and so he has highly symbolic fantasies, and even these are repressed. In simple terms, the psychoanalytic view is that the fantasies are the cause of an unconscious aversion to coital orgasms. My view is that these fantasies represent, in exaggerated form, the feelings that the retarded ejaculator is already having. His is the mentality of the trapped; he is already castrated.

No matter how horrible are his unconscious fantasies, what analysts miss is that the retarded ejaculator is unable to have a good reason to dislike sex with a partner. He has no way to feel entitled to complain about feeling turned off by a partner's demands. Analysts miss this because, like behavior therapists, they assume that he should like sex with a partner and that he should want coital orgasms. In this normative context, it is a foreign notion that he might need a good reason to refuse coital orgasms.

The second causal conception summarized by Fenichel is that the retarded ejaculator is unwilling to "give." This kind of explanation seems to me to be especially glib, being based on the simple logical device of assuming that the consequences of a symptom must represent its unconscious goal. Unfortunately, retarded ejaculators are typically accused of not wanting to "give" by their partners. As Masters and Johnson note of their relatively large sample: "Although only three men constrained their ejaculatory processes to frustrate their wives [at least by their own admission], many more were accused of this motivation by their partners" (1970, p. 129ff.). The idea that the retarded ejaculator is withholding seems to be a superficial interpretation of the lack of coital orgasms. It reflects the partner's view and the social consensus.

Contrary to the way Ovesey interprets the retarded ejaculator's unconscious fantasies, I contend that the retarded ejaculator thinks that everyone *wants* him to have coital orgasms. If we respect his own experience, it is hard to avoid recognizing that he *cannot* be withholding, that he cannot stop giving. In all of my cases, the retarded ejaculator is a classic example of the partner who is unable to take, to be selfish, or, as the current jargon has it, to be responsible for his own satisfaction. It is only when he is alone that he can enjoy his own sensations without worrying about the partner's satisfaction. In fact, I am tempted to say on behalf of the retarded ejaculator, "How much *more* can you give?" As I have characterized him, he is the workhorse of sex, doing the work of ten.

Behavioral Explanations

The chief behavioral explanation of RE is that it is an inhibited reflex and that the causes of this inhibition are irrelevant to its treatment. This interpretation of RE is evident just from the diagnostic labels used by Masters and Johnson and by Kaplan. For Masters and Johnson, it is "ejaculatory incompetence," a label that has not achieved currency probably because only Masters and Johnson can keep in mind what it means—that the reflex and not the person is incompetent. Kaplan heads her chapter in *The Illustrated Manual of Sex Therapy* (1975): "Retarded Ejaculation—Ejaculatory Overcontrol." She (1974) offers the clearest statement of the reflexogenic interpretation of RE:

> Clinical evidence suggests that all the traumatic factors . . . can result in retarded ejaculation. It may be speculated that the mechanism by which these various factors impair the ejaculatory reflex involves an involuntary, and unconscious, conditioned inhibition. According to learning theory, the ejaculatory response has become inhibited because of its association with a painful con-

tingency. The response is blocked just exactly as though the patient anticipated punishment by an electric shock each time he
ejaculated or even had the impulse to ejaculate.

The precise nature of the original painful contingency becomes irrelevant when it is considered in this conceptual context.
(p. 327)

Kaplan goes on to propose that RE is similar to "constipation, which
results from inhibition of the defecatory reflex, globus hystericus,
which is due to an inhibited swallowing reflex, and spastic colitis due to
impaired peristalsis" (p. 328).

Kaplan's diagnostic conception makes no distinction between
masturbatory and coital anorgasmia. The true retarded ejaculator's
orgasmic "inhibition" is specific to one particular context. Constipation is not. Also, one wonders whether this formulation would be put
so definitively if it were recognized that the retarded ejaculator is easily
orgasmic in masturbation.

The reflex conception is stated more explicitly by Kaplan than by
Masters and Johnson, perhaps because she had fewer cases to contend
with, so few in fact that she does not give the number, only saying that
her experience "has been too limited to be statistically significant"
(1974, p. 336). Some of Masters and Johnson's cases are difficult to
reconcile with the reflex conception, since these patients make their
lack of coital orgasms look like the result of something more like a
choice than a reflex. In fact, one failure case, though it was still included in their total sample of 17, was that of a couple "who should not
have been seen in therapy, as there really was no specific ejaculatory
dysfunction. This was only a case of a man's complete rejection of the
woman he married" (p. 134).

The Treatment of Retarded Ejaculation

The Demand Strategy

As a result of this reflex conception, RE comes to look like a male
version of vaginismus. Where muscles should be responsive, they are
locked in a clonic spasm. A major difference from the treatment of
vaginismus is that the spasm is "forced" abruptly in the case of RE
rather than gradually as in the case of vaginismus: The female partner
is encouraged "to manipulate the penis demandingly," so as "to force
ejaculation." Once this has been achieved, she is to manipulate her
partner nearly to orgasm and then to execute "rapid intromission."

(This is what Kaplan calls the "male bridge maneuver.") If orgasm does not follow, she is to "demandingly" manipulate the penis, "quickly" reinserting (Masters & Johnson, 1970, p. 129ff.).

Masters and Johnson's treatment of *female* "RE," that is, of female coital anorgasmia, is, of course, strikingly different. Their whole point with women is to avoid precisely the demand pressure that they require for men. Whereas with men, Masters and Johnson advise a demanding style of pelvic thrusting, in the case of female coital anorgasmia, their advice is just the opposite: Coitus is to be done "without any concept of a demanding thrusting pattern." Whereas with a man, the female partner is advised to force ejaculation, with a woman, the male partner is advised that she should have "the opportunity to express her sexual responsivity without any concept of demand for an end-point (orgasmic) goal," and that a "forceful approach will not contribute to facility of response." With men, the objective is to build up sensation almost before they realize it; with women, Masters and Johnson warn that if "a high level of biophysical tension is reached before the psychosocial concomitant has been subjectively appreciated, the woman experiences too much sensation too soon and finds it difficult to accept" (pp. 304, 307, 309).

Since Masters and Johnson rarely mention subjective arousal, they nowhere state that the female with "RE" is not aroused, but it is apparent from their treatment strategy that this is how they see it. It seems equally apparent that the male with RE is assumed to be aroused, and this can account for Masters and Johnson's diametrically opposed strategies for treating female versus male RE, as Williams (1977) suggests. Undoubtedly, the retarded ejaculator's sustained erections led Masters and Johnson to the assumption that he is already erotically aroused. The nondemand strategy may have been seen by Masters and Johnson as required only when the process of arousal is blocked. What they consider blocked in RE is the orgasm reflex, not the process of erotic arousal.

Masters and Johnson classified 10 of their 17 cases of RE as treatment successes. The effects of their demand strategy do look, at least in Masters and Johnson's cases, the way the process of reflex disinhibition would be expected to look. As Sadock and Sadock (1976, p. 474) put it, once "the spell is broken" by the experience of one coital orgasm, "successive attempts become easier." The patient appears to have learned that, as this etiological conception goes, there will be no traumatic consequences resulting from the disinhibition of the orgasm reflex.

Effects of the Demand Strategy: An Alternative View

My way of understanding the success of the demand strategy with RE is to see it as an accommodation to the retarded ejaculator's need for rough, heavy stimulation. Unlike many premature ejaculators whose penises are exquisitely sensitive to touch, the penis of the retarded ejaculator is insensitive. In Kaplan's case discussed earlier, the patient's penis was seriously numbed by a spinal cord injury. His wife used a rough leather glove to simulate him manually and he used a towel to masturbate with. Similarly, in the intact retarded ejaculator, penile numbness is overcome by rapid and heavy stimulation.

My explanation does not account for why, at least at other treatment centers, a single experience of coital orgasm or even, as Masters and Johnson report, the experience of some of the ejaculate entering the vagina can result in successively easier coital orgasms. Our cases have not shown this all-or-none responsiveness. The first coital orgasm has not led, by itself, to dramatic changes. (Similarly, Kaplan, 1974, p. 332ff., reports both "stable" and "unstable" results.) This has also been true of vaginismus in our population: We have only seen cases of intermittent vaginismus, so there was no "spell" to break.

In this treatment model, no distinction is drawn between RE and masturbatory anorgasmia, which makes the results difficult to evaluate. My guess is that "stable" results are more likely with masturbatory anorgasmia, paralleling the prognostic difference between masturbatory and coital female anorgasmia.

When the treatment of RE *does* have an all-or-none outcome, however, it does look like a spell has been broken, directly confirming the conception of RE as an inhibited reflex. My alternative interpretation of this treatment effect is that what gets broken is not a spell but a set. The retarded ejaculator's sexual set is to satisfy the partner. In the strategy recommended by Masters and Johnson and by Kaplan, the partner is helped to overcome her feeling that there is no way to do anything for him. She is brought out of her withdrawal and transformed into a singlemindedly aggressive partner, determined to *give* no matter how unreinforcing it is for her. The result is that what I have characterized as the retarded ejaculator's numb response to the partner's touch is overcome, although we cannot tell from published reports whether coitus and coital orgasms become as exciting as masturbatory orgasms for him, and whether the partner's touch comes to rival the patient's own.

A serious drawback of this strategy appears in its effect on the patient with whom it fails. When it succeeds, it undoes the patient's oppressive compulsion to satisfy the partner. When it fails, it seems likely that its effect is to strengthen this compulsion. The patient's own belief that he should be having coital orgasms has now been supported not only by the therapist's authority but by the belief that his partner is now doing everything humanly possible for him. As a result, he would feel even less entitled to experience being used, even though he would be all the more convinced that if he were to have a coital orgasm, it would be his partner's and not his own. It would be the prize that she had worked so hard to produce and that he owed her for her efforts.

Although I will not discuss the depth therapist's strategy for treating RE since there is not a strategy specific to RE, from my vantage point there is not much difference between the depth therapist's approach and the behavior therapist's approach to RE. Both approaches are based on the assumption that the retarded ejaculator should want and like coital orgasms. In effect, the patient is treated as if he must overcome feeling used and resentful. This seems clear enough in the case of the depth therapist: The patient's unconscious aversion to coital orgasm is treated as irrational and groundless.

A Counterbypassing Strategy

As I see it, the RE not only should not have a coital orgasm, he should not have an erection. The functionalistic model makes such a formulation sound odd only because the phenomena of functioning with inadequate erotic arousal have been conceptually overlooked although they are familiar to everyone. Treating the problem at the orgasm level may be what makes RE the condition that is the most difficult to treat with current methods.

The standard sex therapy approach begins with the assumption that the male with RE is aroused. It is also assumed that he does not suffer from performance anxiety since his anxiety is believed to be associated with *having* coital orgasms rather than with *not having* them. My approach begins with the opposite assumptions. I see the RE patient as turned off by a partner but nevertheless compelled to perform. In my view, his performance anxiety is at least as intense as that found in any other sexual disorder, but it drives him into performance rather than nonperformance in the excitement (erection) phase, only resulting in dysfunction in the orgasm phase.

The treatment of RE is an instance in which diagnosis and treatment are closely related. If those using the standard approach were to see the retarded ejaculator as not aroused and as driven by a performance compulsion, they would not use their present strategy. They would be more likely to use a strategy like the one Masters and Johnson use to treat female coital anorgasmia. This, at least, is the basis of my own approach.

In the treatment of female coital anorgasmia, Masters and Johnson's goal is to train the woman to be in control of her sexual context. During penetration in the female-astride position, the male partner is to remain passive while she meditatively regulates thrusting movements, learning to attend closely to her own sensations and to not cater to her partner. She learns, in effect, to take possession, not just of her body, as it is sometimes put, but of her sexual relationship. However, this can be difficult to accomplish with couples whose basic rapport is not up to the Masters and Johnson standard. The woman cannot as easily shed her insecurity about ignoring her partner, and the man plays a passive role only in the sense of biding his time. In such a couple, these tensions cannot be bypassed.

Such a couple can still reach the same objective by switching to a *counterbypassing,* expressive technique in which the woman is helped to verbalize her worries about her partner's impatience. However, a merely expressive technique in the style of bioenergetics or Gestalt therapy is of limited value unless the woman's worries are validated, that is, unless she is helped to feel entitled to them by virtue of recognizing that her worries are valid. This is not at all difficult to do, since the therapist always has the choice of picking up either her sensitivity (resulting from childhood experience, later trauma, guilt, inhibition of assertiveness, etc.) or the external reasons that her sensitivity is engaged.

In the instance just described, the therapist might demonstrate that the partner was, in fact, impatient and that his impatience was the result, perhaps, of a fear of being turned off and losing his erection if he is too passive. Having her reactions validated is a form of endorsement that helps give the woman a way to feel more like a sexual encounter is for *her*.

Such a counterbypassing strategy raises the specter of precipitating an inconclusive and interminable depth therapy. However, I would argue that this only happens when an expressive or uncovering approach *has the same objective* as a bypassing approach, that is, to extinguish negative feelings. Thus, RE can be seen as the outcome of "an unconscious refusal to ejaculate" (as an anonymous journal consultant put it in response to a manuscript submitted by one of my colleagues). The implication is that this is an inappropriate response and even that it is repressed because it is inappropriate. However, as I see it, the patient must be helped to make a *conscious* "refusal to ejaculate." It is the attempt to get the patient over his unconscious refusal that can result in an interminable or at least extensive uncovering therapy.

I think of counterbypassing as a more direct way to break the retarded ejaculator's compulsive sexual set and as less likely to reinforce this set when it fails. This means introducing the idea to the RE patient that he is the kind of person who may need to be erotically aroused before he can have a coital orgasm. Although he may protest that he *is* aroused, it should be easy for him to recognize how much more aroused he is in masturbation than he is with a partner, and, of course, he is well aware of how coitus feels like drudgery. He can then be introduced to the next idea, which is that he does not feel entitled to complain about his experience with a partner. The therapist can then present the view that anyone might feel left out, ignored, or used when he is getting very little out of sex at the same time that his partner is multiorgasmic. Since the patient invariably expects to be treated as if he is abnormal for not having coital orgasms, this strategy can be immediately relieving. A complaining assignment can then have equally immediate results, as this next case will illustrate.

Case 3: An Illustration of Counterbypassing

It is unfortunate that most of our RE cases were treated in individual body-work sex therapy, since this modality is unique to our center. It is a revision of Masters and Johnson's surrogate-partner program in which the substitute-partner concept is discarded in favor of the use of paraprofessional staff members who function both as cotherapists in the therapy sessions and as body-work therapists in sessions comparable to those in which couples carry out their assignments (for further procedural details, see Williams, 1978). The principles of treatment we have developed in individual sex therapy are also used by us in couple sex therapy, and I will draw these parallels.

One advantage in presenting material from the treatment of patients in individual body-work sex therapy is that I have much more information available about the cases, since the body therapist serves as a participant/observer. Another advantage is that we would have seen only three or four cases of the 12 if we were treating only local patients in couple therapy and in individual counseling.

To quickly illustrate how this strategy is applied to RE, I will take the case of a Canadian architect, age 36, who requested individual sex therapy at his second wife's urging. (Although she was an American citizen, an outstanding legal problem made it risky for her to reenter the United States, and she also had concerns about confidentiality that made it difficult for her to obtain couple sex therapy in her area.) In her telephone contact with us, she complained that her husband was turned off, a unique perception in my experience for the partner of an RE. He said that he gradually became turned off while thrusting but went on in the hope of becoming aroused again, although he never did. He described the typical retarded ejaculator's automatic erection, mentioning that once when he was hospitalized after a sports accident, he was tormented by having erections when being washed by the nurses. No matter what strategem he tried, he was unable to avoid having continuous erections during this process. However, he said that he was otherwise grateful for his constant erections because his partners never had to know how turned off he was.

He had read Kaplan's *The Illustrated Manual of Sex Therapy* (1975) and had perfected the bridge maneuver with his wife. Using it, he was able to reach coital orgasms about 50% of the time but found it tedious and unrewarding.

Although this patient was only seen for 1 week of body-work therapy, he was quick to learn counterbypassing. He felt liberated with unusual suddenness when he was coached to express the components of his performance anxiety while being stroked by the body-work therapist. He got high—and this turned into sexual excitement—when he told her how he hated sex, how it was an ordeal, a job, how he had to just put himself through it, measure up, and how afraid he was that the body therapist would feel insulted by his expressing these feelings. This is the kind of turning point we look for. Out of this can come an insight, a body insight as well as a cognitive one, about what has been turning the patient off and what it will take to turn him on. When such a turning point is reached, it is not unusual for the patient and the therapists to feel that the job has been done. In contrast, one *performance* success is much more likely to be experienced as a random event, a fluke, and performance anxiety is intensified.

When the body-work therapist went on to manual stimulation, the patient got turned on by talking about how little he was getting out of it and how frustrating it was going to be for her, as well as by talking about how "the electric feelings" came and went. He enjoyed this so much that he could not wait to try it out on his wife and so returned home before we could go further. The questionnaire follow-up on this case was ambiguous, but I offer this case only as a brief illustration of our strategy before going on to a more extensive case presentation.

Case 4: A Successful Course of Treatment

Background

Frank, 20, a college student, complained of being unable to have a coital orgasm. He was unusually experienced sexually for his age, having had two 2-year relationships and several other briefer ones. He described himself as obsessed with sex and masturbated frequently and easily (two to three times daily), becoming aroused by intricate and extensive fantasies. His principal fantasy was of being a male prostitute (heterosexual) who aggressively "raped" women at their request.

He was concerned enough about not having coital orgasms to have investigated artificial insemination in the event that his problem continued into marriage. However, after several counseling hours it became clear that his primary complaint was that the reality of his sexual experiences never matched his fantasies. Although this is not in itself unusual, it became clear that he got very little satisfaction from his sexual encounters. Further, his continuing sense of sexual frustration and ubiquitous sexual fantasies were seriously undermining his ability to concentrate, threatening a loss of scholarships and making it necessary for him to consider interrupting the career line he had planned. He was unambivalently devoted to his field and had no history of previous work inhibitions.

Sexual contact with women was a proof of masculinity for him and a way of satisfying them, but masturbation was far more enjoyable. He was able to reach orgasm with a partner through manual stimulation, but only if he could call up his fantasies. However, he found it very difficult to maintain a fantasy in the presence of a partner, and when he did reach orgasm by this means, it did not seem worth the effort. He had not experienced fellatio, and his lack of interest in it seemed consistent with his interest in being an aggressive "phallic" partner as in his fantasies.

His actual sexual role was, as in his fantasies, the compromised form of passivity represented by being aggressive on demand. A clue to this was his report that his partners were all easily orgasmic. They apparently were assertive and freely able to control their sexual contacts with him. His account also suggested that they encouraged rather than disliked the long-sustained coital thursting toward which Frank was inclined. He shyly admitted that he was regularly told that he was a great lover, and this seemed based solely on his no-frills approach to thrusting and his reliable and sustained erections. He was a partner who could be easily controlled and safely ignored.

His background was white, middle class, stable, suburban, and sexually liberal. Both parents were alcoholics, although this apparently did not interfere with their duties and was not out of place in their social circle. He saw himself as the sexual tutor of his 5-years-younger sister, who, he proudly recounted, was already sexually active and experienced.

He came to us wanting a "surrogate" in response to the December, 1972, *Newsweek* cover story that widely popularized sex therapy. He had been in once-a-week psychotherapy for a year and reported that although he now had some insight into his problem, nothing had changed. The insight was that he was afraid of losing control and was unable to "give."

Initial Treatment Findings

He was initially given a masturbation assignment as an aid in diagnosis, and from his reports on this assignment it was evident that his masturbatory style was "psychogenic." He had an unusually nonspecific masturbatory technique, and it seemed evident that he did not focus on penile sensation. Orgasm depended heavily on the intensity of his fantasies and his involvement in them. When he was instructed to focus on sensation, he was unable to reach orgasm. Thus, it could be inferred that he had the relatively "numb" erection that we have found in the seven RE patients seen in individual body-work therapy. In none of them could this feature be determined from the clinical interview alone.

He did not have a current partner and had to make a 400-mile round-trip commute from his campus, which limited partner availability. Although the much higher fees for individual sex therapy as compared with couple sex therapy put him under pressure to work out an arrangement with a partner, he was unable to accomplish this. We offered to reduce the fee in exchange for his seeing a body therapist in training, and he agreed. He was seen in once-a-week sessions, a practice that we subsequently discontinued. His was one of the cases that persuaded us that daily sessions could have shortened treatment by perhaps a third from the 18 sessions he was actually seen.

He was frightened of seeing a surrogate but was somewhat reassured when he was told that she would not be a surrogate, but a body-work therapist who worked as a cotherapist with me as the review therapist, and that we worked one session at a time rather than on the basis of a fixed number of sessions. It was apparent from the first body-work session that, as Frank had reported, he had the automatic erections that I have suggested are characteristic of RE. He has been our most extreme case of this to date. Whereas full erections lasting as long as a half hour are uncommon, Frank's erections would last almost the entire body-work period, which could be as long as 2 hours out of a 2½-hour session. The body therapist reported that it was not until the 10th session that she saw Frank's penis in a flaccid state.

As Frank had previously reported, his level of arousal was not at all commensurate with his "excitement-phase" functioning. He claimed to feel nothing and said that his penis felt numb. This was corroborated by the way the body therapist felt: She found herself feeling bored and aimless. Perhaps because this was her first case and it also was early in the development of our treatment model, we let ourselves be persuaded to go on to penetration. The body therapist felt some relief at this and, as we later realized, responded as his partners had. She became aroused, and they went on to penetration and thrusting for almost 2 hours. She felt relieved of the stress of Frank's tension, only to discover in the review session that he had not enjoyed it and, further, that he was recriminating himself for not being as aroused as she was. This event is another indication that our treatment of this case represents an early model. The result of such "premature" functioning has typically been the prolongation of treatment.

The Necessity for a Focus on Level of Arousal

In order to keep treatment brief, we have found it necessary to monitor closely the patient's level of arousal and to make it the focus of our efforts. It eventually became evident to us that it is easy to do too much body work, that is, to outstrip what the patient can encompass and to move him into functioning relatively autonomous from feeling. Masters and Johnson have already pointed out that this can easily happen with women (see above). With this recognition, we have increasingly centered on events that occur early in the body work and now find it rarely necessary to go on to penetration.

Frank was a clear case in point. We found that when he was involved in coitus, he felt isolated, passive, and helpless. At this point, Frank invoked the interpretations that he had been given in his previous therapy: These ideas were that he needed to learn to lose control and to be more willing to "give." We pointed out that he condemned himself with these interpretations while, in reality, he was being left out by the body therapist when she withdrew from him into a sexually aroused state. He criticized himself rather than criticize her.

In the review session with Frank and me following their engaging in coitus, the body therapist reported being shocked at having lost track of how turned off Frank was. She said that she had just "tripped out" in a way that she had never thought possible for her. She had had this done to her many times by men but had never thought that she could herself be an "oppressor," as she put it. This was a climactic event for Frank, suggesting to him that at least part of his problem was that he "gave" *too* much, and that, in contrast to his partners, he was not *in* control at all.

It began to dawn on Frank that he had no way to withdraw into sensation the way the body therapist had just done and the way his partners had. I reminded him that just as he was unusually dependent on fantasy to masturbate, so he was unusually dependent on his partner and on the relationship at any given moment for psychogenic stimulation. I pointed out that this dependency did offer an increased potential for intimacy, but that for this potential to be realized would require him to develop communication skills that others could get by without.

Inappropriateness of the Reflex Model

As I have indicated, the generally accepted strategy with RE in couple sex therapy is to increase sensation in a forceful and goal-directed way. This strategy is even more difficult to apply in individual sex therapy than it is in couple sex therapy. As the cases reported by Masters and Johnson and by Kaplan, Frank required his partners to work hard at stimulating him manually for him to reach orgasm. The body therapist was unwilling to do this. She reported that if she felt more aroused, it might be possible to become more vigorous in stroking Frank, but as it was, it just seemed too dreary. The relationship seemed too tense, and Frank already seemed under too much pressure.

As the three of us investigated her reaction further in review sessions, the body therapist also realized that as matters then stood, to work on physically arousing Frank would make her feel used. This fascinated Frank, and he questioned her at length about it. He had never felt entitled to feel used, as had just been demonstrated by the climactic incident in which he had been, as we had put it, *taken advantage of* by the body therapist during coitus. We used this way of describing what she had done for its shock value, since he, of course, considered such moral language to be, at best, quaint. However, it communicated with a deep vein of feeling in him. If he had felt anything in his previous sexual contacts, it would have been to feel used, but he had had no cognitive structure to accommodate such a feeling.

This brings up the question of whether the partner in couple sex therapy should be encouraged to take the risk of being seen as rejecting, a risk the body therapist can take because her responses are likely to be seen by the patient as having a clinical rationale. The demand strategy used with couples in the standard approach to RE requires more subordination of the partner's needs than does the treatment of any other sexual disorder. She must aggressively stimulate the patient, either manually or orally, until he comes close to ejaculatory inevitability. This typically requires heavy, prolonged, and uninterrupted application to the task, followed by rapid intromission, also executed by the partner. Thus, it is in Kaplan's (1974) chapter on RE that she raises the problem of the effect on the partner of being required as Kaplan puts it, to "service" her husband. Kaplan warns that this may be a lot to expect of the partner unless the relationship is "good enough":

> If the woman is mature enough to withstand temporary frustration without hostility, and if the couple's relationship is good enough to make her generosity psychologically rewarding, treatment can proceed smoothly under these conditions.
> However, the wife's intrapsychic conflicts and consequent marital discord may be evoked by the man's progressive improvement and the fact that she is required to "service" her husband. (p. 332)

"Generosity" may not be the most accurate word for the spirit with which the partner carries out her assignment. She can hardly avoid feeling obliged to comply. The alternative is to sacrifice the patient's chance to overcome his symptom. Add to this the fact that the female partner is usually the one who brings the patient into treatment, and we have what amounts to a contractual obligation on her part.

This is not to say that the partner necessarily resents this obligation, at least at first. However, recall that most of the partners in Masters and Johnson's sample experienced "a real concept of personal rejection" and a level of frustration "beyond comprehension." Some were rejected by their husbands as physically unappealing, but probably for most of them it was their husband's unresponsiveness that they took as a rejection. (Unlike the therapist and the patient himself, the partner cannot avoid recognizing that the retarded ejaculator is not aroused by her.)

This treatment strategy depends on the partner being "mature enough," as Kaplan puts it, and on the couple's relationship being "good enough" for the partner to stand further frustration and feelings of rejection. More than that, it depends on the partner's ability, not just to tolerate such feelings, but not to communicate them unduly by the way she stimulates the patient. It is easy to imagine her being a bit too aggressive—or not aggressive enough.

Further, even when the partner succeeds, she is modeling conscientiousness for the patient, an unfortunate reinforcement of his sex-as-work philosophy. As for the virtues of a nondemand approach, Masters and Johnson themselves have written the text. Thus, the body therapist ideally models a resistance rather than a submission to sexual demands, and this would be my objective with the patient's partner as well. She can be helped to have *her* complaints about the patient's unresponsiveness and about his lack of joy. He can then be helped to say his side of it—"But I'm doing it all for you"—something she undoubtedly has never realized and would then insist was not at all what she wanted. This is how their compulsive set would begin to break up.

Psychogenic Arousal

To return to the case, when the body therapist first said that she found herself reluctant to do manual stimulation, Frank was unbelieving. At first he thought it was a pose or a trick, but when he decided it was a reaction she really was having, he accused *her* of being unwilling to give. This gave him a chance to watch her cope with the same accusation that had been flung at him by one of his partners and put as an interpretation by his previous therapist. To his surprise, the body therapist responded that she did not know why he wanted her to stroke him so vigorously, even though she could understand it intellectually. To condense this three-way discussion: Frank acknowledged that he did not know that you needed reasons to do things and that he had always just done what he was supposed to do. The body therapist was able then to say that she found little to respond to in him and that if she did not *know* that he was obsessed with sex, she would have thought that he had no interest in it.

This seemed to liberate Frank to be critical of the body therapist for the first time. He told her that she just did not turn him on, and then suddenly felt a surge of sexual feeling. This was the turning point in the case. Much like the turning point I noted in Case 3, it was an example of becoming aroused by counterbypassing. At first, Frank was disturbed by it. He reported it to the body therapist at the time and both of us in the review session with some embarrassment, thinking that it must be abnormal. We reassured him that this had become a familiar occurrence to us and encouraged him to go further in this direction.

At this point, he reported more sensation in his penis, though this soon disappeared as he reacted with renewed performance anxiety. He then responded with despondency, and we helped him articulate this through our technique of script construction. The patient is instructed to review his experience with the body therapist, and they both construct and shape a list of statements that he can subsequently use to identify and make contact with what he is experiencing. Frank's list included such lines as: "I am afraid of feeling hopeless"; "I'm afraid there is something really wrong with me''; ''I'm afraid you're going to give up on me''; and, in a different vein, ''I just don't know what you want.''

In reaction to saying these lines, especially the first one, Frank again experienced sexual feelings. Simultaneously, he no longer had his automatic erection, and it rarely appeared in the subsequent sessions. Although he still had erections quickly, they were typically accompanied by erotic feeling, and when his mood shifted, at moments that were usually clearly distinguishable, his degree of erection reflected this. For example, whenever he lapsed into compliance, he now would lose some, or all, of his erection. These shifts all took place during genital stroking, and the body work was confined to this during the remaining sessions.

Uncovering Residual Performance Anxiety

During this period, signs of pelvic tension were noted and related to what he was experiencing. He and the body therapist also located tension in his pubococcygeus muscle, which then reminded him of past difficulties urinating in public men's rooms. In addition, he said that when the muscle was especially tight, he would ejaculate without orgasm during masturbation. (Whether pubococcygeal muscle tension is a factor in those who have retarded orgasm but not retarded ejaculation, a symptom identified only by Kaplan, 1974, we have not yet been able to determine, since this was not investigated in our three other cases with this symptom. It may be of interest to note that one of these cases was a premature ejaculator, not a retarded ejaculator).

Although Frank was now noticeably more relaxed, he still had not reached orgasm, our goal for the genital stimulation. He then reported that his masturbatory fantasy had changed: Instead of being paid to ''rape'' women, they now paid him to do female-superior coitus. It was just as aggressive, but they did most of the moving. He revealed that he had begun trying to fade his fantasy women out of the fantasy and to bring the body therapist into the fantasy just before orgasm in the hope of associating her with erotic feeling.

A Complaining Assignment

We felt fortunate that in Frank's spontaneous self-assignment of stimulus fading we had stumbled on a clue that he still felt it was up to him to generate erotic feeling. We said that this feeling of responsibility was the last hiding place of his performance anxiety and then gave him a complaining assignment to do during the genital stroking. While it was going on, it was his responsibility, not to get turned on, but to complain about what the body therapist was doing. He found himself enjoying saying, "I'm not feeling anything." When the body therapist jokingly responded, "Well, I'm doing the best I *can*," he felt close to orgasm but only reached it when he said, "This *really* feels mechanical."

This was Frank's only orgasm during the treatment period. Although this might be a minor event if the standard strategy were used, what happened in this instance was a "spontaneous" orgasm, something Frank had not experienced with a partner before. With the experience of an orgasm, this whole treatment context is then reinforced and internalized. Generalization to a partner is to be expected. Indeed, I would not expect an "accidental" coital orgasm to generalize. Thus, if Frank had had a coital orgasm during his earlier episode of coitus with the body therapist, I would not expect this to affect his sexual responsiveness with other partners, or, for that matter, with the body therapist herself. Nothing would have happened to change his sexual set. Regardless of the source of stimulation, what is needed is a "spontaneous," that is, psychogenic orgasm. This is what is likely to generalize to coital orgasms, as it did in Frank's case. This is the basis for my earlier argument that the coital specificity of RE is not dynamically meaningful, that what is dynamically meaningful is the retarded ejaculator's insensitivity to a partner's touch relative to his own.

In the next session, Frank tried to repeat the series of events that had led to an orgasm, but, as usually happens, it had become a formula, and, to his disappointment, neither he nor the body therapist felt aroused.

He then had a sudden financial setback and had to interrupt the treatment. His father's alcoholism had finally cost him his job, and he had borrowed Frank's savings on a short-term loan to get started in a business venture. It failed, and Frank could not afford further treatment or to return to school.

Treatment Effects

I saw him again 5 years later. He was now in his last year of a professional school and reported that although his sexual "obsessions" no longer interfered with his work, his sexual experiences had been only partly satisfying. He reported now being able to have an erection without assuming that this required him to go on to penetration and also being able, at least at times, to stop the action when he felt out of contact. He appeared to retain awareness of his dependency on psychogenic stimulation and reported being able to tell his partner when he was turned off. He claimed to have coital orgasms easily when he felt aroused, although this was not often. It was difficult to evaluate this claim, since he knew this was what I wanted to hear, and he was still essentially the same person, someone whose first impulse is to satisfy the other.

For such a person, changing partners can be a solution, and it became clear that Frank had made a truly inspired choice. He apparently had instinctively shied away from the enthusiastic performers who would have reinforced his sexual compulsions and instead had a 3-year relationship with a woman who was not coitally orgasmic. This did help reverse his order of priorities, but he found toward the end of that relationship that he did not *want* to have coital orgasms, although he was somewhat less reluctant about having extravaginal orgasms. He was disturbed about not wanting coital orgasms, and it was for this reason that he wanted to resume body-work therapy. However, I thought what he needed was some reassurance and a redefinition of the problem.

Fear of Being Exploitive

Bearing in mind that what makes a retarded ejaculator is *having* to have coital orgasms, my strategy was to help Frank stay with his reluctance rather than to help him overcome it. True to type, Frank thought that he should not feel this reluctance, seeing it as unmanly of him to be so squeamish and foolish as well to feel that he was using his partner if she were not equally orgasmic, since she reassured him that she enjoyed it when he had coital orgasms.

Given our sexual norms, it is all too easy for the clinician to share Frank's concern and to believe that he should be helped to overcome his ambivalence. However, in accordance with my conception of the pathogenesis of RE, my expectation is that an intervention of this kind would have led to a recurrence of Frank's RE.

I congratulated Frank on being able to acknowledge his ambivalence about having coital orgasms, since to experience sex as exploitive can in these times make one feel unenlightened. I told him that I thought RE is created by having to deny and overcome this ambivalence, and that when the feeling of being exploitive returns (from repression), it comes back in concretized form as a fear of soiling or impregnating.

I also suggested that needing his partner to have coital orgasms reflects the retarded ejaculator's inability to "take." I reminded him of what I have here called the "climactic" incident with the body therapist in which we said that *we* thought he had been used by her, and I suggested that on this basis, his worry might be at least partly iatrogenic. He agreed, but added that this had made him realize how he had always felt used and how he could hardly imagine it otherwise, even in his masturbatory fantasies. Now that he could have coital orgasms, he worried that his partner would feel used just as he had, though she might not be aware of it, or if she were aware of feeling this way, she might be just as skilled as he had been at concealing it. He then realized that this worry resolved into his being afraid that she had to like everything, just as had been true for him. This turned his attention to the possibility of helping her, or a future partner, to be freer to have her dislikes, as by doing a better job of having his own.

Two Failure Cases

Case 5: A Missed Arousal Deficit

Two failure cases are of interest. The first patient was 23, unmarried, and a college dropout who drove a cab in a Midwestern city. He was the only retarded ejaculator we have seen who bragged openly about his sustained erections and about how capable this made him as a sex partner. This was a 1-week individual sex therapy case, a patient who, as other retarded ejaculators, had an erection in the first session, could masturbate easily on day 3, but in the fifth session reached his first coital orgasm. He then terminated, feeling he could no longer justify the expense of continued treatment. His coital orgasm might best be thought of as what I earlier called an "accidental" orgasm, in that the therapists saw no evidence that the patient's sexual set had changed in any way. It was a relatively joyless experience, and the therapists believed that he had never really been turned on and that he was relieved to terminate before his turned-off state was exposed. My impression is that such a performance success is experienced by the patient as a fluke that he is afraid he will never be able to repeat. I have not found the "one good experience" to be reassuring unless it is accompanied by an increase in sexual pleasure.

This patient has not returned in the ensuing 6 years. We now might treat this case differently, having learned to resist the pressure to go ahead with the body work when the patient is not turned on. However, this can be a difficult determination to make and to be done effectively requires an experienced cotherapy team.

Case 6: A Failure to Relieve Performance Anxiety

The second failure case was 43, never married, and a tutor in the humanities at a British university; he had just completed a 7-year analysis. As in the previous case, he was obviously proud of his sustained erections, advertised in British swinger-style magazines, and had maintained active, though necessarily infrequent, contacts with over 30 women. He nevertheless found masturbation more satisfying and had never come close to a coital orgasm. He had only reached orgasm four times with a partner, all with the same partner, by masturbating and then switching to fellatio only at the point of ejaculatory inevitability.

He was a highly urbane man who made the memorable comment, "Girls just don't have the touch" (the comparison being with himself, not with men). What he seemed most attracted to in women was neatness, cleanliness, quietness, and decorum. He denied that this suggested that he did not see women as sex objects. In the body-work sessions he was cool and impersonal, but our efforts to reflect this back to him were interpreted by him as a sign that the body therapist was disappointed. Some work was done with muscle relaxation, and this led to somewhat greater responsiveness. He said that he had never enjoyed manual stimulation of his penis before, but he (perhaps correctly) attributed it all to the use of Albolene (our preferred genital lubricant). His defensiveness continued, and he became difficult to control in the body-work sessions. Contrary to our advice, he would keep his eyes closed when stroked and also would make thrusting movements. However, we were able to get him in touch with some of the components of his sexuality. He said that it felt like a sacrifice to penetrate a woman, as if he had given them a part of himself, but at the same time it was an honor to be allowed this act of chivalry. He also said that he was afraid that if he reached orgasm, he would be "under a woman's dominion." (I see the presence of this fear as a symptom of his low level of arousal in the face of the pressure he felt to perform.) He was able to recognize, seemingly for the first time, that he felt no warmth from women and that he wanted to be held more than he wanted to reach orgasm.

Despite his gaining these insights, we lost control of the therapy. The body therapist felt incapacitated, and this proved difficult to present properly to the patient. He felt at fault and became alarmed when, for the first time, his erections were no longer as firm. When the typical 2-week limit was reached, he was obviously relieved to have a pretext for termination. Although we were only guardedly optimistic, we encouraged him to continue, saying that we thought his case might simply be long-term (3 or 4 weeks). He did not continue and, despite his expressed intention to return, probably will not. Looking back on this case, the failure seems unavoidable. I do not think that a more aggressive body-work therapist or the use of techniques of vigorous manual stimulation and rapid intromission would have been any more effective in this case. He may have been most like the relatively content nonclinical retarded ejaculators who have elaborated their symptom into a life-style and, as I speculated earlier, may represent the majority of men with this disorder.

References

Apfelbaum, B. A contribution to the development of the behavioral-analytic sex therapy model. *Journal of Sex and Marital Therapy,* 1977, *3,* 128–138. (a)

Apfelbaum, B. The myth of the surrogate. *Journal of Sex Research,* 1977, *13,* 238–249. (b)

Apfelbaum, B. On the etiology of sexual dysfunction. *Journal of Sex and Marital Therapy,* 1977, *3,* 50–62. (c)

Apfelbaum, B. Sexual functioning reconsidered. In R. Gemme & C. C. Wheeler (Eds.), *Progress in sexology.* New York: Plenum Press, 1977. (d)

Fenichel, O. *The psychoanalytic theory of neurosis.* New York: W. W. Norton, 1945.

Kaplan, H. *The new sex therapy.* New York: Brunner/Mazel, 1974.

Kaplan, H. *The illustrated manual of sex therapy.* New York: Quadrangle, 1975.

Masters, W. H., & Johnson, V. E. *Human sexual inadequacy.* Boston: Little, Brown & Co., 1970.

Ovesey, L. Inability to ejaculate in coitus. *Medical Aspects of Human Sexuality,* 1971, *5,* 121.

Razani, J. Ejaculatory incompetence treated by reconditioning anxiety. In J. Fischer & H. L. Gochros (Eds.), *Handbook of behavior therapy with sexual problems* (Vol. 1). New York: Pergamon, 1977.

Sadock, V. A., & Sadock, B. J. Dual-sex therapy. In B. J. Sadock, H. I. Kaplan, & A. M. Freedman (Eds.), *The sexual experience.* Baltimore: Williams & Wilkins, 1976.

Williams, M. H. *An unnoted inconsistency in Masters and Johnson's use of nondemand techniques: Retarded ejaculation.* Unpublished paper presented at the California State Psychological Association Convention, Los Angeles, March, 1977.

Williams, M. H. Individual sex therapy. In J. LoPiccolo & L. LoPiccolo (Eds.), *Handbook of sex therapy.* New York: Plenum Press, 1978.

Sex Therapy with Special Populations

IV

Introduction: Sex Therapy with Special Populations

As our attitudes toward sex have become more enlightened, and as we have made advances in sex therapy, the special needs of certain groups have gained our attention. These needs may involve attitudes on the part of the therapist, specialized knowledge, or special equipment.

The populations that could be covered in this section are many, including the aged, patients with special medical conditions (e.g., spinal cord injury, myorcardial infarction, diabetes), and individuals whose sexual practices typically have been viewed negatively by society, such as homosexuals. From among the many special situations that might have been selected, we have chosen three: treatment of the cardiac patient, treatment of the homosexual couple, and treatment of sexual deviations. The three chapters presented are representative of the unique knowledge and skill that are necessary in treating certain populations. They also reflect how far we have come in legitimizing the importance of sex in the lives of all individuals.

10

Sexual Counseling and Coronary Heart Disease

RICHARD A. STEIN

A variety of physical diseases and disorders can affect sexual functioning. Among the most obvious are diabetes, spinal cord injury, and myocardial infarction. With diabetes, it has been estimated that sexual dysfunction may occur in up to 50% of the male and female diabetic population, with possible impairment of erectile ability and ejaculation, loss of desire, and impaired ability to achieve orgasm. With spinal cord injury, erectile capability and ejaculatory capability usually depend on the site of the lesion. Males with higher-level lesions or incomplete lesions are more likely to retain erectile capability, while ejaculatory capacity appears to be greater in males with lower-segmental lesions or incomplete lesions. Orgasmic quality and quantity in both males and females is variable, although it is often different from the preinjury experience. In postcoronary patients, sexuality may be affected greatly, partially, or minimally. In many postcoronary and diabetic patients, it is not the disease itself, but the psychological sequelae and erroneous expectations of the patient and his/her family that determine subsequent sexual adjustment. Furthermore, if sexuality is narrowly conceived as penile–vaginal intercourse, more disruption is in store for the patient and his/her partner than if it is more broadly conceived as the exchange of physical and emotional intimacy. The sex therapist working with physically disabled or handicapped individuals must recognize that sexuality can be expressed in a multitude of ways, that loss of potency or orgasmic ability does not involve loss of ability to love or to feel, and that sexual scripts are private and can be altered in a variety of ways to accommodate physical realities.

Richard Stein's chapter concerns the return to normal sexual functioning of individuals who have been hospitalized for myocardial infarction. The problem is significant in terms of the number of individuals affected (in the United States, three-quarters of a million patients survive myocardial infarction yearly) and in terms of the important psychological consequences associated with continued interruption of sexual functioning. Dr. Stein illustrates the need for sensitivity to patient anxieties concerning the resumption of sexual functioning. For example, it is estimated that only 25% of the patients resume normal sexual functioning! He calls for a recognition on the part of the physician that counseling in this area is an essential part of treatment during the recuperative phase. His approach involves the participation

*of the patient's partner and an emphasis on the actual work require-
ments associated with sexual intercourse.*

*Of course, the question of treating sexual functioning as an impor-
tant aspect of the recovery from an illness extends far beyond the
specific myocardial infarction. While other illnesses are not discussed,
this chapter does provide a model for the treatment of a patient's (or
couple's) sexual functioning as part of the more general process of
recovery from illness.*

*Richard A. Stein is Director of the Coronary Heart Disease
Treatment and Prevention Program, Downstate Medical Center, State
University of New York, and Assistant Professor in the Department of
Medicine.*

Introduction

To the patient lying in the hospital coronary care unit, life apparently
sustained by tubes and electrical monitoring devices, concerns about
the resumption of sexual activity are not paramount. In the majority of
such cases, however, the patient will be ambulating free from all
monitoring and intravenous equipment in only 5–7 days and will be
discharged home 7–10 days later. When the immediate fear of death is
no longer paramount, concerns about adjustment to living and the various parameters of life performance that make up the constellation of
factors termed "self-image" become manifest. Significant among this
constellation is the individual's view of himself or herself as a sexually
capable person. This has been assaulted by the disease, the intensive
monitoring following the infarction (which would convince any individual, were he not previously convinced, that he was indeed "sick"),
and a great body of folk myth, which is startlingly ubiquitous, that
conveys the message that one's sex life is finished after a heart attack.

The enormity of the problem can easily be understood when we
realize that over three-quarters of a million patients will survive
myocardial infarctions in the United States each year and that only
25% of couples who were sexually active prior to a myocardial infarction will resume sexual activity after a heart attack. This reduction in
sexual activity is by and large unnecessary in terms of medical or
physiological limitations. If one considers the profound impact on
one's self-image and views of oneself as a "whole person" that is
implicit in the giving up of one's sex life, the need for intelligent,
appropriately timed, and sensitive sexual counseling becomes obvious.

Pathophysiological Background

During any form of exercise, the working muscles of the body will
require an increased supply of oxygen-rich blood. To meet this in-

creased demand, the heart must increase its pumping capacity (cardiac output) to a degree proportional to the exercise requirement. The heart does this to a limited extent by increasing the amount of blood it ejects with each heartbeat (stroke volume) and to a large extent by increasing the heart rate. Concomitant with this increase in heart rate is an increase in the oxygen requirement of the heart muscle itself. This requirement can only be met by an increased flow through the coronary arteries, the vessels which supply the heart with arterial blood. If these vessels are narrow and the maximum flow through them significantly limited, then during exercise a point will be reached where the oxygen requirement of the cardiac muscles exceeds the supply capability of the coronary arteries. This imbalance between oxygen requirement and oxygen supply is termed ischemia.

When ischemia occurs during exercise, various clinical findings and physiological alterations occur. Most significant among these is the onset of chest pain, termed angina pectoris. This pain is usually a pressing, significant midline pain that can radiate up toward the left arm or neck and is usually relieved within minutes of cessation of exercise. Additional clinical symptoms may occur, including the sensation of irregular or rapid pulse, usually reflecting a cardiac arrhythmia (irregularity in heartbeat), or exhaustion and difficulty in breathing, reflecting an alteration in the pressure–volume relationship of the left side of the heart secondary to this ischemic phenomenon. Concomitant with these complaints, changes in the electrocardiogram (most commonly, a depression of the S–T segment of the EKG or a cardiac arrhythmia) occur.

For the given patient with coronary diesease, the limitation of his/her physical activity is determined by the amount of external work that he/she can perform prior to onset of cardiac ischemia.

A general sense of the patient's exercise limitations can be obtained from questioning with regard to whether or not the patient can climb steps, walk briskly, or perform various occupational or recreational tasks with or without pain, undue fatigue, or shortness of breath. A far more precise evaluation can be obtained by "exercise electrocardiography." During this evaluation, a patient performs increasing workloads while blood pressure and EKGs are continuously monitored. The point at which ischemia occurs can be more or less precisely noted, and an accurate quantification of the work required to achieve this ischemic threshold is easily obtainable. The comparison of a patient's exercise capacity with his occupational or recreational work requirements is termed a "work evaluation" and is best performed in a specialized exercise laboratory.

The Realities with Regard to Sexual Intercourse

The work requirements, and thus the cardiac oxygen requirements, of sexual intercourse have only recently been accurately assessed. Initial data obtained by Masters and Johnson (1966, p. 174) showed very high heart rates, and thus cardiac oxygen requirements, during sexual intercourse, but these data were obtained from observed college-aged students with unfamiliar sex partners. A more physiologic evaluation was performed by Hellerstein and Friedman (1969), who used portable EKG recorders to allow patients to record their EKGs continually throughout the day, including during sexual intercourse in their own home setting with an established partner. Their study showed that the mean heart rate obtained during orgasm was approximately 117 beats per minute and that this value was frequently exceeded during the day by occupational or recreational activity requirements. They went on to test several of their subjects to estimate the amount of external work that these patients would have to do to obtain similar heart rates to those reached during sexual intercourse and found that the peak heart rate was approximated by having the patient climb two flights of steps at a moderate pace.

The significance of these data obtained by Hellerstein and Friedman, and confirmed in subsequent studies by Stein (1976, 1977), is that the energy requirement of coitus and the cardiac threat associated with coitus and orgasm are not very significant. These data support the hypothesis that the majority of angina and postmyocardial infarction patients could physiologically resume sexual intercourse confident that the energy requirements would be substantially below their ischemic threshold. The majority of such patients should have no symptoms during coitus or orgasm, and the exercise load should not represent an appreciable risk in terms of ischemic episodes, second infarctions, or potentially lethal cardiac arrhythmias.

The Evaluation of the Patient with Coronary Heart Disease with Regard to Ability to Perform Sexually

Sexual counseling of the postmyocardial infarction patient must be based upon a comprehensive evaluation, including medications, the presence of vascular occlusive disease or neuropathies, and an assessment of the limitation of exercise consequent to coronary occlusive disease.

Coronary heart disease often occurs in the presence of cardiac arrhythmias or elevated blood pressure requiring medications which operate by blocking various sympathetic reflexes. Several of these drugs are associated in some patients with sexual dysfunction, either erectile or ejaculatory. Where problems of this nature exist and the patient is on such medications, the use of an alternative drug should be considered. In making changes of this sort, the patient must be aware of the rationale. The relative difficulty of control of arrhythmias or blood pressure with alternative medications must be weighed against the importance of a satisfying sexual life. This is a decision that can only be made with the full awareness and agreement of the patient, physician, and patient's spouse. A list of drugs with which sexual dysfunction has been associated is presented in Table 1.

An additional consideration is the presence of vascular occlusive disease—especially disease involving the lower aspect of the aorta. Since erection requires the engorgement of the corpus cavernosa and spongiosa tissue, significant obstruction of arterial blood supply to the penile organ will be associated with problems of developing and sustaining a satisfactory erection. Diabetes mellitus is an endocrine abnormality associated with a significant increase in the incidence of cornoary atherosclerotic disease. In the coronary patient who has diabetes mellitus, sexual dysfunction may be due to a neuropathy or inflammation and damage of the autonomic nerves that are responsible for erection and ejaculation. Prognosis in the latter two conditions— peripheral vascular disease and diabetes mellitus—for a satisfactory

TABLE 1

Commonly Used Drugs Which May Be Associated with a Decrease in Libido or Sexual Dysfunction

---

1. Barbiturates (sedatives)
2. Corticosteroids
   Cortisone (used for allergic conditions, renal diseases, collagen–vascular diseases)
   Prednisone
3. Anticholinergic drugs
   Pro-Banthine® (used for peptic, gastric disorders)
   Atropine
   Quarternary ammonium compounds
4. Hypertension drugs, antiadrenergic drugs
   Reserpine
   Guanethidine (Ismelin®) (used for hypertension)
   Methyldopa (Aldomet®)
   Propranolol (Inderal®) (used for hypertension, cardiac arrhythmias, and angina pectoris)
5. Chlorphentermine (Pre-Sate®) (used for weight loss)

---

resumption of sexual activity is a true challenge to the sexual counselor. With the exception of the patient in whom vascular surgery is
possible (not a significant number), the majority of the patients will not
be able to perform sexual intercourse, and the ability to obtain sexual
gratification will require the use of additional techniques.

Sexual dysfunction due to coronary occlusive disease is a significant factor in the patient whose ischemic threshold is below the level of
exercise associated with coitus and orgasm. Here we are talking about
the patient who has chest pain or shortness of breath or significant
palpitations at heart rates of 115 beats or below and at work loads that
are mild to moderate in intensity. This patient must be either treated
with medications or surgery sufficient to allow an increase in achieved
heart rate or exercise capacity or counseled to avoid coitus.

An additional group of patients consists of those in whom on an
exercise EKG evaluation, changes of ischemia or symptoms of chest
pain or shortness of breath are noted at heart rates between 115 and 125
beats per minute. These patients fit within a "marginal group" with
regard to the stress of coitus, and effective sexual counseling frequently incorporates the use of a nitroglycerine-type preparation. (This
drug is associated with an increase in obtainable heart rate and work
load prior to ischemia.) In rare instances, coronary bypass surgery, if
otherwise indicated, will frequently increase obtainable heart rates and
work loads without ischemia being manifested. The third group of patients identified on evaluation consists of those in whom the exercise
capacity and heart rates exceed 125 beats per minute without clinical or
EKG evidence of ischemia. These patients, representing the largest
number of previously sexually active postmyocardial infarction patients, will be limited so far as the resumption of sexual intercourse is
concerned only by misinformation, fears, inappropriate sexual counseling, or anxiety on their part or on the part of their spouses.

Scope of the Problem

In a recent review by Papadopoulos (1978), 135 patients were surveyed
after myocardial infarction, and 75% of the previously sexually active
couples had not resumed sexual intercourse by 6 months after the
patient's heart attack. Where reasons were given by the patients for
failing to resume sexual activity, over 80% explained their failure to
resume intercourse either by impotence (for which there was frequently no physiologic or anatomic basis) or by fear on the part of the
patient or his/her marital partner. The failure to resume sexual inter-

course reflects not only a loss in self-image and assessment of one's ability or self-worth as an individual but also, in many instances, entirely reversible fears based on misinformation. The source of this information is ubiquitous, and only in part relates to the myocardial infarction episode. Numerous patients have heard of someone dying from a myocardial infarction during sexual intercourse, and in a review of 60 patients seen at our exercise laboratory, 95% of the patients thought they knew of such a case or had heard of the actor John Garfield's reported demise during sexual intercourse.

Another significant factor is the tremendous impact that the coronary care and the postcoronary period have on the patient. It is not possible for an individual to deny the serious and significant nature of his/her illness after 4 days of monitoring and intravenous life-support mechanisms have been instituted and after seeing the faces of concerned and fearful relatives and friends. When this situation is combined with vague advice on the part of the physician concerning when and how to resume sexual intercourse and when and how to resume other active parts of the patient's life-style, then the pattern is set for a fearful response to the resumption of sexual intercourse and often the failure to resume an active sex life (Green, 1975). The previous sections of this chapter have pointed out that in the majority of patients, the resumption of sexual activity is not only physiologically safe, but its oxygen demand is well below the ischemic threshold of most of the patients, and in a significant number of other patients, manipulation of drug regimens or the use of exercise training may allow the safe resumption of a satisfying sexual life.

Although there is a great deal of value in providing information for the general public concerning the safety of resuming sexual intercourse and the relative safety of sexual activity after a myocardial infarction, the physician's role must be more patient-directed. Objective, specific, patient-oriented counseling at the time of hospital discharge, combined with supportive counseling throughout the recuperative period, offers the best opportunity for an individual who can physiologically resume sexual activity to do so without unnecessary fears or inhibitions.

Counseling Sessions

Our experience in counseling patients concerning resumption of sexual activity following a myocardial infarction can be distilled down to a sequence of counseling sessions and specific topics and approaches. A number of these sessions can be scheduled with nonphysician health care personnel, but at some point the physician, in whom the patient feels resides the greatest knowledge concerning his/her physiological capacity to resume sex, must play an active and specific role.

The First Counseling Session
The first counseling session of the patient with a myocardial infarction usually occurs prior to hospital discharge; in the majority of instances, this occurs from 14–21 days after the actual myocardial infarction. At this point, a great deal of information is being conveyed to the patient, including information about permissible levels of activity, diet, use of drugs, and resumption of occupational activity. In the midst of this information, the concern on the part of the patient with regard to sexual activity may be lost. Physicians may feel it inappropriate to bring up the topic at this time, and patients may either be embarrassed or feel that there are other areas of more significant concern and that this topic can be dealt with at a later time. It is our feeling, however, that for the patient in whom there has been an uncomplicated course and in whom there is apparently a good ability to resume moderate levels of physical activity, specific information with regard to the safety and advisability of coitus should be given. Although the couple may certainly wish to delay resumption of coitus until some time has elapsed and they have confidence in the patient's physical ability, the opportunity of the physician to combat the ubiquitous folk myth about the resumption of coital activity and cardiac death is best taken early. In our center, patients are routinely given a predischarge activity evaluation on a bicycle ergometer prior to discharge. This evaluation incorporates a mild amount of graded exercise to a submaximal heart rate or to a level of work slightly over that in which the patient is expected to participate at home during the first 6–9 weeks (Stein, Walsh, Fernaine, & Frank, 1978). On the basis of this kind of activity, it is often possible to tell the patient with some certainty about the relative safety of sex after myocardial infarction. Also, at this interview, specific information is given about the improbability of death from a myocardial infarction or arrhythmia during sexual intercourse. We quote specifically the work of Ueno (1963) in Japan, where only 34 of 5559 cases of sudden death after a myocardial infarction were related to coitus. (Only about half of these deaths were due to cardiac abnormalities, and 70% of these occurred with other than a marital partner.) In a smaller recent review of 100 cases of sudden death after coronary disease, no patient was recorded as having died during or soon after coitus (Myers & Hewar, 1975). An approach that we have found valuable is having the spouse observe the patient during the exercise test. Seeing the patient exercis-

ing safely does more to relieve anxiety on the part of both the patient and the spouse than all the verbal reassurance in the world.

Later Counseling Sessions
The patient is usually seen approximately 3 weeks after hospital discharge, and we try to determine whether or not sexual activity has been resumed and, if it has not, why not. If the patient still expresses a fear of resuming sexual activity, then we repeat the relevant information, provide the patient with reprints of the material showing the safety of exercise, and discuss with him/her the specific physiological demand of coitus in terms of heart rate and cardiac oxygen requirement and how this fits with the patient's specific exercise capacity. A number of patients will resume sexual activity with either self-or assisted masturbation. There are no good studies comparing the heart rate during masturbation to that during coitus, but preliminary studies suggest that the cardiac requirements of masturbation are significantly reduced as compared to those of coitus. Again, the importance of bringing up the topic of resuming sexual activity cannot be overemphasized. In a review by Tuttle, Cook, and Fitch (1964), patients who had undergone counseling sessions at cardiac rehabilitation exercise centers were questioned about whether or not the physician had brought up the topic of sexual activity. Over 70% of the patients said that this topic had not been discussed, whereas many of the physicians polled specifically recalled bringing up the topic of sexual activity. These data suggest that there is both a high degree of blockage on the part of the patient to both the topic and specific information and a high degree of resistance on the part of the physician to discussing this topic or discussing it within a context where it is clearly appreciated by the patient.

The next, and perhaps most significant, consultation occurs at 10–12 weeks postmyocardial infarction, when the patient (unless in congestive heart failure or having uncontrolled chest pain due to angina or ventricular arrhythmias) is given a maximum-exercise EKG examination. During this test, a precise quantification of the maximum achieved heart rate and workload of a given patient is determined, and specific comparisons of the estimated requirement of sexual intercourse can be made for the patient. Again, it is useful to have the spouse attend this examination if the patient has no objection. The question of resuming sexual activity is again raised after the exercise test has been performed, and these consultations occur with both the spouse and the patient present. For the patient who has a good response to exercise testing, the physician can say that during the exercise test he/she greatly exceeded the cardiac stress associated with coitus, and therefore sexual activity would be imminently safe. Patients should be encouraged to ask specific questions about coital positions, foreplay, or the use of alcohol prior to sex.

A number of physicians still advise patients to resume sexual activity initially or permanently in a female-superior position as opposed to the more traditional male-superior position. Studies by Nemec, Mansfield, and Kennedy (1976) have shown no difference in cardiac stress in either position. It is therefore not reasonable to ask a couple with several "strikes against them" to change coital positions.

Additional Considerations

This chapter has emphasized that a great deal of the restriction of sexual activity that characterizes the postmyocardial infarction couple is physiologically unnecessary and is often based on misinformation or poorly grounded fears on the part of the patient. There is evidence, as presented by Papadopoulous (1978), that intelligent, sensitive, and direct counseling of the couple with regard to the resumption of sexual activity can often lead to an earlier and more satisfying resumption of sexual activity. Excluded from consideration in this chapter, but of real significance to the postinfarction couple, are (1) preexisting sexual problems manifested by a decrease in coital frequency or decreasing satisfaction on the part of one or both partners and (2) the patient who suffers a massive depressive reaction to a myocardial infarction in which failure to resume sexual activity is only part of a spectrum representing a failure of the person to resume a meaningful existence.

In this section, I would like, however, to deal with certain special considerations that are relevant to the postinfarction couple with regard to sexual activity. Since 1969, when Hellerstein and Friedman published their findings concerning the monitoring of patients' heart rates during coitus by use of portable EKG recording devices, several studies, including my own, have used this device to record heart rates during sexual activity in the home setting. It is my opinion that in addition to being a valuable research tool, the use of portable EKG recording devices during coitus in the postmyocardial infarction patient has real clinical value. For our patients who (despite our assurances that their exercise capacity exceeds the demands of coitus) complain of unusual symptoms of pain, rapid heartbeat, or shortness of breath, or still have a great deal of anxiety concerning their hearts' reactions to sexual activity, the wearing of a recorder at home to provide the physician objective data concerning sexual activity is a significant advantage.

When this device is used, the patient has the electrodes placed in the early part of the day and if a full recording is not being done, for other clinical reasons, then the patient is asked to plug the lead wire into the battery and recording device 1 hour prior to anticipated sexual activity. Care is taken to place the leads on the lateral aspect of the chest wall so that they will not be rubbing against the chest of the spouse during coitus; both the patient and the spouse are shown the recording device, the machine that plays back the recording (a cardioscanner), and the type of records obtained. It is important to emphasize to the patient in this setting that only the EKG is being studied. There are no voice recordings being performed, and the observers will in no way be able to judge the quality of the sex act or indeed whether orgasm has occurred. The patient wears the device during coitus and then, following coitus, removes the plug from the recording device (in our instrument, this stops the recording process) and can even removed the leads approximately a half hour after coitus. The precoital and postcoital periods are necessary to obtain baseline heart rate recordings. In some instances, we repeat this a second time if the patient feels anxious about the use of the instrument, and the data obtained may therefore, in part, reflect acclimation to the recording device. Devices of this nature are available in most hospital settings. They provide the clinician with direct evidence of the cardiac response to sexual activity and can often be the basis for intelligent, convincing counseling with regard to the safety of resuming sexual activity in the particularly anxious patient or spouse.

An additional area of concern is the patient who is unable to resume sexual activity because of ischemia at the work load required by coitus. This patient may show abnormal electrocardiographic changes of concern to the clinician or present with chest pain or shortness of breath during coitus. There are several approaches to the management of this patient, and they will, in large part, be dictated by the other symptoms that make up the patient's entire presentation. The first line of attack, I believe, should always be the use of a nitroglycerine preparation. This can be taken 5 minutes prior to anticipated coitus and, in many instances, will allow the patient to complete the sex act without any symptoms. In our laboratory, when a patient manifests significant ischemic abnormalities or chest pain during heart rates below 130 beats per minute, a repeat test is done after the administration of a nitroglycerine tablet. In most instances, this will allow the patient to complete an additional work load at a higher heart rate and thus give us a reasonable basis from which to predict the satisfactory completion of the sex act with the use of such a nitrate preparation.

Studies in our laboratory have shown that postmyocardial infarction patients who undergo successive-interval training programs will reduce their heart rate response to any given work task and indeed reduce their heart rate and cardiac oxygen demands during coitus. Hellerstein and Friedman (1969) reported that patients who were involved in a cardiac rehabilitation exercise program had an increase in sexual frequency and a decrease in symptoms associated with coitus as compared to a control group. Our studies have shown that patients who involve themselves with successful exercise programs have reduced heart rates and cardiac oxygen requirements during coitus and other activities and that this is the physiological basis for the clinical observation of Hellerstein and Friedman. Although the resumption of symptom-free coitus is not the sole justification for a cardiac exercise rehabilitation program, it is certainly one of the benefits that this program offers the patient.

For the patient whose exercise tolerance is severely limited despite the use of drugs, consideration must be given to coronary bypass surgery. This procedure, which creates an alternate pathway for blood bypassing the obstructed lesion in the artery, is frequently associated with a dramatic improvement in exercise capacity and a reduction in pain. We have conducted several studies that document a marked improvement in exercise capacity, a reduction in frequency of chest pain, and a marked increase in the ability to resume coital activity in previously incapacitated patients. This procedure has an associated mortality and morbidity and therefore is, in my opinion, justified only in specific clinical situations.

Illustrative Cases

Case 1

Mr. D. K. was a 49-year-old man with a 23-year history of smoking two packs of cigarettes a day. Mr. K. noted severe substernal chest pain after dinner one evening and was brought to a local hospital emergency room, where an acute interior-wall myocardial infarction was diagnosed. Mr. K. was admitted to the coronary care unit and remained there for 5 days. After an uneventful course, he was transferred to the intermediate care unit and then discharged after a total of 14 hospital days. On discharge, Mr. K. required no medications and complained of no chest pain or inappropriate shortness of breath.

Mr. K. had been married for 22 years and had three children, the oldest of whom was 15 years of age. During his time in the coronary care unit, Mr. K. repeatedly asked the doctors if they were sure he had had a heart attack and was unable to express either fear or anxiety during his entire hospital course. He appeared overtly cheerful and was frequently flirtatious with the nursing staff. In the intermediate care unit, he specifically asked the house staff when he could resume sexual activity, and his major source of concern was his anticipated difficulty in cessation of smoking. At day 14, Mr. K. underwent a predischarge exercise evaluation and achieved a moderate work load with no ischemic changes on his EKG, chest pain, or dyspnea. Mr. K. expressed no anxiety and answered questions concerning fear of resuming sexual intercourse with an "are you kidding?" attitude. Mrs. K. asked specific questions about resuming sexual activity and was interested in the relative exercise capacity requirements of sex as compared to Mr. K.'s predischarge exercise evaluation.

Mr. and Mrs. K. were seen again at 3 months postinfarction, at which time a multistage exercise EKG examination revealed a low-normal exercise capacity associated with changes of ischemia at only near maximum work loads and heart rates. Questioning with regard to sexual activity revealed that the couple had a frequency of intercourse of approximately three times per week and that Mr. K. masturbated approximately once a week. Sexual activity had been resumed by the couple 2 days after hospital discharge, and Mrs. K. reported that they had had intercourse for 3 successive nights but that coital frequency had decreased to once a week since. Mr. K. associated this decrease in sexual frequency with increasing concerns about life plans and jobs and the stresses of family and business life, but upon repeated questioning, acknowledged that he felt somewhat fatigued after sexual activity and on one or two occasions had noted a slight fluttering in his chest about which he was concerned. Mr. K. wore a 24-hour Holter EKG recorder, during which time the couple engaged in sexual activity. A review of these recordings showed a peak coital heart rate of 124 beats per minute, with no irregular heartbeats noted. The couple was assured that there was no physiological reason for abstaining from sexual activity, and when seen at 6 months postinfarction, they had resumed intercourse two to three times per week.

Comment

Denial is a frequent early mechanism for dealing with myocardial infarction, especially in the patient in whom significant angina or failure is not a problem. Part of this denial mechanism is obviously the reassurance to oneself that one is a "complete individual," and oftentimes this involves one's sexual self-image. It is not infrequent for otherwise polite men to become flirtatious and even overtly suggestive with female medical personnel during their time in the coronary care unit. It is important for nursing and medical staff to realize that beneath this "sexual bravado" lies a great deal of fear and uncertainty concerning one's self-image and, indeed, one's ability to perform sexually. Despite the patient's overt expression of lack of concern, a careful discussion with regard to postdischarge sexual activity is very important and helpful.

It is also interesting to note that after a burst of sexual activity upon returning home, no doubt to prove to the patient and to his spouse that sexuality was not a concern, the then-limited coital frequency pattern was more indicative of his underlying fears. Mr. K. here presents with one of the prime concerns of the individual dealing with cardiac patients after infarction, and that is the sudden awareness of these people of minor changes in heart rate or respiratory rate and fatigue that were not of concern to them before. Without recording objective data from a 24-hour EKG recorder, there is no way to be certain that this "fluttering in the heart" was merely an appropriate sinus tachycardia and not an inappropriate cardiac arrhythmia. From our experiences, this enhanced awareness diminishes with time but never completely returns to normal.

Case 2

Mr. J. S. was a 63-year-old man who suffered a myocardial infarction after 1 year of intermittent chest pain diagnosed by his physician as angina pectoris and treated with a nitroglycerine preparation. Mr. S. spent 21 days in the hospital, at which time digitalis and a diuretic were added to his drug regimen because of early signs of congestive heart failure. During his stay in the intermediate care unit, telemetry revealed occasional ventricular premature contractions, and quinidine gluconate, an antiarrhythmic drug, was initiated. At predischarge exercise testing, the patient had moderate chest pain with S–T segment depression at a heart rate of 110 beats per minute achieved at the 1st minute of 300 kilopound-meters per minute of bicycle exercise. Discharge medications included digitalis, a diuretic, quinidine gluconate, and a nitroglycerine-type preparation.

Questioning of Mr. and Mrs. S. with regard to sexual activity revealed a prehospitalization pattern of sexual activity that included coitus on a biweekly basis. Both Mr. and Mrs. S. assumed that their sexual activity was finished because of the myocardial infarction, and Mrs. S. said, "That part of our lives is over."

The couple was counseled to abstain from sexual activity until their 3-month postdischarge evaluation but were informed that the resumption of sexual activity was entirely possible. After 3 months, Mr. S. was no longer taking a diuretic, and the antiarrhythmic drug had been stopped. The digitalis and the nitrate preparation were still being used. His exercise capacity at 3 months was improved, and he achieved a heart rate of 125 beats per minute with only mild to moderate pain; a repeat evaluation after nitroglycerine showed an ability to perform 20 ml/kg/min of oxygen requirement—work without significant EKG changes of ischemia, chest pain, or dyspnea. At this time, the couple was shown Mr. S.'s exercise evaluation and counseled with regard to the relative safety of resuming sexual intercourse if a nitroglycerine preparation were obtained and taken 15 minutes prior to anticipated coitus. The relative cardiac safety of sexual activity with a long-standing partner in a familiar setting was reviewed.

Both Mr. and Mrs. S. listened intently and seemed relieved by the improvement in Mr. S.'s condition, but neither expressed a desire to resume sexual activity.

Comment

When preinfarction sexual frequency is limited and one or both of a couple is subconsciously or consciously looking for an "acceptable reason" to stop entirely, then a myocardial infarction will often signal the cessation of sexual activity. The relative age of the couple is a consideration but not an absolute one, since everyone involved in sex counseling is aware of an increasing number of couples in their 60s and 70s who have active, satisfying sex lives. I think that the attitude of the counseling staff should always be that the couple can resume sexual activity, but that it is unwise and unrealistic to portray an attitude that they must do so.

Case 3

Mr. J. D. was a 53-year-old attorney who suffered a myocardial infarction 3 months prior to evaluation in our laboratory at Downstate Medical Center. For 1 year prior to his myocardial infarction, Mr. D. had noted chest pain on exertion and had been treated with a nitroglycerine preparation by his attending physician. Since his myocardial infarction, Mr. D. experienced chest pain upon climbing one flight of stairs and required both propranolol and an oral nitroglycerine preparation (Isordil) for control of his pain. Mr. D. did not resume sexual activity since his mycardial infarction and was fearful that he would have chest pain and possibly a heart attack if such activity were to resume. His wife shared this concern and verbalized no concern about the failure to resume their preinfarction sexual activity. Questioning with regard to sexual activity prior to the myocardial infarction revealed a frequency of coitus of one to two times per week and that this frequency had been stable for the past 3 years. There was no history of diabetes, and the patient did not take any other medications. On evaluation in our laboratory, the patient had severe changes of ischemia associated with chest pain and a feeling of shortness of breath at the 3rd minute of exercise on our treadmill protocol (this is at an oxygen consumption of approximately 13 ml/kg/min) and a heart rate of 115 beats per minute. The patient was rested, given a nitroglycerine tablet (1/200 g), and reexercised. This time, the patient was able to complete 6 minutes of exercise and achieve a heart rate of 140 beats per minute prior to the onset of chest pain or significant EKG evidence of ischemia. After the exercise testing, consultation sessions were held with the patient and his spouse and the above-quoted information with regard to coital frequency and resumption ascertained. The couple was shown the patient's EKG records and the heart rate and work load capacity of the husband after nitroglycerine. They were counseled to resume sexual activity with nitroglycerine used a half hour prior to the resumption of coitus. The patient was seen 3 weeks later, and at that time, the patient had not yet attempted coitus despite specific counseling. More detailed questioning showed a persistent anxiety on the part of both the patient and the spouse about possible dire consequences of resuming coitus even after the use of a nitroglycerine tablet. The couple was shown the Holter EKG ambulatory recording device, and the record obtained from such a device was presented to them. The patient then wore the Holter for the entire day at work and in the evening during coitus. He reported feeling better about wearing the device and about resuming coitus because it were almost as if "someone was watching my heart." The recording obtained was shown to the patient, and the heart rate achieved was 123 beats a minute, substantially lower than that obtainable during exercise with nitroglycerine. At a 6-month follow-up, the patient had resumed a coital frequency of one to two times per week, and he reported that they found their sexual activity enjoyable and relatively free of anxiety. The patient had no symptoms during coitus.

Comment

This is a good example of the patient with a marginal exercise capacity in whom coitus would represent a substantial physiological stress. The use of the nitroglycerine preparation prior to coitus allows the safe continuation of coital activity. The problem, of course, is that whenever a patient must take a drug such as nitroglycerine prior to performing an activity, there is a great deal of anxiety associated with the activity, since the drug is usually taken for pain due to coronary disease. In this case, that was overcome by having a Holter recording taken during coitus, and the patient was able to view the actual recording in comparison to the stress-test results. In Hellerstein and Friedman's (1969) study, exercise that created a heart rate response equal to that of coitus was in the area of 16 ml/kg/min of oxygen requirement. This is about the 3rd minute of the Bruce treadmill protocol used in our laboratory. Therefore, the completion with nitroglycerine of the 3rd minute of one stage higher (approximately 24 ml/kg/min of oxygen requirement) assures the safety of coitus in this individual.

Case 4

Ms. A. R. was a 42-year-old woman with a history of smoking for 21 years and of using oral contraceptives for 5 years prior to her myocardial infarction. The patient had no chest pain prior to her myocardial infarction and was seen 4 weeks after an uneventful hospital and posthospital course. At the time of exercise testing, the patient had not resumed sexual activity. The topic of sexual activity was brought up prior to the exercise test when her husband expressed an interest as to whether or not this test would show if the resumption of sexual activity would be safe. The patient exercised to a heart rate of 160 beats per minute. There were no ischemic changes, and an adequate work load was achieved. The patient was counseled that her cardiovascular response to exercise was excellent, that there was no evidence of ischemia or significant irregularity in the heartbeat associated with exercise, and that coitus would represent a stress significantly less than that seen in the testing. The patient was very concerned about "how we knew it was safe." The relevant literature was reviewed, and Xeroxed copies of articles by Hellerstein and Friedman (1969), Stein (1976, 1977), and Green (1975) were given to the couple. The patient entered a cardiac exercise training program and was next seen 3 months later for an upgrading of her home ergometric exercise prescription. At that time, the patient had resumed a coital frequency of three to four times a week without the use of any medications and expressed no anxiety about the stress of coitus. This patient performed 30 minutes of strenuous ergometric exercise daily to a heart rate of 145 beats per minute, and was aware that the cardiac stress associated with coitus was significantly less than that of this daily exercise training session. It is interesting that although there was no significant inhibition about resuming sexual activity, once medical advice concerning its safety was provided, both the husband and wife were aware of relatives or friends who had died during coitus. When pressed to name the specific individuals, they were in both cases friends of a friend. Since neither Ms. R. nor her husband had received any specific advice from either physician or nurse, they had delayed the resumption of sexual activity until a suitable postcardiac evaluation was performed.

Comment

Although statistical data are lacking, there is an impression on the part of many busy clinical cardiologists of an increasing number of young, premenopausal women with coronary disease. This may be due in part to the fact that we are seeing our first generation of women who have smoked for most of their adult lives and who have histories of contraceptive use. An additional factor of unknown significance is the increase of business and life stresses associated with changes in the life-styles of many women.

This patient, of course, had an excellent exercise capacity, and the only concern about resuming sexual activity was the necessity of reassuring the patient of its complete safety and advisability. Even in this couple, for whom the resumption of sexual activity was of primary concern, the failure of the discharging physician to specifically and explicitly discuss the topic caused them to delay, out of fear, engaging in sexual activity until the topic was explicitly handled.

Conclusion

This chapter has reviewed the relevant literature and has given an outline for the management of the patient with coronary heart disease with regard to sexual activity. The resumption of sexual activity is one of the constellation of processes that comprise the successful "rehabilitation" of the patient after a myocardial infarction. It often reflects not only physiological ability but also self-image and is an important aspect of a satisfying life for many of our patients. The major emphasis of this chapter is on initiating discussion of sexual activity with patients at frequent points along the therapeutic rehabilitative path. Physicians often find such topics embarrassing or feel that they will be embarrassing or of no concern to the patient. My own experience indicates that this is not the case. The patient may be unwilling to bring up the topic of sexual activity or may feel that the failure of the physician to mention it means that it is proscribed. I feel that intelligent counseling based on knowledge of the physiological requirements of sexual activity and including an education of the patient with regard to the cardiac stress associated with coitus in comparison to his/her own exercise ability is as much an important part of treating the patient with coronary disease as is discussing his/her medical regimen, activity regimen, or diet. If the physician does not give the patient specific and informative counseling with regard to sexual activity, then the patient will, of necessity, create a program based on misinformation provided by well-meaning friends and associates and will, in most instances, resume sexual activity hesitantly or not at all. In most cases, this totally unnecessary burden can be removed by specific counseling. An additional concept with which I would like to conclude this chapter is the need for exercise testing in the overwhelming majority of post-myocardial infarction or angina pectoris patients. It is only by observing the cardiovascular response to given levels of stress that the physician, or sex therapist can provide intelligent counseling to the patient with regard to the resumption of any occupational or recreational activity, including coitus.

References

Green, A. W. Sexual activity and the post myocardial infarction patient. *American Heart Journal*, 1975, *89*, 246–252.

Hellerstein, H. A., & Friedman, E. H. Sexual activity and the post coronary patient. *Medical Aspects of Human Sexuality*, 1969, *3*, 70–96.

Masters, W. H., & Johnson, V. E. *Human sexual response*. Boston: Little, Brown & Co., 1966.

Myers, A., & Hewar, H. A. Circumstances attending 100 sudden deaths from coronary artery disease with coroner's necropsies. *British Heart Journal*, 1975, *37*, 1133–1143.

Nemec, E. D., Mansfield, L., & Kennedy, J. W. Heart rate and blood pressure response during sexual activity in normal males. *American Heart Journal*, 1976, *92*, 274–277.

Papadopoulos, C. A survey of sexual activity after myocardial infarction. *Cardiovascular Medicine*, 1978, *3*, 821–826.

Stein, R. A. Resuming sexual relations after myocardial infarction. *Medical Aspects of Human Sexuality*, 1976, *10*, 159–160.

Stein, R. A. The effect of exercise training on heart rate during coitus in the post myocardial infarction patient. *Circulation*, 1977, *55*, 738–740.

Stein, R., Walsh, W., Fernaine, A., & Frank, F. Value of pre-discharge exercise testing in post-myocardial infarction patients. *Clinical Research*, 1978, *26*, 607A. (Abstract)

Tuttle, W. B., Cook, W. L., & Fitch, E. Sexual behavior in post myocardial infarction patients. *American Journal of Cardiology*, 1964, *13*, 140. (Abstract)

Ueno, M. The so called coition death. *Japanese Journal of Legal Medicine*, 1963, *17*, 535.

11

Treatment of Sexual Dysfunction in Homosexual Male Couples

DAVID P. MCWHIRTER AND ANDREW M. MATTISON

The evolution of changing attitudes toward homosexuality over the last century has been mirrored in the treatment efforts of the helping professions. For the greater part of the twentieth century, homosexuality was viewed as pathological, if not criminal. Consequently, treatment strategies centered on means and methods of eliminating homosexual arousal and replacing it with heterosexual arousal. Despite the significant lack of success achieved in most of these efforts, attempts continued and, regrettably, are still being practiced, even with individuals who are content with their orientation.

Thanks in large part to the increased outspokenness on the part of gays in cities and towns across the country and the "coming out" of thousands of influential, successful homosexual individuals, sex therapy services for homosexual couples are becoming available. The goal of such treatment is not extinguishing the pleasure that comes from same-gender attraction and arousal, but rather the elimination of anxiety and guilt and the remediation of whatever difficulties plague sexual and relationship functioning.

McWhirter and Mattison's chapter on the treatment of the homosexual couple illustrates several important points. Sex therapy with homosexual couples and individual clients is not significantly different from sex therapy with heterosexuals. The same dysfunctions exist, and the same techniques are employed in treatment. What is critical, however, is a lack of homophobia on the part of the therapist and a commitment to assisting the homosexual individual or couple in overcoming his or her own homophobia.

Although this chapter focuses on the treatment of male homosexuals, the treatment of lesbian couples and individuals requires the same sensitivity as the treatment of homosexual males. Additionally, competency in treating the whole gamut of female sexual disorders is necessary.

David P. McWhirter is Assistant Clinical Professor of Psychiatry at the School of Medicine, University of California, San Diego, and Andrew M. Mattison is Assistant Clinical Professor of Community Medicine (Family Medicine) at the same institution. Both are in private practice at the Clinical Institute for Human Relationships in San Diego.

A New Perspective

In this time of increasing awareness about homosexuality, researchers have turned from searching for causes, etiologies, and incidence to developing typologies and phenomenological exploration. Homosexual persons have developed an increasingly healthier acceptance of themselves as more social and psychological research is applied to better understanding. The homosexual community is instilling pride and visibility to a formerly closeted and oppressed sexual minority, albeit a large minority. Until recently, it would have been almost unthinkable for therapists to provide treatment for sexual dysfunctions in homosexual men, and speaking publicly about such a formerly taboo topic indicates the distance we have traveled in overcoming our prejudices and biases toward same-sex sexual relationships.

The literature on homosexual men in relationships is almost nonexistent. The stereotyped notion that homosexual men are unable to sustain long-term relationships because of arrested psychosexual growth and development does still prevail. There were a few early voices in the wilderness (Hooker, 1957) pointing to the evidence that homosexual men were as well adjusted as heterosexual men. It was still 17 years later before homosexuality per se was dropped from the psychiatric nomenclature. Homosexual men and women have looked upon themselves with new acceptance since the American Psychiatric Association took the step in 1973. Of course, a change in the diagnostic nomenclature opened the door for therapists to focus on other types of emotional and psychological problems that homosexual persons might have.

The recently published work of Bell and Weinberg (1978) from the Institute for Sex Research provides a new and somewhat unfortunate typology for homosexual men and women. The interviews for the study were conducted at a time when the homosexual community was only beginning to be organized. Homosexual men and women in the Bell and Weinberg study did not have the benefit of the "liberation" movement—to see and share in homosexual pride, to see openly homosexual persons elected to public office, to experience the economic power of the boycott, to have national homosexual representatives welcomed at the White House, etc. These conditions have led to a healthier and more positive self-evaluation by many homosexual people and were not present when the data for *Homosexualities* were collected.

In the not too distant past, the therapeutic focus for homosexuality was on changing sexual orientation. The behavior therapy literature was replete with papers and chapters on various behavior-modification approaches to converting homosexual orientation to more normative heterosexual behaviors. The brave and insightful presentation by Davison in his presidential address to the Association for Advancement of Behavior Therapy in Chicago in 1974, calling for a moratorium on aversive techniques for sexual orientation change, did introduce some sanity into the behavior therapy research with homosexual persons. Prior to that time, the literature abounded in psychoanalytic attempts at sexual orientation reversal (Bieber *et al.*, 1962). The dominant position regarding causality for homosexuality stemmed from psychoanalysis. The belief that the causes of homosexuality could be discovered by retrospective examination of parenting and development proved unsuccessful due to the many flaws in the research methods and biases of the investigators. The social scripting theories of Gagnon and Simon (1973), along with their clear thinking along sociological lines, introduced new insights into research and therapy. Persons with homosexual orientation began seeking therapy for problems other than their homosexuality. Fewer and fewer therapists offered treatment specifically for sexual orientation change. The development of homosexual centers and homosexual counseling services around the country has introduced new perspectives for therapy with homosexual people. Organizations and training programs for homosexual therapists are beginning to appear. It is not surprising, then, to find that sex therapy for homosexual men is now becoming available. Although such therapy for heterosexual persons has been available for many years, similar therapeutic services for homosexual men have only been available in the past 4 or 5 years. The models used for treating sexual dysfunction in heterosexual persons are being applied to homosexual relationships. Although this chapter is about treatment for homosexual men, therapy for sexual dysfunction among lesbian couples is also being done.

Our own work with homosexuals arose from clinical needs. More and more, same-sex-oriented men were seeking help from psychotherapy to improve their quality of life, not to reverse their sexual orientation. As we began seeing healthy homosexuals, we recognized the lack of information concerned with how gay men live together in loving, sexual, and intimate relationships. Over the past 5 years, we have interviewed 156 homosexual male couples in which the length of time in the relationship ranged from 1 to 34 years, with a mean of 7.4 years. The ages of these men ranged from 21 to 68 years. The full data on that study will be published elsewhere in the near future. There are no in-depth published studies in the literature specifically dealing with homosexual male couples. The invisibility of this group of people may tend to make research with them more difficult.

The Homosexual Couple

The classification and treatment of sexual dysfunction in the last 20 years represent incalculable progress in the field of human sexuality. Since the pioneering work of Masters and Johnson, which awakened investigators and clinicians to the human suffering attendant to problems of sexual functioning, thousands of people have been treated successfully. Interestingly, homosexual couples (for this chapter, a "homosexual couple" is defined as two males who live in the same domicile and who identify themselves as a "couple") also are seeking help for sexual dysfunction. Homosexual couples experience the same range of sexual dysfunctions as do heterosexual couples, and these sexual problems, for the most part, can be treated successfully.

This chapter describes our 5 years of experience in treating homosexual male couples with some form of sexual dysfunction. An ongoing caseload of heterosexual couples with sexual problems has provided an available resource for contrasts and similarities in the treatment of homosexual male couples. The age range of these homosexual patients has been from 20 to 60 years, with the average age being in the early 30s. The duration of their relationships has ranged from 1 to 26 years.

Establishing the incidence of sexual dysfunction among the population in general has not been accomplished. Masters and Johnson estimate that 50% of American marriages experience sexual dysfunction at some time (Haeberle, 1978). Only recently has there been mention of problems of sexual dysfunction among homosexuals. There have been some preliminary data which indicate that the incidence of dysfunction in male homosexual couples is lower than that in heterosexual couples (Haeberle, 1978; McWhirter & Mattison, 1977). In the recently published work *Homosexualities* from the Institute for Sex Research (Bell & Weinberg, 1978), the researchers do not report the percentage of incidence of various sexual difficulties in black and white male homosexuals, but they do report the existence of dysfunctions and the degrees to which the respondants experience the sexual difficulties as being problematic.

Theoretical Approach

The basis for our therapeutic understanding in work with homosexual men is firmly founded in psychodynamic principles. The treatment methods vary according to the individual's and/or couple's needs. The psychodynamic assessment and treatment of Kaplan's (1974) and Masters and Johnson's (1970) methods are interwoven. The nomenclature derived from Kaplan's psychophysiologic model is used. The useful breakdown of desire-phase, arousal-phase, and orgasmic-phase disorders provides a more clear-cut and unified diagnostic nosology. The new phenomenologically oriented categories of the Diagnostic and Statistical Manual III (DSM III) provide a more precise descriptive diagnosis for sexual dysfunctions that apply to both heterosexual and homosexual persons.

In desire-phase disorders (inhibition of sexual desire, DSM III), two basic varieties of dysfunction are found: (1) lack of interest or diminished interest in sex, wherein one partner or the other lacks the drive to seek or initiate sexual activity with his partner, but once such activity is begun, the disinterested person does participate and function, and (2) aversion, wherein one partner manifests disgust for all sexual activity. In heterosexual couples, aversion to general sexual activity has been found. In homosexual male couples, we have not seen a case of generalized aversion to all sexual behaviors, but rather aversion to some specific type of sexual activity in which one partner wishes to engage. Some examples are aversion to anal intercourse (the most common), aversion to fellatio, or aversion to mutual masturbation.

Arousal-phase disorders (inhibited sexual excitement, DSM III) run the gamut from the individual who is completely unable to obtain penile erection to the individual who is able to obtain penile erection but loses it early in the sexual contact or prior to ejaculation. Understanding arousal as an autonomic parasympathetic reflex helps in diagnosing and ruling out the organic or drug-related causes of erectile dysfunction.

Orgasmic-phase disorders present with two basic dysfunctions: (1) Early or premature ejaculation ranges from the individual who ejaculates at the onset of sexual contact to the individual who is able to "last" for some period of time but ejaculates as either oral or anal penetration is initiated. This condition seems to be seen less frequently in homosexual males than in heterosexual males. (2) Delayed or retarded ejaculation is a condition in which an individual is unable to ejaculate and/or to reach orgasm with oral or anal penetration. In heterosexual males, the condition usually means that the person cannot ejaculate intravaginally, and it is seen relatively infrequently. Among the homosexual men in our caseload, however, it is the most common orgasmic-phase dysfunction. The individual usually is unable to reach orgasm with a partner except by autostimulation that is prolonged and vigorous. The nondysfunctional partner may complain of inability to tolerate the vigorous activity required by the dysfunctional partner to reach orgasm, or he may experience feelings of rejection or hurt when he is not able to help the dysfunctional partner obtain sexual satisfaction. The increased number of homosexual males with this dysfunction may parallel the similar orgasmic-phase disorders seen in females.

Treatment Format

Our therapeutic approach incorporates the general principles of dynamic psychotherapy, considerable education, including the use of films, videotapes, and reading material, along with directive behavioral therapy, sometimes including desensitization and relaxation techniques. We are hesitant to admit it, but our general principles include the "anything that works" approach with the exception of direct contact with our patients other than the physical examination itself. We have used surrogate partners on a few occasions in the past, but generally insist that the person seeking assistance find his own partner. Although we do follow a general format for treatment, no two cases progress in exactly the same lock-step fashion. We had some previous notions that the format itself was therapeutic, but discovered quite early that there is no magic in the process.

In the course of therapy, issues regarding homosexual orientation do arise, and frequently there is a need for the therapist(s) to provide some consciousness-raising for partners in a homosexual relationship. However, this is not as common a difficulty as might be expected.

A certain flexibility is required in treatment formats. In some instances, as illustrated in Example 1, intensive short-term treatment was most appropriate.

> *Example 1.* A couple with a 7-year history in the relationship presented with one partner having had erectile dysfunction for the preceding 18 months. The partners were both in their early 30s, well educated, highly motivated, and most eager for treatment once the initial session was finished. They pressed for more frequent sessions than once a week, then cut down to twice a week and, finally, to once a week as resolution of the erectile dysfunction was achieved.

In desire-phase disorders, such as Example 2, one person was seen several times per week while the couple was seen only once per week.

> *Example 2.* This couple had been together for 11 years. Both partners were in their late 30s. One person had completely lost interest in sexual contact with his partner. This situation of 2 years' duration had severely damaged the relationship. The partner with the lack of interest was seen on a twice-weekly schedule

to work through some of the developmental problems that laid the groundwork for lack of interest. We always find that some individual therapy is required with the person presenting with desire-phase disorders. In addition to the individual sessions, conjoint therapy with the couple proceeded on a once-a-week basis.

In other cases, as in the following example, the couple was seen conjointly once or twice weekly for a total of approximately 15 sessions.

Example 3. This young couple, ages 25 and 26, presented with one partner complaining of premature ejaculation. During the evaluation phase of treatment, the couple was seen twice weekly, but after the evaluation, a slower, more integrating approach with the couple seen on a weekly basis was effective.

In general, the initial four visits include the first diagnostic interviews, individual sessions with each member of a relationship to secure a detailed sex history and psychosocial background, and a conjoint physical examination. This physical examination serves the purpose of ruling out organic difficulties and provides a unique opportunity for discussing information about physiologic issues as well as providing the partners with education about their bodies and the opportunity to ask questions that might not otherwise be asked.

The fifth, or "roundtable," session briefs couples with information gathered during the evaluation process. Sensate-focus exercises are usually started at session 5. The couple is encouraged to experiment with nongenital sensate pleasuring on at least two occasions during the first week. When this has been accomplished without genital touching, genital sensate-focus pleasuring is introduced. As always, this process depends upon the type of dysfunction and the individual's and couple's response to the therapy. The course and duration of therapy with homosexual couples is approximately 15 sessions, including the five evaluation visits, and is quite similar to that for heterosexual couples.

Following the introduction of sensate focus, an interdiction is given regarding genital sex—provided the couple has made a verbal contract with the therapist(s) to follow all instructions carefully. We usually use only one therapist, unless a clear-cut reason for the conjoint model is present. Comparable effectiveness has been achieved by using a single male therapist, and this approach is less costly to the couple in treatment. Indications for the use of two therapists include when (1) one partner is in therapy with one of the cotherapists and clear-cut transference is occuring; (2) there is evidence of strong competitiveness between partners in gaining the support of a single therapist; (3) the evaluating therapist has an initial impression of difficulty in working with one of the partners; (4) severe communication difficulties are evident in the relationship; in such cases, treatment is more effective when cotherapists are present to "model" communication skills for the couple; and (5) concern exists about confusions in the therapist's countertransference feelings.

Illustrative Case

The following detailed case provides an example of a combined approach using the dual-therapist model. It is presented in the sequence in which the events occurred so that the reader will gain some insight into the process and into variations in the treatment methods that can be required with homosexual male couples.

The first contact in this case was by telephone when Ed called for an appointment. He was 20 minutes early for that first appointment (with D. P. McW.). He was a tall, medium-built, blond, blue-eyed, attractive man who appeared considerably younger than his 36 years. He was neatly and fashionably dressed in casual clothes, smiling almost artificially while demonstrating some psychomotor slowing. He sat tensely and almost rigidly in the chair for the first 15 minutes, and he said that he had never seen a psychiatrist before and was worried about it. His depression was causing loss of appetite, insomnia, and difficulty functioning. With some initial reassurance, he shared his story. The current crisis revolved around the threats of his lover, Dave, to terminate their 11-year relationship. Ed did not want that but was feeling incapable of preventing it. He described a general decline in the amount of time spent together and an increasing number of disagreements which moved into arguments that would last for several days at a time. Ed was bewildered and saddened over what was happening. As part of the usual and routine questioning, Ed was asked about their sexual communication. That question opened the floodgates. Through his sobs, Ed told of his "impotence" of the past year—a generalized inability to maintain erections during lovemaking or sex play with Dave. Ed injected the usual questions: "What's the matter with me, Doc? Am I too old? Is it physical? Am I really screwed up?"

Dave, his partner of 11 years, had always been sexually active, not only with Ed but with others as well. Over the previous 6 months, Dave had withdrawn from Ed, sometimes sleeping in the spare room, spending more and more time in gay bars and baths. He had brought home pubic lice on at least two occasions. Ed himself had tried to have sexual contacts outside the relationship but found himself unable to function sexually in any situation. With autoerotic behavior, he was able to obtain erections, but some slight negative feelings about masturbation were detectable at the first session. Prior to the last few weeks, he had experienced erections on morning waking at least five or six times weekly.

Ed's developmental history was significant in the following areas: He was born into an upper-middle-class family; his father was a professional man and his mother worked as an administrative assistant in a research institution. Ed was the third child, with a sister 2 years older and a brother 4 years older than he. His father died of coronary artery disease when Ed was 7. His mother remarried when he was 11, and he claimed never to have gotten along with his stepfather. He had always played rough-and-tumble games with boys, but recalled very early erotic fascination with males. He was essentially a "good boy" until the hormone flow of adolescence and his stepfather's discipline brought rebellion and conflicts to his life. Ed always did well in school, was on the football team, and dated girls, but he was preoccupied with thoughts of leaving home. He admitted to occasional homosexual experiences with friends, including "circle jerks," fellatio, and anal intercourse. He would disobey his stepfather's wishes and would be punished by restrictions and occasional whippings until age 16. He had one juvenile scrape with the police for "joy riding." Graduating from high school at 17, he enlisted in the army, which greatly disappointed his parents, who expected him to attend college. He was sent to Officers' Candidate School and eventually became an officer. He recalled that his 6 years in the service were sad and frustrated years sexually. He was always fearful of his homosexual feelings. While in the army, he went to an occasional prostitute with his servicemen friends but found no satisfaction despite his ability to function. He became introverted and studious and completed correspondence courses for college credit. He read extensively and developed a fine library of his own.

Upon discharge, he decided to join the mass of backpacking American travelers and set off for a year in Europe, where he visited the art galleries and centers of ancient culture. During that time, he became active homosexually. He recalled several instances of erectile failure during this time but discounted their importance.

He returned to the United States at age 24 to finish college and "find myself." He felt lonely and isolated and gradually slipped into a homosexual life-style while working in a library and continuing his studies for his college degree. He read everything he could about homosexuality. He had two or three brief relationships with other men but was looking for a long-term partner when he met Dave again. They had originally met 2 years previously while both were in the army. Dave was a medic. They had experienced some mutual attraction at that time, but Ed had avoided any serious contact. When they met in a gay bar, Ed was overjoyed at the encounter. Dave had a good job in a local hospital and was also attending school, where he was specializing in horticulture. Ed recalled how good he felt about finding Dave. They saw each other frequently and began a sexual relationship after the first week. Over the next 4 or 5 months, they gradually drifted into a relationship without verbalizing a commitment. They moved into an apartment together 6 months later.

No expectation of sexual fidelity was assumed or ever discussed. Each partner had some sexual contacts outside of the relationship. After the first year, they would occasionally go to the bars together and bring another couple or another single male home for a "four-way" or a "three-way" encounter, although Ed seemed to have more ambivalence about this than Dave. Dave discontinued his horticulture courses, and Ed finished his bachelor's degree in English. He briefly considered teaching, but because of his love for books, he began working in a relatively low-paying job in a library. Eventually, they bought a house together and had fun and excitement in redecorating their home and working in the garden. Dave's dedication and interest in plants and flowers kept him outdoors most of the time, while Ed focused his energies on the library and the kitchen. They had limited mutual interests. Ed tended to be extremely intellectual and continued to read voraciously. Dave read newspapers and magazines but could hardly tolerate reading an entire book unless it was about gardening. When Ed initiated conversations about their relationship, Dave would use such opportunities to initiate sexual activity. Their sexual behavior together included both mutual oral and anal intercourse as well as mutual manual manipulation. Both claimed that their sex lives together had been satisfying and fulfilling until 1 year ago when Ed began to experience erectile dysfunction.

At the conclusion of the first session with Ed, he felt much better and stated that he had not realized how much his erectile difficulties had contributed to his depression. After explaining to Ed that sexual dysfunction is best viewed as a problem of the relationship and that effective treatment involves the couple, I asked if both he and Dave would be willing to come in for a session with myself and another male cotherapist. Ed was not sure but said he would like to see me for a few visits before giving that approach serious consideration. I encouraged him to talk with Dave about it anyway.

The second session was 4 days later. Ed gave me more information about himself and his background and talked expansively about his hopes for the future, which included owning his own store, writing a novel, and becoming more active in homosexual community affairs. He avoided issues regarding his erectile dysfunction and did not indicate if he had shared with Dave the fact that he had entered therapy. When I brought up the subject, he stated that he did not have the courage to mention it to Dave. It took two more individual sessions before he asked Dave to come in with him.

During those individual sessions, I obtained a more detailed sexual history. Part of Ed's resistance to talking with Dave about the erectile problems was his conviction that the problem was his own and that he had to "work it out alone." He believed that Dave would stay with him and once again find him an attractive sexual partner only after the dysfunction was resolved. I had to convince him that he was assuming all of these things about his lack of attractiveness and what Dave was thinking and feeling.

I instructed Ed to begin some autoerotic exercises by the third session and explained that self-loving was a part of being able to love and to be sexual with others. It was at that time that he told me of his abhorrence for masturbation when he was younger. His stepfather had discovered him masturbating once at age 14 and had whipped him, telling him, "only queers do that." Despite his highly intellectualized verbal approval, Ed continued to feel guilt and anguish over masturbation. Also, he felt angry and embarrassed that Dave would masturbate openly around him, although he found himself sexually aroused by the behavior. He had not previously recognized this cognitive and affective dichotomy. Ed was instructed to take some special time for his own autoerotic experience, to use body lotion or oils, to pleasure himself all over by rubbing his chest, face, neck, buttocks, thighs, and genitals, and to use fantasy or pornographic material to assist his arousal. Also, he was encouraged to spend at least half an hour for the exercises on three occasions before seeing me again. I asked him to write down his thoughts and feelings about the experiences. He reported that the exercises had been much more difficult than he had imagined, since they raised the old negative feelings about masturbation. In fact, he stated that he could not continue treatment if that were all I could offer him.

At this point of new resistance, I applied the general principle of "going with the resistance"; that is, I agreed with him that it was difficult. He was told that he would not be asked to do that again for the present. He seemed much relieved. The psychogenetic history of masturbation inhibition had not been recognized adequately, nor had the depth of his own negative self-image. The hyperintellectualized defenses and the slick verbal acquiesence had covered these symptoms.

"Going with the resistance" in this treatment format means recognizing the patient's need to object to certain types of behaviors. Instead of discussing these objections, exploring the feelings and the underlying dynamics, the therapist simply accepts the objections, stops giving the instructions to which the patient is objecting for the time being, and takes a different therapeutic approach. In offering resistance to certain sexual behaviors, the patient is always telling the therapist something about him/herself. In our experience, listening, accepting, and responding to that resistance, allowing the patient to have control in that area, especially in the early phases of sex therapy, consolidates trust and almost invariably allows the resistance to be overcome relatively quickly, sometimes without its being mentioned again.

Finally, after the first five sessions, Ed invited Dave to accompany him, and Dave was more than pleased to be asked. The conjoint session was arranged with a male cotherapist (A. M. M.).

The Therapists
It is most important for the therapists to have their own attitudes toward homosexuality clear. The single most important factor in the treatment of male homosexual couples is the total absence of unresolved homophobia in the therapists. If the therapist (or therapy team) has not resolved his/her own feelings about homosexuality and does not possess a strong supportive orientation toward the viability of same-sex relationships, the therapy is doomed to failure (McWhirter & Mattison, 1978).

Approach to Initial Evaluation
Not all couples using sexual dysfunction as the "ticket of admission" to therapy are suitable candidates for sex therapy. We are frequently asked how a decision is made for or against sex therapy as the treatment of choice. We have worked out an assessment scheme that makes this decision less difficult. Once this clear method has been applied, we have fewer "failures" in applying the general principles of directive sex therapy. Using the following four diagnostic categories, we focus on that area which seems to have the greatest impact on the function of the dyad: (1) diagnosis of the sexual dysfunction; (2) diagnosis of the relationship interaction; (3) diagnosis of the individual

personality defenses; and (4) diagnosis of medical problems, if any exist.

The Sexual Dysfunction

Determining the nature of the dysfunction can be very different when one person tells the story as opposed to the couple checking and balancing each other in the conjoint interview. Questions from the therapists must be very explicit. Detailed answers should be gently extracted from the patient.

In this case, Ed reported occasional erections despite his inability to maintain them. Dave reported that Ed rarely got erections with him and that he felt Ed did not care about him anymore. Ed's knowledge was far more sophisticated than Dave's. He feared that he would lose Dave because of his poor sexual performance. Dave reported getting firm erections whenever he was near Ed, which to Dave was a sign of Ed's sexual attractiveness to him. At this time, some concerns about Ed's not desiring sex as much as Dave did also surfaced.

The working diagnosis for the sexual dysfunction was arousal-phase disorder, erectile dysfunction (Ed), with a question about desire-phase dissonance.

The Relationship Integrity

The two therapists had a strongly positive response to the relationship integrity. Although decisions are not made on the basis of the therapists' feelings, we have learned to trust and use them as part of the instruments for assessment. Both Ed and Dave had expressed concern for the other and a deep commitment to the relationship, but we found them both to be withholding from the other for fear of exposing their individual fears of loss. Much of the hostility and avoidance behaviors present were a consequence of total communication failure. Ed was hurt, angry, and fearful that Dave no longer cared for or loved him. Although there was work to do on the relationship, there were no serious obstacles to sex therapy.

In other homosexual male couples, the therapists sometimes find such hostility and total dependence on sex, such lack of mutual concern and caring that work on the relationship must then take precedence over sex therapy.

Individual Personality Defenses

With Ed, an intellectualized defensive pattern with a tendency to process and rationalize his feelings had been interrupted by the threat of the relationship loss. With Dave agreeing to come for therapy, the break in defenses that had precipitated Ed's crisis call was temporarily repaired. Ed's long-standing problems of self-esteem, partly rooted in his same-sex orientation as well as in earlier developmental difficulties, were defended against by some reaction formation and occasional obsessional thinking. Although the therapists felt that some individual treatment would be useful, Ed's quick responses to the first sessions boded well for conjoint sex therapy, although the challenge that his defenses offered was recognized.

Dave, more quiet and withdrawn, had a passive–aggressive pattern of response. His withdrawal from intimacy, the denial as well as the low self-esteem, seemed defended against by a hypersexuality. He found his greatest worth in sexual prowess. His difficulty in verbalizing his feelings, together with his singular style of feeling, rather than thinking about himself, were in sharp contrast to his partner.

The therapists believed that a few individual sessions with Dave would help determine his ability to explore these areas as well as establish a strong rapport with the other cotherapist, who could help him explain himself to Ed and even model the communication suggestions if necessary.

Medical Assessment

A quick review of the individual organ systems in both Ed and Dave revealed no significant medical problems. There was no family history of diabetes and some history of cardiovascular disease in both families. During this time, some concern about aging developed.

This section of the initial assessment should not be avoided. Sexual dysfunctions can be caused by early or late disease states, by drugs for certain medical conditions, etc.

Partner's History

Three days after the initial conjoint meeting with Ed and Dave, the cotherapist had an individual appointment with Dave to begin building rapport and to obtain a developmental and sexual history. At the conjoint meeting, we saw him as somewhat tentative and halting in talking about himself and his relationship. Nonetheless, a strong concern for his partner and a commitment to their relationship emerged. Dave's demeanor at this meeting was markedly different from that in the conjoint session. He bounded into the office with a broadly smiling face and began chattering superficially about his morning's activities as if he and the therapist were long-time friends meeting for lunch. Clearly, he was reluctant to return to the business of the interview but nonetheless began volunteering information in response to any inquiries, provided they were specific and asked in a direct manner. He experienced difficulty in recalling early childhood events or tended to gloss over the information quickly. As the interview proceeded, he relaxed noticeably, speaking spontaneously at times, yet with thoughtfulness and detail. We suspected from the outset that an adequate history would be difficult to obtain with the usual one interview.

Dave was a 35-year-old man from a second-generation Italian background; he was born and reared in a small farming community in a western state. The middle child of five, he remembered his parents as warm and affectionate, hardworking, and very poor. He was reared in the Roman Catholic tradition, but did not attend parochial schools. His father owned a small farm which was operated primarily by the immediate family. Dave reported with enthusiasm his recollections of the chores that were his responsibility at an early age. The rule of the household was to preserve peace and harmony at any cost. Conflicts and involvement in arguments were strongly frowned upon by Dave's parents. He was an average student in school. While he was generally quiet and shy, he recalled being friendly and outgoing with his small group of friends. He was a relatively passive person who rarely would initiate activities but would become involved with projects and hobbies once begun.

Dave enjoyed some childhood sex play with the neighborhood boys, which included mutual masturbation and fellatio, but he did not associate this activity with anything more than childhood play. He masturbated alone with regular frequency from early adolescence and recalled little guilt. He began dating girls in high school but always stopped short of sexual play. During the last year in high school, he began seeing himself as basically same-sex-oriented, which caused some amount of conflict and tended to diminish his already shaky sense of self-esteem and confidence. After graduation, he joined the army and began training as a medic. He had fleeting and impersonal sexual contacts with men over the next 3 years in the service and remained conflicted with his homosexual orientation. He continued to live in the western city in which he was discharged and shared an apartment with a few friends. He obtained a good job in one of the local hospitals. Dave developed a large network of social relationships which were primarily homosexual. He began to feel more at ease with his own homosexuality and began to enjoy frequenting the gay bars and baths. While becoming more socially outgoing, Dave hoped to settle down with one man and develop an ongoing primary relationship.

This individual interview confirmed our initial impressions of Dave. He experienced a great deal of difficulty in identifying his feelings and then in articulating them. In addition, he dealt with stress by denial, passive–aggressive and passive–defensive behavior, and sullen withdrawal. Intimacy was defended against by hypersexuality and coy regression to sweet talk and "campy" expressions.

Conjoint Sessions

After Dave's initial session with the cotherapist, a subsequent conjoint session was held to share our assessment and to outline the treatment plan.

Both therapists agreed that Dave needed a few individual sessions prior to or in conjunction with the sex therapy. It was also realized that Dave would feel singled out and might sabotage the treatment if, from the beginning, the planning did not include specific work on the sexual dysfunction. Therefore, sensate-focus exercises were begun along with the plan for continuing the individual sessions for both partners.

Both partners were very positive at this session and aware of each other's personal and developmental background for the first time. The treatment plan consisted of some sensate-focus exercises in order to reassure the couple of our intentions to treat the sexual dysfunction. The couple also entered into a contractual agreement with us to refrain from sexual activity outside the relationship until such time as we gave "permission" for this activity again. We carefully explained the reasons and emphasized that the whole focus for them over the next few weeks needed to be on each other. While Ed was quick to agree, Dave was more hesitant, but he did make the requested verbal contract. In retrospect, he may have felt "bullied" into this contract, much as he felt that Ed sometimes "bullied" him by his skillful verbalizations. Instructions were given for nongenital body touching, and we emphasized the importance of taking all "performance pressure" off Ed (i.e., lots of body touching without the expectation or even permission for sexual contact). Both partners seemed to understand the rationale for this. Dave even talked about what it would be like for him to have difficulty with erections. Ed seemed very pleased with the instructions. As mentioned above, included in the treatment plan was the recommendation that both Dave and Ed have a few more individual sessions with the cotherapists between conjoint meetings. We both felt that Dave was the partner in need of some individual work at this point, but it would have been too difficult for Dave to have been singled out.

In the individual sessions, Dave continued to talk more easily and effectively and to define his feelings more clearly. Ed's individual sessions focused on his difficulty with his homosexual orientation, his feelings of lowered self-esteem, and his erectile problem. Neither cotherapist would talk about the exercises at the individual sessions, but left that area for conjoint meetings.

The next conjoint meeting started with the revelation that Ed had obtained an erection and maintained it and that Dave had initiated anal intercourse by inserting Ed's erection. Ed had ejaculated but felt badly that the instructions had been violated. Dave felt that the encounter had been very successful because they had "used" Ed's erection. Dave had reached orgasm by fellatio, which Ed stated he had performed to avoid an argument.

The cotherapists had anticipated the possibility of this event with the recognition of some passive–aggressive behaviors in Dave which might have precipitated this action. Several approaches were open to us. The response could have been irritation and remonstrance or acceptance and passivity. Recognizing the developing resistance to the instructions, the original instructions and rationale were reviewed, and the couple was given additional information about their sexual physiology. They were then instructed to repeat the nongenital sensate-focus exercises and to alternate initiation of the exercises over the next week.

The next conjoint session was almost a repeat of the first session. It was as if Dave were asking the therapists to rebuke him for his behavior. In what seemed to be an adolescent manner, Dave seemed to be testing our limits. Once again, applying the principle of "going with the resistance," and in an attempt to regain the therapeutic control of the "exercises," the importance of nondemand was emphasized; we suggested that sexual activities would be permissible other than during the requisite exercise times. We were attempting to reduce Dave's rising anxiety over lack of sexual involvement, since we recognized that his hypersexuality was a defense against intimacy, especially with Ed.

This procedure was effective, and Ed did obtain erections, which Dave did not use, during the sensate-focus exercises. At other times, Dave did intiate sexual contract, and Ed did not obtain erections. Instructions were given for genital touching without expectation of erection or orgasm. Sexual contact at times other than during exercises was still allowed.

The next conjoint session focused on mutual communication problems—especially Ed's irritations at what he considered Dave's thoughtlessness around the house, for example, leaving hall cabinets open which Ed hit his head on, letting dishes pile up in the sink, and leaving hair in the shower drain. All these minor points of annoyance that added up to expressions of anger needed ventilation and remediation. Dave, on the other hand, retreated to his more characteristic behavior of initial withdrawal, then seductive coyness toward Ed in this session. Ed responded with more anger at the behavior. Feeling assaulted and accused, Dave was almost in tears. Dave's cotherapist moved to his defense, and the two therapists modeled the behaviors by means of a short psychodrama for the couple. The treatment format with our individual and conjoint styles is flexible enough to allow such role-playing, which helps to focus the patients' attention on their interactions by providing some mirroring. The patients have a chance to respond to what they perceive of themselves in this role-playing. Such slips into psychodrama can save hundreds of words of explanation, description, and discussion.

The last few minutes of the session centered on the sensate-focus exercises. There had been some change in Dave's sexual pressure during the week, and the couple had done the exercises as prescribed without sex in between. On both contacts, Ed had obtained an erection and lost it during the genital touching. Ed clearly realized how his worries about having the erection were responsible for its loss.

The therapists repeated the instructions for sensate focus with genital touching, adding the encouragement for each to masturbate in the other's presence. Ed was not sure that he could do it, but he agreed to try. Dave smiled broadly. The session ended on an upbeat note.

The couple did not have individual sessions during the week. The next conjoint session focused on Dave's anger at Ed for what Dave considered to be his frivolous and cavalier attitudes toward spending money. Dave's anger had been triggered when he discovered that Ed had purchased a new shirt during the week. During the session, Ed confessed that he had purchased two new shirts but did not tell Dave about the second one for fear of an even angrier response. The therapists had not considered Ed's attitude toward money to be irresponsible. On the other hand, Dave kept a very tight hold on the household budget, and Dave's developmental history of poverty and Ed's history of relative affluence were clearly part of the trouble here. Ed recognized this more easily than Dave. Individual sessions helped to work out some compromises in this area.

The important issue in this session was Dave's inability to allow his anger to surface and to be expressed without Ed's retaliation. During the course of the session, there were several intense, emotional moments, and at one point, the couple spontaneously embraced. In retrospect, the therapists should have focused more on Dave's anger and dealt better with his passive–aggressive tactics as well as his sexual defenses. The following week, Dave had several sexual encounters outside the relationship, and the couple made only one attempt at sensate focus and genital touching. Ed did not obtain erections during the exercises. Ed learned how much of his sexual withholding was connected to his anger, and Dave saw how his anger manifested itself in such passive–aggressive methods. The session was filled with tears, recommitment, and promises to try harder.

Both patients experienced a breakthrough at this session. The therapists remained relatively unintrusive and allowed the couple to "do their own therapy" at this point. In retrospect, this was a very important management issue. It was suggested that the couple take a week off with no instructions with regard to sexual activity. Some sexual contact was encouraged. Ed had successfully masturbated with Dave and felt very good about it.

Again, no individual sessions were held during the week. The next session went smoothly. Both patients had been working on communication. Ed announced that he had been successful with erection and anal penetration on three occasions during the week. Ed expressed his conviction that his sexual dysfunction was reversed! It was indicated to him that he indeed was well on the way to reversal but that more work was needed. Ed felt that he could now keep Dave sexually happy at home, and Dave would not be seeking outside partners as frequently. The couple agreed reluctantly to one more session. They were seen 2 weeks later, and the situation had remained stable.

Dave called 3 weeks later, asking for an individual appointment with his cotherapist. Ed had been depressed the previous 2 weeks. During that time, Dave had not had outside sexual partners, and he did not understand Ed's withdrawal now that they had been having successful sexual contact.

This couple was seen at least five more times without any focus on sexual functioning. Once Ed began having erections, he began ruminating about his own homosexuality. We had neglected to pay sufficient attention to his latent homophobia. With subsequent sessions, we helped both partners to see their individual difficulties with accepting their homoerotic orientations. The clear lack of adequate role models for homosexual male couples was a constant weakness in our therapy. Telling these two men how other men lived together and managed their worlds came only from our limited experience and contact with other male couples. We were able to point out to Ed and Dave the adversities in the world around them that were not supportive of their life-style.

Results

1. Improvement of Erectile Dysfunction. Ed's original complaint of erectile dysfunction was reversed, although he did continue to experience occasional difficulties with Dave. His ability to function sexually in groups and in more casual situations such as the baths was not significantly improved.

2. Improved Understanding of Individual Differences. Ed and Dave understood in a new and clearer fashion that each of them had a past history that was separate and individual and that their individual histories caused some of their different attitudes and behaviors. The resulting behaviors did not originate in the relationship, and the relationship was not at risk for these individual differences.

3. Reduced Expectations. Each partner experienced far less need for the other to conform to his expectations. This relieved much of the pressure for conformity.

4. Improved Play. The couple reported more fun together with fewer rough spots. Activities that were previously divided became more shared, and less tension resulted.

5. Expression of Feelings. Dave was better able to identify his feelings, especially the negative ones, and share them with Ed.

Lack of Results

1. Erectile Dysfunction in Certain Settings. There was no reversal of Ed's erectile dysfunction in groups and during casual sexual encounters. Some additional therapy for Ed was recommended. It was pointed out to him that perhaps he should not consider this to be a dysfunction, inasmuch as he admitted to not enjoying such casual sex, as at the baths, but felt some generalized pressure to have outside sexual contacts.

2. Limited Degree of Intimacy in One Partner. There was some increase in the degree of intimacy in the relationship, but Dave's defense of hypersexuality against intimacy was unaltered. Recognizing that work in this area should be done in ongoing individual treatment, we elected not to focus on this as part of the therapy.

3. Low-Grade Depression. We identified a long-standing, low-grade depression in both partners which was not directly approached during treatment.

Ed and Dave have continued to see one or both cotherapists several times each year since the termination of sex therapy. Usually one or the other calls for a conjoint appointment at some crisis point that has little or nothing to do with their original sexual problem. They have now been together 14 years and feel that the next 14 will be easier.

Similarities and Contrasts

In this section, we will discuss some of the similarities and contrasts between sex therapy with heterosexual and homosexual couples. These factors need to be understood in the treatment process.

Similarities

1. Communication Difficulties. This problem has been present in every case that we have seen. With some couples, the difficulty may be more severe than in others, but the problem is present to some degree. When sexual dysfunction exists in a relationship, the couples' listening, hearing, and feeling responses to each other are also in trouble. The case of Ed and Dave is a good example of this problem. Another example is that of Joe and Jeff.

This couple had been together for 4 years. Joe was 38 and Jeff 27. Their backgrounds were very different. Joe was from an affluent, single-parent home, has parents divorcing when he was 2 years old. He was the only child and was pampered by his mother and two maiden aunts. Jeff was from a less affluent family with five siblings. Jeff's family belonged to a fundamentalist Christian religious sect incorporating austerity and emotional control. Although these two men claimed to love and care about each other, Jeff could only hear the negative comments from Joe, and Joe perceived Jeff as only wanting to frustrate his wishes and desires. No sex therapy could be initiated for their desire-phase disorder until extensive relationship therapy was accomplished.

2. Inability to Know or Even Think about One's Individual and Relationship Needs. For some reason, our society mitigates against individuals thinking about their own needs, wishes, and desires. This feature is so common to most people that it needs no further explanation.

3. "Spectatoring" One's Own Sexual Behavior with a Partner. Regardless of the dysfunction (desire, arousal, or orgasmic phase in heterosexual or homosexual couples), some degree of performance observation exists in dysfunctional persons. Our initial impression in working with homosexual male couples was that there was less spectatoring among them. This observation has not proven to be factual. It is essential for the therapist to identify this occurrence.

4. Pressure Demands for Sexual Relations from the Nondysfunctional Partner. Sometimes the demands from the nondysfunctional partner may be subtle or unintentional, but they are always there until the therapist points them out and the couple makes serious attempts to eliminate the pressure for sexual relations. Removing all pressure from sexual performance in the early phases of treatment may be the single most important factor in therapy. On the other hand, allowing some sexual interaction between nongenital sensate-focus exercises can help the nondysfunctional partner feel less "deprived" during the several weeks of sensate-focus work. When both partners present with sexual dysfunctions, complete removal of the expectation of sex must occur when the sensate-focus exercises are introduced. Explanations are given, and the couples are asked to repeat their understanding of the explanations. In the case of Ed and Dave, the couple was not asked to repeat the reasons. This may be the partial explanation for their initial introduction of anal intercourse when Ed first had an erection with nongenital touching.

5. *An Incidence of Serious Underlying Psychopathology*. The following situations are strict contraindications to sex therapy in both homosexual and heterosexual couples: (a) an active psychotic process; (b) untreated substance abuse, such as alcoholism or polydrug abuse in one partner or both; (c) severe depression in one or both partners; and (d) the presence of unshared "secrets" that influence or affect the relationship. A current sexual affair outside the relationship, which is not known or willing to be shared with the partner, or a history of sexual trauma which might include incest are examples of such secrets. Another example is the presence of a sexual deviation such as sadomasochism or transvestism which is not shared.

One partner in a male couple, who was seen for erectile dysfunction, had a long history of sadomasochistic behavior. He was not willing to share that history with his partner of 1 year because of the partner's clearly stated aversion to such practices. However, the dysfunctional partner entertained current fantasies of such behavior and refused to share this with the nondysfunctional partner. We find that such cases are not amenable to treatment unless the "secret," which usually has some obsessive qualities about it, is shared.

6. *Similarities in Resistances*. These resistances include avoidance of the exercises, complaints of lack of time, missing appointments, and focusing on new areas of initiation. All are examples of the most common resistances we encounter regardless of whether the couple happens to be homosexual or heterosexual. Working with the resistance, in some cases "going with it" or confronting it directly, produces similar good results.

7. *Lack of Knowledge about Sexual Anatomy and Physiology and Tenacious Belief in Old Myths about Human Sexual Response*. While this phenomenon is more common in heterosexual couples, the problem often is seen in homosexual couples. However, with homosexual

couples, often there are different myths. For example, many homosexual men believe that same-sex male relationships do not survive. A high incidence of negative attitudes about sex exists for both heterosexuals and homosexuals.

Contrasts

1. "Open" Sexual Relationships. A majority of male homosexual relationships are "open" sexually; that is, there is an allowance for sexual activity outside the primary dyad. This is infrequently the case in the majority of heterosexual relationships. It is important that therapists who are treating these couples realize and understand this aspect of male same-sex relationships. Although jealousies and other difficulties in this area are encountered, generally speaking, relationship primacy does not reside in sexual fidelity as it does among so many heterosexual couples. This sexual openness can be an accepted part of the homosexual life-style and is not necessarily a major obstacle to the longevity of such a relationship. C. A. Tripp discusses this issue extensively in *The Homosexual Matrix* (Tripp, 1975).

2. Less Rigidity in Sexual Attitudes among Homosexual Males. This can perhaps be attributed to the fact that homosexual patients already find themselves in a somewhat "deviant" segment of the population and therefore participate in more "deviant" sexual experiences than most heterosexual couples.

3. Little or No Assumption of Traditional Cultural "Roles." The old stereotypic notion that one partner must assume the feminine and the other the masculine role in a relationship is a myth. The activities of daily living seem to fall to whichever partner is most interested, with each assuming some responsibility for those tasks neither enjoys. There are decided advantages in not having to deal with role definitions. However, homosexual male couples are essentially breaking new ground in this area, since they find few, if any, models upon which to draw for their interactions.

4. Decreased Likelihood of Laying "Blame" for the Sexual Dysfunction on the Relationship. Since each partner in the homosexual couple usually continues sexual encounters outside the relationship, and the dysfunction seems to persist, the relationship is not held culpable for the problem. A major therapeutic stategy with homosexual couples involves having both partners accept responsibility for reversing the dysfunction and not allowing the dysfunctional person to feel that he must "go it alone."

5. Greater Empathy and Understanding between Partners over the Effects of a Dysfunction. We believe that this is due to the narcissistic sameness of anatomy, physiology, and emotional makeup of the partners.

6. Lack of Institutional Support. With the lack of institutional support systems such as marriage and traditional families for the existence and longevity of same-sex relationships, there is a tendency among homosexual couples to associate stress in the relationship with considerations and fears of dissolution of the relationship.

7. Possibility of Relationship Termination. For some homosexual male couples, sexual difficulties raise the possibility of relationship termination. The relationship lasts as long as "things are going well." The first signs of trouble are not seen as problems to work on, but more as threats to the relationship. Frequently, this delays the couple's seeking help.

Conclusion

Although we have been working with homosexual male couples with sexual dysfunction for over 5 years, we realize that more research and study must be applied to this particular group. As noted above, there are numerous similarities between the work with sexual dysfunction in both homosexual male couples and heterosexual couples, but a number of significant contrasts also are present. The encouragement to innovate is important once the therapists have a basic grasp and understanding of the more standard techniques of sex therapy.

In conclusion, the most important issues for the therapist working with homosexual couples are (1) a lack of homophobia and clear understanding of his/her own homosexual feelings and (2) a conviction in the viability of homosexual relationships. With the new freedom and pride that homosexual people are experiencing, more people are coming to therapy for improvement in their quality of life. Until the present, most work in the area of sexuality and relationships of homosexual persons has been based on previous research and treatment with heterosexual dyads. While the homosexual community owes much to this previous work, it is hoped that what can be learned from work and research with homosexual couples will have value for work with heterosexual couples, since many homosexual couples are breaking new ground in developing alternative models of relationships and pair-bonding.

NOTE

This chapter was written prior to the publication of Masters and Johnson's *Homosexuality in Perspective*, and none of their findings are included herein.

References

Bell, A., & Weinberg, M. *Homosexualities: A study of diversities among men and women*. New York: Simon and Schuster, 1978.

Bieber, I., *et al. Homosexuality: A psychoanalytic study*. New York: Basic Books, 1962.

Davison, G. *Presidential address*. Presented to the eighth annual convention of the Association for Advancement of Behavior Therapy, Chicago, November, 1974.

Gagnon, J., & Simon, W. *Sexual conduct: The social sources of human sexuality*. Chicago: Aldine, 1973.

Haeberle, E. *The sex atlas*. New York: Seabury Press, 1978.

Hooker, E. The adjustment of the male overt homosexual. *Journal of Projective Techniques*, 1957, *21*, 18–31.

Kaplan, H. S. *The new sex therapy*. New York: Brunner/Mazel, 1974.

Masters, W. H., & Johnson, V. E. *Human sexual inadequacy*. Boston: Little, Brown & Co., 1970.

McWhirter, D., & Mattison, A. *Homosexual male couples*. Paper presented to the Society for the Scientific Study of Sex, Las Vegas, November, 1977.

McWhirter, D., & Mattison, A. The treatment of sexual dysfunction in gay male couples. *Journal of Sex and Marital Therapy,* 1978, *4,* 213–218.

Tripp, C. A. *The homosexual matrix*. New York: McGraw-Hill, 1975.

12

Treatment of Sexual Deviations

DAVID H. BARLOW AND JOHN P. WINCZE

Despite the prevalence of individuals displaying various forms of sexual misconduct, most sex therapy clinics are reluctant to offer treatment to the exhibitionist, pedophile, or sexually aggressive individual. Several factors explain this reluctance. Sexually deviant individuals are typically unwilling to enter treatment voluntarily and infrequently do so unless compelled by some agent of the law or society. If they do arrive at the therapist's office, they often display ambivalence about "giving up" their particular sexual proclivity. Frequently, treatment outcome is poor, and recidivism is high. Further, many clinicians dislike the sense of fear, anxiety, or indignation they may experience when confronting an individual with unusual or aggressive sexual appetites, and they may feel at a loss as to how to proceed with treatment. Other clinicians, while intrigued by the treatment challenge, are hesitant to undertake treatment because they do not want to become involved with legal issues. Often, treatment of the sexually deviant individual lasts longer and involves more active monitoring than does the treatment of sexually dysfunctional individuals.

Nevertheless, treatment for sexual deviation is necessary and can play a significant role in prevention of further mishaps. While what gets defined as sexual misconduct varies from culture to culture and reflects societal, legal, and religious norms, any definition of sexual deviation usually involves a consideration of potential harm to the individual or society, the degree of informed consent, and chronicity. It is disconcerting for many to realize that although statistically infrequent, all individuals are probably capable of deviant sexual arousal and even sexual misbehavior at some time and under some circumstances.

In their chapter, Barlow and Wincze present a comprehensive model for the assessment and treatment of sexual deviation. They suggest that deviant behavior consists of three major components: (1) sexual arousal and behavior which may involve either arousal excesses or deficits; (2) social skills and emotional factors associated with sexual interactions; and (3) gender-role deviations. Therapy may focus on each or all of these components, and each component is conceptualized as being independent of the others.

Further, the authors suggest that to be effective in cases involving sexual deviation, ongoing assessment of these three components is necessary, since any one level may be problematic. Assessment must be ongoing, occur in several modalities, and not involve total reliance on the patient's self-report. Too often, an individual describes little sexual arousal to the deviant behavior at the same time that physiological assessment reveals continued arousal. In such cases, premature termination is possible, and the likelihood of relapse is high.

The authors present two cases. One involves incest with a daughter, while the other involves multiple deviations, including a history of voyeurism, exhibitionism, and incest. Barlow and Wincze clearly present methods for ongoing assessment and describe the host of treatment interventions utilized in each case. While one case terminated as a success and the other as a failure, the treatment dilemmas posed by each are striking. Innovative methods of intervention are employed, and the continuous assessment facilitates decision-making throughout treatment.

David H. Barlow is Professor of Psychology at the State University of New York at Albany. He has a long history of involvement in the treatment and conceptualization of sexual deviation. John P. Wincze is Associate Professor of Psychiatry at Brown University in Rhode Island. Both Barlow and Wincze have authored numerous articles in the field of sex therapy.

Introduction

One of the most neglected problems in psychiatry and psychology is the treatment of sexual offenders. This is not because of lack of interest on the part of mental health professions and theorists. From the earliest days, psychopathologists have described cases of sexual deviation in great detail (Ellis, 1915). Descriptions of cases of sexual deviation are also found in most textbooks of abnormal psychology, but revealingly little on the treatment or etiology of this problem is presented beyond pure speculation. Unlike many sexual problems presented in this book which constitute a concern only to the clients involved, the problem of sexual offenders directly impinges on society and is of great concern to our courts and legal systems. Society's most common solution has been incarceration, but due to the early recognition that the basic problem of sexual offenders is psychological, some compromises have been made. In most states, separate programs for the treatment of sexual offenders now exist, albeit within correctional systems, and in some states, whole institutions are devoted to at least the custodial care, and in some cases the treatment, of sexual offenders. The number of sexual offenders incarcerated at great cost to society, as well as the threat these people present to society, have made this a major social problem. Frisbie and Dondis (1965), for example, report that of 1921 admissions to a state hospital for "sexual psychopaths," 79% of admissions were diagnosed as pedophiliacs, 13% exhibitionists, and 4% sexual aggressives. Frisbie and Dondis (1965) report that one-sixth to one-eighth of all inmates in Michigan prisons were sex offenders. Most recently, the government has taken a direct interest in sexual offenders, with the creation of the National Center for the Prevention and Control of Rape. This new agency within the National Institute of Mental Health is funding research into the assessment and treatment of sexual deviation, an area long neglected by federal funding sources.

A relative lack of attention to the development of assessment and treatment procedures for sexual offenders may have been due in part to the extremely poor prognosis associated with treatment. Even if clients with problems of sexual deviation seek out treatment voluntarily (a condition which does not always obtain, particularly with sexual offenders), the prognosis is poor, with low rates of "success" and high rates of recidivism. Early series (e.g., Curran & Parr, 1957; Woodward, 1958) demonstrated no more than 10 to 15% of the cases effecting successful alterations of sexual arousal patterns. Freund (1960) examined the results of 20 seemingly successful cases originally referred by the courts or other social agencies and noted that none of these subjects exhibited lasting improvement.

Several years ago, we presented a new model or a new way of looking at sexual disorders (Barlow, 1974, 1977). This model, or minitheory, was presented with full realization that historically the field of sexual disorders has been plagued with an overabundance of theory and a paucity of data. The fact that theory may not necessarily advance a field is best exemplified by the fact that the major breakthrough in sex therapy in the early 1970s was accomplished by two clinicians working from a pragmatic and largely atheoretical point of view (Masters & Johnson, 1970).

In the field of sexual deviation, however, there seemed at least two good reasons for proposing a new model. First, past approaches to assessment and treatment, whether from a behavioral or psychodynamic point of view, have been very narrow. Reasons for this will be discussed below. Second, and perhaps more important, past approaches to assessment and treatment have been very static. As with many formulations in psychology and psychiatry, the assessment and treatment of sexual disorders usually consists of an initial broad label such as "sexual dysfunction" or "exhibitionism," followed by a standard treatment which may or may not relate to that label, such as psychotherapy or behavior therapy. This approach is static, since it is a closed conceptual system that leaves out the individual. Instead, it is directed at the average exhibitionist or sexually dysfunctional patient who, of course, does not exist. More importantly, it discourages an initial individual assessment of the variety of behavioral and emotional excesses and deficits which may exist within an individual carrying one of these labels, such as exhibitionist. This may not strike a responsive chord in most clinicians who pride themselves on individualized assessment and treatment, but one only has to listen to clinicians' attributions concerning their failures to verify this static model which forms the basis for so much intervention. The psychodynamic clinician will often cite resistance as the reason for failure of psychotherapy, and the behavioral clinician will point to the countervailing contingencies in the environment. Often, there is little in the way of ongoing assessment during either of these treatment approaches, and therefore there is little or no chance for modifying components of treatment based on individualized feedback of the effects of a given intervention. Similarly, because of this lack of ongoing feedback, it is very difficult to handle novel situations which might arise during treatment.

The model presented below is formulated to provide a better predictive link between a comprehensive assessment and subsequent treatment. The hope is that this model will facilitate the development of truly individualized approaches to clients with ample opportunity to alter treatment, if treatment proves ineffective. Recognizing the basic complexity of sexual problems in general and sexual deviation in particular, and the possibility of intervening with a number of different "treatments" in a given case, another function of this model would be to provide at least the possibility of a deliberate ordering or sequencing of treatment interventions from the least intrusive to most intrusive or, in other words, do not do five things if one thing is sufficient.

This approach is, of course, a clinical extension of the single-case experimental design strategy in clinical research which highlights the intensive study of the individual across time (Hersen & Barlow, 1976). The key ingredient in this approach is repeated measurement during treatment rather than merely pre–post measurement, which is a necessity in any open system. In terms of assessment, this model is also influenced by the problem-oriented treatment approach (Fowler & Longabaugh, 1975). As it has evolved, this model breaks down sexual behavior into three basic categories or components, each requiring at least a thorough initial assessment with subsequent ongoing assessment as indicated. After a brief presentation of this model, two cases that were treated within the context of this model will be described.

The first compoent of sexual behavior requiring assessment involves problems with sexual arousal or behavior—specifically, the genital component of sexual behavior, which is a chain of events beginning with early aspects of sexual arousal through sexual contact of some kind. In the case of sexual deviation, the subject of this chapter, it is possible that several problems can coexist within the general category of sexual arousal and behavior problems. For example, some clients may have problems with undesired pedophiliac arousal as well as difficulties with deficient heterosexual arousal. Another possibility would be the presence of strong and functional heterosexual arousal accompanied by excessive pedophiliac arousal. In sexual deviation, "deviant" arousal and desired, usually heterosexual, arousal are assessed and treated separately, since evidence indicates they are most often independent of one another (Barlow, 1977; Barlow & Agras, 1973; Brownell & Barlow, in press).

A second component is comprised of social skills and emotional factors associated with sexual interactions. Most cultures have developed elaborate social patterns of behavior surrounding the genital aspects of sex. In our culture, many clients may not have adequate arousal patterns and the necessary behaviors to engage in the type of heterosocial behaviors necessary for meeting, dating, and relating to desired persons. In addition, emotional factors such as anxiety might inhibit sexual performance in some way.

The third component in this model is comprised of gender-role deviations. A percentage of clients, particularly those with certain patterns of deviant arousal, may have some gender-role deviations in which a preference for the opposite sex role is reported, to a degree where some conflict between biological and psychological sexual identity exists. When opposite-sex-role behavior is completely adopted and the patient consistently thinks, feels, and behaves in the opposite sex role, this mistaken gender identity is called transsexualism.

Biochemical variables might comprise a fourth component of sexual behavior. Based on the evidence now available, biochemical variables, particularly hormonal variations, do not seem to be a factor in the majority of sexual problems. For this reason, we have stopped routine assessment of hormonal variables in our laboratories for the time being.

This model also encourages an assessment of various factors which may contribute to the problems within each of the components listed above. These "contributing factors" may be roughly divided into three main categories:

1. Individual characteristics—knowledge, intelligence, health, self-image, assertiveness, and age.
2. Past experiences—trauma and childhood upbringing.

    3. Current circumstances—partner relationship, substance abuse,
        job pressures, and living arrangements

Very often in clinical practice, the factors listed above contribute to the
manifestation and severity of the presenting sexual problem. For
example, it is not uncommon for an exhibitionist to experience an
increase in sexual offenses following difficulty in his job or marriage. In
such a case, the initial focus of therapy may be on stabilizing the work
situation or marriage instead of directly dealing with the deviant behavior. Since each case is quite unique, the comprehensive assessment
advocated here would suggest which tactic of therapy is best for each
client. Each component of sexual behavior should be analyzed in light
of the contributing factors and an individually tailored therapy program
developed.

    Finally, one basic assumption of the model is that the components
exist independently of each other and that influencing or modifying one
component does not necessarily produce changes in a second component. For example, changes in gender-role behavior may occur independently of changes in heterosocial skills or sexual arousal patterns
(Barlow, Abel, & Blanchard, 1979; Barlow, Reynolds, & Agras,
1973). Similarly, increasing heterosexual arousal does not insure the
ability to follow through on this arousal if the appropriate heterosocial
skills are not present. Finally, decreasing deviant arousal, as attempted
in the cases to be presented, does not insure that alternative sexual
arousal patterns will fill in the void (e.g., Barlow, 1973; Barlow &
Agras, 1973).

    It was noted above that previous approaches to assessment and
treatment have been very narrow. For example, in treating pedophiliac
patients, behavior therapists throughout the 1960s and early 1970s
would concentrate on deviant arousal but would neglect to assess or
treat any possible deficiencies in heterosexual arousal or heterosocial
skills. The implicit assumption was that if one could eliminate deviant
arousal, then these other factors would demonstrate spontaneous improvement. This is an example of a static model of sexual disorders
which discouraged an individual assessment of excesses and deficits in
the multiple facets of sexual behavior.

    Interestingly, the psychodynamic view of sexual deviation also
presented a static model in the 1960s and early 1970s (Barlow, 1974).
Here the emphasis was most usually on heterosocial relations and anxiety surrounding sex. Treatment most usually included resolving fears
of relationships with adult women in those adult males with sexual
deviation and, of course, examining the sources of these fears in early

childhood experiences. Little attention was paid to patterns of deviant or heterosexual arousal or to gender-role deviations.

The Issue of Deviance

Many factors are involved in a decision to label a particular behavior as "deviant." As Ullmann and Krasner (1975) point out, the label "deviance" most often refers to the sociocultural context of the behavior rather than any properties inherent in the behavior itself. With this view, a pattern of sexual arousal or type of sexual behavior that is labeled deviant may change from time to time or from culture to culture. This phenomenon seems to be occurring today relative to homosexual arousal patterns. It is well known that the American Psychiatric Association recently removed homosexuality from its list of deviant sexual behaviors. It is possible that social attitudes toward other sexual behaviors which currently are candidates for treatment may also change. All sexual arousal patterns which either involve cooperative partners or no partners, such as transvestism and some fetishes, may come to be regarded as reasonable expressions of sexual behavior by society in the future. Those deviant sexual arousal patterns which involve noncooperative partners or children are likely to remain a concern of society. The most common patterns encountered in the clinic are pedophilia, exhibitionism, and the violent expression of sexual behavior, including rape.

The model proposed above eschews demarcations between what is normal and what is abnormal within the various components of sexual behavior. All components, including gender identity, seem to be on a continuum (e.g., Stoller, 1969), and sexual arousal patterns are no exception. For example, Freund and his colleagues (Freund, McKnight, Langevin, & Cibiri, 1972) have demonstrated that most "normal" males have some sexual arousal to prepubertal children. For this reason, it seems presumptuous to make decisions unilaterally on whether or not to treat a sexual problem. This decision must be made by the client after reviewing with the therapist all the evidence of a detailed assessment and after considering in some detail the original motivations for seeking assistance. Obviously, there may be some instances in which the therapist does not agree with the client's choice for moral or other reasons, but ideally these issues should also be discussed before any therapeutic contract is consummated. In this respect, the therapist acts as a consultant to help achieve goals set by the client.

In our experience, adequate safeguards exist within the therapeutic process with voluntary clients if for some reason a therapeutic contract is drawn up which does not truly reflect the client's goals. These safeguards take the form of the various countercontrol procedures, some of which have been described by Davison (1973). The one exception involves those clients with sexual deviations such as pedophilia which bring them in contact with the legal system. It is our experience that these clients, who come for treatment on the orders of judges, probation officers, etc., are not always interested in their stated goals of changing their arousal patterns, but are merely responding to legal contingencies. For this reason, we insist in our clinics that legal consequences of the behavior be settled independent of the treatment process and before any therapeutic contact is negotiated. Others can support a different approach. Maletsky (1978) reports no difference in success rates in the treatment of exhibitionism between court-referred and self-referred clients. These issues, of course, extend beyond assessment and treatment of sexual behavior to most behavioral and emotional problems, but they deserve mention here since sexual deviation has become a focal point for many of these issues in recent years.

Treatment

The last 10 years have witnessed a remarkable series of advancements in the assessment and treatment of sexual disorders, but it is beyond the scope of this chapter to review these developments here. For extensive reviews on the assessment and treatment of all four components of sexual behavior, see Barlow (1977), Brownell and Barlow (in press), and Caird and Wincze (1977). Since the two cases discussed below are concerned with difficulties in patterns of sexual arousal, a brief review of treatments for sexual arousal patterns is an appropriate background.

Increasing Deficiencies in Sexual Arousal

If both deficits in desired patterns of arousal as well as excesses in unwanted patterns of arousal exist, the first step is always to increase deficient arousal, since there is some evidence that occasionally deviant arousal might diminish after this step is taken (Barlow & Abel, 1976; Barlow & Agras, 1973). One procedure that has proven effective has been termed "fading" and its variations. In the original experiment (Barlow & Agras, 1973), the procedure was based on the assumption that deficiencies in desired sexual arousal may be due to problems in stimulus control; that is, a partial response, in this case sexual arousal, occurs only in the presence of one particular type of situation or person. The purpose of the intervention, then, is to alter stimulus control such that the sexual response occurs in the presence of the desired stimulus. Originally, two slide projectors were positioned such that they both focused on one point on the screen. The slide depicting a person who respresented the desired sexual arousal pattern was inserted into one projector, and the undesired sexual arousal pattern was represented by a slide in the second projector. Both light bulbs in the projectors were attached to a rheostat so that as one brightened the other diminished. Since the slides were very closely matched, the image appeared to alter. In the case of a pedophile, a slide of a young boy would be projected at 100% brightness and the slide of an adult woman projected at 0% brightness initially. The basic idea was that sexual arousal would occur to the first image in the sequence, and, if the change is gradual enough, it will continue to occur in an errorless discrimination fashion until it is also occurring to the desired image.

This gradual fading procedure was successful in a series of cases such that heterosexual arousal increased. A variety of procedures using fantasies rather than images projected from slide projectors have built upon this basic finding of gradually introducing desired stimuli in the presence of sexual arousal (e.g., Abel & Blanchard, 1976).

A second, more widely used procedure clinically is orgasmic reconditioning or masturbation training. In this technique, sexual arousal produced by masturbation is usually paired with sexual fantasies which are new or different to the client. This procedure forms a part of many treatments for sexual deficiencies, particularly sexual dysfunctions, and has been recently suggested as clinically effective in a program designed to enhance sexual arousal in women (Lobitz & LoPiccolo, 1972). However, there is no clear evidence at this time on what is really happening, since it has been difficult to determine experimentally that this procedure works. Recently, Conrad and Wincze (1976) attempted to analyze this technique on a group of four patients using more objective measures and found that self-reports of heterosexual arousal did increase, but there was no increase in heterosexual arousal when objective physiological measures were used. In a recent article, however, Kantorowitz (1978), exploring the effects of orgasmic reconditioning with nonpatient college students, demonstrated that some increments in sexual arousal do occur during this procedure. These results, of course, would have to be extended to the clinic. This area is in need of considerably more development in order to determine the most effective procedures for increasing arousal.

Decreasing Undesired Arousal

At present, the evidence is somewhat clearer on the treatment of choice for decreasing unwanted arousal. The procedure used most often is covert sensitization (Cautela, 1967), in which aversive scenes are paired in imagination with the undesired sexual arousal. Although noxious scenes of nausea and vomiting were used early in the history of this procedure, more recently, realistic scenes depicting actual consequences of the behavior as they might occur in each individual case are employed. For instance, an exhibitionist might imagine exposing himself and then very quickly being apprehended by the police, much to his own embarrassment and that of his family. After early demonstrations of the effectiveness of covert sensitization on undesired arousal patterns (e.g., Barlow, Agras, Leitenberg, Callahan, & Moore, 1972), Callahan and Leitenberg (1972) compared covert sensitization with electrical aversion while treating a series of sexual deviations. Covert sensitization proved superior on some measures and in no instance was it inferior to electrical aversion. Considering that covert sensitization requires no expensive apparatus and can be self-administered, it seems more practical than other forms of aversion therapy and has the added advantage of being entirely a self-control procedure which allows the patient to use the technique as he or she wishes. In a more recent article, Brownell, Hayes, and Barlow (1977) treated a series of patients with multiple sexual deviations using covert sensitization. Once again, covert sensitization was effective in reducing deviant sexual arousal, but multiple deviant arousal patterns seemed to be independent of one another even within the same client. For example, decreasing transvestite arousal in one patient with covert sensitization had no effect on an existing pattern of sadistic arousal in the same patient. This further buttresses the notion of the independence of various patterns of sexual arousal and behavior.

With this brief review, it is possible to describe in some detail the application of this model and the treatment techniques currently available in two cases of sexual deviation. The first is a more detailed description of a case originally presented in Harbert, Barlow, Hersen, and Austin (1974).

Case 1: A Case of Father–Daughter Incest

The client, Tony, was a 52-year-old married television repairman. He reported that 10 years ago, he began having incestuous relations with his oldest daughter, who was 12 years old at the time. Initially this activity consisted primarily of light kissing and some fondling, but gradually this escalated to heavy petting and finally mutual masturbation, which continued until his daughter was 17 years old. Tony's relationship with his wife was extremely poor at this time, and he described her as very rejecting. During their sexual relations, he often ejaculated prematurely. Following the birth of his oldest daughter, sexual intercourse occurred infrequently, and occasionally Tony would have sexual intercourse with other women. By the time his oldest daughter was in her early teens, his wife expressed an interest in resuming a normal sexual relationship, but this was rejected by Tony since he was already involved in an incestuous relationship with his daughter.

When his daughter was 16 years old, his wife learned about the ongoing incestuous relationship. This resulted in separation and eventual divorce. The family drifted apart shortly thereafter, and his oldest daughter stayed with her mother. For a period of 5 years, Tony did not visit his daughter, although they would exchange letters occasionally. During this period, Tony remarried and was generally happier in his second marriage than he had been in his first marriage.

After a 5-year separation and just before Tony's initial contact with our clinic, he had occasion to visit his daughter, who was living alone in a different city. A second visit, shortly after the first, led to a recurrence of the incestuous behavior. At this point, Tony became extremely depressed and told his wife the full story. His wife took responsibility for initiating his contact with the clinic, with his full cooperation, while his daughter, who was now 22 years old, obtained private psychiatric treatment in her own city.

Tony's early sexual history contained a number of events of possible etiological significance. Between the ages of 9 and 10 years, he was encouraged by an uncle to observe a game of strip poker which the uncle was carrying on with a neighbor's wife. During this period, he also observed his uncle fondling a waitress at a drive-in restaurant and shortly thereafter was instructed by his uncle to fondle his young female cousin. Thus, he had an early model for mutual fondling and masturbation, and obtained some sexual pleasure from interacting in this way with young girls. When Tony was approximately 13 years old, he engaged in mutual manipulation with a sister and her girlfriend. He also remembered this as a pleasurable experience. Later on, when Tony was 18, a brother-in-law brought him to a prostitute, with whom he first experienced sexual intercourse. He remembered this as unsatisfactory, however, since during this visit and subsequent visits to prostitutes, he ejaculated prematurely. In contrast to his early experiences with young girls, his first experiences with adult women were entirely unsatisfactory. When Tony joined the army, shortly thereafter, and was sent overseas, he remembered occasional sexual contacts, but particularly enjoyed sexual relations with younger girls, often as young as 12 years of age. Tony also reported, during his initial interviews, that his sexual fantasies during intercourse with both his previous and present wife most often concerned his daughter.

Tony was seen in our clinic before the model described above was fully worked out, and therefore a full assessment of the three components of sexual behavior, including both deviant and desired sexual arousal, was not carried out. In retrospect, he obviously had no problems in the area of gender-role behavior or gender identity, nor were there any apparent difficulties with his heterosocial skills, since he was 52 years old, reasonably happily married, and was generally compatible with his wife on attitudes and behaviors surrounding their sexual relations, which were reasonably frequent. Nevertheless, the strength of his sexual arousal with his current wife was not assessed but was assumed to be adequate, since he reported regular sexual relations with her. The lack of formal assessment in this area led to subsequent problems during the followup, to be described below.

Since incestuous behavior was clearly the major difficulty, as reported by Tony, and since his moderate depression was clearly reactive to his renewed incestuous behavior, all attention was focused on the incestuous sexual arousal. Levels of incestuous arousal were assessed in two ways, one attitudinal and the second physiological. First, Tony's attitudes or "attraction to" deviant sexual behavior with his daughter were assessed by means of a card-sort technique (Barlow, Leitenberg, & Agras, 1969; Barlow, 1977). Five scenes depicting Tony interacting sexually with his daughter were typed on individual cards. For example, in one scene it said on the card, "You're along with your daughter in your truck. You put her hand on your penis." These scenes would then each be placed in one of five envelopes, labeled 0 to 4. Zero represented no desire, and 4 represented very much desire. Thus, if Tony put one card in the No. 2 envelope and a second card in the No. 3 envelope, his score to that point would be 5.

Since we had not worked with incestuous behavior before, one issue that arose before implementation of therapy was the necessity of preserving, if at all possible, a desire to interact in a normal, fatherly way with his daughter. It was thought that use of an aversive procedure, even covert sensitization, might have the effect, if successful, of eliminating any desire to interact with his daughter. It was decided to go ahead with treatment, in view of the severity of depression and the patient's strong desire to eliminate his incestuous fantasies, but to assess as carefully as possible his desire to interact in a normal, fatherly way with his daughter, in addition to his sexual inclinations. Thus, additional scenes were made up and included in the card sort depicting normal father–daughter interactions. For example, one scene read, "You're alone with your daughter in her apartment—you begin discussing her future plans." A total of 10 scenes were given to Tony during 4 baseline days and before every treatment session, as well as at follow-up. This repeated assessment of incestuous and fatherly attitudes allowed a close monitoring of treatment as it progressed.

In addition to attitudinal measures, objective measures of sexual arousal, specifically, penile circumference changes to incestuous material, were also assessed and repeatedly monitored during treatment (Barlow, 1977; Barlow, Becker, Leitenberg, & Agras, 1970). The stimulus materials in this case consisted of photographs of the daughter, brought in by Tony, as well as audiotaped descriptions of incestuous activity with the daughter which were made up based on Tony's descriptions. These 1-minute audiotaped descriptions were screened and finally approved by Tony for accuracy and arousability before being included in the formal assessment. This audiotape method has been fully described elsewhere (Abel, Blanchard, Barlow, & Mavissakalian, 1975), and is very useful for measuring objectively the content of erotic fantasies and also for the assessment of those sexual deviations that do not lend themselves to visual representation by slides, movies, etc. Since the procedure is somewhat involved, the reference cited above should be consulted for details of its use. Full descriptions of the physiological assessment of sexual arousal in both males and females are presented in Barlow (1977) and Caird and Wincze (1977). The emphasis here will remain on the clinical aspects of this case.

As noted above, the first goal of treatment in this case became the reduction of incestuous arousal, and the five scenes depicting sexual interaction with his daughter on the card sort were chosen for use in covert sensitization. Initially, the noxious scenes which Tony was to imagine in conjunction with the incestuous scenes included nausea and vomiting, but Tony's report and the early indications on the card sort indicated that these were not effective for him. At this point, the scenes were reassessed, and Tony suggested scenes that were more realistic and important to him, such as discovery by his current wife, his father-in-law, or, most important, his family priest. He was also very concerned about the negative effects of this activity on his daughter, and this aspect was also incorporated into the scenes. While realistic consequences are now routinely included in covert sensitization, this was not true when Tony was treated, but careful monitoring of his repeated measures, along with his report, allowed a change to be made before any negative consequences of an ineffective treatment were encountered. The typical scene used in a session is presented below:

> You are alone with your daughter in your trailer. You get the feeling that you want to caress your daughter's breasts. So you put your arm around her, insert your hand in her blouse and begin to caress her breasts. Unexpectedly the door to the trailer opens and in walks your wife with Father X [the family priest]. Your daughter immediately jumps up and runs out the door. Your wife follows her. You are left alone with Father X. He is looking at you as if to ask for some explanation of what he has just seen. Seconds pass, but it seems like hours. You think of what Father X must be thinking as he stands there staring at you. You are very embarrassed and want to say something, but you can't seem to find the right words. You realize that Father X can no longer respect you as he once did. Father X finally says, "I don't understand this; this is not like you." You both begin to cry. You realize that you may have lost the love and respect of both Father X and your wife, which are very important to you. Father X asks, "Do you realize what this has done to your daughter?" You think about this and you hear your daughter crying; she is hysterical. You feel like you want to run, but you can't. You are miserable and disgusted with yourself. You don't know if you will ever regain the love and respect of your wife and Father X. (Harbert *et al.*, 1974, p. 82)

Usually these scenes are most effective if relayed by the therapist with a bit of drama and force. After the client reports experiencing the full impact of the scene, he is asked to create it himself. This is followed by a period of alternating therapist-originated and client-originated scenes until the client is self-administering the scenes exclusively. With Tony, however, the therapist administered all scenes during a period of 15 days, at which point Tony was discharged from the hospital and began administering his own scenes. Intermixed with these five covert-sensitization scenes per day were five scenes involving normal father–daughter relations, also taken from the card sort. In this procedure, Tony was described imagining this type of interaction and then feeling happy, relaxed, secure, etc. His daughter's feelings were also presented in terms of her love and respect. This facet of treatment once again reflected our insecurity in regard to the possible generalized effect of covert sensitization, where all interactions with his daughter would be aversive. There was no a priori evidence that this therapeutic tactic would prove effective, but as so many of our clinical interventions, it seemed useful to attempt to set up a situation in which Tony would have a chance to make this discrimination, and thus it was included.

Results of Treatment

Mean penile circumference changes to audiotapes depicting sexual interactions with his daughter and to photographs of his daughter are presented in Figure 1. On Probe Day 6, the realistic scenes involving Tony's most feared consequences of his incestuous desires were substituted for the scenes of nausea and vomiting. This was correlated with a large drop in sexual arousal, objectively measured, which continued throughout the rest of the treatment.

The results of the card sort reflecting Tony's attitudes toward his incestuous behavior as well as his attitudes toward normal father–daughter relationships are presented in Figure 2. During baseline, Tony highly valued both deviant and nondeviant interactions with his daughter, but on Probe Day 6, his sexual relations with his daughter began to be devalued, until reaching a point close to 0. Fortunately, Tony's desire for normal father–daughter interactions remained high throughout treatment. It is, of course, not clear from this case whether the

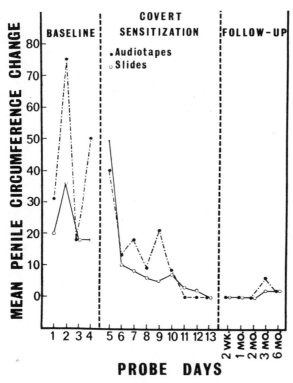

Figure 1. Mean penile circumference change to audiotapes and slides during baseline, covert sensitization, and follow-up. (From "Measurement and Modification of Incestuous Behavior: A Case Study" by T. L. Harbert, D. H. Barlow, M. Hersen, and J. B. Austin, *Psychological Reports*, 1974, *34*, 79–86. Copyright 1974 by *Psychological Reports*. Reprinted by permission.)

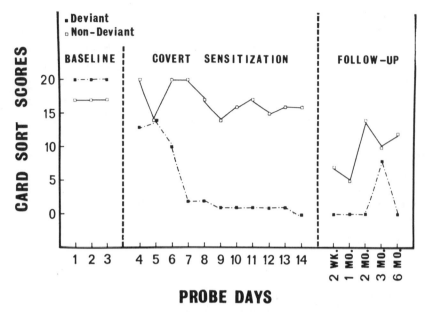

Figure 2. Card-sort scores on probe days during baseline, covert sensitization, and follow-up. (From "Measurement and Modification of Incestuous Behavior: A Case Study" by T. L. Harbert, D. H. Barlow, M. Hersen, and J. B. Austin, *Psychological Reports*, 1974, *34*, 79–86. Copyright 1974 by *Psychological Reports*. Reprinted by permission.)

presentation of the "positive" scenes involving normal father–daughter interactions during treatment was responsible for this discrimination. It is entirely possible that he may have made this discrimination without these scenes, but the scenes involved little extra time and seemed a reasonable clinical strategy.

Follow-ups were obtained at 2 weeks, 1 month, 2 months, 3 months, and 6 months, as indicated in Figures 1 and 2. Incestuous arousal, as measured objectively by penile circumference changes and subjectively by the card sort, remained negligible for the first 3 months. During this period, an unexpected finding was a drop in desire for normal father–daughter interactions. There was no indication of this in Tony's report, and only after some questioning did Tony say that he had been sending gifts, Christmas cards, letters, etc., to his daughter to which she had not responded. He pointed out that he could understand her unwillingness to respond to him at this point, but he was still hurt, resulting in a drop in his nondeviant card sort. Shortly after this, his daughter began responding to some of his initiatives, and he felt much better about the whole situation, as reflected in the card sort.

One of the most interesting results during follow-up, which was also unexpected but if unchecked could have undermined the whole treatment, occurred at the 3-month follow-up. At this point, a slight increase in sexual arousal to his daughter, as measured by penile circumference change, was noted. This increase was also reflected in the card sort. He "confessed" that his sexual relations with his wife were less than satisfactory and that in the past several weeks he had begun having more generalized marital difficulties. Although he had successfully suppressed incestuous fantasies during relations with his wife, these occasions with his wife provided the most powerful cues for his incestuous fantasies. Thus, after the onset of marital difficulties, these fantasies began to reappear. A more careful assessment and monitoring of his appropriate sexual behavior and fantasies might have uncovered deficiencies in this area much earlier, allowing appropriate interventions, but the incomplete assessment in this case led to discovery of this deficiency only by interference, that is, during an unexplained rise in incestuous arousal. When this was discovered, booster sessions of covert sensitization were initiated along with some clinical interventions to increase sexual arousal with his wife and to correct the current marital difficulties. These efforts seemed to be successful, based on his report and from the observation of his incestuous fantasies and arousal, which returned to 0 at 6 months.

In retrospect, this case had a positive outcome clinically, but there were many "choice points" during the course of treatment at which the wrong decision might have led to failure rather than success. First, the incomplete assessment of desired heterosexual arousal and behavior would most likely have led to failure if not for the somewhat accidental discovery at the 3-month follow-up of difficulties in this area. Fortunately, Tony had not moved away, stopped his follow-up visits, nor been terminated at this point, allowing this discovery to be made. It was also fortunate that the assessment procedures were continued at these follow-up intervals to pick up these important changes. Second, the noxious images involving nausea and vomiting which were used in covert sensitization might well have been continued if Tony had not spoken up about his reactions to the scenes. There are many clients who undoubtedly do not speak up, and if daily or weekly repeated measures are not in effect, these cases will be failures, and the conclusion will be that covert sensitization is just not effective with everyone. Finally, an important factor in outcome was the discrimination made by Tony between incestuous relations and normal father–daughter interactions. It is not clear if the "positive" scenes had anything to do with this discrimination; this procedure may have been "excess clinical baggage." There is other evidence that aversive therapy, including covert sensitization, has extremely specific effects (Barlow, 1978; Marks & Gelder, 1967), but as so often happens with clinicians, we were very conservative in this case, choosing the excess baggage over the possibility of not making this discrimination. The second example describes a more complex case of sexual deviation and illustrates a component analysis as well as an analysis of contributing factors.

Case 2: A Case of Multiple Sexual Deviations

Presenting Problem

Robert was a 31-year-old married blue-collar worker with a somewhat irregular employment record and a history of alcohol abuse. He reported that he first started "peeping" in windows when he was age 14. He would ride around at night on his bike, and when he spotted a female through a window, he would stop and stare. These early experiences were almost always accompanied by feelings of arousal and erection. Eventually, his peeping led to masturbation and orgasm. Although peeping was Robert's first sexual experience, he also reported exposing himself at age 14 or 15.

When he was old enough to drive a car, he would drive around until he spotted some prepubescent girls and park his car near them. Before calling the girls over to his car, he would unzip his fly and pull out his penis to insure that he would be in full view of the onlookers. He would then call the girls to his car and attempt to engage them in conversation. Remarkably, he reported, none of the girls ever seemed upset by the experience, and, in his judgment, many seemed to enjoy it.

By his late teens, he had been arrested several times for peeping and exhibiting, but in no way was deterred by his incarcerations. On the contrary, he found it more sexually arousing when there was a threat of arrest. His exposure behavior seemed to take on a compulsive nature, and he was soon exhibiting several times a week. On some occasions, he was able to talk young girls into mutual masturbation and fellatio.

He was a smooth talker, indeed, a flatterer who could approach children without threat. He often played on their innocence and curiosity. For example, one of his ploys was to open a pornographic magazine and pretend to be reading while a young girl was nearby. Upon seeing that she was curious, he would remark, "Someday you may look like this." He would show the girl a picture of the nude woman and discuss the picture in a nonthreatening, educational way. If the girl continued to show interest, he would discuss sexual behavior and eventually attempt to extend his "educational" endeavors to sexual ones.

At age 23, Robert met a divorced 25-year-old woman in a bar. She was friendly and made Robert feel comfortable—a feeling Robert was unaccustomed to in the presence of adult women. After only 1 month of dating, Robert married her and became the stepfather of her two daughters, ages 4 and 5. At first, the marriage was workable, but after about 6 months, Robert's wife began putting on weight and working at two jobs. Left alone much of the time and discouraged by his marriage, Robert began drinking heavily and was soon yielding to his former sexual urges of peeping and exhibiting.

His marriage "rocked" along for 7 more quarrelsome years, until his stepdaughters entered puberty. He took notice of this and became sexually attracted to the eldest daughter and soon began stroking her while she was sleeping. On some occasions, his stepdaughter was awake and yielded to his advances. This ritual, which eventually led to sexual intercourse, occurred almost nightly, while his wife was at work. The eldest daughter felt guilty about her relationship with Robert and told her mother. The mother became extremely upset with this news and asked Robert to leave. At this point, Robert turned for help and was referred to our clinic.

Etiology of Problems

There are a number of factors in Robert's background which are of possible etiological significance. Robert was raised by a very stern, authoritarian father and a passive mother in a small Texas town. His father, who was a firm believer in old-time Southern Baptist religion, often preached the evils of sexual intercourse to his family. It is not surprising that Robert learned little about sex from his father, other than the strong message that it was bad. This is not an unusual experience for many men expressing sexually deviant behavior—information given to them about sex is often cryptic and negative and sexual urges and arousal are often suppressed in normal heterosexual situations because of the negative feelings associated with them. Consequently, as many deviant men, Robert grew up feeling uneasy around females his own age and, for the most part, actively avoided heterosocial situations.

Robert's deviant behavior was, on the other hand, reinforcing to him in at least two ways. First of all, it provided a sexual outlet and a source of pleasure, and, secondly, he seemed to derive some gratification from being arrested and disgracing his father. The courts treated him lightly (this is not unusual), and his father was publicly humiliated. Robert's family, in fact, moved away from their small Texas town following his arrest.

Behavioral Analysis and Therapy Plan

Robert sought psychiatric help following the rejection by his wife. When he entered the clinic, he had been drinking alcohol excessively for several weeks and had been living in a small apartment by himself. Initial interview assessment revealed that he had not been getting along with his wife for most of his marriage and that he was never comfortable with her sexually. Although his marital difficulties contributed to his feelings of stress, it was clear that his marriage was beyond salvation and that marital therapy was not indicated. Furthermore, his deviant sexual behavior enjoyed a long history which had been brought into the marriage. Of importance for the conceptualization of Robert's problems was that, although he had acquired basic heterosocial skills, he did not feel sexually attracted to adult women and, in fact, expressed feelings of discomfort.

Robert spoke freely of his peeping, exhibiting, and pedophiliac experiences and indicated a high frequency of sexual urges accompanied by fantasies of these behaviors. Following several interview sessions, physiological assessment (strain gauge) was conducted to determine his degree of erectile response to slides. Physiological sexual arousal was measured in terms of average pen deflection during stimulus exposure. Slides were selected which portrayed stimuli characteristics of the three deviant responses. For example, the "peeping" slides portrayed a woman in various stages of undress viewed through a window. Slides representing heterosexual stimuli portrayed nude women alone, as well as women involved in sexual activity with a male.

Robert was also instructed to record his subjective feelings of arousal during the slide presentations by moving a lever along a calibrated scale from 0 (not aroused) to 10 (extremely aroused). The use of the hand lever has been previously described by Wincze, Hoon, and Hoon (1978). Robert also sorted 20 cards which described his involvement in the one normal and three deviant categories of sexual behavior described above. Five cards were representative of each of the four categories, and the cards could be sorted into any of five intensities of sexual arousal. Robert's task was to read each card and judge how sexually aroused the described scene made him feel.

Data were collected for 5 consecutive days and analyzed before a therapy program was initiated. The physiological and subjective arousal data from this assessment period are presented in Figures 3 and 4.

These data, along with the interview and card sort, assisted in formulating the treatment plan. The most pressing problem was the

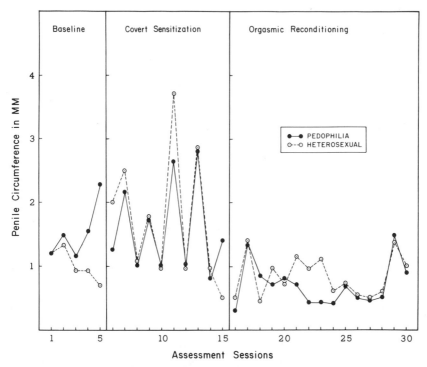

Figure 3.   Mean penile circumference changes, as measured in mm pen deflection, during exposure to stimulus slides. Data are from baseline-assessment phase, covert-sensitization phase, and orgasmic-reconditioning phase.

sexual attraction to and activity with pubescent females. As shown in Figures 3 and 4, the greatest arousal was expressed in the presence of slides of pubescent females. The initial treatment plan was designed to help him control and suppress this deviant arousal. Since his sexual arousal to adult heterosexual stimuli was well below his sexual arousal to pubescent females, the second part of the treatment plan was aimed at increasing this aspect of his sexual arousal pattern. Finally, the multilevel analysis of Robert's sexual behavior revealed that he expressed no problems of gender identity and only minor problems of heterosocial approach. It was decided that the latter two areas would not be a focus of therapy. During treatment for his sexual problems, Robert was an inpatient, restricted to a hospital ward, and he did not have any opportunity to drink alcohol while therapy was in progress. Since Robert did not have a long history of alcohol abuse, however, treatment plans for this problem were developed with a cooperative institute following the sexual therapy program.

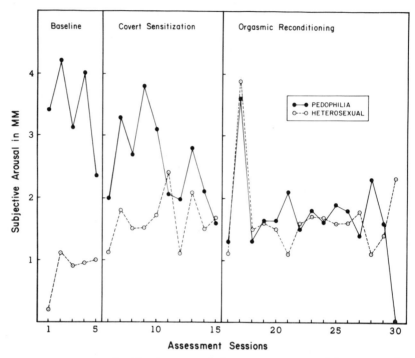

Figure 4. Report of subjective arousal changes, as measured in mm pen deflection, during exposure to stimulus slides. Data are from baseline-assessment phase, covert-sensitization phase, and orgasmic-reconditioning phase.

Therapy and Results

A covert-sensitization procedure which focused on sexual arousal and behavior with pubescent females was implemented for 20 sessions. Throughout the entire sexual therapy program, assessment procedures continued following every other session. The results of the covert-sensitization procedure are presented in Figures 3 and 4.

As shown in Figure 3, there was negligible overall suppression of the physiological arousal to pubescent female stimuli during the covert-sensitization program, but this procedure seemed to produce increased variance in the sexual arousal level to all categories of stimuli.

With the exception of assessment session 10 (Day 25), all categories of sexual arousal seemed to covary. The data from the cognitive lever (Figure 4) suggest some overall suppression in the reporting of sexual arousal during this phase as compared to the baseline phase. The card-sort scores also showed a drop from a mean score of 19.5 for pubescent females during the baseline phase to a mean score of 12.5 during the covert-sensitization program. Robert reported feeling less arousal to pubescent females at this time, although there appeared to be almost no suppression of physiological responding to deviant stimuli. After 20 sessions of covert sensitization, it was decided to attempt an orgasmic-reconditioning procedure to increase the arousal value of adult females. This procedure employed a modified fading technique in the laboratory, in which arousal was initiated in the presence of slides of pubescent females and culminated in orgasm in the presence of slides of females a couple of years older. When Robert was able to masturbate in the presence of these "new" stimuli 75% of the time without losing his arousal, another "new" slide was introduced depicting a female a couple of years older still. In this step-by-step procedure, Robert eventually was able to masturbate to orgasm without losing his arousal using adult females as stimulus cues.

In spite of the success of this conditioning procedure conducted in the laboratory, there did not appear to be any increase in arousal to adult females in probe sessions conducted after 34 conditioning sessions. These data support the findings of Conrad and Wincze (1976), who also found no conditioning effect of orgasmic-reconditioning procedures with clinical patients. However, as in the Conrad and Wincze (1976) study, the patient did verbalize improvement in his interest in and arousal to adult females.

Robert was released shortly after the orgasmic-reconditioning procedure and was referred to an alcoholic treatment unit at another hospital. Following an inpatient course of treatment at this unit, Robert managed to "stay dry" for 6 months. However, he began drinking again after 6 months and once more yielded to his deviant sexual urges. He was seen in our outpatient clinic following a 3-day drinking spree and stated that he had lapsed into pedophiliac and exhibitionistic behavior once again. Although he was scheduled for additional treatment sessions, he failed to show for his appointments and has not made contact with our clinic in over a year.

Discussion

The model of sexual disorders proposed in the Introduction offered a comprehensive approach to analyzing Robert's multiple sexual problems. This assessment allowed the development of an individually tailored treatment program which began with covert sensitization. The ongoing assessment procedure allowed a continuous monitoring of the effects of therapy. Although a great deal of variance was present in all categories of sexual behavior, no other strong trends were noticed throughout 20 sessions of covert sensitization. This procedure was then abandoned because of the absence of any trends in the data.

Similarly, the orgasmic-reconditioning procedure failed to yield any encouraging trends in the ongoing data and was stopped after 32 sessions.

In spite of the lack of success of this case in terms of clinical outcome, the case is a valuable illustration of the use of the model of sexual deviancy to which we ascribe and of the use of an ongoing multilevel assessment procedure. The model allowed a development of a priority-ordered treatment plan, and the ongoing assessment prescribed the timing of intervention strategies. If trends had been observed in the assessment data, therapy would have been continued for many more sessions. The data predicted, however, that continued therapy was a waste of valuable therapist time. Data from other clients in our program are often predictive of success, and therapy time course can be projected fairly accurately.

It is difficult to conclude why there was a lack of success in this second case. However, analysis of some important clues allows some speculation. Robert did not show real commitment to the program and seemed to be motivated in therapy only because of his desperate situation in his marriage. He did not seem to have a real desire to alter his deviant behavior and probably would not have sought treatment if he were not so destitute. His lack of commitment to changing his deviant behaviors may have interfered with the intensive therapy program.

In addition, no attempt was made in either the sex therapy program or the alcoholic treatment program to help Robert deal with social and work-related stresses. He apparently did not develop adequate problem-solving skills in either program and found himself once again faced with considerable stress once outside of the hospital. Stress led to a resumption of his drinking, and deviant sexual behavior followed shortly after.

Other Therapy Concerns with Deviants

Involvement of Partner

Many child molesters and other sexual deviants are married and have children of their own. In such cases, it is often advisable to involve the wife and sometimes even the children in the therapeutic process. The involvement of the marriage partner will offer an additional source of information for assessment of the problem and will provide an ongoing monitoring of the patient's behvior outside of therapy sessions. Also, in many cases of deviancy, considerable stress in the marriage may be contributing to sexual offenses. It is not uncommon for a child molester, exhibitionist, or rapist to commit deviant acts in anger following a marital feud. Involvement of the marriage partner in such cases may serve to reduce stress, if the couple is actively involved in marital counseling. Such counseling may focus on either sexual or nonsexual aspects of the marriage.

In cases of incest, it may be important to involve the children as well as the wife in therapy sessions. A family therapy approach to incest may be facilitative in helping the family to reestablish normal family functioning. In addition, such an approach will provide the therapist with more sources of data for an ongoing evaluation.

Involvement of the wife in the therapeutic process may be concurrent with other ongoing therapeutic procedures. For example, a client may be involved in a program of covert sensitization, orgasmic reconditioning, and marital counseling sequentially or simultaneously, depending on the ability and motivation of the client.

Visualization Problems in Therapy
At times, there are clients who have a great deal of difficulty in becoming engaged in the covert-sensitization procedure. They may have difficulty imagining scenes, or they may report that they are experiencing little or no aversive impact from the scenes. In such cases, it is often helpful to reanalyze the content of the scenes to insure that realistic and appropriate stimuli are being presented. A more careful physiological assessment with audiotapes may help expand on appropriate erotic cues (Abel *et al.*, 1975). In addition, it is helpful to engage the client in recreating his own covert-sensitization scenes out loud. Such oral rehearsal will help some clients to become more involved in the scenes and bring the procedure under their own control.

Outpatient Treatment
Since therapists dealing with outpatients have little or no control over their clients outside of sessions, care should be taken not to unwittingly stimulate a client through exposure to erotic material. Exposure to explicit slides, audiotapes, or videotapes during an assessment session may leave a client sexually aroused to a point they cannot control. Mann (1970) has shown that exposure to erotic material may significantly increase a heterosexual couple's sexual activity for at least 48 hours following the exposure. There is every reason to believe that deviant individuals may also increase their sexual behavior following such exposure. Whenever possible, assessment sessions should be conducted while a client is an inpatient. If an inpatient stay cannot be arranged, then the therapist should warn the client and his partner of

such a danger and monitor the behavior as carefully as possible. For rapists and other dangerous individuals, the therapist may be best advised not to conduct an assessment with outpatients which includes exposure to explicitly arousing material.

Summary

The two cases presented illustrate the utilization of an assessment and treatment strategy for sexually deviant behavior. Deviant behavior is, first of all, conceptualized as having three components: (1) sexual arousal/behavior, (2) social skills and emotional factors associated with sexual interactions, and (3) gender-role deviations. The focus of therapy may be on one or more of these basic components. A second aspect of the model is that within each component, various factors which may be contributing to the manifestation of the problem are considered. Treatment may focus on the component of behavior or on the nature and urgency of the problem. A third and final aspect of the model is that sexual deviancy is assessed on multilevels: behavioral, subjective, and physiological. Thus, reliance on only one modality of assessment, such as self-report, may mislead one into false assumptions about the success of the process.

This rather complex model of assessing and treating sexual deviancy helps to target the key problems and individualize the treatment program. Since assessment is ongoing, it allows the therapist to continuously evaluate the impact of therapy. When therapy seems to be effecting little change in the client (as in Case 2), therapy procedures can be altered or abandoned and save the client and therapist time. The decision to alter, stop, or continue treatment can be based on objective criteria rather than subjective impressions alone. It should be noted, however, that the utilization of objective data is not yet entirely a scientific process, and we often have to rely on past clinical experience to assist in our treatment predictions. As more data are gathered using our model, we can look forward to more and more reliance on objective criteria and less and less reliance on subjective impressions.

At present, our sophistication in assessment procedures far surpasses our treatment effectiveness for sexual offenders. Although we can often describe a client's arousal pattern in detail (Abel et al., 1975) and predict dangerousness (Abel, Barlow, Blanchard, & Guild, 1977), we still do not have effective treatment strategies with the chronic offender (Walker, 1978). Walker (1978) points out that with the chronic sex offender, there is little evidence that psychodynamic or behavioral approaches to therapy will produce a dramatic change in the person's sexual behavior. The changes are often too little and too late! Case 2 is a good illustration of this predicament. Walker (1978) advocates a combined treatment of antiandrogen therapy and psychotherapy for the chronic offender, but this very controversial procedure is not available for most sexual offenders in this country.

However, the utility of this model for assessment and treatment is far from negligible. The assessment procedure does help to separate high-risk offenders from occasional offenders through detailed examination of data from the assessment sessions and behavioral records. In addition, dangerousness can be predicted, and a prognostic picture for most clients can be developed. The assessment procedure will also help to set priorities for the treatment strategies and deal with the most crucial problems first.

Our model does not tell us who should be labeled and treated as a sexual deviant; such labeling is of cultural and legal concern. Walker (1978) has addressed this concern in depth and has concluded that an answer to such a question often requires analysis of harm, consent, and chronicity as well as the consideration mentioned above that most of these attributes are on a continuum. Even so, as therapists, we are called upon to interpret subjectively these parameters and to make some weighty decisions. The proposed model encourages interpretation and application of these parameters for each individual case. By so doing, it should be easier to include patients in therapy who need it and exclude those who do not.

References

Abel, G. G., Barlow, D. H., Blanchard, E. B., & Guild, D. The components of rapists' sexual arousal. *Archives of General Psychiatry*, 1977, *34*, 895–908.

Abel, G. G., & Blanchard, E. B. The measurement and generation of sexual arousal. In M. Hersen, R. Eisler, & P. M. Miller (Eds.), *Progress in behavior modification* (Vol. 2). New York: Academic Press, 1976.

Abel, G. G., Blanchard, E. B., Barlow, D. H., & Mavissakalian, M. Identifying specific erotic cues in sexual deviation by audiotaped descriptions. *Journal of Applied Behavior Analysis*, 1975, *8*, 247–260.

Barlow, D. H. Increasing heterosexual responsiveness in the treatment of sexual deviation: A review of the clinical and experimental evidence. *Behavior Therapy*, 1973, *4*, 655–671.

Barlow, D. H. The treatment of sexual deviation: Towards a comprehensive behavioral approach. In K. S. Calhoun, H. E. Adams, & K. M. Mitchell (Eds.), *Innovative treatment methods in psychopathology*. New York: John Wiley, 1974.

Barlow, D. H. Assessment of sexual behavior. In A. R. Ciminero, K. S. Calhoun, & H. E. Adams (Eds.), *Handbook of behavioral assessment*. New York: John Wiley, 1977.

Barlow, D. H. Aversive procedures. In W. S. Agras (Ed.), *Behavior modification: Principles and clinical applications* (2nd ed.). Boston: Little, Brown & Co., 1978.

Barlow, D. H., & Abel, G. G. Recent developments in assessment and treatment of sexual deviation. In W. E. Craighead, A. E. Kazdin, & M. J. Mahoney (Eds.), *Behavior modification: Principles, issues, and applications*. Boston: Houghton Mifflin, 1976.

Barlow, D. H., Abel, G. G., & Blanchard, E. B. Gender identity change in transsexuals: Follow-up and replications. *Archives of General Psychiatry*, 1979, *36*, 1001–1010.

Barlow, D. H., & Agras, W. S. Fading to increase heterosexual responsiveness in homosexuals. *Journal of Applied Behavior Analysis*, 1973, *6*, 355–367.

Barlow, D. H., Agras, W. S., Leitenberg, H., Callahan, E. J., & Moore, R. C. The contribution of therapeutic instructions to covert sensitization. *Behaviour Research and Therapy*, 1972, *10*, 411–415.

Barlow, D. II., Becker, R., Leitenberg, H., & Agras, W. S. A mechanical strain gauge for recording penile circumference change. *Journal of Applied Behavior Analysis*, 1970, *3*, 73–76.

Barlow, D. H., Leitenberg, H., & Agras, W. S. The experimental control of sexual deviation through manipulation of the noxious scene in covert sensitization. *Journal of Abnormal Psychology*, 1969, *74*, 596–601.

Barlow, D. H., Reynolds, E. H., & Agras, W. S. Gender identity change in a transsexual. *Archives of General Psychiatry*, 1973, *28*, 569–579,

Brownell, K. D., & Barlow, D. H. The behavioral treatment of sexual deviation. In E. Foa, A. Goldstein, & J. Wolpe (Eds.), *Handbook of behavioral intervention*. New York: John Wiley, in press.

Brownell, K. D., Hayes, S. C., & Barlow, D. H. Patterns of appropriate and deviant sexual arousal: The behavioral treatment of multiple sexual deviations. *Journal of Consulting and Clinical Psychology*, 1977, *45*, 1144–1155.

Caird, W., & Wincze, J. *Sex Therapy: A behavioral approach*. Hagerstown, Md.: Harper & Row, 1977.

Callahan, E. J., & Leitenberg, H. Aversion therapy for sexual deviation: Contingent shock and covert sensitization. *Journal of Abnormal Psychology*, 1972, *81*, 60–73.

Cautela, J. R. Covert sensitization. *Psychological Reports*, 1967, *20*, 459–468.

Conrad, W. K., & Wincze, J. Orgasmic reconditioning: A controlled study of its effects upon the sexual arousal patterns and behavior of adult male homosexuals. *Behavior Therapy*, 1976, *7*, 155–166.

Curran, D., & Parr, D. Homosexuality: An analysis of 100 male cases seen in private practice. *British Medical Journal*, 1957, *1*, 797–801.

Davison, G. C. Counter-control in behavior modification. In L. A. Hamerlynck, L. C. Handy, & E. J. Mash (Eds.,), *Behavior change: Methodology, concepts, and practice*. Champaign, Ill.: Research Press, 1973.

Ellis, H. *Studies in the psychology of sex* (Vol. 2), *Sexual inversion*. Philadelphia: F. A. Davis & Co., 1915.

Fowler, D. R., & Longabaugh, R. The problem oriented record: Problem definition. *Archives of General Psychiatry*, 1975, *32*, 831–834.

Freund, K. Some problems in the treatment of homosexuality. In H. J. Eysenck (Ed.), *Behavior therapy and the neuroses*. New York: Pergamon Press, 1960.

Freund, K., McKnight, C. K., Langevin, R., & Cibiri, S. The female child as a surrogate object. *Archives of Sexual Behavior*, 1972, *2*, 119–133.

Frisbie, L. V., & Dondis, E. H. *Recidivism among treated sex offenders*. Research Monograph No. 5, Department of Mental Hygiene, State of California, 1965.

Harbert, T. L., Barlow, D. H., Hersen, M., & Austin, J. B. Measurement and modification of incestuous behavior: A case study. *Psychological Reports*, 1974, *34*, 79–86.

Hersen, M., & Barlow, D. H. *Single case experimental designs: Strategies for studying behavior change*. New York: Pergamon Press, 1976.

Kantorowitz, D. A. An experimental investigation of pre-orgasmic reconditioning and post-orgasmic deconditioning. *Journal of Applied Behavior Analysis*, 1978, *11*, 23–34.

Lobitz, W. C., & LoPiccolo, J. New methods of the behavioral treatment of sexual dysfunction. *Journal of Behavior Therapy and Experimental Psychiatry*, 1972, *3*, 265–271.

Maletzky, B. M. Assisted covert sensitization in the treatment of exhibitionism. In D. J. Cox & R. Daitzman (Eds.), *Exhibitionism: Description, assessment and treatment*. New York: Garland, 1978.

Mann, J. *Effects of erotic films on sexual behavior of married couples*. Paper presented at the annual meeting of the American Psychological Association, Miami, Fla., September, 1970.

Marks, I. M., & Gelder, M. G. Transvestism and fetishism: Clinical and psychological changes during faradic aversion. *British Journal of Psychiatry*, 1967, *113*, 711–729.

Masters, W. H., & Johnson, V. E. *Human sexual inadequacy*. Boston: Little, Brown & Co., 1970.

Stoller, R. J. Parental influences in male transsexualism. In R. Green & J. Money (Eds.), *Transsexualism and sex reassignment*. Baltimore: Johns Hopkins Press, 1969.

Ullmann, L. P., & Krasner, L. *A psychological approach to abnormal behavior* (2nd ed.). Englewood Cliffs, N.J.: Prentice-Hall, 1975.

Walker, P. A. The role of antiandrogens in the treatment of sex offenders. In C. B. Qualls, J. P. Wincze, & D. H. Barlow (Eds.), *The prevention of sexual disorders: Issues and approaches*. New York: Plenum Press, 1978.

Wincze, J., Hoon, E., & Hoon, P. Multiple measure analysis of women experiencing low sexual arousal. *Behaviour Research and Therapy*, 1978, *16*, 43–49.

Woodward, M. The diagnosis and treatment of homosexual offenders. *British Journal of Delinquency*, 1958, *9*, 44–59.

13

Conclusion: Overview of Some Critical Issues in the Evaluation and Treatment of Sexual Dysfunctions

LAWRENCE A. PERVIN AND SANDRA R. LEIBLUM

The preceding chapters have covered a wide variety of dysfunctions, methods of treatment, and general issues. Each author has given an account of the perspective and treatment program utilized in the course of sex therapy. Clearly, sex therapy is not a routine, workbook procedure. Treatment requires skill, sensitivity, and patience on the part of the therapist. The chapters point out the variability in procedure that applies not only among different therapists but, to a certain extent, within each therapist as he or she considers the unique problems and needs of each person or couple. In the course of reading these chapters, many important issues become apparent. Let us now take stock of them.

Diagnosis and Incidence

A number of the contributors have pointed out the difficulty in making certain diagnoses and the relevance of one's model of normal sexual functioning. By and large, we are able to proceed in our work without working out a careful diagnostic scheme. The focus is on the problem of concern to the patient, and generally this is clearly defined. However, the limits of our understanding become clear in more subtle cases or where partners disagree concerning the nature of the difficulty. Often the male with the problem of premature ejaculation wants to know how long he should be able to continue before ejaculation. Is there an answer that can be given? A woman wants to know how much stimulation should be required to have an orgasm. Is there an answer that can be given?

As noted in the chapters by LoPiccolo and by Zilbergeld and Ellison, such questions become particularly acute when one considers the problem of low sexual desire. How often is reasonable? Again, at the extremes, the task may be easy, and often we may not have to worry about this question. But equally often there is a discrepancy between the desires of the partners involved, and this requires some

377

consideration of the issue. Perhaps the answer is as Zilbergeld and Ellison suggest—the problem can only be defined in relationship terms. In this sense, the person with minimal desire is not dysfunctional as long as the partner's desire is at a similar level, and the same holds true for the person with a tremendous appetite for sexual activity. While the goal in sex therapy thus may be to work out some mutually satisfactory arrangement between the partners, sex therapists generally do have some of their own estimates as to what is "normal" and "desirable" and probably are biased in the direction of "more is better." To a certain extent, the basic problem of a lack of definition concerning healthy functioning is no different from that in treating other psychological dysfunctions, but that is a basis for caution rather than cheer. Awareness of this relationship should help to sensitize us to potential biases that may enter in as a result of personal values, societal norms, and scientific-professional models. The issue of personal bias is sensitively addressed by McWhirter and Mattison in their chapter on the treatment of sexual dysfunctions in homosexual male couples.

While diagnosis may not be a key part of sex therapy, assessment certainly is. Throughout the book, an emphasis has been placed on the careful monitoring of a person's sexual functioning as well as other aspects of his or her physiological and psychological functioning (Lazarus). The emphasis on assessment includes evaluation of the person's general psychological status, evaluation of contributing medical factors (Ellis; Leiblum, Pervin, & Campbell), evaluation of potential factors contributing to progress or resistance (Barbach), evaluation of relationship strengths and weaknesses (Perelman), detailed evaluation of rates of progress and changes in patterns of sexual functioning (Barlow & Wincze), and, in cases of cardiac difficulty, careful evaluation of the patient's limits for physical activity (Stein).

The issue of scientific models to be used in assessment is specifically addressed in the chapters by Apfelbaum and by Zilbergeld and Ellison. What is suggested is that the response cycle or phase models of Masters and Johnson and of Kaplan may not be adequate. Instead of a stage model of the sexual response (e.g., excitement, plateau, orgasm, and resolution stages), a component model is suggested. The components suggested by Zilbergeld and Ellison (interest, arousal, physiological readiness, orgasm, satisfaction) clearly bear some relationship to the stage model. However, it is also clear that there are some distinguishing aspects, and, as the authors suggest, these may influence what we consider to be the problem and how we treat it. Perhaps of the greatest significance here is the shift in emphasis from a strictly physiological model to one that includes psychological–

experiential components. In particular, the cognitive construction of the events and the subjective experience now become important, points also made in the chapters by LoPiccolo, Apfelbaum, Ellis, and Lazarus. In the words of the supporters of the component model, "something important was missing in the conceptual apparatus and in the treatment approaches—a concern for the subjective elements of sex" (Zilbergeld & Ellison, p. 66). In addition, these authors suggest that the components are at least potentially independent of one another.

The introductory chapter discussed the relationship between developments in sexology and sex therapy and changes in societal values. To what extent have our earlier models reflected a concern with quantity rather than with quality, with performance rather than with satisfaction? How often is an ejaculation equated with an orgasm in the male? Is the criterion of an orgasm in the female her subjective report or physiological data? What difference does it make if the patient sees a change in his or her condition strictly as a result of relabeling an experience? Clearly, bringing in subjective experiences helps to broaden and deepen our perspective of human sexuality, but whether it will help to solve some of these difficult diagnostic issues remains to be seen.

Of course, without a clear diagnostic criterion, it is difficult to consider questions of incidence in definitive terms. Many sex therapists have suggested that different problems are now being seen in treatment centers—more often than in the past, they are difficult to treat and involve problems of desire (LoPiccolo). Are these changes real? Are they due to the utilization of self-help books by many people who thereby do not need formal treatment? Are changes in society resulting in the development in different problems, in changes in labeling of difficulties by patients, or in changes in labeling of difficulties by therapists? In any case, the patient population seen at treatment centers cannot be used as a basis for estimating the frequency or distribution of difficulties in the larger population. Patients are selective about the kinds of problems for which they will seek treatment and often will use a problem as a "ticket for admission" to treatment. And, with all of our increased acceptance of and sophistication about sexuality, a significant proportion of the population remains seriously inhibited in this area and reluctant to seek help for its difficulties.

Causal Factors and Antecedent Events

For the most part, sex therapy does not concern itself with the etiology of sexual dysfunctions. In a pragmatic fashion, the concern is with treatment of the problem and not with how the problem developed. It is fortunate that it is possible to proceed with treatment in the absence of such understanding, for the factors contributing to specific sexual dysfunctions are extremely puzzling. Despite the availability of different theoretical interpretations, we are at a loss to specify in any meaningful way the critical developmental and/or traumatic events that lead to difficulty. Nor are we in any better shape when we consider the personality characteristics that predispose one to develop various difficulties. Anxiety is often mentioned as an important factor, but anxiety can lead to excessive sexual desire or lack of desire and to premature ejaculation or retarded ejaculation. Lazarus notes that many factors enter into dyspareunia and that no single factor appears to be essential. Ellis remarks that many men with problematic sex histories have no sexual difficulties, while others with positive histories develop serious difficulties. Even with the same person, it often is difficult to ascertain why the problem appears at some points but not at others or why the same male may experience a problem of erectile dysfunction at one point and a problem of premature ejaculation at another point. Under such circumstances, it is tempting to turn to explanations in terms of constitutional differences. However, it is hard to see how such differences would account for some of these shifts, particularly shifts between exaggerated desire and minimal desire.

The list of early developmental factors and precipitating sources of stress is a long one. Barbach notes that there are multiple interacting causes of anorgasmia—an absence of information or presence of misinformation, problems in early socialization experiences, skill deficits, and more or less profound psychological disturbance. Similarly, the chapter on vaginismus (Leiblum, Pervin, & Campbell) emphasizes the variety of potential contributing factors—lack of information, early traumatic sexual events, and basic characterological difficulties. In almost every case of sexual dysfunction, we can find problems of guilt, misinformation, trauma, or disturbed patterns of relationships that are part of the developmental past. In those cases in which such events cannot be found, it is typical to attribute this to limitations in history-taking and patient recall, an attribution which probably makes a great deal of sense. The problem is, however, that so often patients have siblings who grew up in similar environments and experienced similar or even more severe trauma, yet do not experience the same problems in sexual functioning. Environments are never the same, and events are never equally traumatic, but just how differences in these developmental events make for normal or disturbed sexual functioning, or for one or another form of sexual dysfunction, remains puzzling indeed.

How often is it the case that we come across a person who for every known reason "should" have been a premature ejaculator, or had a problem of erectile dysfunction, or been unable to achieve orgasm, and yet the problem is not present?

If one goes from early developmental factors to current personality style, the picture is not any clearer. As Perelman notes, "the diversity found among premature ejaculators defies classification beyond the PE itself" (p. 202). Similarly, the specific role of precipitating events and situational–relationship factors often is puzzling. Most everyone would agree that a person's sexual functioning is expressive of his or her personality and that the nature of the sexual relationship with the partner is expressive of more general aspects of the relationship. However, here, too, we do not find simple one-to-one relationships. Stress at work leads some to find solace and comfort in the sexual relationship, while it leads others to experience disruptions in sexual functioning and further blows to self-esteem. Although partners often feel that they can only enjoy sex when things are "smooth in the relationship," other couples find that sex is what helps to bring them back together, and some report that it is never better than when they are at odds with one another. Sexual functioning and interpersonal relationships are individually complex. Is there any reason why we should find a lesser degree of complexity in the relationships between them?

An important distinction is made by social learning theorists between the conditions that contribute to the acquisition of a response and the conditions that elicit the response and maintain it (Bandura, 1977). Thus, while an understanding of the etiological factors may be difficult and unnecessary for treatment to proceed, assessment of eliciting and maintaining conditions is an important part of sex therapy. While even here it is sometimes difficult to determine why the person has the difficulty with some partners but not with others, on some occasions but not on others, generally such determination is possible and contributes greatly to progress in treatment.

It is easy to suggest that biological–constitutional factors, developmental factors, and situational factors all play a role in sexual dysfunctions, but does this really enhance our understanding? Indeed, are we any clearer about the factors that contribute to "normal" sexual functioning? The problems in understanding here are equally great for those with a psychoanalytic orientation and those with a behavioral orientation. Although etiological events, characterological defenses, and situational conditions often can be pinpointed, it is also often the case that they cannot. The therapeutic techniques that are used relate much more to what has been found to work in the past and to a therapist's own personal predilections than to any clear understanding of the factors contributing to the sexual dysfunction itself. It is perhaps useful to keep this fact in mind as we consider the techniques that are used, the question of rationale for the utilization of one or another therapeutic technique, and our understanding of therapeutic success and failure.

Treatment Methods and Issues

The field of sex therapy contains a wide variety of techniques. Some of these techniques are specific to a particular dysfunction (e.g., Semans technique and premature ejaculation, the use of graduated dilators and vaginismus), while others are used more broadly (e.g., sensate focus, systematic desensitization). Some techniques tend to be used for particular problems (e.g., covert sensitization and fading described in the chapter by Barlow and Wincze), though one would imagine that their therapeutic potential is far broader. Whereas some of these techniques are somewhat specific to sex therapy, others have been borrowed from the broader field of psychotherapy and behavior change. In addition to variation in technique, there is variation in format—individual, couple, and group, as well as an individual therapist or a cotherapist team.

With all of the techniques that are available, what can be said concerning the general issue of therapeutic approach and rationale? Is sex therapy art, skill, or mechanics? Do we operate on the basis of hunch and "hit or miss" or on the basis of fairly explicit relationships between types of patients, types of problems, and types of procedures? In fact, it is probably the case that after the development of an initial therapeutic strategy, there is a great deal of work that is done on an intuitive or semidefined basis. Although there may be considerable agreement among sex therapists concerning initial strategies, increasing variability becomes apparent as difficulties in treatment arise. In fact, this has been one of the purposes of this book—to consider how various therapists go about handling all phases of the treatment process.

In terms of rationale, Annon's (1974) PLISSIT model serves as an illustration of a rationale for the sequential utilization of various treatment procedures. In his conceptual scheme, Annon suggests that one can move from an initial level of problem difficulty, where perhaps only permission is required for progress to occur, to a final level of difficulty, where treatment may involve intensive therapy. Annon suggests that each level requires a great degree of therapist skill and competence. He also suggests that the necessary level of treatment and preferable procedures to be used can be determined by an initial assessment; in other words, in contrast to many other situations, there should be a close linkage between assessment and therapeutic approach. A similar argument is made by some of the contributors to this volume (e.g., Lazarus; Barlow & Wincze). However, it remains questionable as to just how close a connection exists between assessment and therapeutic approach. The linkage would appear to be close in the work of Barlow and Wincze, but this is because systematic assessment is an ongoing part of their program. On the other hand, one would wonder about how explicit the rationale is for selection of an alternative treatment procedure once assessment suggests that the current procedure is not working. Again, one would guess that as cases become more difficult and as problems in treatment arise, variability in therapeutic practice increases and rationales for practice become less articulated. To what extent, then, is sex therapy somewhat like earlier, and in some areas current, medicine? There are some treatments which we use pretty much independently of the problem, some which we have a fairly good idea will work with specific problems, and some which we hold in reserve to try as problems in treatment emerge.

Part of the problem here goes back to our inadequate understanding of the determinants of sexual dysfunctions and, more generally, to our inadequate understanding of the processes of therapeutic change. Many techniques were developed independent of an understanding of the causes of a difficulty, and in many cases, a rationale for a technique has been developed after the successful utilization of the technique. Kaplan (1974) has made an excellent effort to develop a theoretical base for understanding the connections between various problems and treatment procedures, but this effort has followed the development of new practices and has not itself led to the development of new techniques. The approach is somewhat different in the cases of therapists such as Ellis and Lazarus. These therapists have attempted to develop a general understanding of dysfunctional behavior and therapeutic change and then to apply this understanding to the treatment of sexual dysfunctions. What is particularly striking is the wide array of contributing factors and therapeutic procedures that is considered. Ellis' contribution is noteworthy in its emphasis on cognitive, affective, and behavioral aspects of dysfunction and treatment, as is Lazarus' emphasis on consideration of all components of the BASIC ID.

Both Ellis and Lazarus place considerable emphasis on cognitive aspects of their treatment procedures. The emphasis on cognition has been a striking trend in the field of psychology in general and the field of behavior therapy in particular. Thoughts, images, and fantasies have always been important parts of sex therapy. But there is something new here, both in the degree of emphasis and in its connection with the broader field of psychotherapy. In a similar vein, the chapter by Zilbergeld and Ellison is illustrative of this point. The emphasis there is on the labeling and relabeling of internal areas—an aspect of the attribution process that has received considerable attention in the field of psychology. In terms of this connection, one wonders about the possible adaptations to sex therapy of other cognitive procedures that are now being developed. For example, does Bandura's (1977) work on modeling and self-efficacy suggest an understanding of why films and videocassettes often are helpful, and does it suggest other potential developments in modeling procedures? Does Meichenbaum's (1977) work on stress-inoculation training and coping through cognitive control (coping self-statements or positive thinking of one form or another) suggest new directions in sex therapy?

Most of the therapeutic techniques popular in sex therapy were borrowed from behavior therapists. As many writers have noted, it is perhaps ironic that psychoanalysis, with its prominent place in the history of sexology and psychotherapy, has offered so little to recent developments in sex therapy. The main reason for this would appear to be the contrast between the pragmatic, dysfunction-specific approach of most sex therapy as opposed to the underlying conflict-resolution emphasis of psychoanalysis, though the reaons may go deeper than this. While psychoanalysts have not been represented in this volume, there are analysts who also are sex therapists, and the analytic point of view does continue to be a part of the field. Perhaps this is most explicitly the case in relation to the issues of resistance and transference—two of the major points of emphasis in psychoanalytic therapy.

Concern with the problem of resistance has been expressed in many chapters in this volume, and, as cases get more difficult, increasing attention is being paid to it. The term is used by therapists of varying persuasions, so that it cannot always be considered within a specifically psychoanalytic context. Whereas initially the term "resistance" was used in a very limited sense to apply to a patient's noncompliance with the free-association rule in psychoanalysis, it began to be used more broadly in analytic writings to refer to lack of therapeutic movement due to internal conflict about change. At this point, the term is used by therapists of other persuasions and is defined by Gottman and Leiblum (1974) as follows: "We define resistance as occurring when the client(s) is not meeting the therapist's expectations regarding meaningful, goal-oriented therapeutic work"(p. 6). In its most general usage, resistance refers to all behaviors on the part of the patient that run counter to therapeutic agreements and interfere with progress. While we all are familiar with the problem, and many cases of resistance are obvious, in many ways it is a complex and poorly understood phenomenon. Of particular importance here is the danger of using the concept of resistance to blame patients for failures ("The therapy didn't work because of the resistance of the patient"), rather than recognizing our own errors or the limitations of our techniques. Another danger is that of assuming we understand something because we have a term for it. Resistance is a useful term for pointing to certain phenomena (e.g., missing appointments, not doing assignments, not talking about conscious thoughts and feelings) which share something in common and for pointing to an important area for therapeutic consideration. It is not a useful term if it serves as a device for focusing blame or for disguising inadequate understanding. This point is made by Gottman and Leiblum (1974), who note that resistance is a description of events and behaviors on the part of the client and not an explanation of lack of progress. According to them, resistance can occur because of threats associated with change, because of inadequate skills on the part of the client, because the environment fails to support change, or because of problems in communication or control between client and therapist.

Not only are there problems in being sensitive to and aware of resistance, but often considerable skill is needed to move beyond the impasse. There exists considerable variability among therapists in how problems of resistance are typically handled. A few contributors (McWhirter & Mattison; Perelman; Zilbergeld & Ellison) suggest bypassing the resistance, going with it, or working around it. Does this make sense as a general principle? If not, under what conditions does the principle apply? Barbach introduces the interesting approach of raising the issue at the outset with the patient: How do you think you would go about sabotaging treatment? This presumably makes it easier to address the question later, but ultimately, how useful is this procedure? Kaplan's approach is to proceed with behavioral techniques until one runs into difficulty and then explore, interpret, or analyze the resistance. A case recently seen at the Rutgers Sexual Counseling Service is illustrative in this regard. The husband had a problem with erectile dysfunction. Each time the couple made progress, there followed a period of retreat and noncompliance with the suggested homework exercises. When this pattern was pointed out, it emerged that each had fears about successful intercourse, and each was struggling with the issue of control in the relationship. This paved the way for discussion of their common concerns and for further progress in their sexual relationship. Whether prescribing other exercises or otherwise handling the problem would have been equally productive or more productive remains an open question. The point here is that the handling of resistance is a problem of increasing concern to sex therapists, a problem whose solution often makes for the difference between success and failure.

Perhaps the best way to summarize this section is to recognize that with all of sex therapy's available techniques and clear delineations of dysfunctions, there does not exist a real cookbook guide for the sex therapy practitioner. While self-help manuals are often of assistance, and we can often depend on the effectiveness of certain procedures, much of the work in sex therapy continues to involve some combination of experienced clinical judgment, intuition, hunch, and trial and error.

Outcome: Evaluation and Interpretation

As in other areas of therapy, sex therapy involves complex questions of evaluation and explanation. One of the most complex questions here concerns the criteria for success or failure. This issue may be somewhat simpler to handle than in other areas of therapy, since in sex therapy generally there is a specific dysfunction that is being treated, which is not always the case in psychotherapy. However, this is not always the case even in sex therapy, and what initially was presented as the problem may not turn out to be the problem in the long run.

In terms of the question of criteria for evaluation of success and failure, one question that can be asked is, which reports are to be treated as valid—patient reports, partner reports, therapist reports, questionnaire data, behavioral indices? Each of these methods has its advantages, and in an ideal world, there would be considerable agreement among them. The problem is that often this is not the case—partners disagree, patients and therapists differ in their evaluations, and objective indices may differ with patients and/or therapists (Strupp & Hadley, 1977). Considering the latter, what is one to do if a patient reports that she still does not experience an orgasm, whereas physiological recordings give clear indications of an orgasm? Does it make a difference if frequency of intercourse significantly increases or declines in the course of sex therapy? How do we evaluate treatment if a couple comes in with one member having a dysfunction and in the course of treatment this problem is alleviated but the other member experiences a dysfunction? Are we treating individuals or partners?

Does it make a difference how generalizable the improvement is—whether the man with an erectile dysfunction can now have an erection during masturbation, during intercourse with his regular partner, or during intercourse with an occasional partner, or whether a previously anorgasmic woman can have orgasms during masturbation, during intercourse with her regular partner, or during intercourse with an occasional partner? The problem becomes easier to handle clinically when patient and therapist agree that the dysfunction is no longer present. But often there is some difference of opinion here, and therapists certainly vary in the criteria they use for considering termination of treatment—successful or otherwise. In fact, it has been interesting for the editors of this volume to read the case reports and to occasionally find themselves in disagreement with the contributor as to whether the case should be considered a success or a failure.

Other questions need to be considered concerning criteria for evaluation. For example, at what point in time is the evaluation to be made? Most therapists would recognize the importance of follow-up data and the potential for relapse. In some instances, studies of the results of sex therapy have been outstanding in this regard; that is, many evaluative studies in this area do report follow-up data for a considerable period beyond the termination of treatment. Though partial and complete relapses do occur, in general, the follow-up data suggest considerable stability in gains made in sex therapy. Which gains are most likely to be maintained, and why, remain important theoretical and practical questions. Many clinicians feel that occasional "booster sessions" can go a long way in helping to maintain gains, but this is a view that desperately needs to be tested systematically.

One final question to be noted here, alluded to previously, concerns whether we are treating a dysfunction, a couple, or what? For the most part, sex therapists tend to be problem-focused and pragmatic. However, almost all sex therapists view sexual functioning in an intrapersonal as well as interpersonal context. Once we consider sexual functioning in terms of psychological experiences as well as performance aspects, we begin to take seriously questions concerning the person's ability to enjoy sex and the couple's ability to enjoy sex together as well as questions concerning whether each can perform sexually (Apfelbaum). In its extreme form, this question involves whether the problem is "one of general psychopathology more than a sexual problem" or "one of the relationship warranting marital therapy rather than sex therapy." These are important and complex questions in their own right, but often the issue is more subtle, and dividing lines cannot be drawn so neatly. A number of papers, particularly those on low sexual desire, have emphasized the importance of considering the subjective aspects of sexual functioning. As we increasingly attend to these experimental and motivational aspects as well as performance aspects, we can expect questions concerning evaluation to become even more complex.

It is hard to consider systematically the question of why therapy succeeds or fails when we do not have established criteria, but such efforts can be made and are important to the profession. In fact, this was one of the major questions that we asked our contributors to address: What determines success and failure in sex therapy? The question is an interesting one to raise for a variety of reasons. First, it brings home the point that therapists do not like to talk about failure. How often does one read a paper about treatment failures? At a recent conference on sex therapy, a speaker focused on failures in treatment to the surprise, and admiration, of the audience. We all recognize that failures occur and that something can be learned from them, but we shy away from discussing them, particularly publicly and in print. Therefore, the contributors to this volume are noteworthy in their efforts to approach this problem in a forthright way. A second reason for the importance of this question is that it highlights areas of inadequate understanding and potentially removes the mystique from certain therapeutic practices. Whereas many explanations are offered for success, often they turn out to be questionable in the light of failures. Perhaps most puzzling is the case in which treatment is a failure but shortly thereafter the patient shows dramatic improvement, as was true of the third case in the chapter on vaginismus (Leiblum, Pervin, & Campbell). Did therapy play any role in the improvement? If so, which aspects of therapy? In general, are the effects of various treatments specific to those techniques, or is there some more general effect that is independent of any specific procedure?

Explanations for varying degrees of success and failure have tended to focus on patient characteristics, dysfunction characteristics, therapist and/or treatment characteristics, and patient–therapist/treatment relationship characteristics. Most attention generally is given to patient characteristics that make for successful or unsuccessful treatment. Often, it is suggested that patients high in motivation, with relationships to build upon, and without severe psychopathology are the best candidates for sex therapy (LoPiccolo). Such criteria seemed relevant in the three described cases of vaginismus, and the high success rates of Masters and Johnson have often been attributed to their careful selection in this regard. On the other hand, one of the failure

cases presented by Perelman also seemed to have all of these characteristics. Ellis suggests that failures are due to the patient's unwillingness to work, to the presence of a powerful irrational belief that the
patient "refuses" to surrender, or to the presence of serious general
emotional disturbance. Each of these criteria makes some sense, but
is there any systematic evidence suggesting that they could be used
to predict success or failure?

Turning to dysfunction characteristics, we again confront some
puzzling phenomena. Erectile dysfunctions generally are perceived as
more difficult to treat than cases of premature ejaculation. Is there any
reason why this should be the case? Does the difference express differences in personality characteristics in members of the two groups
(and, if so, which), or does it express differences in the availability of
effective treatment techniques? Why, as is pointed out in the chapter
by Barlow and Wincze, is the recidivism and relapse rate so high in
cases of sexual deviation? Why, as Barbach suggests, should primary
anorgasmia be easier to treat than situational anorgasmia? One could
speculate that differences here, as in the broader issue of patient
characteristics, relate to an ability to form meaningful interpersonal
relationships and to the place of the problem in the person's general
psychological functioning. The latter suggests that a sexual dysfunction
can be more or less related to other parts of the individual's personality
functioning, a systems view which is questioned by some of the contributors to this volume. Whatever the potential merits of either of these
explanations, systematic research support for them is missing.

Finally, one comes to therapist and treatment characteristics. It is
noteworthy that about a third of the contributors have addressed this in
a serious way. Ellis is perhaps most explicit in his treatment of this
question, suggesting the following therapist impediments to success: an
erroneous theory, low therapist frustration tolerance, utilization of
only one or two methods, and personal emotional blocks. McWhirter
and Mattison similarly emphasize the importance of therapist attitudes
and feelings, a problem also emphasized by psychoanalysts in the concept of countertransference. Concerning treatment procedures, many
of the chapters raise interesting questions: What is the rationale for
selection between individual therapy and group therapy? Does one
treat a couple whenever possible, or, as Ellis suggests, is it sometimes
preferable to treat the individual? What are the criteria for deciding
between psychotherapy, marital therapy, and sex therapy? Is it necessary, as Ellis and Lazarus suggest, to consider cognitive, emotional,
and behavioral aspects of the problem, or is it possible to have a more

limited focus? Can one trust in the efficacy of certain procedures, or, as Zilbergeld and Ellison suggest, is it often the case that we have "no way of predicting when it will be useful"?

Attempts at explanations for success and failure in sex therapy confront us with the vast array of factors that enter into the therapeutic process. As recent reviews indicate, generally there is good support for the efficacy of sex therapy, but most studies have serious methodological weaknesses, and conclusions concerning effective therapeutic agents are impossible (Kilmann & Auerbach, 1979; Reynolds, 1977; Sotile & Kilmann, 1977). The many patient, therapist, and treatment components not only make individual contributions but also interact in complex ways. This is no less true for sex therapy than for the field of psychotherapy in general. Speicific treatment procedures do exist for specific problems, but a generally effective rationale for selection among procedures and a generally plausible explanation for failures remain to be developed.

Additional Issues

In addition to the issues previously discussed, a number of other issues are worthy of consideration. These involve questions of ethics, questions of training, and questions concerning the place of sexology and sex therapy in relation to other parts of the human sciences and in relation to the broader field of psychotherapy and behavior change.

As the field of sex therapy expands and becomes both more widely practiced and more generally available, questions concerning values and ethics become increasingly important (LoPiccolo, 1978; Masters, Johnson, & Kolodny, 1977). As was indicated in the introductory chapter, sex therapists both respond to and influence values and attitudes in the prevailing culture. No less than other people, sex therapists have their own deep-seated and strong feelings about sex in general and about specific acts in particular. What is communicated, then, if the patients want to know whether the door should be open or closed when they are having intercourse, whether it is all right for the children to see them nude, whether or not enjoying oral sex expresses an inhibition or "hang-up," or whether extramarital affairs are permissible or express a problem in the relationship? Most therapists would agree that their role is to assist the patients in coming to their own conclusions, but how often do attitudes get communicated explicitly or implicitly? Recently, a therapist met with a woman who was upset because her husband wanted her to be involved with him in his cross-dressing rituals and to lead him around on a chain. The therapist had some concerns as well as questions about these practices, but wondered whether this response was not an expression of her own social and sexual biases. In another case, a group of male and female sex therapists discussed the issue of surrogate sex therapists. Not only did individuals differ in their views, but there were striking differences between the male and female therapists concerning the desirability of male and female surrogate therapists. These differences expressed surprisingly different attitudes toward the meaning of sex for men and women.

The issue of ethics and values is an important question in all kinds of therapy. Is there any reason for it to be different in relation to sex therapy? Some factors would suggest that this might be the case. First, sex remains an emotionally charged area for most people, which lends itself to bias on the part of the therapist and vulnerability on the part of the patient. Second, many individuals practice sex therapy without having had more general formal training and without an adequate emphasis on ethical issues as a part of their professional training. Third, sex therapy generally is short-term and directive. In contrast with long-term and less directive therapies, sex therapy involves specific recommendations to patients and often involves direct reponses to patient inquiries. While this does not necessarily lead to more personal bias affecting the treatment decisions, it does suggest that there is a greater potential for the values of the therapist to affect treatment. To a certain extent, the boundaries of sex therapy remain ill defined as the practitioners struggle to define themselves as members of a profession.

A second question involves our interpretation of the place of sex in the more general psychological functioning of the individual; that is, how realistic is it to treat sex independently of other feelings toward the self and toward people generally? The psychoanalytic approach has generally been criticized for its emphasis on underlying conflicts and personality problems that underlie sexual difficulties. Sex therapists point to their therapeutic achievements independent of consideration of such conflicts or underlying problems. But the full dimensions of this problem perhaps remain to be explored. Do such questions become more relevant as we consider the subjective, experiential aspects of sex as well as the performance aspects? Do such questions become more relevant as we treat more difficult cases? For example, one wonders about the long-term effectiveness of brief sex therapy in cases of primary and/or chronic desire deficit. It should be recognized that one can consider these questions seriously without necessarily adopting a psychoanalytic point of view. Thus, for example, Ellis emphasizes the place of changes in sexual functioning as part of more comprehensive personality change while remaining critical of many psychoanalytic emphases. Perhaps the issue here is most succinctly stated by Perelman, who suggests that while some effects in sex therapy are limited, "the maintenance of symptomatic improvement may be a function of the nonsymptomatic changes in the dyad" (p. 224).

A third important question, related to the second, concerns the relationship between sex therapy and psychotherapy. One aspect of this involves procedural questions, another training questions. While almost all would agree that sex therapy is a form of psychotherapy and does require the sophisticated clinical skills of a psychotherapist, one wonders to what extent it is possible to combine traditional psychotherapy with sex therapy. Most behavior therapists see no problem with this—sexual problems are handled as another form of behavioral dysfunction and treated in a fashion similar to the treatment of other difficulties. Most psychoanalytically oriented therapists, however, would hold a somewhat different view. In general, they suggest that one can introduce some dynamic, insight procedures into sex therapy, but one cannot introduce the directive approaches of sex therapy into more traditional insight therapy. The rationale given for the latter is that it upsets the transference, but many therapists these days are struggling with the question of whether it is not indeed possible to integrate psychodynamic and behavior therapy (Wachtel, 1977). As has been noted, such questions become particularly critical as one considers problems of resistance and difficulties in treating relationship problems as well as sexual problems. If sex therapists are viewed as technicians, then the relevant skills can probably be acquired in a relatively short period of time. On the other hand, if sex therapists are sensitive clinicians capable of recognizing and responding to a wide range of difficulties, then highly specialized training is necessary. The issue is put by LoPiccolo (1978, p. 514) as follows: "Is it [sex therapy]... a complex, multifaceted psychotherapy procedure to be used only by those with formal training [and a license] to practice psychotherapy? Is it, as many sex therapists argue, a form of educational activity not requiring psychotherapeutic skills on the part of the sex therapist? Is sex therapy merely a form of physical skill training like golf or tennis lessons?"

A final question to be addressed concerns the relationship of sex therapy to other fields and disciplines. Sex therapy will stagnate unless it remains in touch with developments in other fields. Many of the questions posed in this chapter have been addressed by psychologists, psychiatrists, social workers, and sociologists investigating the effects of psychotherapy. Many of the techniques currently in use have been borrowed from other forms of therapy, and developments in areas such as modeling and biofeedback hold promise for the future. Conceptualization of the nature of human sexuality stands to gain from advances in biology, anthropology, sociology, and psychology. Thus, a final issue for the field concerns its ability to remain in touch with and profit from contributions in other areas as well as contributing to developments in these areas.

Conclusion

In this chapter, we have considered a vast array of complex questions and highlighted some of the contributions that have been made by the authors in this volume. When we undertook to edit this volume, we had in mind a book which would realistically portray what sex therapists do and how they struggle with the difficult issues that confront them. In this goal, we believe that the contributors have served us well. They were chosen, in part, to reflect the diversity of approaches and thinking that currently exist, and their chapters evidence the rich variety of approaches that exists in the field as a whole. The contributors were invited to consider their successes and failures, and they were generous in sharing these experiences with us. We believe that what has been portrayed here is reasonably representative of the successes and failures one finds in the practice of sex therapy. As the introductory chapter indicated, sex therapy has made amazing advances in a short period of time. As this final chapter suggests, much work remains to be done.

References

Annon, J. S. *The behavioral treatment of sexual problems*. Honolulu: Kapiolani Health Services, 1974.

Bandura, A. Self-efficacy: Toward a unifying theory of behavioral change. *American Psychologist*, 1977, *84*, 191–215.

Gottman, J. M., & Leiblum, S. R. *How to do psychotherapy and how to evaluate it*. New York: Holt, Rinehart, & Winston, 1974.

Kaplan, H. S. *The new sex therapy*. New York: Brunner/Mazel, 1974.

Kilmann, P. R., & Auerback, R. Treatments of premature ejaculation and psychogenic impotence: A critical review of the literature. *Archives of Sexual Behavior*, 1979, *8*, 81–98.

LoPiccolo, J. The professionalization of sex therapy: Issues and problems. In J. LoPiccolo & L. LoPiccolo (Eds.), *Handbook of sex therapy*. New York: Plenum Press, 1978.

Masters, W. H., Johnson, V. E., & Kolodny, R. C. (Eds.). *Ethical issues in sex therapy and research*. Boston: Little, Brown & Co., 1977.

Meichenbaum, D. *Cognitive-behavior modification*. New York: Plenum Press, 1977.

Reynolds, B. S. Psychological treatment models and outcome results for erectile dysfunction: A critical review. *Psychological Bulletin*, 1977, *84*, 1218–1238.

Sotile, W. M., & Kilmann, P. R. Treatments of psychogenic female sexual dysfunctions. *Psychological Bulletin*, 1977, *84*, 619–633.

Strupp, H. H., & Hadley, S. W. A tripartite model of mental health and therapeutic outcomes. *American Psychologist*, 1977, *32*, 187–196.

Wachtel, P. L. *Psychoanalysis and behavior therapy*. New York: Basic Books, 1977.

Author Index

Subject Index